THE UPSCA NEWSLETTERS
2nd Edition

UPSCA stands for University of the Philippines Student Catholic Action. This organization has existed from pre-war times to the present. Over the years, membership has reportedly ranged from a high of a few thousand to just a handful at the lowest. From within that group who entered college in the late 50s, sets of friends have maintained close contact with each other. Starting from the early 90s, the internet played a big part in keeping them in touch. This cyber group of UPSCAns, known as the Loop, are about 150 strong, and span the college years from the late 50s to the mid 60s.

A good number of these friends happened to be in Los Angeles, and they did have parties when the occasions arose, especially when visiting UPSCAns were passing through.

On Christmas 1994, a printout of names and addresses of these friends was distributed, and this eventually started the UPSCA newsletters.

Below is a listing of all the 17 issues over a 20 year period, followed by all the newsletters. Most of the issues were produced as b&w hardcopy, and mailed out to the members. These have been have been scanned to PDF. The last two issues were electronic files in color, emailed out to members.

This compilation, however, is all printed in b&w.

Fernando "Danny" Gil   22 February 2016

Addenda to this 2nd edition: many of the original files were retrieved and converted directly for clearer prints, but with some weird results. Where practical most of the detailed postal, email and telephone data was expunged, or the entire directory page was not included.   15 March 2016

ISSUE	DATE	HEADLINE
Num 1	Dec 25 1994	UPSCA ROLADEX
Num 2	1st Qtr 1996	A BELATED HAPPY AND NEW YEAR TO ALL!
Num 3	1st Qtr 1997	ALL HEP ABOUT LAKBAYAN USA '98!
Num 4	3rd Qtr 1997	SOUTHERN CRUISE FELL THRU, BUT LAKBAYAN WON'T
Num 5	1st Qtr 1998	TIME TRAVEL CLAIMED BY SOME UPSCANS
Num 6	2nd Qtr 1998	FUND RAISER ON FOR DELANEY HALL
Num 7	3rd Qtr 1998	A TALE OF TWO PARTIES
Num 8	4th Qtr 1998	WORDSMITH BOOK WINS AWARD!
Num 9	1st Qtr 1999	EMAIL LOOP LINKS UP AND DOWN!
Num 10	2nd Qtr 1999	THE TRIBE INCREASES AS OLD MEETS YOUNG
Num 11	3rd Qtr 1999	THE LOOP GOES TO A HIGHER TECH PLANE
Num 12	Spring-Summer 2000	BOOKS ON FR. DELANEY COME OUT
Num 13	Special Edition 1st Half 2001	LAKBAYAN BECOMES A REALITY!
Num 14	Summer 2001	LAKBAYAN AGAIN IN 2003, IN PROVANÇE?
Num 15	Late Summer 2003	PHOENIX? RESURRECTION? WE'RE BACK!
Num 16	March 2007	RESURECTADO. ON BATANES LAKBAY.
Num 17	Fall 2014	THE GREAT PHILADELPHIA GATE CRASH

PSCA
newsletter

19002 horst av • artesia ca 90701
tel 310/402-5098

Volume 1 Number 1　　　　　　　　　　**Sunday, December 25, 1994**

Taken May 1992
at Danny and Lisa
(née Señeris) Gil's,
during a despedida
given by L.A. UPSCAns
for NVM Gonzales.

(L–R, all in glasses)
José Alzona,
Enteng Batas,
Jimmy Abad,
Danny Gil,
Tony Estrera
and Johnny Balaoing

Perhaps to most of you non–Los Angeles residents, this mailing will come as a surprise. But for the past three years, we UPSCAns of the vintage from late 50's to early 70's have been meeting periodically, and in the course of these get–togethers, we've come up with a mailing list of UPSCAns in the U.S. (next page). Most of these names have been garnered thru networking; others thru the modern technology of the CD-ROM phone book in most libraries: so long as you're listed, we can track you down.

We have an informal UPSCA Alumni Association of Southern California. We now want to expand it into a national association, and would like to set a tentative date wherein perhaps as many of us as possible can get together. We are looking to Saturday, May 29, 1995. This is a three–day weekend just before summer.

So please contact us soonest. Send more data on yourselves so we can have a newsier Newsletter. Let other UPSCAns whom you may know also contact us. My address and phone/fax is above.

A Merry Christmas
and a Happy New Year!

UPSCA Rolodex　　Christmas 1994

Arthur & Cher Adiarte
767 Fairmount Av
St Paul MN 55105
(612) 222-3825

Offie (Peñaflorida) & Ken Aid
12628 Lemming St
Lakewood CA 90715
(310) 865-2034

José Alzona
370 Temple Av #7
Long Beach CA 90814
(310) 438-0728

Myrna Aquitania
643 Hillcrest Dr
Camarillo CA 93012
(805) 389-9513

Primo & Lindus Arambulo
11921 Old Gate Place
Rockville MD 20852
(301) 984-7923

Noli Arong
8973 Patrick Av
Arleta CA 91331
(818) 768-5039

Sisoy Arong
8119 Concho St
Houston TX 77036
(713) 776-2818

Johnny & Alda Balaoing
3399 Holyoke Dr
Los Angeles CA 90065
(213) 258-1453

Nina Los Baños
5916 Edrene Av
Las Vegas NV 89108
(702) 646-8056

Enteng & Mely Batas
44123 Camellia St
Lancaster CA 93535
(805) 946-8911

Jun & Cynthia (Reyes) Calejesan
159 Kermit Dr
Monaca PA 15061
(412) 264-4483

Manny Castillo
875 E Buchanan Ct
Brea CA 92621
(714) 671-2989

Tessie Chua Chiaco
24262 Walnut #7
Newhall CA 91321
(805) 259-3199

Bing (Ferrer) & Anthony Dubitsky
6608 Oliver St
Riverdale MD 20737
(301) 577-7567

Manny & Lee Espejo
28141 Newbird Dr
Saugus CA 91350
(805) 296-8820

Tony & Josie Estrera
17403 Niagara Av
Cerritos CA 90701
(310) 809-3342

Baby (Mangosing) Evangelista
4820 Welford
Alexandria VA 22309
(703) 780-5404

Susan (Rodriguez) Fagan
345 E. 54th St #217
New York NY
(212) 759-3673

Malu (Barrios) & Oids Garcia
12458 Timbercreek Lane
Cerritos CA 90701
(310) 404-1195

Danny & Lisa (Señeris) Gil
19002 Horst Av
Artesia CA 90701
(310) 402-5098 or 402-1890

Erwin & Alita Gomez
401 Shorewood Ct
Valparaiso IN 46383
(219) 465-1034 or 980-1307

Ruben & Maria Habito
7422 Villanova St
Dallas TX 75225
(214) 360-0595

Effie (Sta Romana) Hall
2545 Brambleberry Ct
Bettendorf IA 52722
████████████

UPSCA *ALUMNI ASSOCIATION, USA*

NEWSLETTER   NEWSLETT ER   NEWSLETTER

A M D G   Vol 1, Num 2 (1st Quarter 1996)   Published by UPSCA Alumni Association, USA

A BELATED AND HAPPY NEW YEAR TO ALL !

A Happy New Year to All!! We hope you had a wonderful Christmas, And we hope you will have a Happy New Year.

***

So sorry for all you people who missed our first 1996 bash: a potluck party held in Danny & Lisa Gil's place Saturday, February 17. You will rue the day! The food was so good, the singing better, the jokes and stories more hilarious, and the dancing (spontaneous as it was totally unplanned) was the highlight.

But not to worry. We voted to have another one like it on May 11, more specifically a jam session complete with dancing instructors (Rey & Ollie Sanidad for the Tango, Danny & Lisa Gil for the Salsa, and whoever else is willing to try). By then, we also should have more definitive plans for a summer picnic, or the like.

***

Johnny Balaoing was the earliest to appear, mainly to tell us that he had two other commitments that night so he wasn't so sure about coming back, but he left the more important stuff: the kaldereta dish, and all the data for the forthcoming concert by one of us Upscans, *Maurie Borromeo*. If you remember, Maurie was one of the more active organists at the Chapel, and a piano accompanist during the Choir practices. She stayed for some years in the East coast, finishing her ethno-musicology degree, and has since gone back to the Philippines. She will be back on May 17 with the *U.P. Kasarinlan Cultural Group* in a concert at the Glendale Civic Auditorium sponsored by the Fil-Am Community of St. Bernard, of which Johnny is an active member. Johnny would like us Upscan Alumni to jointly support the event. During the party, we discussed and agreed to raise $250 for a one page advertisement on the souvenir program, and in addition,

This is a photo taken during an Upsca party about two years ago. Try to identify the people (some of them were guests and so don't wrack your brains too much). In the next issues, we will be scanning and printing "before and after" photos from the Philippinensian Yearbook and from more recent photos of the same individuals. So be game and send in your photos now. We can retouch them if you want. See next page for an example of what time has done to some of us, for better or for worse.

to attend the concert. We made a headcount and for those who committed, we will be enclosing the $15 tickets for the concert, and a form with instructions on how to remit the amount (including the share for the advertisement) to Johnny.

***

Another item of transition is that *Tony* and *Josie* (nee Angeles) *Estrera* have been made president and co-president starting this year. So finally, yours truly (Danny Gil) can bow away.

***

Here are other fairly recent news items which should be reported. Loida Nicolas Lewis came over a few weeks ago for the paperback book launching of her late husband's biography."*Why Should the White Guys have All the Fun*". This event was sponsored by a number of Filipino organizations. Myrna Aquitania brought our attention to the luncheon at a plush Beverly Hills restaurant. It was there that we got the latest address of Divsy Astraquillo from her sister Ludy Onkeko, a columnist of the Business Daily and a prominent member of the Filipino community in LA.

***

Ok, let us recount what the Upscans here in Southern California did as a group last year We had our usual "post Christmas get together" mid-January. Then we had a party in May, and a camping in July. And of course, in between all those, there were those family birthday parties, and weekend biking and/or tennis sessions among the closer neighbors (mainly Tony, Oids and Ken). But so far, we haven't yet feted anyone from out-of-State. Let's make that a priority for one of these forthcoming get-togethers.

So for you guys out there, contact us whenever you are passing through LA, and we'll set up a party! It's a date.

***

IT'S A DATE

Saturday, May 11, 1996 - Party and jam session at Danny & Lisa's place.
Sunday, May 19, 1966 - UP Kasarinlan Cultural Group Concert with by Maurie Borromeo at Glenndale Auditorium.
Sometime July - picnic and/or camping (just like last year) - to be announced in next Newsletter.

Before: 1964   After: 1996
The ravages of time on the physiognamy. Guess who?

Editorial
by Danny Gil

*The following is a writeup made over a year ago, after the enthusiam following the first Newsletter in December 1994, which mainly was just an address list with an introduction. This writeup was to have been included in the next Newsletter. Since the next issue never came out until now, I'm including it just the same, albeit a **bit stale**. And since many things have happened since then, let me preface it by the more important item, the obits:*

Gerry Gil - July 26, 1995
Violy Calvo - sometime late 1995

***

As far as we know, there are generally two distinct Upsca groups in the LA area. The older set are those who were in UP from the late 50's to early 60's, such as the Basement Bugs *Johnny Balaoing, Manny Espejo, Enteng Batas* and *Noli Arong.* Johnny and Manny have been here since the mid 70's. Together with other Upscans before our time (such as *Fe Tolentino, Zeny Roxas, Angel Sta Maria and George Carlos*), they already had a thriving camaraderie in their church group at the north part of LA. The other set are the younger ones (UP vintage late 60's) such as *Tony and Josie (nee Angeles) Estrera, Malu (nee Barrios) and Ed Garcia, Ofie (nee Peñaflorida) Aid, Mario Manansala (eng'g), and Manny Castillo (MD)*. When *Ping Tan* visited a couple of years ago, this group hosted a party, and through Tony and Josie, Lisa and I did get to meet them. Tony and Josie are relatively new to LA, having immigrated from Australia, where they had stayed long enough to become citizens there. Johnny Balaoing is notable as the first and possibly the only Pinoy heart transplant patient. He had had a number of heart attacks early on, and finally got a new heart about 4 years ago. *José Alzona* moved to LA about 7 years ago, after spending most of his post-UP life in the East coast in high tech jobs. He's shunned it all for now, and is doing freelance writing on the LA scene. He's the one we see most often, as he has a key to the house where he does his faxing, xeroxing, scanning, or laser printing. José tells of having met a number of Upscans in the East coast some years back, such as *Arthur Adiarte, Jun and Cynthia Reyes-Calejesan, Bing*

Ferrer-Dubitsky, Erwin Gomez, Baby Natividad and a few others. Most of their addresses comes from *José*. A number of the East coast addresses comes from *Rory Abrera Somerstein*, who runs two schools in upstate NY, and mentions that *Helen Samson* resides in Germany with her army officer husband. Until *Ernie Panganiban* and his wife *Jessie* moved further out to the valley, our families did get to see each other very often. *Berryl Silva* is in the singing/musical scene. Other contemporaries are *Jessica Infante* who is a nurse at Kaiser Hospital, and *Tessie Chua-Chiaco* who runs her own music studio. *Myrna Aquitania* who lives further north at Camarillo, is active in many of the LA Filipino groups. There are others whose names wouldn't ring a bell, but they are all out there somewhere, and there are others who have moved on. For instance, we can't trace *Nilo Cruz* who used to be in LA, then moved to San Francisco and may be in Texas now. He still was around when *Tigi Barcelona* came to visit in '88. Then there was "retiree" *Tony Nievera*, who had settled in SF after a very successful career in top managerial slots in a number of Philippine firms, including IBM. He apparently has gone back to Manila or unto bigger things elsewhere.

But the most outstanding in terms of corporate and financial visibility is *Loida Nicolas Lewis* (UP law 67?), who met her future husband when she was a post-grad student at Harvard. When he passed away 2 years ago, he was considered the most successful black business man in America. He had stunned Wall Street by pulling a billion dollar leveraged buy-out of TLC Beatriz International, a food conglomerate. I understand that for a year, her husband's brother took over running the corporation, but Loida has since replaced him and and is doing very much better. Loida's business interests are mainly Europe based, and she spends a good portion of her time there. The late husband, Reginald, was a generous philanthropist and gave UP one of the biggest grants it's ever received.

As for the Upscans who stayed home in the Philippines, *Gerry Gil* is the associate editor of the Manila Standard, and very often deals with many of the politicians. *Jess Javelona* is nearing retirement at PRC after having spent years in various positions including stints in Thailand and Europe. Similarly, *Johnny Reyes* has been with Shell Phils for a long time and had various assignments in Australia. The last time I heard, he is now in Holland. *Lino Faelnar* still is with the Asian Dev Bank. I believe some of their kids (wife is *Maureen*, nee Holazo) studied here in the US but are back there now.   *Melvyn* and *Susan* (nee *Paulin*) *Martin* run their own PR firm. *Jimmy Ong* and *Mon Pasicolan* are big-wigs in San Miguel. They've visited a couple of times and always manage to drop by and/or stay with us. *Jimmy Abad* and *Mercy* (nee *Rivera*) visit now and then, and have a daughter presently in Boston taking her masters degree. Among the older set contemporaries, *Eli Alampay* and wife *Sonia* (nee *Alday*) also come and go, and so has *Noel Soriano*. All these above Upscans still meet very often and the group also includes *Tigi Barcelona, Jimmy Valera, Lallie de Vera, Eddie Magtoto, Romy Manlapaz, Ping Tan, Beth* (nee *Arcellana*) and *Bong Nuque, Isagani Cruz*, and others. *Freddie Santiano* was central in that group until he passed away unexpectedly in June of 1992. It happened the day the entire family and I arrived for a visit. During the wake, I did meet some friends whom I hadn't seen since the school days in the '60s such as *Eleanor Laya* and some engineering schoolmates.

Bobby Neri, Art Ferrer, Mat Sanchez and *Ibarra Gonzales* are Jesuit men of the cloth. The only other Upscan Jesuit I know, *Ruben Habito* (of the younger set) is now an ex-Jesuit. His is a very interesting case which deserves an complete article in itself. See page 5. He sent me a xerox of the clipping which I scanned and OCR'd.

For those at the other side of the world, *Mon Casas* is settled down in Strasbourg with a family. *Bernie de Castro* is married to a Frenchman and from what I understand, spent a year or so the Philippines on some foreign service assignment.

Chit Inciong and I had an interesting time when I went East last summer to visit two of my children We hadn't seen each other in 20 years. He came to the US in '83, a year after I did. Chit's wife *Vicky* is with the UN and presently is in Lebanon for a job assignment. He has two boys still in school. All are musically inclined just like the father. Their daughter is studying in Switzerland. He says he meets almost weekly with *Cecille* (nee *Gordon) Mueller* for prayer meetings. She is now based in Maryland, although her navy-officer husband is temporarily in Haiti.

My brother-in-law who resides in a relatively small city in Michigan has coined the term "herd instinct" which he defines as the desire to meet more of your kith and kin as time passes. This probably explains the success of the hometown organization of Lisa, dubbed Tanjay USA. Tanjay is a "small town" just north of Dumaguete. We have a couple of activities every year, and at one time, we had to rent the guest house of the Dodger Stadium at LA to hold the 350 guests we had for a dinner-dance.

In similar vein, I guess this attempt of reaching out to the other Upscans is also a herd instinct, with the Upsca Diliman of the '60s being the "small town".

Any other theories?

***

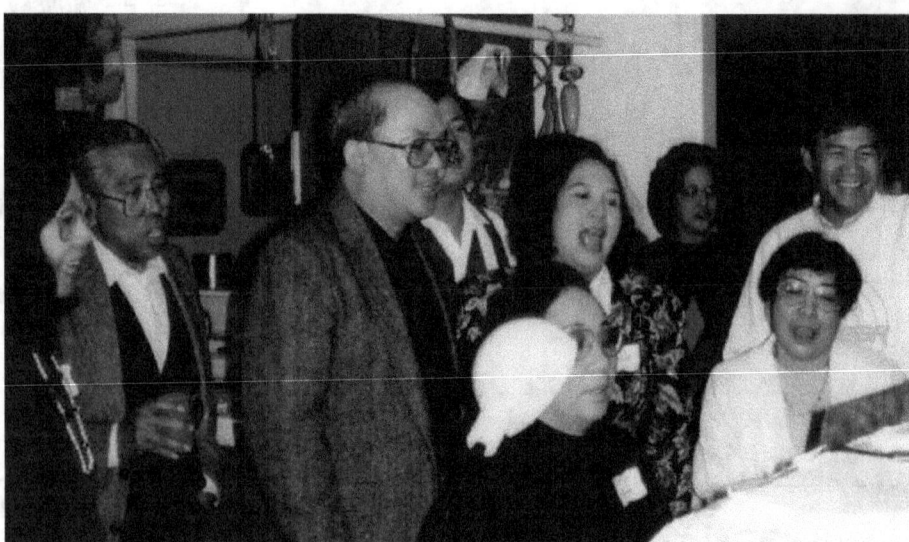

Singing in action! Left to right: Josie Angeles-Estrera, Johnny Balaoing, Manny Castillo, Oids Garcia (partly hidden), Zeny Roxas-Ramirez (at the piano behind lamp), Malu Barrios-Garcia, Alda Balaoing, Lisa Señeris-Gil, Ernie Pangilinan.

***

After Gerry Gil passed away, I made copies of his computer floppy disks and have found a lot of fascinating tidbits in his writings (which among others include over a thousand editorials over his 5 year stint as Opinion Editor of the Manila Standard). Since it is almost Holy Week, and some of us may be attending spiritual retreats, I'd like to share with you a letter which Gerry wrote to a friend's daughter. Here it is fully reproduced:

***

7 July 1989

Dear Joe-Ed:

Your mother has told me that you're taking off this weekend for your first closed retreat and that you're a trifle concerned about the prospect of three days of silence. All of us who have gone through such retreats had similar concerns the first time around.

In fact, this concern never leaves us: it is with us every time we start a closed retreat. And yet, at least in my case, there is a certain fascination with closed retreats: when I start an open retreat, I sometimes wish it were a closed one (your mother and father, who regard me as one of the most talkative characters they know, will almost certainly be surprised by such a statement coming from me).

There are a number of points I'd like to share with you about the silence of a closed retreat.

First, there is more to the silence of the closed retreat than the mere silence of the mouth — which is all we observe when we merely "shut up." Much as our retreatmasters may urge us to shut up, keeping silent in this sense is not sufficient to enable us to make a good retreat.

You can say absolutely nothing, but "make up" for this silence by keeping all your other senses wide open: you can make your eyes wander over the environment you have often taken for granted; you can strain your ears to catch the noises that sound just at the level of consciousness — as did a friend of mine (who rose to be a big executive with Coca-Cola Export Corporation) who spent one entire closed retreat observing how wasps make a hive!

There is such a thing, then, as the silence of the senses — a little harder to keep than the silence of the mouth. But even the silence of the senses is not sufficient to enable us to make a good retreat.

We may shut up, we may keep our eyes and ears closed, but we can still let our minds run riot — recreating in our minds the last book we read, the last movie we saw, or imagining the most outlandish things we can think of. To the silence of the mouth and the silence of the senses, we must add the silence of the mind.

Here, you may ask, "What is the point to all this? Why do we have to keep these three kinds of silence?"

The best answer I can give is that keeping these three kinds of silence makes it possible for us to "hear" whatever message the good Lord wants to tell us.

Remember the story of the little boy Samuel, who was living in the temple with the high priest Eli? In the dead of the night, he heard a voice call him, and thinking that Eli was calling him, he went to the high priest, who said he had not called. The third time this happened, Eli told Samuel that it must be the Lord who was calling and that Samuel must respond, "Speak, Lord, for thy servant hears."

It is this kind of receptiveness to the message of the Lord that retreat-masters hope to develop when they require silence.

Of course, not all of us can maintain all three kinds of silence during the full three days of the retreat. Too often, we manage to succeed only in shutting up. Sometimes, we manage to shut our other senses down. It is perhaps for only a few brief periods that we manage to keep the silence of the mind.

But in the periods where we succeed in keeping the silence of the mind, we can and do come to grips with ourselves. We start asking ourselves such fundamental questions as, "What am I?" "What do I want to be?" and "In what direction am I moving?"

True, these are all very human questions that we can ask ourselves and even answer — even outside the context of the closed retreat. But the closed retreat puts these questions in a larger, non-worldly context: "What do these questions mean — and what do our answers mean — in the context of eternity, in the context of heaven and hell, in the context of our relationship with God?"

And this is why the silence of the closed retreat can be somewhat frightening, because it forces each individual to confront himself, judge himself, not so much in terms of whether he is bright, popular, or otherwise successful in the eyes of his family, friends, and acquaintances as in terms of whether he is a good man in the eyes of God.

I don't know whether you noticed, but in the last paragraph, I started using the term "individual"; in previous paragraphs, I used the term "we." This is because the question of where one stands in the eyes of God has to be answered on an individual basis. Because ultimately, it is you who decide what "being a good man" means to you, it is only you — not I, not your parents, not your friends — who can give the best answer to the question of where you stand in God's eyes.

And this is the other reason why a closed retreat requires silence. We do not speak to other people; we do not compare notes with other people. Rather, each person communes with himself to answer the basic question, "Where do I stand on the road to eternity?"

There is something somber, even frightening, about a closed retreat, Joe-Ed, because sooner or later, no matter how much the retreat-master may try to sugarcoat the message, we cannot run away from the fact that sooner or later, each of us is going to die: this is the unstated premise of the question of "Where do I stand on the road to eternity?"

And each of us dies alone; our friends stand sad and silent, powerless to give us aid; alone we will stand before the throne of God...and it is for this reason that when a man poses to himself the question of where he stands on the road to eternity, it is best that he confronts the question alone.

And yet, because we are human, we do not like to ponder about death. To a young person like you — with your full life still ahead — the question of death seems by and large irrelevant.

And so, I wouldn't be surprised if your retreat master does not dwell on this question too much. He may give one or two talks on death (this was "standard operating procedure" in my time), but, by and large, the talks will direct your thoughts toward more spiritual things: even the practical guides to living a good and happy life will be couched in moral and spiritual terms.

There is something to be said for this approach: we must learn that many of the things our day-to-day existence consider to be important — such as power, wealth, beauty, strength, prestige, and glory — are not so important after all in the context of eternity.

So many people, Joe-Ed, make their lives unnecessarily miserable because they lose out on the honor roll, a scholarship, an election, a job opportunity, a friendship, or other things that are merely of passing value. It is human, of course, to feel disappointed when one loses something he values. It is human to feel angry, even vengeful, when we feel that life is unjust to us. And yet, we must realize that when we make such losses and injustices warp our very lives, it is we, not those who offended us, that sin most grievously against ourselves.

The silences of the mouth, of the mind, and of the senses enable us to step away from the cares of the day-to-day world, to place these cares in a larger context, and to keep our eyes on the more important question of whether we are becoming the kind of human being each of us would want to be.

And this is the larger message of the closed retreat: that we should develop the skill of lapsing into the three kinds of silences whenever we want to. Later in life, we will not often have the chance of taking off for a day or even three days to reflect on how our lives are going. And so, it would be desirable if we learn from our closed retreats how we can "retreat" into the three kinds of silences for a few minutes, for a few hours, whenever we feel it is necessary to do so.

By the way of nothing at all, I close this letter with a few verses that I used to reflect on during the retreats I took when I was your age:

I walk down the Valley of Silence, down
   the dim, voiceless valley —alone;
And I hear not the fall of a footstep around
   me save God's and my own;
And the hush of my heart is as holy as
   hovers where angels have flown.
Long ago was I weary of voices whose
   music my heart could not win;
Long ago was I weary of noises that fretted
   my soul with their din;
Long ago was I weary of places where I
   met but the human — and sin.
I walked in the world with the worldly; I
   craved what the world never gave;
And I said, "In the world, each ideal that
   shines like a star on life's wave
Is wrecked on the shores of the real and
   sleeps like a dream in a grave."

My best wishes for a truly silent retreat.

Gerry Gil

***

Help!

We need your articles, letters, pictures, jokes, and other items of interest for the forthcoming issues. Also, names and addresses of other Upscans. Do send them in to either Tony Estrera or Danny Gil (see addresses on last page). Alternately, you can e-mail them to ferngil@aol.com or tonyest@aol.com.

If you want to e-mail something to one of the Upscan *barkada* in the Philippines, try Isagani Cruz at clairec@dlsu.edu.ph

Hope to hear from you guys out there!

One priest's spiritual journey

Two very different paths brought a Christian practitioner of Zen to a new family and a new life in Dallas

By Thomas Huang
staff writer of The Dallas News

He had studied many of Zen's ancient spiritual questions, but none were as puzzling as the stirrings Ruben Habito now felt in his heart.

In the autumn of 1988, the Jesuit priest and student of Zen discovered he was in love.

He was at odds with himself. At 41, Ruben Habito had devoted more than two decades of his life to God and to religious studies in Japan. But his feelings for Maria Reis, a doctoral student of Chinese religions, transcended infatuation and could not be ignored.

He took a leave of absence from the Tokyo university where he had been teaching courses in religion and returned home to the Philippines. For months, he prayed. He consulted with his family and friends. He had to make a decision about his priesthood and his vows to celibacy.

Mr. Habito ultimately chose a path, he said, guided by this principle: That to lead a spiritual life, he had to truly know himself and be honest with himself; to recognize that life has many callings and that one must pay attention to them; to engage the real world, not flee from it.

Spirituality is "a constant attempt to listen to the inner voice and follow it fully" said Mr. Habito, 47, now a theology professor at Southern Methodist University and a teacher at a local Zen center.

"The spiritual is the innermost core of the human being——that which opens us to touch the transcendent, what is most intimate to us."

But following your inner voice does not mean doing things simply because they please you, Mr. Habito said. The world is not to be used for selfish ends, but it is the field where you open yourself to others and to the sacred.

Deepening your spirituality does not mean becoming self-centered, either. "It's not just an inward turn," he said. "As we touch the core of our inner selves, we can better feel connected to one another. It is not a center that excludes everything."

Up until his moment of crisis in 1988, Mr. Habito had led a life that was bold, yet somewhat cloistered at the same time.

Edward Poitras, a theologian at SMU, described his friend this way: "He's a person who has a gyroscope, an inner direction, an inner stability, where he can keep going in the direction he has set, even though it may mean changes in his life."

The son of teachers, Mr. Habito grew up in Cabuyao, a rural Philippine town south of Manila. At an early age, he saw people living in destitution, beggars on the streets, impoverished children dying from malnutrition and pneumonia. As a precocious young-

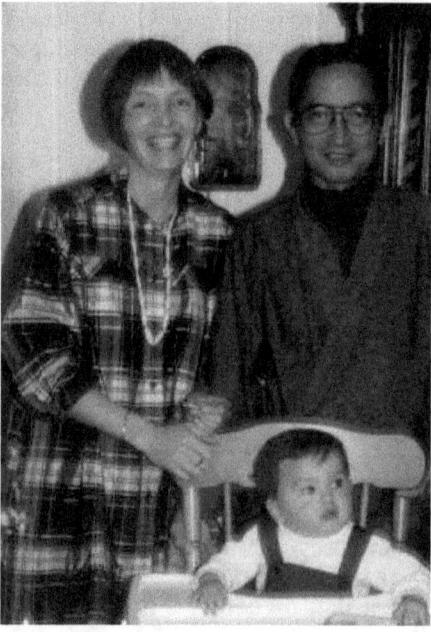

Ruben and Maria Habito with first child.

ster, raised Catholic, Mr. Habito asked himself questions: "What's the point of living? How can we live in a way that we could lessen the suffering in this world? Does God really exist? If he does, why do all these inequalities exist.

Those questions created a thirst in him to read philosophy. In 1964, Mr. Habito left a physics scholarship at the University of the Philippines and entered the Jesuit order at he age of 16, despite some initial resistance from his parents, who thought he was too young.

After graduating with a philosophy degree from a Jesuit-run college in 1969, Mr. Habito volunteered to serve as a missionary in Japan. There, he was ordained as a priest.

In 1971, curious as ever, Mr. Habito practiced Zen under a master to understand Japanese religions in more than an academic way. Zen meditation "enhanced your sensitivity for the sacredness of things around you." Mr. Habito said. "I found that enriching."

In Zen, Mr. Habito found an affirmation of the spiritual exercises of St. Ignatius of Loyola, who founded the Jesuit order in the 16th century.

Mr. Habito "doesn't throw away the past and go to something new," said Mr. Poitras. "He keeps the past and keeps the traditions he has, and builds on them. He didn't compromise his Catholic faith when he became a Zen practitioner, but he added that on."

By the late 1980s, Mr. Habito had entered his 40s, and his life appeared set. He had become fluent in Japanese. He was teaching philosophy at Sophia University in Tokyo. Having completed his kaon training, he also began to teach Zen to others. Kaons are questions asked of a student to force him, through contemplation, to a greater awareness of reality.

Then he met Maria Reis. At an academic conference, they struck up a friendship. They corresponded. She was a native German studying Chinese Buddhism in Japan. He saw in her an openness, a depth of spirituality, and a sensitivity to others.

In Mr. Habito, Maria Reis, now 35, says she saw "kindness, humbleness and intelligence. I feel that intelligent people easily get aloof from others, but he's very open to people and humble at the same time."

After a year of friendship, their feelings for each other blossomed. He withdrew to the Philippines to reflect. After months of prayer and meditation, he discussed his quandary with a Jesuit spiritual director.

Mr. Habito said the director told him: "When you are faced with a decision like this, I caution you not to make a decision based on what other people will think. Listen to the depths, what you feel in the deep stirrings of your own heart."

A moment of clarity came. "If I chose to forget Maria and not see her, it would be based on my reputation, on people expecting me to be a priest, to not fall in love." Mr. Habito recalled.

He made his decision.

In May 1989, Mr. Habito asked to leave the Jesuit order with the intention of marrying Ms. Reis. He still considered himself a member of the Catholic Church but he agreed to no longer practice as a priest.

Still, matters were far from settled. The couple agreed to live apart for one year to confirm their feelings, to give themselves space for a solid decision.

Through a professor who knew him, Mr. Habito was invited to join the faculty of the Perkins School of Theology. He moved to Dallas in the fall of 1989.

Ms. Reis, who was completing her doctoral research in Japan, passed up a coveted job at a research center in Germany and, in 1990, moved to Dallas. In April of that year, the couple were married at the chapel at Perkins. With marriage came a true calm. "The tremendous peace was an indication there was something deep here I could rely on." Mr. Habito said.

At SMU, he teaches world religions and spirituality. He also teaches Zen and leads meditation at a Zen center that holds its meetings at Grace United Methodist Church at East Dallas.

The Habitos attend Holy Trinity Catholic Church on Oak Lawn Avenue. They now have two sons, Florian, 3, and Benjamin, who will be 2 in mid February.

Mr. Habito's role as a husband and father is "something I've found very eye opening. I wouldn't trade it for anything," he said.

"Spirituality, as I've learned, is not something that takes you away from ordinary life and the struggles of a human being, but it re-engages you in all of that."

"My semi-monastic way of life turned to full engagement". He can recognize something meaningful in mundane events -- like changing diapers." he said with a smile.

***

In Memoriam: Gerry Gil 1942-1995

Remembering Gerry

Cipriano S. Roxas
Editor in chief

Reprinted from The Manila Standard, February 9, 1996

How I wish this article wouldn't have been written. And how I wish I didn't have to write it myself.

For even now, almost seven months after **Gerry Gil** bade goodbye to the **Standard** newsroom because he felt he was "coming down with a touch of the flu," never to come back again, his memory still lingers.

How can we at the central news desk forget the sight of Gerry, wearing a brown jacket, his right arm still in a sling (he had figured in a car accident and broken his collarbone three weeks earlier) telling us that he was knocking off early, and yes, the editorial for the next day was done, thank you.

Sure, said we, jokingly adding "Take two aspirins and call me in the morning. Sleep easy, my friend."

When he bought the farm two days later, all of us were stunned. How could this man, still frisky as a colt at middle age, this man with that inveterate, puckish sense of humor, this man who was the lender of last resort in the newsroom, pull such a cruel joke? Why, said I, even corporate executives gave the company at least two weeks' notice before they left, right?

But then, the finality of it all began to dawn on all of us. And the memories of our association with the man came cascading.

We first met Gerry in the old *Philippines Herald*, where **Oscar Villadolid**, then editor in chief, brought him along with **Jimmy Ong**, the late **A.G. Sto. Tomas**, and two or three other young writers. Gerry was given the rank of associate editor. He also wrote a regular column for the paper. Even then, his wit shone.

We had to put our association in the back burner for a while after someone signed Proclamation 1081 one night in September 1972, putting an end to the glorious history of the venerable *Herald*.

Years later, **Standard** publisher **Rod T. Reyes** was shopping around for a new chief editorial writer who would also edit the opinion pages because the incumbent was leaving for greener pastures.

Enter **Butch del Castillo**, the paper's business editor with the question: You know anybody named Professor Gil? For a while there I thought he was doing a takeoff on the Broadway musical *The*

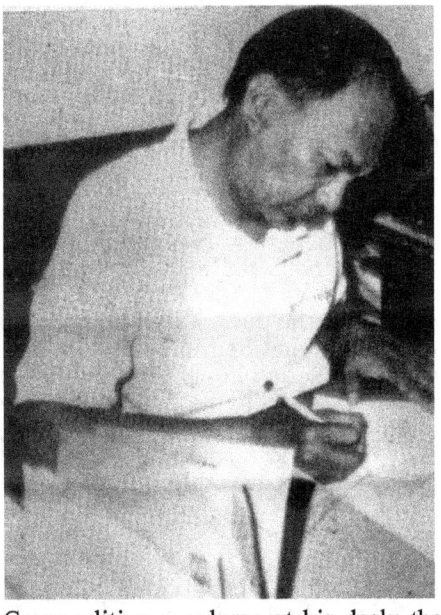

Gerry editing a column at his desk: the typewriter his alter, the cup of coffee his chalice, and the cigaret his sacred host.

Music Man (the chief character is named Prof. Harold Hill). "I mean Gerry Gil, you dingbat," says Butch. "Met the fellow last night, and I offered him the post."

"Go get him," said I, and reported the "find" to Rod Reyes.

Gerry assumed the editorship of the **Standard's** editorial pages two days later. And we picked up where we left off a decade and a half earlier.

He was the perfect foil for my role as the Attila the Hun of the newsroom. He didn't have the stomach to cashier the recalcitrants. I was heartless when it came to those things.

And we developed an almost-nightly routine after the paper had gone to bed. He, Butch del Castillo, and, sometimes, **Amante Bigornia** would repair to my office, aptly called "Bistro Cipriano" because it was the only room in the **Standard** offices with a liquor license.

"Mr. Roxas, is the bar open?" he would invariably ask. It was my signal that all was well with the opinion pages.

There were rare occasions though, when he would preface his entry with a terse "Zip, we have to talk." I knew I was in trouble.

On those rare occasions, we would forego the Bistro routine and our other stop, a watering hole hole for newsmen called "The Other Office." On those occasions, Gerry and I would do our spiritual exchange at my apartment, there to discuss the problems currently plaguing the paper.

And the editorials he wrote. What sizzlers!

Once, he asked me if I had a copy of the Bible in my office.

"I know you're spiritual, Zip, but this time, I don't mean the bottled variety. I'm looking for the real thing," he said.

"Sure," said I. "I must have a copy stashed away somewhere in that mess of an office. You'll find it."

I didn't quite appreciate it at the moment, but Gerry, the stickler for accuracy that he was, wanted to doublecheck some figures for the paper's editorial the next day.

The editorial dealt with the privilege speech delivered by a congressman who had savaged the reputations of several newspapermen, including the memory of the late **Louie Beltran**, who had died months earlier.

The congressman compared the newspapermen to Judas Iscariot, "who betrayed Christ for 36 pieces of silver."

"A slight mathematical inaccuracy here," Gerry wrote. "The Bible says 30 pieces of silver. Unless, as is his won't, the good congressman tacks on 20 percent to every transaction."

We never heard from the congressman.

Days after his passing, reams and reams of copy were written about Gerry. One of the best tributes came from his friend Jimmy Ong, vice president of San Miguel Corp., a college buddy at the University of the Philippines.

In his piece: *"Gerry Gil: The priest who might have been,"* Jimmy recounts that one late night at the old *Herald* newsroom, Gerry reflected, wistfully, that his contemporaries in the seminary were, one by one, being ordained. If he had stayed the course, by 1972 or thereabouts he might have made it to the priesthood.

Jimmy continues:

"The order of Melchizedek never lost its fascination for him: on a similar occasion, he said of his newsman's job: The typewriter is my altar, the cup of coffee is my chalice, the cigaret is my sacred host."

"In the cold light of day the comparison sounds mawkish and melodramatic. But when you come down to it, Gerry was sacerdotal, in a raffish sort of way.

"Certainly he observed two of the three great vows. In this country, you virtually take a vow of poverty if you hope to be a decent newspaperman or teacher; and Gerry was both. He was celibate, too; though there was a time at Stanford when I thought that if he only could bring himself to declare his feelings for a special lady, she'd have raced him to the nearest bed, or altar.

"The vow of obedience was the hard part. The story goes that within his first month at the seminary, he found his way to the cellar and got drunk on altar wine. Obedience would be particularly tough on

Gerry—he had too much of an impish sense of humor, too much of an eye for the absurd and the fatuous, to submit without question to authority.

"And lord! how he loved to skewer officialdom. All newsmen do; one does not join the profession out of a sense of modesty. But Gerry Gil's editorials could be particularly irritating because they were devoid of vituperation or scalding rage; their tone was one of patient, good-humored explanation of the obvious to a prize idiot.

"Gerry's editorials were inimitable in other respects. They weren't always aimed at the foibles of the mighty. He had an editorial, would you believe, on the novels of Isaac Asimov. He was masterful on the subject of educational testing and statistics—again, hardly your everyday editorial fare. And he had this habit of scanning the liturgical calendar or the day's gospel, and spinning it into an editorial on some saint or parable.

"This last, of course, is a standard ploy of a preacher looking for a likely sermon; another indication, then, of Gerry's ministerial disposition.

"It is an odd thing to dwell on, when there is so much else to write about Gerry; that he was ninong to heaven knows how many of his friend's children; that he probably yearned to be better known as a professor of research methods than as a journalist; that he wrote letters to the editor, reams of them, using different names and typefaces, sometimes one letter to refute another that he had written, and thus carrying on a debate with himself; that he was the truest friend one could ever hope to have.

"But it is as a priest that I will remember him; a priest who might have been, and, as it turns out, really was; one who felt he heard the calling, and fashioned an offbeat and lovely response."

Gerry's favorite quote came from the opening lines of Scaramouche, and it could very well have applied to himself. *"He was born with a gift of laughter, and a sense that the world was mad."*

POSTSCRIPT: Gerry died of complications arising from pneumonia.

In a compilation of the tributes to Gerry, his brother **Danny** says that Gerry had been sick for some time already, "but none of us knew it or realized how acute it was getting, until it was too late.

"After his death, we found an x-ray plate taken as a routine procedure right after his vehicular accident a month earlier. The plate was mistakenly brought to the house, where it languished unseen. It showed Gerry's damaged collarbone as expected, and it also showed his lungs clouded by bi-basal pneumonia."

***

With the strong prompting of family and friends, Jimmy Ong is writing a book which is scheduled for release hopefully by March 23, Gerry's birthday. Herein are excerpts from Jimmy's letter to the publisher:

PLAN OF PROPOSED BOOK

For more than a decade after 1972, Gerry did not write for any newspaper. Given the fate of the Philippine press under martial law, he choose not to engage in what he did best —opinion writing. Starting in the early 1980s, the press began testing its freedom. Gerry joined by writing in letters to the editors, often for the sheer fun of adding spice and clarity to the pages of a press that had grown cautious, passive and often careless with its facts.

The proposed book is an anthology of Gerry Gil's journalistic writings-columns, feature articles and letters to the editor — selected for their craftsmanship, lucidity, humor and wit.

In the case of most journalists, an anthology of this nature would be of limited interest because most of what journalist write is timely, topical and therefore quickly stale.

The pleasure one derives from reading Gerry Gil does not stem mainly from the inherent news value of his chosen topics. What sets Gerry Gil's writing apart is felicity of expression—-not what he says but how he says it — a felicity that in turn derives from a highly literate and informed mind, formidable powers of contrast and analysis, a sense of humor that made the objects of his criticism not hateful but ridiculous, and a gift for wordplay in the English language.

Even so, because what Gerry Gil wrote about was in fact timely and topical, I propose to be very selective, and limit the collection to those which will require a minimum of background context and explanation, and which can stand alone over time and lose little of their luster. This will mean, I estimate, about 100-150 editorials, 50 or so columns, about the same number of letters to the editor, and just three or four feature articles.

The primary market for this anthology would therefore be readers with an interest in the craft and practice of journalism —— particularly opinion writing —

at its best. The book can function as a reference or model for journalism professors and students, or simply for those who wish to entertain themselves with literate, stylish and often mischievous commentary on the Philippine scene.

***

In November, family and friends of Gerry in the Philippines raised enough funding to endow a professorial chair in Journalism at the University of the Philippines. See picture below. This group, headed by Peter Garrucho, Jimmy Ong and Mrs. Avelina Gil (Gerry's mother) are now trying to raise funds from friends of Gerry who are abroad. With this funding, they hope to launch a program wherein promising literary talent is

A professorial chair has been funded in the name of Gerry Gil at the College of Mass Communication in UP Diliman. Present at the turnover rites were (seated from left) Mr. Generoso Gil, Sr., Mrs. Avelina Gil, UP System Pres. Emil Javier and Mr. Peter Garrucho. (Standing from left) Cecille Garrucho, Prof Honesto Nuqui, SMC VP Jimmy Ong and CMC Dean Luis Teodoro. Gerry taught at the CMC.

encouraged by yearly contests and prizes. We enjoin you Upscans to please consider supporting this drive. Attached herein is a form with all the details.

***

Last year, some of us tried our hand in writing up some feature articles, but none ever got completed. So we're including some of them as is. Perhaps the authors will complete as a "serial" in the next issue. We also are including excerpts from letters and Christmas cards received over the past year and a half, so pardon the mish-mash. We need fillers to complete the last two pages!

***

BACK TRACK
by Malu Barrios-Garcia

Its funny to think that it really is a small world with odds of meeting each other in another country or state can be In the range of one in a eight billion, we suddenly encounter ourselves in Southern California. Who would have thought that after some twenty-some years our paths would cross, all paths leading to a small-town-city-unknown, Bellflower - midway between L.A. and Orange Counties. It was so easy to pick up where we left off even after a protracted absence. The nucleus consisted of the following interesting characters: Malu (nee Barrios) and Oids Garcia, Ofie (nee Penaflorida) Aid, Manny Castillo, and Mario Manansala.

1982 was the year when Susan (nee Po) Rufino and I were both working at Neiman Marcus in San Francisco. (Sue in the Intimate Apparel Dept and I in the Epicurean Section). It was my first job outside of teaching and it was exciting to be there at the opening of a new store with all its unique items.

1987 saw Manny Castillo and Mario Manansala having a chance encounter at the La Palma Library one lazy afternoon. Manny just moved to sunny Southern California from Chicago where he practiced as a pathologist from some ten years and got tired of Chicago's harsh winters and bone-chilling winds. Mario just got accepted at an engineering firm and had just arrived from Manila with wife Myrna and two little lovely daughters by the name of Theresa and Sophia. It really was a serendipitous encounter but the thing was Mario still had that deep baritone voice and I knew that it had to be him. Since then, the nucleus has expanded to include old stalwarts Bess Silva and visits by Alex Cuejillo from Washington, DC.

...to be continued.

***

Excerpts from a fax that Danny Gil sent to Mercy Abad in July of 1994 after he received a Happy Birthday fax bearing about 20 signatures signed during a recent party at Ping Tan's house:

"Two weeks ago Lisa and I accompanied our aunt to a PGH Nursing

The impromptu dance, Feb 17. Showing backside, L-R: Oids Garcia, Malu Barrios-Garcia, Lisa Señeris-Gil. Facing front: Offie Peñaflorida-Aid, Ernie Pangilinan, Manny Castillo. Hidden person is Perla Manapol, Lisa's cousin, who will be teaching the Merringue and Swing in the next dance session. So be there!

reunion dinner-dance at one of the Sheraton's, and although Tia Beth graduated in 1944, most of all those in the party were graduates of more recent vintage. The 1969 class clearly dominated the group: they were a cohesive and fun bunch, coming from all over the place. In one of the program writeups, I read that a certain Alita had married an Erwin Gomez. It was almost midnight when I noticed that item, so I looked around, and sure enough, there was a guy who looked like Erwin, and when I got up to ask, it really was him. He was especially anxious to get in touch with Joe Alzona, whom he had frequent contact with years earlier. So I gave him Joe's number and suggested he call now since Joe sleeps late and wakes late. Erwin and Alita were leaving to go back to Indiana the next day. He did talk to Joe, as I found out later.

Here's another episode of serendipity. About 2 months ago, we were at the airport seeing some relative off, and Lisa takes a double take and shouts "Reggie". It was Reggie Cruz Cailao, and Eddie. They were enroute to the East coast to visit their son. They gave us the news that they also were going to see Primo "Buloy" Arambulo and Lindus Carreon. I got the address from them."

***

More excerpts....

From a Christmas card sent by Effie Sta. Romana-Hall:

"Thanks for newsletter UPSCA list. It sure is great to know where people are. I'm director of college relations for Mount St. Clare College. My parents are in Wisconsin with my brother. Regards to all..."

***

From a card sent by Arthur Adiarte to José Alzona:

"Kumusta ka na JE. I guess that you probably gave our address to Danny for the Newsletter. I recognize a lot of familiar names in the list. We would be interested in an Upsca get-together.."

***

From a card sent by Johnny Reyes:

"In March, six Upsca families came to Tabangao (for the first time in the more than 25 years that we've been living in Batangas) - the Pasicolans, Abads, Javelonas, Faelnars, Martins and Barcelonas. I made a map to guide them. The engineers (P,J and B) were able to follow it, but the lawyers (F and M) got lost and arrived much later. It was a memorable weekend for us, especially since we were about to leave Tabangao then...."

***

Upsca Alumni Association Roster as of January, 1996 - details erased

Arthur & Cherrie Adiarte
St Paul, MN 55105

Tessie Chua Chiaco
Newhall, CA 91321

Danny & Lisa (Señeris) Gil
Artesia, CA 90701

Mario & Myrna Manansala
La Palma, CA 90623

Amelia (Bascon) Rasalan
Bayside, NY 11364

Ofie (Peñaflorida) & Ken Aid
Lakewood, CA 90715

Bing (Ferrer) & Anthony Dubitsky
(301) 577-7567

Erwin & Alita Gomez
Valparaiso, IN 46383

Baby Natividad
Toronto, Canada

Beryl Silva
Long Beach, CA 90808

José Alzona
Long Beach, CA 90814

Lolly Aquino
Los Angeles, CA 90042

Myrna Aquitania
Camarillo, CA 93012

Primo & Lindus Arambulo
Rockville, MD 20852

Noli Arong
Arleta, CA 91331

Sisoy Arong
Houston, TX 77036

Divsy Astraquillo
Shorewood, WI 53211

Latest group picture Feb 17, 1996 at Gil residence for Upscans and friends, front row L-R: Rey Sanidad, Ernie Pangilinan, Danny Gil, Manny Castillo. Back row L-R: Tony Estrera, Josie Estrera, Mely Batas, Jessie Pangilinan, Ollie Sanidad, Lee Espejo, Manny Espejo, Enteng Batas, Malu Garcia, Lisa Gil, Oids Garcia, Ofie Aid, Ken Aid. Sorry to cut you off at the neck, Rey, but one of the kids who took the picture did just that and the second shot was too blurred to scan.

Johnny & Alda Balaoing
Los Angeles, CA 90065

Manny & Lee Espejo
Saugus, CA 91350

Ruben & Maria Habito
Dallas, TX 75225

Ernie & Jessie Pangilinan
Mission Hills, CA 91345

Bernie (Abrera) Tjarks
Dallas, TX 75224

Nina Los Baños
Las Vegas, NV 89108

Deo & Aleli Estacio
Altadena, CA 91001

Effie (Sta Romana) Hall
Bettendorf, IA 52722

Lina (Soliman) Plantilla
Brooklyn, NY 11229

Girlie (Alzona) & Tito Valbuena
Astoria, NY 11102

Olga (Cruz) Barrios
Williamsville, NY

Tony & Josie Estrera
Cerritos, CA 90701

Chit & Vicky Inciong
Maplewood, NJ 07040

Greg Santillan
San Gabriel, CA 91775

Sari Valenzuela
Brooklyn, NY 11215

Enteng & Mely Batas
Lancaster, CA 93535

Baby (Mangosing) Evangelista
Alexandria, VA 22309

Jessica Infante
Los Angeles, CA 90065

Angel & Stella Sta Maria
Pasadena, CA 91103

Where are these others? We know they're around somewhere.

Nancy (Cruz) Binel
Kensington, MD 20875

Susan (Rodriguez) Fagan
New York, NY

Raquel (Celera) & Ric Lejano
Torrance, CA 90503

Rory (Abrera) Somerstein
Garrison, NY 10524

*Christie (Borromeo)
Mario Songco
Nilo Cruz
Rachael (Zaraspe)
Vic Vitug
Susan (Po) Rufino
Dolly (Orendain)
etc.*

Jun & Cynthia (Reyes) Calejesan
Rio Piedras, PR 00926

Dette Feliciano
Los Angeles, CA 90020

Loida (Nicolas) Lewis
New York, NY 10019

Zeny (Roxas) & Sixto Ramirez
Los Angeles, CA 90041

Joe & Cielo Carlos
Northridge, CA 91326

Terry (Dapilos) Gamboa
Patchogue, NY 11772

Manny Castillo
Brea, CA 92621

Malu (Barrios) & Oids Garcia
Cerritos, CA 90701

Editorial Box

Published by members of the Upsca Alumni Association in Los Angeles supposedly every quarter but more so whenever it catches their fancy.

19002 Horst Ave   e-mail: ferngil@AOL.com
Artesia, CA 90701   tonyest@AOL.com
tel/fax (310) 402-1890   supermario@AOL.com

UPSCA ALUMNI ASSOCIATION, USA

NEWSLETTER   **NEWSLETTER**   **NEWSLETTER**

A M D G   Vol 1, Num 3 (1st quarter, 1997)   Published by UPSCA Alumni Association, USA

ALL HEP ABOUT LAKBAYAN USA '98!

THE MANILA UPSCANS ARE GETTING ITCHY FEET (i.e., wanderlust, not the fungal variety). THERE ARE TWO MAJOR PROJECTS IN THE OFFING: *SOUTHERN CRUISE '97* and *LAKBAYAN USA '98.*

It is best that we hear from the *Loyalistas* (more on that later). Quoted below are excerpts from Johnny Reyes' email:

The above two projects were conceived by **Jimmy** *and* **Mercy Abad** *in consultation with several other UPSCA couples during a dress-up dinner they organized last Saturday 22 February at Hotel Intercon in Makati. Present were the* **Javelonas, Martins, Cruzes, Tans, Reyeses, Pasicolans, Faelnars, Beth Nuqui***, and the* **Abads** *themselves. Others were expected, but either declined or injunned. In any case, a quorum existed.*

Southern Cruise '97 *is a projected trip to the Visayan Islands, Palawan, and/or Mindanao aboard one of the new luxury ships which turn around (from Manila and back) within 4 to 5 days. Preferred stopovers are Boracay Beach (reputedly one of the best in the world), Puerto Princesa, and Camiguin. The choice of carrier and route will depend on cost-effectiveness, novelty, and safety. Families will be included. A bit remote from where you American folks are located.*

Lakbayan U.S. '98 *- another Abad brainstorm - is a planned motorcade across continental America by UPSCAns mostly coming from here in the Philippines, but augmented by United States-based UPSCAns who have both the time and the interest to take time off from work and to tag along. An estimate mentioned last 22 February of the optimal time required was 12 days. Two couples at a time can probably share a rented Plymouth Voyager, with room enough for baggage (no kids this time). The intention is to design the route so that it passes near as many UPSCA residences as practicable, without sacrificing the potential for sightseeing. The resident will be expected to provide advice on the most scenic routes in his*

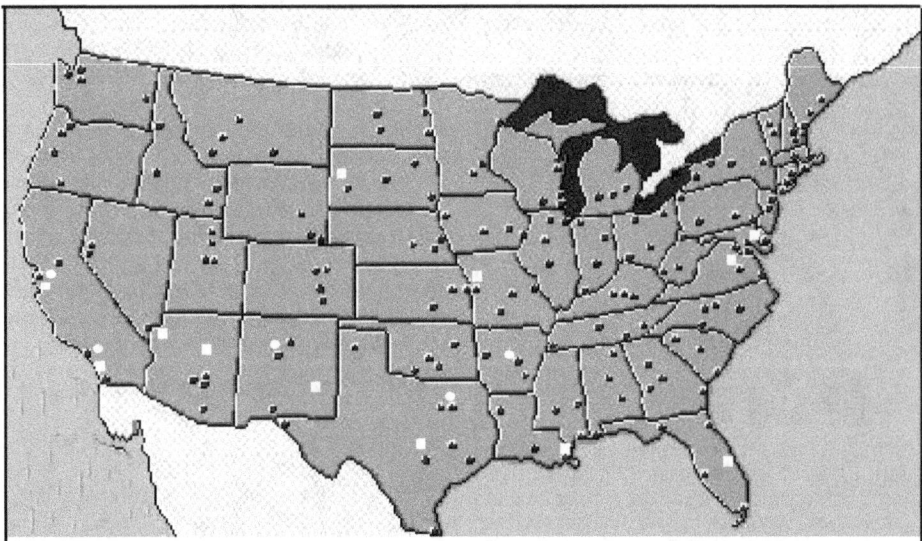

Here's the USA map with dots showing major cities. Draw in a most suitable route to pass through the circles (where there are known Upscans who are glad to be visited) and the squares where the sightseeing is good. Consider the roadways, although unfortunately not shown. Mark up other areas of interest and communicate with Mercy Abad and/or Johnny Reyes.

area; point out where decent overnight accommodations can be obtained at an affordable price, and act as a communication center so that stragglers who lose their way can reestablish contact with the rest of the group via only a local call. Why wait until next year? So we will have time to save up for the trip - hoping that when September 1998 comes around, we are all still physically fit.

Tony Estrera (Los Angeles), **Christie Borromeo-Kawal** (Albuquerque), **Susan Po-Rufino** (San Francisco) and **Nancy Cruz-Dienel** (Little Rock) then joined into a lively email exchange, pointing out especially the problem of trying to cover too much ground. As Nancy said:

If you plan to go coast to coast, you would need more than 12 days (unless you do it the Nippon way - click your camera and go!); it would be an awful lot of driving. Is this trip strictly sight-seeing or kind of outdoors, activity-related, i.e. short hikes in and around National Parks/Forests such as Yosemite, Grand Canyon, Mesa Verde, Carlsbad Caverns in New Mexico, etc or NYC Broadway Theaters cruise? Or probably mixed activities for everyone?

So Johnny gets more excited, becomes an eager advocate, and starts applying some engineering equations and what-if scenarios:

I was hoping we could go a bit farther east than Colorado— meaning the Atlantic Coast. This exercise is not something we can do every year, so we should really maximize. But it's such a good idea I'm getting carried away with it. My only problem is that they want it next year—not this year—

Johnny Reyes, then, in 1964 yearbook.

but I feel there is so little time left, and we're not getting any younger. **Jimmy** *and* **Mercy** *are the Project Managers,* **Danny Gil** *is the Senior Consultant, and* **I am the MEA (Most Eager Advocate)***. I hope that during his visit to the Philippines in July 1997, the Senior Consultant can come up with (a) a Project Definition and Scope (including a Menu of Options); (b) a plus-or-minus 10 percent Estimate of the Costs; (c) and Sensitivity Considerations (the answers to "What if -"*

questions, such as *"What if too many or too few couples decide to participate?"*; *"What if it becomes unseasonably cold in September?"*; *"What if the peso-dollar rate changes drastically?"*; *"What if the Philippines severs diplomatic relations with the U.S.?"* Another important piece of information is the cost penalty when you return a hired car at a city different from where you picked it up - How does it compare with the added cost of designing your route so that you ultimately come back to your starting point (an inefficient way of making a sightseeing trip)?

Johnny Reyes - now, or almost so. Taken in July 1992 at Mon Pasicolan's QC house during a get-together. Notice the similar type of smile on Johnny's face? Can someone remember the adjective used to describe his smile? Beside him is wife Mila (nee Garcia).

2. You are right in saying that there is a risk we may be trying to cover too much ground, and ending up not enjoying ourselves. My own pet interest is the driving from coast to coast (and exploring the major cities at either end), which is really a once-in-a-lifetime activity. I am not so interested in sightseeing the national parks in America's backyard—after you have seen the Grand Canyon, what else is new?—but I don't know what the preference of the majority is. I already said to Mercy that I am just a follower, and am prepared to go along with whatever the majority want.

*3. It may also liven up the trip if we hold a little competition between the **EXPATRIADOS** (Danny, Tony, and the rest of the U.S.-based crowd, who are familiar with the terrain) and the **LOYALISTAS** (we who are Philippines-based, and coming in cold), to see who get to the important milestones first.*

4. The prize for winning could be six bottles of Champagne—to be consumed at the end of the trip (real Champagne, not the soda pop made in California).

5. I hope people will make time available in 1998 to join this little adventure,

because I am confident it will be an enjoyable and unforgettable experience. Moreover, as a group activity it is an opportunity which will come only once in a lifetime (I don't think anyone will want to cross the U.S. more than once—there are other things to do).

6. Willingness and ability to drive in the U.S. will be useful, but are not essential. For example, I am prepared to take a non-driving couple along with us (I can't relax anyway when somebody else is at the wheel), provided they will share the cost of the car rental and the fuel.

Johnny goes on with spreadsheets on time and distance data, and compares it with his family's sojourns in Europe during his overseas assignment in Holland. And hopefully with tongue-in-cheek says:

Guys, inasmuch as we seem to be already mulling a five-year planning period, how about the following project proposals:

1999 - Vladivostok to St. Petersburg by train (via Moscow).
2000 - Rio De Janeiro across the Andes to Machu Picchu.
2001 - Kampala to Lagos via Rwanda/Zaire.
2002 - Sydney to Perth by camel.

Somewhere among the email exchanges, the idea of getting too old and geriatric came up, and of course, there's its consolation, per Nancy:

I can't help but comment: who is thinking of a geriatric trip?? That is not in our vocabulary at all, not yet, anyway. They say, it is all in the mind (mind over body?). In reference to Mercy's note,

before Alzheimer or whatever else sets in, we better do this trip while we can and while we can still recognize one another. On the other hand, if it reaches that stage (meaning having Alzheimer's tendencies, may we all be spared!), it is really <u>like being in a new place every time</u> since your short-term memory comes and goes, you won't know if you have been to a place or not!

Susan (Po) and Guilly Rufino sign up right away:

Yes! Guilly & I would definitely love to act as area marshals for San Francisco and the Bay Area for fellow UPSCANs touring the US. I'd like to join the group at some point, too!

And finally, Mercy wraps it all up:

Dear Johnny,

Please consider us as a non-driving couple. Gemino drives but his style drives me crazy (often times he fancies himself as Steve McQueen). If you make Gemino drive, I'm taking the bus and see you at the next station. I intend to enjoy this trip and have a lot of laughs.

All this e-mail conversation is heightening the anticipation! I can't wait for 1998. What if Pres Ramos decides to run and we have a revolution? For sure I'm going back to the streets, this time with weak knees. How I miss Gerry and Fredie.

Best regards,

Mercy

At Hoover Dam, while en route from Las Vegas to Grand Canyon, during the 1992 visit of the Abads. L to R, younger daughter Cybele, (now a medical student in UP), Jimmy flanked by adopted twins Diego and David, Mercy, tour guide Lisa Gil and Cyan. Cyan, now teaching at Ateneo, was in LA until last year where she took further post-graduate courses after a 2 year stint in Boston.

For those who didn't catch the significance of Mercy's last sentence, here's some news, albeit stale, but relevant nonetheless especially for us who felt the loss dearly.

Gerry Gil passed away July 1995, a case of walking pneumonia. He was opinion editor of The Manila Standard for the past 5 years, and a selection of his writings were collected by Jimmy Ong and published last year as "*Wordsmith with a Slingshot, the Gerry Gil Book*". The book is available for $15 and part of the proceeds goes towards the Gerry Gil Foundation for Best Journalistic Writing Awards.

Fredie Santiano passed away July 1992 from a heart attack. It happened a few days before a get-together hosted by some Upscans for Danny & Lisa Gil and family who were visiting. Many of the pictures shown herein are from that gathering.

Pre-1984 photo showing some of the *barkada*. Sitting, L to R, Melvyn Martin, Danny Gil, Jimmy Abad, Mon Pasicolan, Noel Soriano. Standing, Jimmy Ong, Lino Faelnar, Fredie Santiano, Gani Cruz, Ping Tan, Tigi Barcelona, Gerry Gil, Ruben Rivera. Can anyone recall the date/occasion?

EDITORIAL

What is a newsletter? This question becomes all the more relevant as the proliferation of computers makes it so simple for almost anybody to whip up a sheet or two of printed matter. While the word "news" implies that the topics are recent, this isn't always the case. The contents could vary from manifesto-like pronouncements on pet issues and opinions, to gossipy chatter, or to a mish-mash of communications (written or emailed) amongst a common group. Many a newsletter - especially those originating from various office departments in large government bureaucracies - are tools of propaganda. Newsletter names can be catchy. For instance, in an agency dealing in pest control, someone suggested that the newsletter be named either "The Pest Times" or "The Pest of Times", obviously punning Dickens' famous opening line. Many newsletters, however, fall under the category of the "vanity press", which means that the editor(s) and/or the contributors alike are frustrated writers who still keep on trying.

However the case may be for this UPSCA Newsletter, the intent of those behind it is to bridge the distance and the years that have separated those who met in the late '50s to the mid '60s at the Chapel Basement of the University of the Philippines, made fast and lasting friendships, and now look back fondly on that segment of their lives as formatively ennobling and memorable.

Perhaps this paper should be renamed "Upscans Reminisce Times." Nicely ambiguous, isn't it?

Any other suggestions?

The advent of email has spawned an avalanche of fast communication. Whereas before, one had to scrounge around for something to say and write so as to fill the few pages in a newsletter for the amusement of the target audience, now it's so much simpler: merely import the saved files and reprint them. So, here goes (of course, some of the passages are lifted off from the more conventional snail mail files):

From Susan (Po) Rufino last year regarding the previous Newsletter:

First of all, thank you for reprinting Gerry's letter to a friend's daughter. I'm still re-reading (and thinking) about some lines there. You know, I only got to know him better after my UP days when I was already working at the Department of Foreign Affairs and he was with the Press Foundation of Asia. My work at the DFA (as one of the originals in the 3-man office of the ASEAN Secretariat) entailed a lot of interaction with the press and that's how Gerry and I got re-acquainted.

As for me now, I've been working as a realtor in San Francisco since 1991. My husband Guilly (for Guillermo) and I work as a team with TRI Realtors-Jon Douglas Co. So, spread the word and refer your friends to us!

From Rory (Abrera) Somerstein early 1996 regarding the query about her email name:

Caniki is an island owned by my family in Palawan; hence the name CANIKIISLE. Keeps the memory of the Philippines alive for me (the coconut trees, white sandy beaches and the China Sea)! We're presently developing it into a private resort.

Nice to hear about old friends. It's like being Rip Van Winkle, waking up after 20 years!

When you write the next newsletter, you can say I'm still running my two schools and am also very busy with my TV show. Presently I'm scheduled to interview the former editor of Life Magazine. Also have the first black model of the USA lined up and the CEO of Starbucks Coffee! Also do community service at a nursing home on Sundays for 8 hours. The residents are lonely, need visitors and lots of help. I provide that. Very fulfilling and satisfying work for me.

My eldest son is 27 and my daughter is 22. Both finished college and are working already. [The youngest], Marc is in 8th grade.

Later last year, they drove cross country and daughter Sandra enrolled for further studies in Arizona.

Rory and daughter Sandra hamming it up in a Ghost-town wild West scene.

From Jun and Cynthia (Reyes) Calejesan in Puerto Rico, late 1995:

Jun is in his second year as General Manager of 3 plants for Cutler-Hammer. Two are in PR and the other is in the Dominican Republic. We originally were supposed to be in PR for 2 years but are now going 5. We have 4 children. Lyn is a senior at Penn State. Eva and Aimee are twins in the 11th grade, Virgil, the youngest is the computer buff. All four grew up as active members of the Samahang Pilipino in Pittsburgh. I guess you might say I'm doing my thing, mainly at school and at church ... volunteer work for Unicef, past PTA president, member of book and gourmet groups, etc., squeezed in between limo service for the kids. Next year when the twins will be ready to step into college, I shall probably have to rejoin the rat race and chase the almighty dollar to help pay tuition costs.

From Priscilla (Bautista) Perez in NY regarding the Gerry book:

The book was really good reading. I also think it amusing that Gerry used my old address in Makati, with some modification, for one of his characters in the letters to the editor.

From Ruben Habito in Dallas early 1996:

Give my regards to our friends out there, among them Tony & Josie Estrera, Malu & Oids Garcia, Berryl Silva, and loads of others. I recall my short but intense period of "hanging around" at the Delaney Hall with fondness and gratitude.

From Christie to Johnny:

Great hearing from you. Regards to Mila. Do you have any kids? We have two, Reena (26 yrs) and Tony (21).

Johnny's reply:

Your question about kids—these are our girls:

Maria Margarita	26
Maria Mercedes	24
Maria Marcelina	14
Maria Matilde	14
Micaela (adopted Maltese)	7

My, my, many members might mistake minstrels like Mauricio and Mila making Mariam markers mandatory as mad mayhem.

(Ed note: I honestly thought at first that Johnny's adoptee was a real maiden, not a Maltese mutt).

Johnny's zeal in reporting the Lakbayan project extended to his mailing of photos where the event was first discussed, such as the one above, captioned thus: "The building at left is the Interconn, where the dress up dinner was held two weeks earlier. Unfortunately no one brought a camera during the dinner itself". Two other photos showing a parking lot and empty stairwell have therefore been omitted due to space considerations.

Regarding Holy week, Nancy mused:

Today, on our way to work at about 7:30 AM, I was suddenly reminded of our typical Good Friday in Manila in the 60's - quiet, not much traffic, no rock music, etc. One almost did not mind the humidity and the heat. Is it still very much the same way? (the quietness, that is) In contrast, in Little Rock (or any other city in USA, I am sure) the traffic was just like any other day and so was the music on the radio. Somehow, I was also reminded of the "retreats" we used to participate in during the Lenten week at U.P. Diliman, topped with the midnight mass at Easter. It was joyful yet so very peaceful; a retreat from the madding crowds but close to friends and family. Are we really getting old(er) when long term-memory-recall keeps tugging at the brain cells?

Johnny answered:

Good Friday in Manila is as quiet nowadays as it was when we were still in college. It is an ideal time to be in Manila, except for the fact that all shops are closed. Everyone else is on his way to Baguio or to some "resort." I say "on his way," because the chances are he will never get there. A big change since the 60's is the current volume of traffic on our highways. Besides being extremely heavy,

the traffic flow is aggravated when a bottleneck arises, and all motorists converge from both sides, taking up every available space like flowing water. The result is gridlock, and although volunteer traffic managers do a heroic job trying to untangle the jam, their efforts are usually futile because they don't have the equipment (walkie-talkies, helicopters, passably high IQ's, etc.) to handle major traffic problems. Last Holy Thursday, the expressway to the north was at a standstill until late at night, according to radio reports.

During the early part of these email exchanges, some confusion was inevitable. Johnny thought that the ncruz@ address was Nilo Cruz. But apparently, he also was confused to be somebody else. As he wrote:

Note to Susan Po-Rufino: I think you are confusing me with Johnny Ramos. I have nothing to do with music, except play tapes and CD's.

Note to Christie, Rory, and Susan: You asked what I am doing, and where I am living. My job is Development and Technology Head at Shell Refinery in Tabangao, Batangas (110 kilometers south of Manila). This e-mail connection is in my bedroom, not in the office.

Incidentally, Johnny Ramos is still at the UP Conservatory of Music, and very active in the lay apostolate group *Opus Dei*.

From Danny to Christie and Nancy:

We've been in LA since 1982. Came over with the three kids. Now, Ramon, the oldest at 29, has been in NY for over three years working as a graphics/arts designer. Babette, at 27, also works in NY as a tech writer for a finance firm. She moved there 2-1/2 years ago when her husband (they met at UCLA) got an MS scholarship. He just finished and is now working at NY, too. So we have one grandkid at 4 years, and he indeed is the apple in the eye. Joey, the youngest at 22 will be finishing his molecular microbiology course at UCLA this year, and intends to go for post graduate studies. Lisa works as a registered pharmacist, and I work in engineering for the State as a licensed PE.

Editorial Box

Typeset by Danny Gil in Los Angeles from unwitting contributors from the Internet and abetted by other accomplices of the UPSCA Alumni Association. Published supposedly every quarter but more so whenever it catches their fancy. Call, write, or fax in your comments, pictures, articles to postal address below, or email as shown.

19002 Horst Ave   e-mail: ferngil@themall.net
Artesia, CA 90701   jmreyes@mozom.com
tel/fax (562) 402-1890   tonest@aol.com

Miscellany

Isagani Cruz is the pioneer in this emailing circle of Upsca friends. However, most of his voluminous output is too intellectual for reprinting, as the cerebrations are south of the waist meridian. For example, here is an interpretation from the bible, which he picked up somewhere and graciously relayed to us:

1. Noah's wife was Joan of Ark.
2. Lot's wife was a pillar of salt by day and a ball of fire by night.
3. Joshua led the Hebrews in the battle of Geritol.
4. Moses went to the top of Mount Cyanide to get the Ten Commandments.
5. The 7th commandment is "Thou shalt not admit adultery."
6. Jesus was born because Mary had an immaculate contraption.
7. The people who followed Jesus were called the 12 Decibels.
8. The epistles were the wives of the apostles.
9. One of the opossums was St. Matthew.
10. Salome danced in seven veils in front of King Harrod's.
11. Paul preached acrimony, which is ano-another name for marriage.
12. David fought the Finklesteins, a race of people who lived in Biblical times.
13. A Christian should have only one wife. This is called monotony.

Which brings to mind his 60's interpretation of AMDG, which every Upscan should know stands for the latin phrase *Ad Majorem Dei Gloriam - for the greater glory of God*. Guess what his AMDG meant, and win a prize: a *free ticket* for the Lakbayan (provided we can get a sponsor). A hint is that his AMDG had something to do with gustatory craving. Along the same vein, in a similar pronouncement years ago, Caesar's **veni, vidi, veci** became **veni, vidi, mandocavi**, which per Isagani, meant *I came, I saw, I masticated (or, I chewed)*.

Most husbands, however, subconsciously mutter *"I came, I saw, I concurred."*

-o-o-o-o-

Here's another printable truth from Gani:

There was a man and lady in an elevator on the 99th floor, when all of a sudden the cable snapped and the elevator started to plummet at an incredible rate. They looked at each other, both pale as ghosts. The lady gasped, ripped off her blouse, and said, "Make me feel like a woman for the last time." With that, the man ripped off his shirt and said, "Here, iron this!"

A 1992 photo of the interior of the Chapel of the Holy Sacrifice, with its rounded structure clearly discernable. Still looks the same as it was in the '60s, with the murals and curved pews.

One day my son **Ramon** was musing about the theory of *"The Six Levels of Connection"* which states that anybody in the world can be connected to anybody else because they personally know someone who, in turn, knows another person, who knows that person in question, and so forth. So for example, he is connected on the third level to the Pope because his grand-uncle Msgr. Raval, a bishop, knows Cardinal Sin, who in turn, knows the **Pope**. The theory states that anybody in the world is connected to anybody else in an average of only six levels (3 levels up to some international figure, then 3 levels down to another nobody). It is interesting to trace such connections. For instance, I have a cousin-in-law who worked for the PLO office in Washington and met Yassir **Arafat**. So all of you Upscans whom I know are only 3 levels away from Arafat. Can anybody trace a closer connection to say, **Elvis Presley** or the **Queen** of England? Send in your answers. There might be another prize!

No, this is not the exterior of the Chapel. It's a look-alike building in Los Angeles that was recently demolished. Used to be an Elks Club.

Here is an 10 year old letter from the late Gerry Gil to Bong Nuqui. If you appreciate it's subtle undertones, then you were "in with the crowd" then:

Dear Bong:

As you predicted, I did make a snide remark about Noel's being made National Security Adviser, but the snide remark, alas, makes sense only to those old enough to remember the former name of ANSCOR.

I told Noel that I understood that the National Security Committee is known in certain media circles as "SORIANO Y CIA."

What I really would have enjoyed would be Noel's appointment to the board of San Miguel Corporation. Such an appointment would not only create confusion in the public mind as to which Soriano is which but also complicate the work of Jimmy Ong and San Miguel's other publicists.

The only way the press would be able to distinguish one Soriano from the other is would be to talk of the "white Soriano" and the "black Soriano;" "the Wharton White" and "the Harvard Black;" "pale Pilsen" and "cerveza Negra;" perhaps even "el insular" and "el indio."

Underlying all this would be the whispered speculations about the possibility that the late Col. Andres Soriano sired a bastard during one of his visits to plant in Cebu.

An additional bonus is the presence of Ramon del Rosario on the board: the press would have a field day gleefully distinguishing between "Boy Blue" and "Boy Black."

But enough of this talk about Noel. We should talk about you for a change. Did you know that ever since you moved over to Fiji, some of your friends have started referring to you as a "Suva-non"?

Gerry

Noel Soriano is still recovering from a stroke. He was with AIM and was running his own consultancy. Any communication for him could be coursed to **Angge** (Alday) Soriano. Let us keep praying for his continued recovery. **Bong Nuqui** is now with the Math Department in UP.

So, hereeeeeeeee's Gani! With his wife Medy during their last visit to LA. Gani is with La Salle and writes in various publications.

The Gil's, *R to L:* Danny, Lisa, grandkid Minkoy, Babette, Joey and Ramon. Son-in-law Ian took the picture, 1993 HS grad time.

More email/snail mail excerpts:

From Melvyn about Christmas:

Here is a fax message I received from an anonymous sender. It is from a sign on the wall of Sjishu Bhavan, the children's home in Calcutta, India. It sort of grabs you because it is so Christian. It is easier read than done. Here goes:

ANYWAY

People are unreasonable, illogical and self-centered, love them anyway.
If you do good, people will accuse you of selfish, ulterior motives, do good anyway.
If you are successful, you win false friends and true enemies, succeed anyway.
The good you do will be forgotten tomorrow, do good anyway.
Honesty and frankness make you vulnerable, be honest and frank anyway.
What you spent years building may be destroyed overnight, build anyway.
People really need help but may attack you if you help them, help anyway.
Give the world the best you have and you'll get kicked in the teeth, give the world the best you've got anyway.

Merry Christmas to you and your loved ones!

From my daughter Babette - Random Thoughts:

1. *If a mute swears, does his mother wash his hands with soap?*
2. *If someone with multiple personalities threatens to kill himself, is it considered a hostage situation?*
3. *Instead of talking to your plants, if you yelled at them would they still grow? Only to be troubled and insecure?*
4. *Is there another word for synonym?*
5. *Isn't is it a bit unnerving that doctors call what they do "practice"?*
6. *When sign makers go on strike, is anything written on their signs?*
7. *When you open a bag of cotton balls, is the top one meant to be thrown away?*
8. *Where do forest rangers go to "get away from it all"?*
9. *Why isn't there mouse-flavored cat food?*
10. *Why do they report power outages on TV?*
11. *What do you do when you see an endangered animal that is eating an endangered plant?*
12. *What's another word for thesaurus?*
13. *If a parsley farmer is sued, can they garnish his wages?*
14. *Would a fly without wings be called a walk?*
15. *Why do they lock gas station bathrooms? Are they afraid someone will clean them?*
16. *Why do people who know the least know it the loudest?*
17. *If the funeral procession is at night, do folks drive with their headlights off?*
18. *If a stealth bomber crashes in a forest, will it make a sound?*
18. *If a turtle doesn't have a shell, is he homeless or naked?*
19. *When it rains, why don't sheep shrink?*
20. *Should vegetarians eat animal crackers?*
21. *If the cops arrest a mime, do they tell him he has the right to remain silent?*
22. *Why is the word abbreviation so long?*
23. *When companies ship Styrofoam, what do they pack it in?*
24. *If you're cross-eyed and have dyslexia, can you read all right?*

From Nancy:

Do you remember Yaying (Pilar Enriquez Ilano)? She visited us about 6 years ago in Maryland; it was as though her last good-bye and it was. She was killed in a car accident on their way to Baguio for the annual pre-graduation rites at PMA - her father, 2 brothers, husband, son, were all PMA graduates.

From someone who'd rather remain anonymous:

I am so deeply saddened by Gerry's leaving us - first Fredie, (only one "d", he always told me), then Gerry - I guess we're all somehow moving into the "waiting room in that train station" taking us to that inevitable journey - to another Upsca get-together! (Was it Tigi who said that? I added the last part).

-o-o-o-o-

A few weeks ago, Lisa decided to clean out the box in which all the past photos and snapshots have been kept, and then set them up in the proper albums. So I helped out in sorting them, and pulled a bunch of Upsca-related pictures which are now printed all over this issue, hopefully with accurate captions on dates and places. As they say, *a picture speaks a thousand words. So here goes:*

Clemencia "Babynats" Natividad flanked by her mom and cousin Danny, at Niagara Falls, Canada sometime 1991. She stays in Toronto.

Erwin Gomez extended his San Diego trip to came over to LA to meet visitor Jimmy Ong in May 1996. Erwin with José Alzona.

Rolly Mesa, Tigi Barcelona and Mercy Abad posing for old times sake, July '92, QC.

The '92 welcome party which also turned out to be a farewell. *1st row, L-R:* Maya Santiano, Peanuts Pañares, Mercy Abad, Maureen Faelnar. *2nd row:* Angge Soriano, Beth Nuqui, Susan Martin, Merle Tan, Tercy Villaruz, Lallie Lacaba, Nora Barcelona, Lisa Gil and Ting Ong.

Picture at right. The July 1992 party at Mon Pasicolan's. It was a house warming, bienvenida for the Gil's, and a farewell for Fredie Santiano, who passed away a week earlier. *L to R, rear to front:* Fr Nim Gonzales, Kit Villaruz (Tercy Mortola's hubby), Gerry Gil (with camera), Ping Tan, Eddie Magtoto, Bong Nuqui, Noel Soriano, Danny Gil, Rolly Mesa, Jimmy Abad, Mon, Melvyn Martin, Lino Faelnar, Tigi Barcelona, Ruben Rivera, Jess Javelona, Romy Manlapaz.

Ely Alampay and Sonia (nee Alday) posing sweetly. Ely runs a law office in Makati. He recently authored a beautiful childrens book "Yahin, Nihay".

Tessie Chua-Chiaco teaches piano and runs a music studio north of LA.

Posing in LA: Angel Sta Maria, Manny Espejo and Jessica Infante. Jessica is a nurse at Kaiser Hospital. Angel and Manny are supervisors at their respective places of work.

At the same gathering as above, drinking a toast to Fredie. Looking very somber, *L - R:* Mimi Pasicolan, Ting Ong, Gerry Gil and Merle Tan. In background is Johnny Reyes and Susan Martin.

Dance session time during one of the LA parties. Leading the pack on the dance floor is Donnie Joaquin, UP Eng'g guest.

A few moments later for another toast, someone must have said something funny about Fredie, or the toasts were getting one too many. Shown clearly are Ruben and Naida Rivera, Mercy Abad, Beth Nuqui, Mon Pasicolan, Noel and Angge Soriano, Josie Magtoto, Nora Barcelona and Maureen Faelnar.

At Gerry's wake July '95: Jimmy and Ting Ong, Danny, Mercy and Jimmy Abad, Maya Santiano, Josie Estrera and Mon Pasicolan. Danny flew in; Josie happened to be in Manila on vacation. Floral arrangements at back are, among others, from Loida (Nicolas) Lewis, and from Pres Ramos.

Johnny Balaoing making announcements the other year at Upsca gathering about the forth-coming visit of a UP troupe featuring Maurice Borromeo. Johnny is literally young-at-heart. He's a transplant recipient since a few years back.

NVM Gonzales and Jimmy Ong at Loyola Cemetery.

At Gerry's wake. Danny Gil, Alex de Leon and Fr Nebres, president of Ateneo. Fr Nebres and Gerry were together in Stanford in the '60s.

Fr Art Ferrer officiating mass at Gil residence in Makati at the 9th day of prayer. Art is dean of the Law School in Ateneo de Cagayan.

In Sep '96, Tigi and Nora passed thru LA on a visit to Florida. A joint Upsca and UP Mech'l Eng'g party was thrown in their honor at Danny's place. Caught candidly while eating is Tigi. Other Up-scans are Mario Manansala (sit-ting at right) and Ernie and Tony (extreme left). Another Upscan surfaced then: Remy Chica.

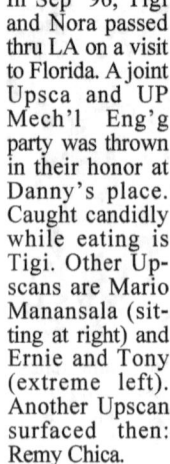

NY '96. Chit Inciong flanked by Lisa Gil and Dennis O'Leary. Chit runs his insurance agency, and wife Vicky was recently on overseas assign-ment with the UN. Dennis was Gerry's contempo-rary in the seminary in the '50s and was a news media person with Jimmy Ong in Cotabato in the early '60s. He now is the "unofficial" historian at the Phil Embassy. Lisa and Danny (who took the picture) were visiting the grandkid.

Listening to a Tigi joke (head barely showing): Mon, Ruben, Eddie, Bong, while Lino and Gani stand behind. At the July '92 party at the Pasicolan's.

First LA visitor for '96, Mon Pasicolan, shown with Tony Estrera and José Alzona. Jimmy Ong and Tigi Barcelona followed shortly.

Nina Los Baños caught surprised on camera while Manny Espejo, Jimmy Abad, Johnny Balaoing and Enteng Batas chat in the brackground. Nina came all the way from Las Vegas to attend the LA party for the Abads.

Manny Castillo cracking his really funny doctor jokes, as Malu (Barrios) Garcia and Alda Balaoing share a laugh just before attacking dessert.

Belting it out with song. Enteng Batas, Ernie Pangilinan (at piano), Josie Estrera, Oids and Malu Garcia, and Lisa's back. A January post-Christmas party.

At the UP Mass Comm library where Gerry's parents donated some of his books, soon after the completion of the fund drive to set up a Professorial Chair in Journalism in Gerry's memory. L - R: Dean Teodoro, Prof and Upscan Georgina (Reyes) Encanto, Prof Carolina Malay, and Mrs and Mr Gil. Georgina recently completed her PhD.

Editors note: this issue should have had a number of more interesting pictures. Christie and Nancy were sending some of theirs, which in an email note, said something about the pictures being necessary so we can recognize each other for the Lakbayan '98! However, as the deadline nears, and this issue goes to press, the pictures haven't yet arrived in the mail. Also, I was expecting some emailed scans of the Oct '96 Gerry Gil book launching in Manila showing a number of political big wigs nervously leafing thru the book to see if their names were in there, while editor Jimmy Ong looks on gleefully. But, no luck, too. As mentioned elsewhere, these photos came out from the big box containing a ten year collection. I could not find those showing the 1994 and 1995 Upsca camping trips to the seashore and to the mountains, or the parties at Johnny's and Angel's houses where the elder of the Arong brothers first made his appearance. Or the July '96 trip home where Swiss resident Bernie (de Castro) Mueller was around. One consolation for all these omissions is that there'll be a stronger incentive to come out with a next issue soon. So you folks out there, send in your pictures, news, jokes, anecdotes, etc.

UPSCA ALUMNI ASSOCIATION, USA

NEWSLETTER   NEWSLETTER   NEWSLETTER

Vol 1, Num 4 (3rd quarter, 1997)   Published by UPSCA Alumni Association, USA

SOUTHERN CRUISE FELL THRU, BUT LAKBAYAN WON'T!

Remember the headline in the last issue? The *Loyalistas*' wanderlust plans? Here's a quote from Johnny, the prolific correspondent:

After all the hoopla, I hope the Lakbayan U.S. '98 project does not fall through. The Southern Cruise '97 project already has—After a date was set (28 April) by the Abads, Pasicolans, Javelonas, and Martins, everybody backed out except us. We had no choice but to cancel also for the meantime.

Regards. Johnny

-o-o-o-

JOIN THE LAKBAYAN! SIGN UP NOW!

The LAKBAYAN'98 will go through. Tentatively scheduled to fly in Friday, 17 April 1998 are the **Reyes'** (with two daughters), the **Abads**, and the **Pasicolans** (who may be a few days late). Other *Loyalistas* who have indicated their interest but have not yet committed are the **Javelonas, Faelnars, Ongs, Nuquis** and **Tans**. *Expatriados* who have committed are the **Gils** and **Tony Estrera**. Others who indicated interest are the **Batas'** and the **Pangilinans**, so far. There most likely will be more locals interested especially after this Newsletter explains the plan for the first time (we haven't had a get-together in ages, though Tony is setting up a party when **Fr Pat** makes his expected visit).

The grand tour is designed to accomodate anybody who *can spare 1, 2 or 3 weeks vacation.* The proposed itinerary has been intermeshed so that all groups can be together the longest possible time, seeing a good portion of the American outdoors, at quite a reasonable cost.

The plan for the *Loyalistas* are as follows: after flying in Friday April 17, they rest and/or do some sightseeing, then local UPSCANs host a get-together Sunday evening at the Gil's residence. On Monday mid-morning, together with **Tony Estrera** and **Lisa & Danny Gil**, we embark on a drive via large van to *Las Vegas* for an overnight cum gambling jaunt, then to *Flagstaff AZ* with side trip to

The LATEST and the MOSTEST of the *Loyalistas*, taken August 2, 1997 at Jimmy Ong's house, on the occasion of an *Expatriado* couple a-visiting. Identified by numbers: 1-2 Jong & Ting Ong, 3-4 Jimmy & Mercy Abad, 5-6 Mon & Mimi Pasicolan, 7-8 Johnny & Mila Reyes, 9-10 Tigi & Nora Barcelona, 11-12 Jess & Jessie Javelona, 13-14 Lino & Maureen Faelnar, 15-16 Bong & Beth Nuqui, 17 Georgina Reyes-Encanto, 18 Anggie Soriano, 19 Maya Santiano, 20 Nilo Cruz, 21 Ping Tan, 22-23 Lisa & Danny Gil.

Hoover Dam or *Grand Canyon*. Next overnight will be *Albuquerque NM* where we visit **Christie** and family, then *Rosswell* for UFO country and *Carlsbad Caverns*, where we stay 2 nights, pitching tent to "rough it out". Next stop is *Dallas TX* where the group splits into the 2-week and 3-week trekkers. The **Gils** and other (if any) 2-week trekkers continue in the van by swinging north for another week. At this point, the **Pangilinans** may fly in from LA as they can spare only a week. The van riders then proceed to *Yellowstone National Park* passing through *Oklahoma, Kansas, Nebraska* and *Wyoming* to *Yellowstone*, then swing south-west through *Salt Lake*, parts of *Utah, Death Valley*, and back to *Los Angeles*. The 3-week trekkers rent car(s) at *Dallas*, and proceed to *Little Rock*, where they see **Nancy** & family, proceed to *Memphis* to see **Elvis**, then drive through the *Appalachians* and *Moonshine* country to *Washington DC*, stay 2 or 3 days visiting museums, **Liliosa** and **Lindus** among others, then proceed to *New York, Boston*, etc. They return the car(s) at *Newark NJ* and fly back to LA or SF, thence to Manila.

Since **Johnny** wanted an estimated cost plus or minus 10%, we worked out some scenarios on spreadsheets, after making inquiries on cost of car rental, local plane fares, motel rates and the like. Within this issue are *two such spreadsheets*, which show the details of all *estimated costs* and *proposed schedules*. Each is based on a "module", an idealized combination of participants for the most economical and comfortable van/car arrangement. The biggest hurdle was in trying to arrange for a one-way rental vehicle without having to pay a hefty drop-off charge.

So please carefully look at pages 8 and 9, then throw in your suggestions, as these schedules will definitely change to fit the group's concensus. Then make your commitment before the end of the year. Remember, the more the merrier.

-o-o-o-

Johnny has defined terms for the project. As he says in an email to the *Loop* (more on that later):

Here is a review of existing terminology:

(a) UPSCAns who migrated to the U.S. in the 60's to seek their fortune - *Expatriados*.
(b) UPSCAns who stayed in the Philippines through thick and thin - *Loyalistas*.
(c) UPSCAns who lost contact - *Desaparecidos*.
(d) UPSCAns who reestablished contact recently - *Resurectados*.

And some new terms:

(e) Those who are planning to join the Lakbayan next year - *Los Atrevidos*.
(f) Those who will finally do it - *Los Majaderos*.
(g) Those who want to do only half of the coast-to-coast - *Media Entradas*.
(h) Those who would prefer a more leisurely pace - *Los Geriaticos*.
(i) Those who would prefer to hire a bus - *Commuters' Chapter*.
(j) Those not included in (i) - *Aquellos-con-nunales-en-sus-pies*.
(k) Those who will cancel at the last minute - *Los Indianeros*.
(l) What the Lakviajeros will look like during the exercise - *Los Refugidores; o La Gente del Barco*.
(m) What the Lakviajeros will be like after the exercise - *Despalinjados*.

-o-o-o-

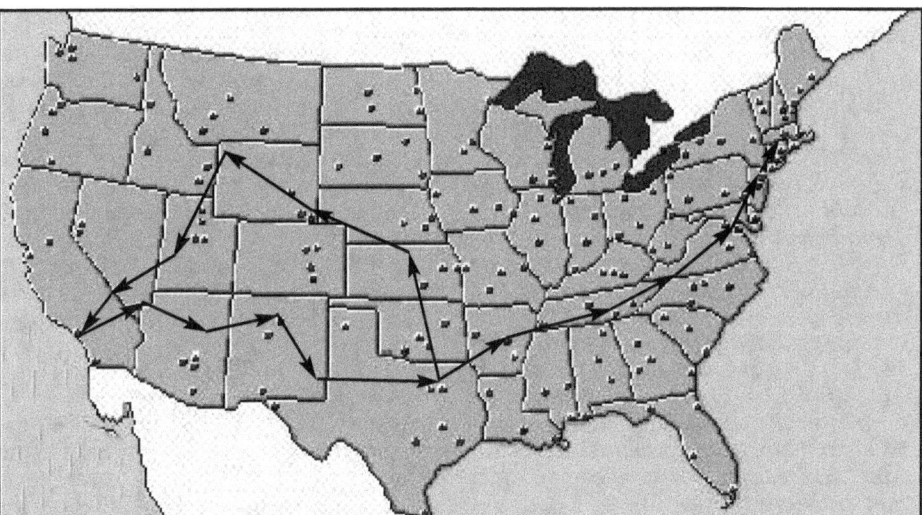

The proposed route plotted out for the *Loyalistas, Expatriados, Media Entradas*, etc. Hope there are no *Indianeros*. We can't reproduce a map with freeways shown as the lines would become too confusing, so the arrowed segments are approximate paths, each representing a days travel. Dots are major cities. The *Loyalistas* and some *Expatriados* go all the way East; the *Media Entradas* loop back to LA from Dallas.

QUIZ SHOWTIME and ANSWERS:
In the last issue, the question was raised about the meaning of Isagani's **AMDG.**

*The question I can answer for you is Gani's AMDG, from a fellow X-J. Of course it's obvious it means **Ang Mga Damulag na Gigil na Gigil**. Historically there has been a mistake in transcription: the medieval monks should have written down AMDGG, to reflect the above (gigil na gigil), but some monk-transcriber ran out of ink on his feather-pen, and only got as far as the first G. That is why it comes down to posterity as AMDG, and therefore the mistaken interpretation, which came to be the overt meaning is in Latin, says something like "**Ad Majorem Dei Gloriam**," but according to the most reliable Jesuit secret transmission codes, the original was in Tagalog, with the above*

meaning made public for the first time. Remember this, and let this open your eyes to the most esoteric tradition that will give you inner spiritual strength, if you repeat it three times every night before going to bed. Ang Mga Damulag na Gigil na Gigil - 3x.

Your friendly X-J,
Ruben Habito

-o-o-o-

*AMDG - **Another Man's Diet Gone**?*

Nancy Cruz-Dienel

[Ed: you weren't that far off!]
-o-o-o-

***"Ang Mga Demonyon Gutom"** that's what it means. First time I heard it was from **Johnny Ramos** in the Commuters chapter meeting. But the full impact only came when I saw **Enteng Batas'** grinning* like one when he introduced me to the rest of the Chapel Bugs like **Manny Espejo**, **Tony de Vera** (of the pet show fame) and another grinning one, **Tinoy Desamito** whom **Gerry Gil** says lives in "poso negro" Pangasinan.... Do I get the prize?

Mon Pasicolan

[Ed: Tinoy comes from Pozurubio. And yes, Mon gets the prize.]

-o-o-o-

Nobody else except **Nancy** offered a better solution to the poser on the *Six Levels of Connection:* Nancy's dentist was the dentist of Chelsea Clinton, or some relationship like that, so it places Nancy two levels away from a president. Close enough. Too bad, there was no prize here.

-o-o-o-

More email debate on the LAKBAYAN:

Hey Guys!

More arguments IN FAVOR of going on Lakbayan U.S. during April and May (instead of September) 1998:

1. As Tony says, April and May are tornado months. I fully agree this will be a wonderful opportunity to experience Mother Nature! (I consider this the really decisive clinching argument.)

2. As Christie says, temperatures in the high desert during April and May are ideal for travelling (10 to 15 degrees Celsius), unlike in September (27 to 32 degrees). I hope you guys are not planning to go all the way to the U.S. and hoping to end up with temperatures like Manila! Might as well stay home and drive to Batangas instead. ----- Johnny

-o-o-o-o

Dear Loyalistas,

April is the second best month to be in Washington (October is the best for me, because I like autumn). The cherry blossom festival with a grand parade takes place around the first weekend, and everyone in the city, Democrats and Republicans alike, are in good spirits. The whole city is in bloom and crawling with tourists. Weather is also great, but some days may still be too cold (in the 30's) so jackets (especially windbreakers) and sweaters are still needed. For those who suffer from allergies, Washington in April is peak season for pollen, so make sure you bring antihistamines and vitamins. In case of severe allergy attacks compounding homesickness, I can prescribe herbal teas, hence I am also known as Liliosa Herbalista ------ Liliosa

-o-o-o-o

Editorial Box

Typeset by Danny Gil in Los Angeles from unwitting contributors from the Internet and abetted by other accomplices of the UPSCA Alumni Association. Published supposedly every quarter but more so whenever it catches their fancy. Call, write, or fax in your comments, pictures, articles to postal address below, or email as shown.

19002 Horst Ave
Artesia, CA 90701
tel/fax (562) 402-1890
email: ferngil@aol.com
tonest@aol.com

A really old photo of **Liliosa**'s birthday showing **Gerry**. Liliosa sent it with the caption: *Danny & Lisa, this is my only copy but perhaps your family has a better reason to keep it. Also in the picture are* **Bobby Neri, Fredie Santiano, Ruben Rivera** *and* **Evelyn Machan.** **Alexi Antonio** *got cut-off. The little boy by the cake is my brother* **Phillip**, *who now is a doctor in New Jersey. Time has flown, hasn't it?*

Now, quickly, another poser: what year was this photo taken? Hint: count the candles, get Lili's age, do some arithmetic, and presto, you might win a prize. Another: what is Alexi up to now? How about Evelyn?

FICTION SECTION

Ghost Story, by Johnny Reyes

We arrived in Baguio rather late in the evening, and spent more time than necessary looking for addresses, because I hadn't been in Baguio since before the Great Earthquake. We finally found the place where the caretaker lived, and picked up the keys to the house where we were going to stay ourselves. She gave us brief instructions regarding the house, and asked if we wanted her to come along to show us where everything was kept— linen, cutlery, etc. I said, don't worry, I have stayed in the house many times before and I know where everything is. OK, she said, I will just drop by on the day of your departure—six days from today. If you need anything before then, just call me on the telephone. Otherwise, you're on your own. I could sense she knew that we knew about the stories about the house.

Of course I put up my sister and her husband in the famous room with the "resident"- the room at the head of the stairs - although my sister herself didn't know about the story. I told myself that what they didn't know wouldn't hurt them. Still, I felt responsible, so I decided that from time to time on the first night I would check whether they were O.K. To my disappointment the night passed quietly - no screams - and when I woke up just at the break of dawn ("*agaw-dilim*") I decided to check one last time. I saw that my sister's maid was already up and about in the hall, sweeping the floor just outside the "room," the door of which was still shut. I greeted her and asked whether her Ate Bay and Kuya Senen were sleeping well, and she said, "*Ang senyora ko po ay nagpapahinga.*" Did they have any problems last night, I asked hopefully. "*Wala po,*" she replied, rubbing the "*balat*" (accent on the first syllable) on her face self-consciously. "*Ano na nga ba ang*

pangalan mo?" I asked, but she didn't answer and instead turned around and went back to her sweeping, so I just shrugged it off. Having received this anticlimactic (and disappointing) report on the events of the previous night, I then went out for my early morning walk in the cold air of Baguio.

Later in the morning, our two families went to the Baguio market and stocked up on fruits and vegetables for the rest of our stay. Mila and my sister Bay (eight years older) prepared a big lunch for our first full day, and in general everyone had a feeling of well-being. There was no mention of anything unusual happening the night before. Our daughters wanted to go horseback riding in the afternoon - without a man leading the horses, they insisted. I said we'd see. "By the way, Bay," I suddenly thought, "Where's your other maid? Has she had any lunch?" "Which maid? I brought two. There they are in the kitchen." "Neither of those two, Bay. I mean the one with the birthmark on her face." "Birthmark? I don't have a maid with a birthmark on her face. Are you joking with me again?"

-o-o-o-

*For Johnny: did you ever consider a second career as a spook writer? That was a good story, realistic details, local color, suspense, and all. Also made me miss Baguio, which I haven't seen in ages. Why don't we all write up our favorite ghost stories featuring our own personal close encounters with the ghostly kind. We can have our very **prize-winning literary man (congratulations, Gemino!)** critique our styles, have it published, maybe even sell the script rights to Hollywood, and give Stephen King a run for his money. ---- Liliosa*

Johnny always has the last say: *By the way, it wasn't just a story I made up. I swear it really happened. Also, I thought spooks were spies, not ghosts?*

-o-o-o-

Actually, there already is a venue for recognizing aspiring literary talent: **GGF** or the **Gerry Gil Foundation**. This foundation was conceived soon after Gerry's demise, and should work in similar manner to the well known Palanca Awards. The incorporation of the GGF, however, hasn't gone as fast, despite the fact that the initial target fund goal already has been reached. So those who remember having *made checks to GGF* may find them *uncashed yet*. If they have gone stale, you will receive a request for reissuance. The president of the GGF is **Ramon Pasicolan**; treasurer is **Mercy Abad**. The rest of the 13 incorporators are Upscan, media, and family friends of Gerry. The board recently reset the target funding to half a million.

A small source of such funding is the sale of Gerry's book "*Wordsmith With A Slingshot*", a compilation of Gerry's best writings by **Jimmy Ong**.

For those who haven't read it, we strongly suggest you buy the $15 book (or donate more), by contacting us. It is very good reading.

Quoted below are sample reactions from two readers:

My faith in the wit and sharpness of thought of the Filipino writer has just been restored, thanks to Gerry's Book.

I would have been one of his readers (I am now) had I stayed in the Philippines but I was already here when Gerry peaked. I think he was several niches above Doroy Valencia and other opinion writers of the time because Gerry attacked issues objectively, researched his material well and articulated his thoughts very clearly. I was in the Philippines on a vacation two years ago this month and sought the old columns and columnists that I used to read with admiration in the sixties. I was disappointed to find that even the best among them (Max Soliven for example) seem to have lost the fire in their articles.

I am half-way through the book and I'd hate to see the last page. I will mention this book to my reading friends here and see if I can get them to buy it. Anyway, thank you for sharing the book with me. It is a must reading for every Filipino. I also think his writing compares well with the best of them in this country, Cronkite, Safire et al included.

Gerry left us too soon.

Baby Miraflor
[Ed: Baby is a townmate from Stanford]
-o-o-o-

*I finally received my copy of Wordsmith sent from Manila. I have started reading the foreword by **Jimmy Ong** and **Cip Roxas** and have gone through some of **GJG**'s writings - **awesome!!!** Always to the heart of the matter!*

Nancy Cruz-Dienel
-o-o-o-

Here are three pictures mailed in by Johnny Reyes which he encaptioned as shown.

Close-up of the honoree Liliosa and hosts Nora and Tigi (Tigi is the one on the right).

Liliosa's double Ellen, who works as a laboratory analyst at the Shell Refinery in Tabangao, Batangas City.

Dinner hosted by Tigi and Nora Barcelona at the very plush *Flavors and Spices Restaurant* in Ortigas Center on 14 June 1997, in honor of balikbayan Liliosa Mangosing-Evangelista.

JOKE TIME!

[Ed: There were comments from the fairer gender about one of the jokes in the last issue as being sexist. I promised not to repeat such transgression. So as an atonement, I'm including one from the other point of view. Hope I don't get flak from the guys.]

Three guys are out having a relaxing day fishing. Out of the blue, they catch a mermaid who begs to be set free in return for granting each of them a wish.

Now one of the guys just doesn't believe it, and says: "OK, if you can really grant wishes, then double my IQ." The mermaid says: "Done." Suddenly, the guy starts reciting Shakespeare flawlessly and analyzing it with extreme insight.

The second guy is so amazed, he says to the mermaid: "Triple my IQ." The mermaid says: "Done." The guy starts to spout out all the mathematical solutions to problems that have been stumping all the scientists in various fields: physics, chemistry, etc.

The last guy is so enthralled with the changes in his friends that he says to the mermaid: "Quintuple my IQ." The mermaid looks at him and says: "You know, I normally don't try to change people's minds when they make a wish, but I really wish you'd reconsider." The guy says: "No, I want you to increase my IQ times five, and if you don't do it, I won't set you free." "Please," says the mermaid. "You don't know what you're asking. It will change your entire view on the universe. Won't you ask for something else, a million dollars, anything?" But no matter what the mermaid said, the guy insisted on having his IQ increased by five times its usual power. So the mermaid sighed and said: "Done."

And he became a woman.

-o-o-o-

[Ed: Now a truly cerebral joke with profound socio-economic implications.]

After applying simple algebra to some trite phrases and cliches, a new understanding can be reached of the secret to wealth and success. Here it goes:

Knowledge is Power; *Time is Money* and as every engineer knows, *Power is Work over Time*. So, substituting algebraic equations for these timeworn bits of wisdom, we get:

$$K = P \quad (1)$$
$$T = M \quad (2)$$
$$P = W/T \quad (3)$$

Now, do a few simple substitutions: Put W/T in for P in equation (1), which yields:

$$K = W/T \quad (4)$$

Put M in for T into equation (4), which yields:

$$K = W/M \quad (5)$$

Now we've got something. Expanding back into English, we get: Knowledge equals Work over Money. What this MEANS is that:

1. *The More You Know, the More Work You Do and*
2. *The More You Know, the Less Money You Make.*

Solving for Money, we get:

$$M = W/K \quad (6)$$

Money equals Work Over Knowledge. From equation (6) we see that Money approaches infinity as Knowledge approaches 0, regardless of the Work done. What THIS MEANS is: *The More you Make, the Less you Know*. Solving for Work, we get

$$W = M \times K \quad (7)$$

Work equals Money times Knowledge. From equation (7) we see that Work approaches 0 as Knowledge approaches 0. What THIS MEANS is:

The stupid rich do little or no work.

-o-o-o-

REACTIONS TO THE LAST ISSUE:
[Ed: last three pages were all pictorials]

I must congratulate you for that Newsletter. Mimi and I were so happy to see the pictures of the party held at our place in honor of you and **Lisa** and of course for old man **Fredie**. Looking at all of us with the exception of **Jimmy Abad**, we are at least 20 lbs overwweight from 20 yrs ago, though **Tigi** looks exactly the same from 40 yrs ago, like the Phantom (the ghost who walks). **Mercy Abad** claims that Tigi's pomade up to now is the *Three Flowers*, a product of *PRC* and as popular then as *Purico, Ang Tibay*, and *Kati-Alis*, a concoction of **Primo Arambulo**'s father.

Mon Paiscolan

Had a lot of fun reading and scrutinizing the pictures in the UPSCA Newsletter. Many I have not seen in almost 35 yrs such as **Ely & Sonia Alampay, Enteng Batas, Johnny Reyes,** etc. Thanks, too, for the Engineering Newsletter. Also recognized a few that I have forgottten all these years. You certainly are helping us reminisce about our "good old days" at UP. It's been fun getting to know how everyone is doing and getting updated on his/her family.

Christie Borromeo-Kawal

Wow, those Newsletters were really cool. I enjoyed every page, and couldn't take off the smile from my face the whole time I was reading them - congratulations for setting up something like this. Sure brings back memories. Best regards to **Lisa**. Will meet with **Liliosa** this Thursday. Must we have a picture taken for the Newsletter?

Miren Dumlao-Santos

Great work in connecting UPSCA Alumni thru Newsletter. Pictures summoned so much memory of UP days just by looking at familiar faces. It's really true: "Life is long - it's just that it goes too fast!" Hope to see more of you all even in pictures. Mabuhay! Love & peace.

Chit Inciong

By the way, you should really revise all your records and have me listed as Liliosa. No one calls me Baby anymore (except by immediate family), after my American colleagues decided that Lili was really more appropriate. My future grandchildren would think "Lola Baby" an oxymoron.

Lili Mangosing-Evangelista

Thanks again. Your "circulars" (encyclicals?) always put me back in time, to those nostalgic days in the chapel grounds at Diliman. Sige, laging nananabik.

Ruben Habito

Danny, you are a repository of so much historical info *cheese miss,* I never realized how much I had forgotten. Can you compile an anecdote book? Lets get all our people to share our reminiscences and document it for history. I nominate Jimmy Abad (**JABAD**) as the main compiler, **JONG & JALZONA** as major contributors, **JEREYES** as commentator and general kibitzer (or should it be **Gani Cruz**?) and so on. Who knows we may create a masterpiece!!!!

Godo Juliano

We loved receiving the last Newsletter and reading all about the proposals re the trips across America. We're adding another proposal which might be a bit simpler. Why not a cruise around the Caribbean islands. Why we could have an entire deck to ourselves if enough people sign up! And , even if we don't have the entire deck, we could still have a rip-roaring good time with several tables full of UPSCAns and their respective families. There'd be no problem of where to stay and where to originate and end. Well, that's our two cents worth.

Cynthia Reyes-Calejesan

Re the Lakbayan, you should let us know details before the spring of 1998. How many are coming (more or less). As you know, Washington's history is rich in scandals, so a survey of preferences may be useful, i.e. take the scandal site of your choice: the Watergate hotel, the US Naval Academy, or the quintessential Lincoln Bedroom of the White House. Or they may opt for a picnic by the Lady Johnson Park from which can be seen the city's skyline, if we could still coordinate sightseeing and reminiscing in one stroke. I even thought of a cruise down the Potomac River but dread the thought of how the headlines would read, should the ship sink. "DELANEY'S FAITHFUL EXPURGATED!"

Lili again

Danny, just received the UPSCA Newsletter and was appropriately shocked. You will hear shortly from my lawyers regarding the libel suit and the charges against breach of privacy.

Johnny Reyes

[Ed: Pulling our legs again]

-o-o-o

A Pictorial Reaction. Soon after the last issue was mailed out, we received a letter and picture of **Ramon de Veyra** and **Eva (Singson) de Veyra** and **sons**. They had a copy reproduced and sent them to others. Per their note ..."*we are always in touch with Noel & Angge, Ely & Sonia, Gene Abril, Nacy Ferrer, etc. Best Regards.*"

The **LOOP** is a group of twenty some Upscans who all have access to email. Some have it on their home computers; others through their office computers. So starting over a year ago, the group started communicating. Inevitably, the email traffic started getting too heavy with messages, letters and jokes, clean and green, recycled or otherwise. So we set up some guidelines and categorized the participants into three groups, Categories 1, 2 & 3. As Johnny explains so succinctly: *It's really very simple. Category 2 comprises normal people so send social email to them. Category 1 comprises all kinds in addition to the above—D.O.M.s, pervies, or just plain liberals like Canikiisle. Send only good jokes else don't bother. Category 3 are those with non-secure e-mail addresses, i.e., accessible to very impressionable children; monitored by the boss; etc.*

Here's an example of a **LOOP** interchange, a first actually: a **CYBER BIRTHDAY PARTY** (all these were sent to all members of the Loop, Category 2):

This is clearly uncensored material. Here goes: It is JOHNNNNNY's birthday on July 28th. There ought to be the equivalent of a cyberspace blowout from the guy who has succesfully been "pulling our legs" with his pranks, jokes, spooky stories and gets away with it. My wife Mimi just reminded me that last July 26th was Gerry Gil's 2nd death anniversary another "Leg Puller" par excellance. So as our collective "gift to Johnnny" let's request Gerry to "pull Johnny's legs " on his birthday. Regards to all.   *Ramon*

Happy Birthday, Johnny! Any special celebration? Wish we could be there to help you in the big "blowout"!

Christie

"Happy birthday, to you, happy birthday to you, happy birthday, happy birthday, Even if I don't know you!" I take that back. I know you're an UPSCAN. And I know you're 70. I'm an UPSCAN too and would like to know more about you in your next e-mail. Enjoy!   *Malu*

Happy seventieth birthday, Johnny! How does it feel to be senile?   *Gani*

[Ed: Johnny's reply]

Oy Guys!

Thank you, thank you. [Bow]

Malu and **Ani**, you are completely wrong about my real age.

Malu wants to know more about my personal circumstances. Well, I was born during a time of unrest, during wartime, during the time when the peaceful life on the islands where I lived was being disrupted by the arrival of men in tall ships, men in long brown robes with little wooden objects that made me uneasy and men in metal jackets and hats. I remember the sound of fighting, and when my brothers and I came down to watch we saw Kalipulaku strike down the bearded man and leave him lifeless at the edge of the water. That was night time, because that was the only time when our group could move around safely. Whenever our foolish brothers *ventured out in sunlight their skin was burned horribly*, so we survivors had soon learned to *stay in the earth until dark*. After we were finished with the bearded man, we *flew back nourished* into the night. That was more than four hundred years ago, but I still remember it vividly because it was near the time of my birth. I can visit you at any hour of night, but when you see me *tapping on the window pane* you must invite me in, or I cannot enter.

Mon, no *one was able to pull my leg* the other night, because I was out the whole time—*flying around*.

Johnny

-o-o-o-

[Ed: I don't know if Johnny reads Edgar Allan Poe more than Carlos Castañeda, or he is just plainly influenced by our aswangs. So I might just as well show a picture which my flash caught soon after the August 2 party was breaking up and everybody was leaving for home. I remember Johnny had said something earlier about taking less than an hour to get home to Batangas.]

HOW CURRENT EVENTS SOMEHOW REVERT TO PAST EVENTS:

Hello Everybody,

We had a get-together with long-time-no-see Upscan **Arthur Adiarte**, who together with his wife **Cherrie** nee Guerrero (also BS Physics but '69) and son **Eric**, were visiting from Minneapolis. Since it was a Thursday night, just **Tony/Josie Estrera** and **Ernie/Jessie Pangilinan** were present.

We had lots to tell each other, after a 32 year gap. They, however, were aware of many of our doings due to the Newsletters we've sent them.

And he, together with Ernie, also joins the Loop. At this stage, we can put them in Category 2, and let them decide to upgrade to Category 1 later.

Let's welcome the two to the Loop.

Danny & Lisa

Hello Everybody (using my Mom's email in Manila),

Just to let both *Loyalistas* and *Expatriados* know that here's another *Ressurecto* who should be welcomed to the Loop - **Nilo Cruz**. Met him last week with **Tigi**. He's based in SF with Bechtel but is on a 3 year Phil assignment. And who should show up at the next dinner table but **Willie Soong**. It was poignant because Nilo, Tigi and I were back stage crew members of Upsca's *"Diary of Anne Frank"* presentation, with Willie playing the part of Mr Duffels, I think. Informatively, **Lino Brocka** played the part of the dentist. Willie of course is known as the *big, big wig in business*, but remembered more among us in **Segi Gazmin**'s song refrain *"Willie Soong in My Heart"*.

Danny

Dear Danny,

Just noted your "poignant" meeting with the construction crew of *Anne Frank*. Gosh, men are sentimental, too!

I heard about **Willie Soong**'s big business from one of our office contractors, **Carlos Esguerra**, who is also a UP grad. He mentioned that Willie did all the electrical installations for the palace of the **Sultan of Brunei**. If you see him again, please say hello din kay Willie.

Liliosa

Hi Danny!

You sure have a way of reviving old memories! Yes, I now recall those good old days with the *Drama Club* and the *UPSCA Dramatic Guild!* What sticks most in my mind is the fact that we had to rehearse for several weeks, and into the wee hours of the morning. I remember having to drop off some of the cast members at their homes after the practices. I also remember the little romances that started up during the rehearsals and during the run of the plays and ending when the plays ended! We also got visitors, outsiders (those who were not of the acting kind), who occasionally watched us practice and made us feel like fools onstage, especially when we flubbed our lines!

In "Anne Frank" I was Mrs. Frank. It was a fun role and I got to wear my mom's favorite white rabbit fur coat in one of the scenes. Unfortunately another cast member got carried away one night at a performance and tore one sleeve completely off. She was a great actress. If I remember correctly her name was **Alma Roque**. Luckily my mom wasn't angry. I guess she figured she wouldn't be able to use the coat anyway, considering the heat and humidity in Manila!

Lino Brocka already showed his great love for the theater then. As Mr. Dussel the dentist, he not only was a great actor and artist (with great ideas about how a scene should be played), he also told great stories about his friendship with the actor who played Dr. Ben Casey on TV. He really had stars in his eyes, even then, so it came as no surprise to me when he eventually became such a luminary in the world of Philippine movies and theater.

I felt quite fortunate to be invited to a showing of his films and meeting him in Manhattan shortly before his car accident in which he died. He looked the same - hardly older but slightly heavier than when we were together at UP practicing for *"Anne Frank."* He talked about how serious he was about the movies he made, that he didn't appreciate other filmmakers who used a lot of "toilet jokes" to make people laugh.

Rory

Dear Rory:

Your memories of the drama rehearsals brought others back!

My funniest memory is of the rehearsal of the play adapted from "*Arsenic and Old Lace*" and directed by **Louie Lagdameo**. I played a bit role as the niece of the parish priest, who was engaged to marry someone (played by **Dick Funk**) whose brother (**Danny Dequito**) and sisters (**Gloria Castro** and **Veronica Nañagas**) were in different stages of insanity. At one point, I started to scream because one of the villains tried to get rough with me. Well, my little brother **Phillip** who was watching the rehearsal started to cry and ran to the stage to hug me and "protect" me from the bad guy! We all stopped and laughed so long and so hard, with Louie saying, "Now I know we are really good. We are so convincing!"

Other hilarious memories were of **Reggie Cruz-Cailao** as the nurse who had to kiss (or get kissed by?) patient **Mundy Gonzalez** (dear departed **Florencia**'s kuya) in "*Dear Brutus*". At this point, the directress, **Linda Caedo**, would yell at them to "Hesitate! You are supposed to hesitate!"

Hope to hear from you again, Rory, and to you and the rest of the Loop, best regards.

Liliosa

-o-o-o

NOW BACK FROM REMINISCING FOR SOME NEWS BEFITTING A SUPPOSEDLY REAL NEWSLETTER:

From Isagani:

The *Evening Paper* congratulates its columnist **Gemino H. Abad** for winning first prizes in the annual Philippines Free Press Literary Awards for 1996 for his short story, "*Introibo*," and essay, "*An Ordinary Day*." Dr. Abad has also been chosen as the 1997 UP Alumni Association (UPAA) Professional Awardee in Literature.

From Jimmy Ong (after a particularly good joke by Isagani):

For more humor in this vein — sex with a sci-fi spin — **Isagani** has a Palanca award-winning short story, "*Once Upon a Time Some Years From Now*," in the recently launched literary quarterly *Pen & Ink*.

From Nancy:

We are back from Boston and New Hampshire for a couple of conferences and a reunion with **Sari Valenzuela, Frine Dimaano, Guia Mendoza, Angioline Loredo, Clara Valenzuela, Noel Calingasan, Carmina Cruz** and **Francis Dayrit**. All UP grads but not all UPSCANS, years 1963 to 1990. We over-

PICTURE GALLERY: Upscans and acquirees who haven't as yet been shown in past issues but have been in touch. Top row, L-R: **Bernie (de Castro) Muller** from Switzerland, **Bert Sandoval** (both taken in July 1996 party in Manila), **Myrna Aquitania, Noli Arong** (both were active Upscans only in their first year or so. Noli went back to Cebu but his 3 younger brothers *Sisoy, Doming,* and *Baby* stayed on). Bottom row, L-R: **Remy & Anching Chica, Don & Christie (Borromeo) Kawal,** and **Gerry & Nancy (Cruz) Dienel.** Christie mailed ink-jet printed color pictures of the family, but the scanner couldn't get a good reproduction, hence these grainy blowups of film prints from Nancy. Send in your pictures! I won't doctor them, I promise.

dosed on seafood especially lobsters and clams since they are rather hard to find here in Little Rock.

From Arthur Adiarte:

Hi everybody! Good news!!! Thanks to you all who wrote letters and/or sent e-mail in support of the Philippine Study Group of Minnesota **Correct the Plaque!** campaign (specially to Isagani Cruz for his timely article *Minnesota Vs. The Philippines* (*Philippine Star*, 7/3/97)), the Minnesota Historical Society (MHS) and the Capitol Area Architectural and Planning Board (CAAPB) met with us yesterday to inform us that they agree that a corrective plaque is needed! *[Ed: Arthur's group has been long fighting to correct gross historical inaccuracies in a plaque at the Minnesota State Capitol].*

From various sources re the Cha-cha:

The Congress is initiating a move to amend the 1987 Constitution via a Charter Change (aka Cha-cha) to remedy what it considers it's nine weak points: review the notion of "national patrimony"; review the powers of the Supreme Court; throw away term limits of elected officials; change from bicameral to unicameral; change from multiparty to two-party system; change from presidential to parliamentary system, de-synchronize elections, etc. It is impossible that all nine amendments will be tackled and proposed for

plebiscite before the elections scheduled in May 1998, which is why most people believe that what the Congress really intends is to simply concentrate on lifting term limits and allow the President as well as themselves to perpetuate themselves in power beyond June 1998.

The official Catholic Church stand is "*Elections Muna Bago Cha-Cha.*" It is also the stand of the Iglesia ni Cristo, of business, of schools, of media, even of some of the ruling party's members, and of easily 99% of the Philippine population. Unfortunately, it is not the stand of those in power. If allowed through Charter change, given his low poll ratings, Ramos can only win reelection through fraud and cheating the way Marcos did 28 years ago. Extension, on the other hand, will rob Filipinos of the thing they love best — elections — and will therefore lead to massive unrest, including armed rebellion from non-leftists. In short, Charter change will lead to a collapse of the economy, to political instability of a scale unknown since Ninoy was assassinated, and perhaps to armed revolution or martial law. This is why Charter changes cannot be allowed at this time, even if some changes are clearly called for on the theoretical level.

There are going to be massive rallies September 21 in the Luneta and other major Philippine cities.

Let us all hope and pray for the best.

LAKBAYAN '98

PROPOSED SCHEDULE and ESTIMATED COSTS for a 3 WEEK TREK for LOYALISTAS starting Friday, 17 April 1998

Scenario: 3 Manila couples stay as guests when in LA. Then with 3 LA couples, share 15 passenger rented van, overnight at Vegas, tour either Hoover Dam or side trip to Grand Canyon on way to Flagstaff, then proceed to Albuquerque, Roswell for UFOs, Carlsbad Caverns, then Dallas where group splits up, and 2-week trekkers take van north. The 3-week trekkers rent full-size Lincoln Towncars (no drop-off charge), 4 to a car, and proceed to Little Rock, Memphis, drive thru Appalachia to Washington DC, New York, Boston, then back to Newark NJ, return cars, and fly back to LA.

#	DAY	START FROM	DRIVE TO & STAY OVERNIGHT	DIS-TANCE MILES	EST SIDE TRIPS MILES	EST AVE SPEED MPH	APPRX TRA-VEL HRS	VAN CAR RENT $	EST CAMP FEE $	GAS EXP $	DAILY TOTAL $	NUM PEO-PLE	SHARE COST PER $	AIR FARES $	CAMP* HOTEL $	AVE MEALS $	AVE MISC $	DAILY TOTAL $	STAY >24 HRS	REMARKS AND OTHER HIGHLIGHTS ENROUTE
1	Fri													$800				$800		fly in, evening
2	Sat																$10	$10		rest/sightsee
3	Sun																$10	$10		sightsee, Upsca party
4	Mon	LA	Vegas	298		55	5.4	$72		$24	$96	12	$8		$60	$25	$10	$111		leave mid mom
5	Tue	Vegas	Flagstaff	263	100	55	6.6	$72	$20	$29	$121	12	$10		$60	$25	$10	$115		Hoover Dam or Grand Cyn
6	Wed	Flagstaff	Albuquerque	345	20	55	6.6	$72		$29	$101	12	$8		$60	$25	$10	$112		side trip Meteor Crater
7	Thu	Albuquerque	Carlsbad	260		55	4.7	$72		$21	$93	12	$8		$60	$25	$10	$110		sightsee Rosswell
8	Fri	Carlsbad	Carlsbad		30	35	0.9	$72	$26	$2	$100	12	$8		$0 *	$25	$10	$52	yes	whole day at caverns
9	Sat	Carlsbad	Dallas	413		55	7.5	$72		$33	$105	12	$9		$60	$25	$10	$112		group splits, rent car
10	Sun	Dallas	Little Rock	334	20	55	6.4	$80		$19	$99	4	$25		$60	$25	$10	$145		see Nancy
11	Mon	Little Rock	Memphis	138	50	50	3.8	$80		$10	$90	4	$23		$60	$25	$10	$140		Graceland visit
12	Tue	Memphis	Knoxville	400		55	7.3	$80		$22	$102	4	$25		$60	$25	$10	$146		scenic route
13	Wed	Knoxville	Wash DC	452		55	8.2	$80		$24	$104	4	$26		$60	$25	$10	$147		scenic route
14	Thu	DC	DC		20	35	0.6	$80		$1	$81	4	$20		$60	$25	$10	$136	yes	Smithsonian, etc
15	Fri	DC	DC		20	35	0.6	$80		$1	$81	4	$20		$60	$25	$10	$136	yes	see Liliosa, Lindus
16	Sat	DC	NJ	230		55	4.2	$80		$12	$92	4	$23		$60	$25	$10	$141		
17	Sun	NJ	NJ			50	0.8	$80		$2	$82	4	$21		$60	$25	$10	$136	yes	visit NY
18	Mon	NJ	Boston	211	40	60	4.2	$80		$14	$94	4	$23		$60	$25	$10	$142		
19	Tue	Boston	Boston		40	35	1.1	$80		$2	$82	4	$21		$60	$25	$10	$136	yes	sightsee, etc
20	Wed	Boston	NJ airport	211		55	3.8	$80		$11	$91	4	$23	$360		$25	$10	$441		night fly to LA
21	Thu	LA																$0	yes	rest
22	Fri	LA												$800				$800		fly out, evening
23	Sun		Manila																	arrive MNL 5:00 am
			Sub totals per couple =							$602			$14	$1,960	$900	$425	$190	$4,077		<= Grand total
													$47	$21	$10	$5	$97		<= 21-day daily ave per person

Road miles driven = 3935
Ave miles per day = 187
Ave cost of gas/gal = $1.35

72.7 hrs driving time
14.4 % on the road
17 ave miles/gallon for van
25 ave miles/gallon for car

Notes on estimated costs:

1. Meal cost averages picnic lunches, motel continnental breakfasts, etc.
2. Motel costs are average mid-class rate, double occupancy.
3. Renting a suite with 6 or so couples sharing (or pitching tent) will be more fun and economical. Early bookings at other motels can lower costs to $40.
4. Above estimates are idealized, but doable, for budget planning.

These costs are based on an idealized economical "MODULE" for comfortable seating of passengers. More participants would just require more modules. Less participants would make this basic module slightly more expensive, as only van/car costs go up.

LAKBAYAN '98

PROPOSED SCHEDULE and ESTIMATED COSTS for a 2 WEEK TREK starting Monday, 20 April 1998

Scenario: 3 couples from Manila and 3 couples from LA share 15 passenger rented van, overnight at Vegas, tour either Hoover Dam or sidetrip to Grand Canyon on way to Flagstaff, then proceed to Albuquerque. Roswell for UFOs, Carlsbad Caverns, then Dallas where group splits up, and 3-week trekkers rent car(s) and head East. The 2-week trekkers may be joined by a 1-week trekker couple who fly in from LA, and they all continue in the van and proceed through Oklahoma, Kansas, Nebraska, to Yellowstone, then Salt Lake, parts Utah, Death Valley, then back to LA.

SCHED #	DAY	START FROM	DRIVE TO & STAY OVERNIGHT	DIS-TANCE MILES	EST SIDE TRIPS MILES	EST AVE SPEED MPH	APPRX TRA-VEL HRS	CAR VAN RENT $	ENT CAMP FEE $	GAS EXP $	DAILY TOTAL $	NUM PEO-PLE	SHARE COST PER $	AIR FARES $	CAMP* HOTEL $	AVE MEALS $	AVE MISC $	DAILY TOTAL $	STAY >24 HRS	REMARKS AND OTHER HIGHLIGHTS ENROUTE
1	Fri																			Manila guests arrive
2	Sat																			
3	Sun																			Upsca party
4	Mon	LA	Vegas	298		55	5.4	$72		$24	$96	12	$8		$60	$25	$10	$111		leave mid morn
5	Tue	Vegas	Flagstaff	263	100	55	6.6	$72	$20	$29	$121	12	$10		$60	$25	$10	$115		Hoover Dam or Grand Cyn
6	Wed	Flagstaff	Albuquerque	345	20	55	6.6	$72		$29	$101	12	$8		$60	$25	$10	$112		side trip Meteor Crater
7	Thu	Albuquerque	Carlsbad	260		55	4.7	$72		$21	$93	12	$8		$60	$25	$10	$110		sightsee Rosswell
8	Fri	Carlsbad	Carlsbad		30	35	0.9	$72	$26	$2	$100	12	$8		$0 *	$25	$10	$52	yes	whole day at caverns
9	Sat	Carlsbad	Dallas	413		55	7.5	$72		$33	$105	12	$9		$60	$25	$10	$112		group splits
10	Sun	Dallas	Hays	560		60	9.3	$72		$44	$116	8	$15		$60	$25	$10	$124		thru Oklahoma
11	Mon	Hays	Cheyenne	423		55	7.7	$72		$34	$106	8	$13		$60	$25	$10	$121		thru Kansas
12	Tue	Cheyenne	Yellowstone	390		45	8.7	$72		$31	$103	8	$13		$60	$25	$10	$121		thru Wyoming
13	Wed	Yellowstone	Yellowstone		20	35	0.6	$72	$30	$2	$104	8	$13		$0 *	$25	$10	$61	yes	whole day Yellowstone
14	Thu	Yellowstone	Cedar City	427		60	7.1	$72		$34	$106	8	$13		$60	$25	$10	$121		see Salt Lake
15	Fri	Cedar City	Death Valley	270		55	4.9	$72	$20	$21	$113	8	$14		$0 *	$25	$10	$63		see Kolob Canyon
16	Sat	Death Valley	LA	290		55	5.3	$72		$23	$95	8	$12		$60	$25	$10	$59		see Ghost Town
17	Sun																			rest
18	Mon																			back to work
19	Tue																			
20	Wed																			
21	Thu																			
22	Fri																			
23	Sun																			
											Sub totals per couple =		$288	$0	$540	$325	$130	$1,283		<= Grand total
													$11	$0	$21	$13	$5	$49		<= 13-day daily ave per person

Road miles driven =   4109   75.3 hrs driving time
Ave miles per day =   316   24.1 % on the road
Ave cost of gas/gal = $1.35   17 ave miles/gallon for van

Notes on estimated costs:

1. Meal cost averages picnic lunches, motel continental breakfasts, etc.
2. Motel costs are average mid-class rate, double occupancy.
3. Renting a suite with 6 or so couples sharing (or pitching tent) will be more fun and economical. Early bookings at other motels can-lower costs to $40.
4. Above estimates are idealized, but doable, for budget planning.

These costs are based on an idealized economical "MODULE" for comfortable seating of passengers. More participants would just require more modules. Less participants would make this basic module slightly more expensive, as only van/car costs go up.

Mailing List   -   Postal and email addresses and tel num erased

Jimmy & Mercy (Rivera) Abad
Antipolo, Philippines

Rory Abrera
Dallas, TX

Arthur & Cherrie Adiarte
St Paul, MN

Ofie (Peñaflorida) & Ken Aid
Lakewood, CA

Letty (Ramirez) Ajodah
Queens Village, NY

Ely & Sonia (Alday) Alampay
Quezon City, Philippines

José Alzona
Long Beach, CA

Nanette (Gadi) & Boy Angeles
Monroeville, PA

Lolly Aquino
Los Angeles, CA

Myrna Aquitania
Camarillo, CA

Primo & Lindus (Carreon) Arambulo,
Rockville, MD

Noli Arong
Arleta, CA

Sisoy Arong
Houston, TX

Divsy Astraquillo
Shorewood, WI

Johnny & Alda Balaoing
Los Angeles, CA

Nina Los Baños
Las Vegas, NV

Tigi & Nora Barcelona
Quezon City, Philippines

Olga (Cruz) Barrios
Williamsville, NY

Enteng & Mely Batas
Lancaster, CA

Lennie (Abellera) & John Blair
Libertyville, IL

Jun & Cynthia (Reyes) Calejesan
Monaca, PA

Ramon O. Casas
Strasbourg, France

Manny Castillo
Brea, CA

Delfin Castro
Bowie, MD
Remy & Anching Chica
Northridge, CA

Tessie Chua Chiaco
North Hollywood, CA

Isagani & Medy Cruz
Malate, Philippines

Nilo Cruz
Makati, Philippines, (temp)
San Francisco, CA

Boy dela Cruz
Quezon City, Philippines (temp)
Cottage Grove, MN

Nancy (Cruz) & Gerry Dienel
Little Rock, AR

Bing (Ferrer) & Anthony Dubitsky
Riverdale, MD

Cir & Rose (Lacebal) Engay
Los Angeles, CA

Georgina (Reyes) & Mervyn Encanto
Quezon City, Philippines

Manny & Lee Espejo
Saugus, CA

Deo & Aleli Estacio
Altadena, CA

Tony & Josie (Angeles) Estrera
Cerritos, CA

Liliosa (Mangosing) & Gene Evangelista,
Fairfax, VA

Lino & Maureen (Holazo) Faelnar
Las Piñas, Philippines

Susan (Rodriguez) & Dick Fagan
New York, NY

Dette Feliciano
Los Angeles, CA

Temy (Dapilos) Gamboa
Patchogue, NY

Malu (Barrios) & Oids Garcia
Cerritos, CA

Pepito & May (Miñosa) Gatchalian
Quezon City, Philippines

Danny & Lisa (Señeris) Gil
Artesia, CA

Erwin & Alita Gomez
Valparaiso, IN

Ruben & Maria Habito
Kyoto, Japan (temp)

Effie (Sta Romana) Hall
Bettendorf, IA

Chit Inciong
Flushing, NY

Jessica Infante
Los Angeles, CA

Jess & Jessie (Quinto) Javelona
Muntinglupa, Philippines
Nanette (Ortega) & Benny Jongco
South Orange, NJ

Godofredo Juliano
Philippines

Christie (Borromeo) & Don Kawal
Albuquerque, NM

Lallie (de Vera) Lacaba
Pateros, Philippines

Clara (Reyes) & Bart Lapus
San Juan, Philippines

Raquel (Celera) & Ric Lejano
Torrance, CA

Gus & Toti (Yuson) de Leon
Quezon City, Philippines

Loida (Nicolas) Lewis
New York, NY

Cheche (Lim) & Delfin Lazaro
Philippines

Dante & Baby V. Liban
Quezon City, Philippines

Eddie & Josie Magtoto
Parañaque, Philippines

Mario & Myrna Manansala
La Palma, CA

Romy & Edna (Zapanta) Manlapaz
Quezon City, Philippines

Melvyn & Susan (Paulin) Martin
Alabang, Philippines

Jess Martinez
Freeport, IL

Bernie (de Castro) & Jurg Muller
Geneva, Switzerland

Clemencia Natividad
Toronto, Canada

Tony Nievera
Douglaston, NY

Bong & Beth (Arcellana) Nuqui
Quezon City, Philippines

Jimmy & Ting Ong
Pasig, Philippines

Ernie & Jessie (Raqueño) Pangilinan
Mission Hills, CA 91345
Ramon & Mimi Pasicolan
Quezon City, Philippines

Lina (Soliman) Plantilla
Brooklyn, NY

Priscilla (Bautista) Perez
Bronx, NY

Susan Po
San Francisco, CA

Sonia (Valenzuela) & Dietrich Quast
Sao Pablo, Brazil

Amelia (Bascon) Rasalan
Bayside, NY
Hermie (Manoto) & Jess Rabe
Cerritos, CA

Johnny & Mila (Garcia) Reyes
Belle Mead, NJ

Ruben & Naida (Uy) Rivera
Quezon City, Philippines

Maya (Arroyo) Santiano
Quezon City, Philippines

Greg Santillan
San Gabriel, CA

Angel & Stella Sta Maria
Pasadena, CA

Zeny (Roxas) & Sixto Ramirez
Los Angeles, CA

Nel Reformina
Nanuet, NY

Nem & Bing (Pascual) Santos
Whittier, CA 90601

Alex & Miren (Dumlao) Santos
Quezon City, Philippines

Miren (Dumlao) Santos
Bethesda, MD (temp)

Berryl Silva
Long Beach, CA

Noel & Angge (Alday) Soriano
Quezon City, Philippines

Ping & Merle (Custodio) Tan
Quezon City, Philippines

Bernie (Abrera) Tjarks
Dallas, TX

Dell & Julz Tocong
Bellflower, CA

Girlie (Alzona) & Tito Valbuena
Astoria, NY

Sari Valenzuela
Brooklyn, NY

Jimmy & Nora Valera
Ontario, Canada
valeraj@iname.com

Mon & Eva (Singson) de Veyra
Quezon City, Philippines

Priscilla (Javier) Weber
Manhattan Beach, CA

Elizabeth (Zaraspe) Yoo
Los Angeles, CA

AMDG

UPSCA *ALUMNI ASSOCIATION, USA*

NEWSLETTER NEWSLETTER NEWSLETTER

Vol 1, Num 5 (1st quarter, 1998)   Published by UPSCA Alumni Association, USA

TIME TRAVEL CLAIMED BY SOME UPSCANS!

Flash! Upscans **Ernie Pangilinan** and **Johnny Reyes** claim to have experienced time travel when they were allegedly abducted by UFOs at separate sites in Batangas, Philippines and Sidona, NM. Both of them were brought together and shipped back into the past, where they managed to roam Diliman and Quezon City in the '60s. According to them, it was like being in suspended animation: they could see and hear the things happening around them but could in no way interfere. Fortunately, they had a camera with them when abducted, and were able to take pictures, some of which are now reproduced herein. What even was more amazing is that Johnny found himself taking pictures of himself! (see picture at right). After a few days of wandering around, they were whisked back to the present reality.

Their experience must also have extended a collective influence on many others. Their circle of friends, known as the "Loop", suddenly exuded a general sensation of nostalgia, as the subject matter on the emailed exchanges turned to past events.

– – – –

Another picture taken in perhaps what could only have been the '60s. Johnny Reyes, Baby Mangosing, Jimmy Abad seated and Arthur Adiarte, Lindus Carreon and Alex Villaflor standing.

Taken after the reception of the Fredie Santiano and Maya Arroyo wedding in 1970 at Camp Crame: 1 Naida Uy, 2 Ruben Rivera, 3 Pong Lustre, 4 Delia Lustre, 5 Rozel Santos, 6 Tony Estrera, 7 Mercy Rivera, 8 Jimmy Abad, 9 Gi Dia, 10 Mon Pasicolan, 11 Gerry Gil, 12 Nora Cunanan-Barcelona, 13 Lisa Señeris-Gil, 14 Danny Gil.

Lakbayan '98 gets a new name as Walakbayan! It won't go through. Trust Murphy's law. Anything that can go wrong will go wrong. And trust Johnny's bantering scenarios during the early planning stages to actually become a reality. His questions then were..."*What if too few couples decide to participate?"; "What if it becomes unseasonably cold?"; "What if the peso-dollar rate changes drastically?"; "What if the Philippines severs diplomatic relations with the U.S.?"*

Presently, 75% of the above scenarios have come true, so the inevitable happened, and after much emailing amongst the Loop *Atrevidos*, the plan was reluctantly called off, at least for 1998. Here are some excerpts:

Johnny: Reason I have been silent about the above exercise for quite a while now, after having been its most enthusiastic advocate since late 1996, is the unspoken subject in everyone else's mind. Some time during the third quarter of 1997, the peso suddenly started depreciating in value from US$ 1/26.50 to about US$ 1/29. I have been watching and waiting, secretly hoping its value would go back up again to 1/26.50, the way it did in early 1995. But this time it continued slipping, slipping until the peso is now worth about US$ 1/40—a drop in value so far of 34% from what it was originally—with no signs of ever recovering. It means that those of us whose limited resources are all in Philippine pesos will need to spend 34% more whenever we go abroad. I continue to watch and wait, secretly hoping also that foreign exchange controls will not be reimposed. Embarrassing though it may be, I am serving notice that the chances of my going through with the coast-to-coast drive in 1998 are rather low at the moment. As my ol' pop used to say about the Philippine economy, the bad news is that this year has been worse than last year, while the good news is that this year will be better than next year!

Lili: Don't worry, Johnny. You can always cross the big water by flapping your wings, visiting any city you so desire, and, while in Washington, roost in the monument of your choice. Now that Walakbayan is out of the

Another back-from-the-past picture: L to R, Danny Gil, Jun Abao, Gani Cruz, Eli Lademora, Jimmy Abad, Tigi Barcelona, Jimmy Ong, Fredie Santiano, Ben de Leon & Gerry Gil. Can anybody remember where and when this was taken? The Chapel Basement?

way, we can figure other means and ways of keeping the loop going (other than sharing jokes). How about a reading club, that is, sharing titles/authors of interesting books and/or reactions to them (including novels, recipe books, non-fiction, how-to books, etc.). Or if that is too corny, how about starting an investment club via eMail (more for educational purposes but with the option of actually pooling a small amount each month and tracking its progress in the stock or bond market)? Alternatively, how about **Clara**'s suggestion of organizing RP-bound short trips, not as extensive as the southern cruise, but travelling to more adjacent areas such as *Baguio-Ilocos* region, or *Subic Bay-Pangasinan* coastal region, *Aklan-Iloilo-Boracay*, etc. If the offers are good and timely, why, we expatriados may even join you guys! We can then have a real reunion with all extant UPSCANs of our time, gathering from all around the world. For example, whatever happened to the likes of **Thelma de Ausen**, **Carol Vera**, **Johnny Ramos**, **Jimmy Lapus**, etc.?

Johnny: Baguio-Ilocos, Subic Bay-Pangasinan, and Aklan-Iloilo-Boracay are probably too ambitious for us. More achievable at the moment is something like *Tabangao-Ambulong-Libjo-San Isidro-Malitam* (Barrios around Tabangao Refinery). **Jimmy Lapus** is now a famous eye surgeon. We are in close touch — he did an eye operation on me three or four years back.

(Ed: The pace shifts beat and soon becomes an exchange of one liners:)

Tony: Did he [Jimmy Lapus] become famous after performing your eye operation?

Johnny: Touché! That was a good one indeed, something I could not have resisted doing myself. Nice to hear from you Tony [Estrera].

Tony: Happy New Year to all. I just couldn't resist that *one-liner*.

Lili: Here's more famous Upscan one-liners:
  Gerry Gil: *Control your passions!*
  Romy Manlapaz: *Such trivialities!*
  Lindus Carreon-Arambulo: *Johnny dah'lin!* (to Balaoing, Ramos, Reyes, et al)
  Alex Villaflor: *What, me worry?*
  Jimmy Abad: *Deutscheland uber alles.*
Does anyone remember any others?

Danny: That was good, Lili. Here's more I remember as often retold by Gerry:
  Lino Faelnar (to Jun Pascual): *How did it happen?*
  Lino Faelnar (again to Jun Pascual after Jun's pained response): *Is there any hope?*

For those who don't know **Jun**, he was a brilliant and hardworking person who, despite a bout with polio, tried to be just like the rest of us. After a meteoric rise in the Makati Stock exchange, he passed away suddenly while here in the US in the early '80s. His wife **Sunta** was in LA for some time, but I understand is in the East coast now.

-ooo-

(Ed: Sometimes, a mere word can cascade into a torrent of exchanges. Here's what happened when Mon Pasicolan first came on line, and how the subject of Ghosts came about):

Danny: Dear Mon, yours is the true ghost appearance. After all these emailings among the circle, I think this is the first time I hear from you. Glad you've been following the exchanges.
  And speaking of ghosts: Johnny, do you remember that time back in college when we went to **Tess Daffon**'s reputed haunted house beside the old Makati

cemetery on November 1 eve, All Soul's Day, and played hide and seek among the graves? **Joe Alzona** brought this topic up (I don't even remember him being with us then, but I know Fredie was there). Has anybody been in contact lately with Tess' group then, such as **Jennifer Romero-Llaguno**? Another girl in that group, **Priscilla Bautista-Perez**, is in NY.

Gani: About Tess Daffon, now named **Terra Daffon** and working with some television network, I haven't seen in decades. About the house, however, I tried to find it recently but it seems that there are all sorts of new buildings all over the place. I remember it was kind of recessed from the street. I'll try again. It was really eerie, as far as I remember. And yes, JE was with us when we went through the house that *unforgettable night of ghosts*. (P.S. Now that you have suddenly made our comments possible material for printed newsletters, we have to be extra careful not to reveal any really personal stuff. From now on, I send only dirty jokes that cannot be printed without violating anti-obscenity laws in every country!)

Johnny: Thanks for copying me in on the *chismis*. On the night you were referring to, I was at home in San Juan. I never joined the wild shenanigans the rest of you guys engaged in, because I was in bed every night by eight after doing my homework and brushing my teeth. If you say I was spotted at Makati Cemetery, it must have been my *astral projection* you saw—present in spirit.

(Ed: Soon after, Johnny wrote his acclaimed Ghost Story featured in the Newsletter issue 4, and other incidents alluding to his kinship with them!)

-ooo-

(Ed: Johnny went on and wrote another story, serialized. It is too long to reprint in this issue, but to titillate those who weren't on the Category 2 Loop and were unable to read it, here are some comments, as assembled by Johnny himself):

Malu: *Ano ito*, not a ghost story, but suspenseful! Continue ASAP. It's soothing to one's tired body at day's end. Great story-teller! For once, not humor-ful, not full-of-corns either.

Christie: As I read your interesting story, it reminded me how cold it could really get in the East Coast, the damp type that "gets through your bones." Fortunately, our cold weather in the Southwest, though temps could be in the teens, is not as bad because it is the "dry" type. Winter in the high desert is invigorating, clear and brisk! Thanks for sharing your adventure.

Ramon: As usual, Johnny, you tell a good yarn.....with the style and texture of Rod Serling's Twilight Zone and One Step Beyond. I also read your recent letter to the *Inquirer* on how to solve the traffic mess and it makes good sense too. Being stuck in Metromanila traffic nowadays is like being in the Horror Zone... More stories please of the Taller variety this time.

Lili: I deleted it as soon as I read it!

Mercy: . . . a laughing matter in the office.

JOng: It seems a tad presumptuous to cc everyone.

Bernie Abrera-Tjarks: Can be quite amusing, but definitely not politically correct!

-ooo-

On Irritating People. *Another lively Loop exchange started when Gani sent a test email to everybody. Excerpts:*

Johnny: What I meant was that presumably Isagani wanted to test whether all those on his "Category 2" mailing list were receiving his message. Unless each of us is asked to acknowledge, in my view his test is meaningless. But I guess that is how the minds of physicists-turned-"literati" function.

Lili: Aren't we getting a little bit unfriendly here, particularly with the last sentence?

Johnny: One of my hobbies is irritating people. I wonder who I can irritate today?

JOng: Irritating people is a fine art and a noble tradition. At Delaney Hall thirtysomething years ago, **Isagani** was known to irritate people just by looking at them. Ditto **Joe Alzona**. But Ani and Joe

learned from the masters — **Gerry Gil** and **Fredie Santiano**.

Gani: All is forgiven, Johnny. You did not irritate me at all! Your efforts were fruitless. And don't worry about it, Lili. Johnny is a literati turned engineer, and has forgotten that computers automatically check if mail is misdirected. Thank you to all who acknowledged receiving the test message.

Lili: Interesting exchange. As I told Jong, if you gents want to become virtual members of the Dead Irritaters Society (with apologies to their kinfolk), why, we should leave you to your own devices. I wish I could hear more from the ladies, though.

-ooo-

Sightings *Aside from UFO and other supernatural sightings, here are some real people sightings:*

Nancy Cruz-Dienel: I forgot to tell you that sometime in 1995 in a mall in Bethesda, MD a couple and a young lady came up to me and asked if I were who they thought I am. Guess who? No other than **Lindus** and family!!! We really did not have a chance to meet again after that since we were getting ready to move [to Arkansas].

Liliosa Mangosing-Evangelista: I myself came to Washington in late 1969 and hoped to move on and see the world. But as fate would have it, I settled here in the Virginia suburbs. How interesting to read about how everyone else is doing after 30-some years. **Lindus** and I find ourselves in this area, and we manage to get together once in a while. We used to discuss the past a lot, although we now find ourselves talking more about the future. What to do as old(er) ladies!

Over the last 3 decades I have seen only a few UPSCAns around this town. I bumped into **Priscilla Javier** at the Smithsonian Museum once, and nearly missed recognizing **Cecile Gordon** in a craft fair. **Johnny Ramos** was once in this area but has long since gone. And **Delfin Castro** was tax officer at the Philippine Embassy once upon a time. **Susan Laya Mysen** (Eleanor's younger sister) says she was an UPSCAn but she doesn't remember any of you. She must be very young. Other sightings over the years: **Joe Halog** in a PAL plane enroute to Manila, **Athena Forteyza** on the subway train. You never know when the next sighting would be.

During the Marcos years, I avoided the Philippine Embassy like a plague. But some important papers needed to be filed once and I had no choice but to go there. A gentleman gave me the forms and offered a table and chair where I could fill them up. I still kept my back to him and minded my documents when all of a sudden he said, *"Did you know that* **Johnny Ramos** *is in town?"* This was like thunderbolt, and I finally faced him, knowing he must be friend not foe, and would have had something to do with my UPSCA past! He continued talking, *"Baby nanam, nakalimutan mo na ba ako? Si* **Delfin Castro***!"* It turned out that Delfin was the Tax Officer at the Embassy at that time. That was enough to make me relax and by the time I had completed the documents, we were chatting about old times.

Ran into **Maria Teresa Montelibano** (Terry to us then, fellow English Major) at the Pfalzgraff factory outlet while looking for discounted china. Was she ever an UPSCAN? Am not sure. But I remember her because she hugged me like a long-lost soul-sister and cried out, **"Liliosa Manotok!** Imagine seeing you here!"

-ooo-

We'll have to ask Ernie or Johnny what year in the past they took this picture, which appears to be in the Marikina house of Danny & Lisa Gil (oops, the timeprint says June 1972): L-R, Naida Rivera, Medy Cruz, Edna Manlapaz, Lisa (standing), Gerry Gil, Nora Barcelona, Mercy Abad, Maya Santiano (back turned) and Miren Santos.

Johnny's UFO abduction started a run on waxing nostalgic:

Johnny: When I was in college, my daily allowance (only on class days, not on week-ends) was two pesos. These are what I could buy with it:

Jeepney, San Juan house to Cubao	P 0.10
Jeepney from Cubao to U.P.	0.10
10 Newport cigarettes	0.25
Lunch at the co-op canteen	0.80
Two cokes during the day	0.20
Jeepney from U.P. to Cubao	0.10
Jeepney from Cubao to San Juan	0.10
Surplus	0.35

If I passed via Quiapo instead, it cost P0.15 to get from San Juan to Quiapo, and from there another P0.20 to get to U.P. Diliman—a costly excursion. On the other hand, I could be clever and take a Divisoria jeep instead, which cost only P0.10 to take me from San Juan to the intersection of Azcarraga and Quezon Boulevard. From that point, it also cost P0.20 to get to U.P., but I would already have saved P0.05.

On those rare occasions when I managed to grab my older brother's blue Packard for the day (the one with the bashed-in right side, which I always parked against a wall so only the good side was showing), I could get from San Juan to U.P. and back with four liters of regular gasoline, costing P1.00 (total, not per liter).

A game of bowling at the old quonset hut across the road leading to Balara from the Student Union cost either nothing (if you won) or P0.60 (if you lost). (It actually cost P0.30 per game per alley.) Shooting pool cost either P0.20 per game (preferred by beginners) or P0.60 per hour (not too cost-effective if you were a bad player, like I was).

Unless I obtained a windfall handout from time to time from my older brothers who already had jobs, I had to save up for dates out of my surplus, if any. (Most of the time, the surplus was dissipated in the poker games played at the men's rooms of the Engineering Building.) But a fried chicken meal at Max's cost only P2.50, so it didn't take that long to accumulate enough funds for a twosome. I also got a windfall sometimes by registering for a laboratory subject, paying with a cheque (because my Pa didn't want to pay in cash), and then dropping it again. The refund was a cool P50.00.

My oldest brother's daily allowance when he was in college was also P2.00, and he was thirteen years ahead of me. Either he was a much better negotiator than I was (with our Pa), or the inflation rate at the time was zero. I read later on that indeed that was the inflation rate in the U.S. in 1955 (when I was graduated from Grade Six).

Try asking your kids nowadays how long they can survive with two pesos.

Nancy: You certainly received more daily allowance than what my father gave his daughters and there was a differential if you could go home for lunch or not. He knew our class schedules more or less. His philosophy was, the less extra money you had, the less was the lakwatsa!! He was probably right on but it did not prevent anyone from doing so.

Bong Nuqui: I don't know whether there already were *ikot* jeepneys during your time in Diliman but when we were sophomores, the ikot started at 5 centavos. When the drivers tried to raise it to 10 centavos, the students gave them a difficult time. Well, guys, it now costs P1.75. Of course it now goes through a bigger circle. Did you know there is now a "toki" jeepney route? This is the route which counterflows the old "ikot" route. I hope you guys can guess why it is called "toki".

JOng: Johnny, now that you've walked us all down memory lane, my daily allowance must have been around P2 also, and I wonder now how I made do after I joined UPSCA.

Although daily busfare could be as low as 30c going and 30c coming back — 10c from Shaw to Crossing, 20c from Crossing to UP — the UP-bound buses along Highway 54 (it wasn't EDSA yet) were few and usually crammed. I was more assured of a seat if I rode from Shaw to Quiapo (15c), then, somewhere near Times or Main theatres, boarded the bus for UP (20c).

What complicated life after joining UPSCA was the barkada of **Primalee Haresco, Susan Paulin** and **Linda Fuentecilla**, whom Danny Gil mentions in an earlier entry. Prim, Susan and Linda all went home from Delaney Hall in a Quiapo-bound bus, and once or twice a week I'd board the bus with them. Linda got off at Hi-way (10c), Prim at Scout something-or-other (15c) and Susan at Quiapo (20c), and of course I'd gallantly pay for everyone. (My misogyny is but an intellectual and philosophical conviction; in practice I can be quite the gentleman.)

And that was just busfare. My financial situation eased up only during the semester that I joined the Collegian, and later, signed up at the Inst of Mass Comm as a student assistant.

Tony: I remember buying siopao at Ma Mon Luk's in Cubao for 50 centavos (?). Now I have to pay $1.50 at Mami King when I go to Daly City, south of San Francisco, and $3.25 for chicken/pork mami. And it is a poor imitation of what I remember. Probably they forgot to include the cat!

Johnny: Guys and Gals! Still on the same topic: Mila commented that the cost of a laboratory subject in U.P. was not really P50 but more like P15! (In fact, our total tuition per semester was only about

P150.) This means my sins were only venial, not mortal.

My old parents always liked to tell me about the good old "Pre-War" days—"before I was born"—when things were dirt-cheap. I guess I never really believed the relative prices they were citing—until now.

By the way, are you all aware that the time when our generation was in college and high school happened to be the *Golden Age* of pop music? I am referring to a fantastic 10-year period between 1955 and 1965—never duplicated before or afterwards in history—when a tremendous amount of talent exploded at the same time. Look who made it to the Top Ten during that period: Elvis Presley! the Everly Brothers! Buddy Holly! Bill Haley! Fats Domino! Neil Sedaka! Paul Anka! Harry Belafonte! the Kingston Trio! Jimmy Rodgers! Patsy Cline! Loretta Lynn! Patti Paige! Teresa Brewer! Connie

Johnny posing with one of his favorite Hollywood couples, Paul Newman and Joan Woodward, and the dog Rin-tin-tin.

Francis! Peter, Paul, and Mary! the Beatles (Phase I only)! And more: Frank Sinatra! Nat King Cole! Joni James! Tony Bennett! Frankie Laine! Johnnie Ray! Pat Boone! Frankie Avalon! Jo Stafford! Julie Andrews! the Brothers Four! Mario Lanza! Jim Reeves! Petula Clark! Doris Day! Marty Robbins! Freddy Fender! Brenda Lee! Bobby Vinton! Jerry Lee Lewis! Ray Peterson! Roy Orbison! Cher! Sammy Davis Jr.! Barbra Streisand! Liza Minelli! the Chordettes! Listening to any of the above performers on tape is guaranteed entertainment even now, and even my daughters (the older batch anyway) concede it is superior to today's quality of pop music. (Songs then had a standard length of two to three minutes only.) Aren't you glad it happened during our time? The 70's tried hard to start a second wave, but they only had a few stars—Tom Jones, Engelbert, Karen Carpenter, the Beatles (Phase II)—so it didn't take off. That ten-year period was also a Golden Age of sorts in movies. It all started with Marlon

Brando and James Dean (who got killed in 1955, but became a cult figure afterwards). Remember the introduction of Method Acting? Compare Marlon Brando's Mark Antony (more or less standard nowadays) with that of Victor Mature in "Samson and Delilah" (the old style of acting). Compare also the Lancelots of Robert Taylor and Franco Nero.

Danny (to Tony & Johnny): Do you remember that Math 102 calculus class under Mrs Ortigas wherein we three bet a hamburger sandwich and coke combo to be paid for by the guy who had the highest grade in the test (as a *consuelo de bobo* prize). Well, when I saw my score of 45, I knew I'd get a free hamburger. Then Tony showed his score of 39, and I wasn't too sure anymore about my freebie. Then Johnny showed his score of 27, and I ended up paying for the blowout. I later dropped the course, but flunked again in the next term.

☺☺☺

(Ed: Expatriados inevitably would have anecdotes about their early years here, especially on culture clashes and the like. Here's my rejoinder to Johnny on Pets).

Thanks for the slew of e-mails you sent over the past days. Indeed, your pet Maltese adoption threw me off. I guess it reflects on my never having been a pet lover. Of yes, we did have a pet dog for about 7 years. Let me digress for it makes an interesting story.

When we were new here in 1982, my daughter Babette, age 12, was pretty lonely, and a neighbor gave her a puppy, which promptly got run over. As it was convulsing before her eyes, my older son Ramon laid it down at the most convenient place which happened to be the outdoor barbeque grille, to which my youngest son Joey, then 6, innocently asked if we were going to barbeque it. This of course threw Babette into a weeping rage, so we agreed to buy her a puppy (hard cash for us at that time). We did, and eventually the dog, whom Babette named Chaz (but whom I referred to as "Stupid Dog"), became our pet. My name was the one that stuck.

It ran off a couple of times, and each time it didn't come home, it inevitably was lodged at the dog pound, and we had to fish it out after paying a hefty fine. On the third occasion, I put my foot down, knowing that if left unclaimed for a week, it would be put to sleep. So there we were driving to San Diego for a visit with my aunt, the seventh day after Chaz left. Then Joey started musing about a dog's soul, what would happen if it died. When I looked over my shoulder, everybody was weeping. All for that stupid dog!

So, we drove back, and fished him out from the dog pound again. He never got caught by the dog catcher after that, but apparently was nocturnally active towards a neighbor's pedigreed prized dog. The neighbor complained so I had Chaz neutered. But the damage was already done. The neighbor's dog died from complications after the owner tried to abort the fetus.

When the neighbor came crying to tell me about it, I happily announced that Chaz was already neutered. She didn't find it amusing at all, and added that they'd probably sue, unless we helped pay for their dog's funeral, which we did. Anyway, to make a long story short, Chaz got pretty old and sick, and eventually I had to bring him to the dog pound to be put to sleep. I must admit I had a tinge of remorse when I lifted him off the car. Poor Stupid Dog.

☺☺☺

JOIN A CONTEST

You are invited to write a short story whose theme revolves around the picture above. Winner will receive a prize and get published in the Newsletter! Email, snailmail or dictate entries to Gani Cruz. His address is on last page.

☺☺☺

PAST, PAST, PAST news:

Before Gerry Gil rejoined the Newspaper game in 1987, he wrote letter after letter to various publications under different names. The 300 plus letters in his files came under 43 different signatories. Many letters went unpublished. Selected ones appear in the book on his writings

"*Wordsmith With a Slingshot*". Herein below are two examples. It is more than coincidence that the pseudonyms he choose have names close to real life persons he knew: Ronan Bernas was his student in Ateneo and a brother to the Jesuit priest, and Margie Gosingco (Holmes) was another Ateneo student who now is a famous writer/columnist.

> 525 Gen. Lacuna Street
> Makati, Metro Manila
> March 12, 1986

Letter to the Editor
Veritas
Quezon City

Our political exiles in the United States led by Raul S. Manglapus, Raul Daza, Bonifacio Gillego, Juan Frivaldo, Heherson Alvarez, etc. have reported on their doings in that country and have given the lie to the epithet, "steak commandoes," coined by a discredited columnist.

I wish our political exiles in China would also report on their doings. While no one ever called them something like "Dim Sum dissenters," very many of us have the impression that they didn't do very much. If this impression is correct, they should tell us why they didn't. Was it because they would not or because they could not? Otherwise, it is just a matter of time before someone labels them the "Peking lame ducks."

> Roman Bernas
> Makati

-ooo-

> 8481 Mercedes Street
> Bel-Air, Makati
> May 15, 1986

Letter to the Editor
Veritas
Quezon City

Women for the Ouster of Marcos through Boycott (WOMB) want to know what name they would give to the coffee shop and lending library they have opened (*Veritas*, May 11).

I assume they would want to keep the WOMB acronym.

If the coffee shop is to be the watering hole for WOMB people waxing nostalgic about what they did during the anti-Marcos struggle, they could name it, "We Once Mounted a Boycott" (which is more truthful than the more impressive "We Ousted Marcos through Boycott").

I suggest "We Offer Merienda with Books" which truly reflects the business they're in. Though modest, it's far classier than "Women Operating a Merienda Business."

> Perla Gosingco
> Makati, MM

SOCIETY PAGE NEWS:

Anonymous Contribution: TIGIBEE CELEBRATES 68TH

Santiago Barcelona Jr. was given a surprise party by his children (organized by eldest daughter **Pompee**) on his birthday Sunday 16 November. Aside from Tigi's **Ateneo** friends, the well-wishers included the following **UPSCANs**: Mercy and Jimmy Abad; Nilo Cruz; Maureen and Lino Faelnar; Jessie and Jess Javelona; Josie and Eddie Magtoto; Susan and Melvyn Martin; Ting and Jimmy Ong; Mimi and Mon Pasicolan; Charito Quintos; Mila and Johnny Reyes; and long-lost pair Leonor and Bert Sandoval.

The affair was held in the two-hectare garden (with the lawn tennis court) of the imposing 100-year-old ancestral home of the Barcelonas on Don Mariano Marcos Street in San Juan. The garden was decorated with photos of Tigi when he was still a cute 3-year-old tot. The guests were all gushing, "Tigi, you haven't changed at all!"

The plan was that all the visitors would be assembled when Tigi walked in—the better to spring the surprise. But because of the perennial Metro Manila traffic problems, only two couples made it on time, the Pasicolans and the Martins, so that by the time a critical mass had arrived Tigi was already in full control of the situation. He was therefore held accountable and made to explain why some stray couples didn't make it through the traffic jams or could not find the place.

We would like to thank all of Tigi's children, family, friends, household staff, ancestors, etc., without which this affair would not have been possible.

(Ed: this anonymous correspondent may have made a mistake in counting because Mercy reported about the same birthday party as being the 60th. Of course, this correspondent may have been the same one who in the last Newsletter, claimed he was at least 300 years old).

-ooo-

Visit by **Pepito** *and* **May (Miñosa) Gatchalian.**

Sometime early October, **Johnny Balaoing** called to set up a get-together for Pepito and May who were passing through from Mexico on their way back to Manila. They were staying with some friends in Cerritos, a stone's throw away from our place in Artesia. On that short notice, we managed to round up **Tony & Josie Estrera, Enteng Batas** and family, and their hosts who happened to be UP Los Baños Upscans, too. We had a fun evening especially when Enteng and Pepito started relating all their shenanigans at the old quonset hut dorms, known then as the chicken coops.

A month or so later, Johnny again called for a get-together with long time Minnesota resident **Moises (Boy) de la Cruz**. We remember Boy was the chief electrician for the lighting and stage effects during the Upsca presentations at the Engineering theater. Unfortunately, Boy and family had other plans and the get-together didn't go through

-ooo-

The Gil's visit to DC to meet Lili, Lindus and Miren:

In November, **Danny & Lisa Gil** visited the two children and the grandkid in NJ, and made a trip to Washington, DC to meet old friends. Unlike California where the freeway system is easy to follow, Danny found the local freeways confusing, and got hopelessly lost trying to traverse the 12 miles from downtown DC, where he picked up **Lili**, to the agreed meeting place at a Mall near Lindus' home and Miren's place of work. This was despite the road maps, Lisa's navigating, and Lili's eventual back-seat driving! Only later did we find that Lili doesn't drive.

Needless to say, we still had fun time having a quick lunch with **Miren** and **Lindus,** who had patiently waited for us. Miren is doing research in the NIH (National Institute of Health) and will be going back to Manila when the project is completed. After lunch, Miren went back to work, while we followed Lindus to her house nearby. Husband **Buloy Arambulo** was at work (same place where Lili works), so we missed seeing him. Lindus showed us her fabulous artwork: hand-tooled aluminum sheets depicting religious figures, icons, sceneries, etc.

We brought Lili back to her work, after taking a good number of pictures of everybody. Unfortunately, after we developed the set in LA, the entire envelope got lost, probably mistaken as junkmail and thrown in the trash can.

Our NY visit with another Upscan **Susan Rodriguez-Fagan** was more productive in terms of pictures, as Susan sent in some of the shots they had taken. Susan recently retired from the UN and together with husband **Richard**, are considering moving out of NY. Picture below shows Richard (extreme left), and Susan (third from right) with friends. The kid is Lisa and Danny's *apo*.

RECENT CORRESPONDENCE, email or otherwise:

This note is long overdue. Nancy has forwarded a note from you eons ago and I never found time to take care of it. But before I go on, let me thank you first for sending me UPSCA newsletters that you circulate. I enjoyed reading them (and have shared them with fellow ex-UPSCANs in the area.)
                    Sari Valenzuela, NY

Thanks for the surprise. I did receive an e-mail from Ferngil but it somehow didn't get through and I had been wondering who on earth it could have been. Of course, I do remember Danny Gil. I still have a picture of us taken together on a branch of a tree in Malolos, at Mario Manio's place, ages ago. The picture is already quite faded. You can include me in category 3 for the time being. I had just printed out the [email address] list. What a list. It will be great to be able to get in touch again.
                    Sonia Valenzuela-Quast, Brazil

I finally found the time to write my holiday messages. I rushed through Manila on my way to Geneva after a hectic conference on global warming/climate change in Kyoto, Japan where we finalized the negotiations for a protocol for 10 days non-stop! Then Christmas with the family, plus all the things I did not do, but should have done, before Christmas, including Christmas shopping. But the intention was there to greet all our friends, which is what counts I guess.
                    Bernie de Castro-Muller, Switzerland

Arthur Adiarte sent in this picture of the new Minnesota State Capitol plaque which correctly portrays the Filipino's struggle for independence.

Thank you so much for the Newsletters. It is wonderful to hear about old friends again. I can't tell you how many warm memories they brought me. Enclosed is a picture with my husband Nem. Please give my regards to Ramon Pasicolan if you get in touch with him.

He was the president when I was chairman of the HE-ED Chapter.

Bing Pascual-Santos, LA

Hey Fern!
I'd like you to look at a photo of me and my colleague at work Ed A. Poe (the one with the moustache), who share a

common hobby — *writing ghost stories*. Ed has a colorful background — he says that before he joined us, he was a student at West Point but got kicked out for drunkenness. Although he has never published a full length novel, he has written many short stories and claims to have been a ghost writer (literally) for Stephen King at least once.

Regards to you, Lisa, and the kids!

Johnny and Mila, Phils

Oy, Johnny, *hirit naman*. Give us more ghost stories! *Kahit na galing kay* Edgar Allan Poe, *basta lang hindi* plagerized. *Baka may stateside flavor pa.*

-ooo-

Editorial Box

Typeset by Danny Gil from unwitting contributors from the Internet as abetted by members of the Upsca Alumni Association in Los Angeles. Published supposedly every quarter. Mail, fax, or call in your articles, pictures, jokes, manifestos, etc. to address below:
19002 Horst Ave Artesia, CA 90701
tel (562) 402-5098 fax (562) 402-1890 email: ferngil@aol.com

FLASH! As we go to press, the news was just relayed to us that **Johnny Balaoing** had an investiture January 11 for *Knight Commander of the Order of Pope Gregory the Great* at the St Francis church. Cardinal Mahoney officiated at the ceremony. Congratulations Johnny!

FINAL REMINDER:

The post Christmas UPSCA party will be held on January 24, Saturday at Danny & Lisa Gil's house.

-ooo-

JOKE TIME! More ERAP jokes.

Little is known of the fact that Erap once applied to Med School. Listed below are the results of his entrance test dug up from some ancient archives. Needless to say he didn't make it...

ANTIBODY: against everyone
ARTERY: the study of fine paintings
BACTERIA: back door to a cafeteria
BENIGN: what you be after you be eight
BOWEL: letters like A, E, I, O, or U
CAESAREAN SECTION: a district in Rome
CARDIOLOGY: advanced study of poker playing
CAT SCAN: searching for ones lost kitty
CAUTERIZE: made eye contact with her
COMA: a punctuation mark

CONGENITAL: friendly
CORTIZONE: the local courthouse
D & C: where Washington is
DILATE: to live longer
ENEMA: not a friend
ER: the things on your head that you hear with
FIBRILLATE: to tell lies
GENES: blue denim slacks
HEMORRHOID: a male from outer space
IMPOTENT: distinguished, well known
LABOR PAIN: hurt at work
MINOR OPERATION: somebody else's
ORGAN TRANSPLANT: what you do to your piano when you move
PARALYZE: two far-fetched stories
PATHOLOGICAL: a reasonable way to go
PHARMACIST: person who makes a living dealing in agriculture
PROTEIN: in favor of young people
RED BLOOD COUNT: Dracula
RHEUMATIC: amorous
SECRETION: hiding anything
TABLET: a small table
TERMINAL ILLNESS: getting sick at the airport
TIBIA: country in North Africa
TRIPLE BYPASS: better than a quarterback sneak
TUMOR: an extra pair
URINE: opposite of "you're out"
VARICOSE: very close
VEIN: conceited

- - - - -

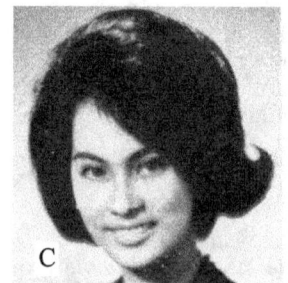

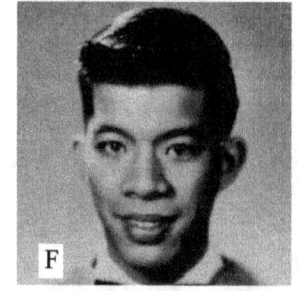

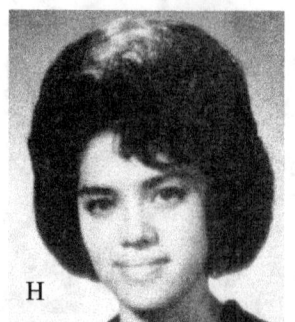

If you have been reading carefully the Newsletters, you should be able to match the lettered pictures with the clues below:
1. The Plaqueman
2. Mrs Frank
3. JOng paid for her fare
4. Son of Katialis inventor
5. Misses cat in his siopao
6. Flaps his wings
7. The Ghost who walks
8. Finds their winter brisk

UPSCA ALUMNI ASSOCIATION, USA

NEWSLETTER　　　NEWSLETTER　　　NEWSLETTER

AMDG　　Vol 1, Num 6　(2nd quarter, 1998)　　Published by UPSCA Alumni Association, USA

FUND RAISER FOR DELANEY HALL

Here is an email 3 weeks ago from Mercy which reproduces the appeal letter for the above drive, shown boxed in below:

Dear All,

I got this letter from **Fr Robert** who is chaplain of the UP Chapel. He is asking for our help to renovate *Delaney Hall*, an important backdrop to our happy college days. I thought, maybe this is a project we could all undertake. Danny, maybe you can take the lead for US UPSCANS.

Mercy Abad

April 14, 1998

Dear _____

Greetings!

We are getting the renovated **Delaney Hall** ready to be blessed on December 20, 1998. The repairs have started. We want the Hall to reflect our continued love and esteem for the man of cloth who helped us build the Chapel of the Holy Sacrifice, now called the U.P. Parish of the Holy Sacrifice.

A bust of Fr John P. Delaney will be cast in bronze by National Artist Napoleon "Billy" Abueva who made the huge Crucifix inside the Church. This bust will remind us of how the "*priest of fire and steel*" (Fr F. Gough) and who died 40 years ago looked like.

We now appeal for your support. Your donations will help us finish the project for the December 20th blessing. You may forward your donations to Parish of the Holy Sacrifice, Diliman, Quezon City or you may call us at telephone numbers 926-9496 and 926-1592 for further information.

Thank you very much.

Yours with the Holy Sacrifice,
FR ROBERTO P. REYES

A week or so letter, another email came from Mon & Eva (Singson) de Veyra:

Dear Danny & Lisa,

Greetings from the Kalayaan Land. We just celebrated the centennial yesterday with a big bang. The whole nation was feted to a lot of historical memories, grandiose parade and a colossal fireworks. We have a lot to thank God for despite our limitations - at least we are free.

We visited **Yolo Sulit** at Cardinal Santos Hospital on June 11- his 63rd B-day. I don't think he recognized us. **Susan** is well, but very much tied up.

Angge sent us the following SOS letter from the present UPSCA chaplain for dissemination to the UPSCANs She said she has already sent you one already for the members in U.S.A. You can always reproduce the letter. Mon thought of sending you one by email, with the permission of Angge. If you have collected some donations, you can send them to Angge.

Last month we feted **Baby Sanciangco-Parker** whom I've not met since 1960. We had as guest **Yeyet Oliveros-Santos, Sonia and Ely Alampay, Angge and Johnny Ramos.**

We've passed on the bulletin you sent us to **Ben de Leon** (Pres Ramos' right hand man) and the other to Johnny Ramos - who is in close contact with Ramon.

Do get in touch. We hope you could solicit from all Upscans there, especially (**Johnny B, Enting B, Manny E, Liliosa M, Jessica I, Zeny R, Sisoy A, etc, etc,**)

Best regards to all.

Mon & Eva

-o-o-o-o-o-

So, everybody, why don't we **pull out the checkbooks,** *especially for those mentioned by Eva. Make your* **checks** *payable to* **Parish of the Holy Sacrifice.** *Remember the adage "Give until it hurts". Unless you can have them somehow get to Fr Reyes, it might be better to mail them here to 19002 Horst Ave, Artesia, CA 90701, and we'll send the checks via courier (with all the friends and relatives coming and going from LA to Manila, it shouldn't be any problem).*

The sign in front of the church. Commercialism notwithstanding, as sign reads "curtesy of Urban Bank. . . . ."

Delaney Hall, or DH, as it was more commonly referred to during our time in the '60s. Picture was taken during July '97 visit, and shows Lisa Gil flanked by her cousin Norma, and son Joey. Original color shot showed the manicured and verdant foliage around the area.

SOME REACTIONS TO THE LAST ISSUE:

From Beth and Bong Nuqui: We received the newsletter just this morning, via messenger from Mercy. I was so entertained by it, I was late for a meeting at PGH. I was giggling away with my hoarse voice from a heavy cold, and didn't realize the time. Thank God for people like you and Johnny Reyes. Thank you for the laughter and memories.

-o-o-o-o-o-

From Gani Cruz: Yes, I received the latest issue but, Danny, that photo you identify as me does not look the remotest like me. Did I really have such a thick moustache? It must have been someone else. Keep up the good work otherwise!

Yes, Gani, it may not have been you at all. Ernie Pangilinan and I spent some time trying to identify all those in the picture, which incidentally was taken at the UP President's residence when Noel was president. Shown in the inset is the mystery man (leftmost) beside the identifiable Eli Lademora, Jimmy, Tigi and JOng. Could it have been Jess Javelona? Any answers from anybody?

-o-o-o-o-o-

Another boo-boo, per Arthur Adiarte:

Danny, the picture [   ] the bronze plaque v 'e not the corrected o ꞁ understanding

-o-(

From JOng: Hi, 1 ꞁ came last week, tha.ꞁ had a grand time, she with the exchange of comments on *Walakbayan*, and I with the trips down memory lane. I guess this happens when you hit 53 or older — you relish these stories coming back to you,

and triggering more and more memories from the dim past. The anecdotes and injokes may limit the newsletter's appeal, to people within a certain age band; but your fiftysomething readers will have so many stories to tell that you should never run out of material.

-o-o-o-o-o-

From Liliosa, re "identify the graduates":

Yes, I think I identified all the mystery graduates. Tony Estrera is the Catman, Arthur is the Plaqueman, Buloy is the son of Katialis (a historical error soon to be corrected, I heard), Primalee was one of JOng's bus muses, Christie likes NM's brisk winters, Rory was Mrs Frank, Johnny is the Canadian goose, and Tigi hasn't changed at all, at all! Did I miss anyone?

The short story contest will be addressed in the next issue, if there is a next issue.

-o-o-o-o-o-

JOng sent this picture with caption: On the assumption that you continue to look for fading photographs of how we looked 30 yrs and 30 lbs ago, for possible publication in the newsletter, here is something from the past. It's labeled "Quezon Conferences II, May 8-11, 1964, Baguio City." The conferences started in **Melvyn Martin**'s time, as leadership training seminars for UP High students. UPSCAns with nothing better to do during the summer break would bring maybe 20 high school seniors up to Baguio for three days or so of lectures. We called them Quezon conferences because MLQ was, then and now, not a bad role model; also, the "Q"in his name could be reworked into a logo that looked vaguely like the UPSCA pin. Because when you came down to it, the Quezon conferences seemed like a handy way to do some advance recruiting among UP High's best and brightest, even before they made it to college. Don't know if the strategy worked very well. Smarrafact, I'm not even sure if the conferences continued after my time. Anyway, the photo: As you can see, it's not easy to tell, from a perspective of 34 yrs

later, organizer from organizee. And of course today I'm unable to name most of the HS students in the picture. But if you start with the *back row*, you'll spot some of the UPSCAns of that era. That's **Mon Pasicolan**, 2nd from left, with glasses and necktie. **Rey Aquino. Celia Morales. Ana Corina Castro. Roddy Suaco. Emy Masigan. Vangie de Castro. Me. Ruben Habito**, not looking at the camera. **Oca Ramos. Alex Dacanay. Edgar Maranan.** *Second row* includes **Digna Dacanay** and **Ping Tan**. To the right, looking considerably less nourished than he is today, **Manny Castillo. Tom Aquino.** Front row has **Fr Pat Lim** and some of the UPHS faculty who tagged along. At the back of the foto, also reproduced, are signatures of some of the people who went, and a dedication that reads: "To Jong, for the ray of light that added to the brilliance of my candle. (sgd.) Bathless Celia." "Bathless," of course, is a reference to the chronic problem of anyone who stayed at Patria Inn — water. *Anybody, want to volunteer some info?*

A TALE OF TWO POLITICIANS-TO-BE

The recent Philippine Elections made the Loop sizzle with political views. A number of members jumped right into the political arena.

Gani *went into REAL politics, and when finally it was over, he wrote to all:*

Raul Roco conceded today, not to the better candidate, but to the candidate that got more votes (Erap). Roco got a respectable third (maybe even second, if you factor in De Venecia's cheating) in the counting. Let us hope that Forest Gump (or Dumb and Dumber) surprises us. Meanwhile, my short stint in politics as Roco's *media handler* has taught me a valuable lesson — you cannot always be right when you are right, and you may not always be wrong when you are wrong.

On the other hand, ***Johnny*** *went into VIRTUAL politics (after all, as the previous newslet issues indicated, Johnny can fly, can teleport and go back in time):*

Yo Guys!

It has not been an easy decision for me to make, but after much soul-searching I have finally taken the step. Public service is a calling which is thankless, punishing, exasperating, and debilitating, but it can also be extremely gratifying. I recall the words of George F. Warren, the 19th President of the United States, who said, "When I was asked to give my share, I did and more. And what did I expect in return? Nothing, save the thought that I had given my best for my nation." Radovan Karadzic, the famous Balkan statesman, said as much when he vowed to "purge my soul, my neighbor, and my country."

Looking around me during the last few years, I have found nothing but paralysis, a state of suspended animation. Nothing has changed, but men seem to be contented with the status quo. It is really the best of times and the worst of times, with the *rich getting poorer* and the *poor getting richer*. And what have I done about it so far? Absolutely nothing!

The supreme sacrifice is to give up one's personal and private life and to throw one's *cat into the ring*, regardless of the chances of success.

Why am I calling upon the help of my friends? Because you are the only hope, the bulwark of democracy, the guardians of a way of life. I call upon you to embark with me upon a voyage of faith, and to lend me your support [as I run for political office].

You may ask, what is my platform? When I flew to Puerto Princesa, I was able to see some of the most spectacular groups of islands in the world. It was then that I learned about the island

The "post-Christmas party" held 24 Jan 98. *Crouching L to R:* Oids Garcia, Manny Castillo, Danny Gil, Greg Santillan. *Standing L to R:* Johnny Balaoing, Angel Sta Maria, Lisa Gil, Bing (Pascual) & Nem Santos, Malu (Barrios) Garcia, Ernie Pangilinan, Myrna's son, Ken Aid, Precy (Javier) Webber, Ofie Aid, Myrna Aquitania, Rose (Lacebal) Engay, Jessie (Raqueño) Pangilinan, Alda Balaoing. Sorry if the names may be mixed up. Greg was the only one with a loaded camera and his emailed color scan of the picture didn't come out too clear when converted to B&W. As usual, the party was all eating, singing and laughter.

province of Samaral and realized the opportunities. I am therefore *running for Representative of Samaral Province (pop. 7)*, with your help and that of Divine Providence.

My platform rests on a single public works project which I intend to carry out as soon as I am elected Congressman of the Second District of Samaral Province (comprising the beautiful Samaral Pequeño Island).

Samaral Pequeño has one problem: At *low tide it goes completely under water, the island disappears*, and the inhabitants (my prospective constituents) have to get on board their boats while waiting for the waters to recede. Needless to say, this is a most unproductive period.

My plan is to *build an undersea pipeline tunnel* which will connect Samaral Pequeño to the bigger island of Samaral Grande (which belongs to the First District), 700 meters away. This will *allow the flood waters to drain away from Samaral Pequeño towards Grande during high tide.* To prevent the water from flowing back during low tide, a check valve (non-return valve) will be installed along the pipeline. My civil engineering advisers have assured me that this solution will work, and that it will solve once and for all the centuries-old problem of Samaral Pequeño, and I will have been responsible for it.

Many of us responded favorably to Johnny's candidacy. From Danny:

And by the way, your years down under in Australia must have reversed your logic too, since at low tide, you claim the island of Samaral Pequeño goes under water. Also, I cannot contribute much to your coffers but I can help by asking some of

my Philippine connections there to terrorize the voters to vote for you.

An email from another supportee also named Danny wrote in:

Good luck to your friend Johnny. Except that I really don't think it's prudent for him to throw his 'cat' into the ring. The Society for the Prevention of Cruelty to Animals detests throwing felines into a den of crocodiles. As for his underwater province, I've heard of flying voters, but swimming voters . . . ? That's a new one.

Just like any good politician, Johnny responded promptly, with an alibi:

Pretty sharp of you to catch the error, but it was just a typo. Of course, I had meant the island of Samaral Pequeño goes under water at HIGH tide, not low tide. (It must have been the hecticness of the campaign getting to me.)

Anyway, the elections are over, and the voter turnout in the Second District of Samaral Province was 100%. The counting was also completed early, thanks to the local Bantay Bayan movement (who I had the feeling were there to watch me, but one learns to take these things in stride). Final results: Jose Gupiling, fisherman, 3. Desiderio Pinagkaisahan, fruit farmer, 3. Juan M. Reyes, engineer, 1. (By the way, I am a registered voter of Samaral Pequeño Island.) It was not a bad showing for a first attempt, considering I was only two votes short of the winner. Also, in percentage terms I scored a decent 14.3%, not very different from the way some of the presidential candidates have been scoring so far.

HOW POLITICS AFFECTED THOSE WHO VENTURED IN IT.

Gani underwent a complete metamorphosis and waxed eloquently on these words of wisdom, or at least it seemed so at first (list was shortened):

INSTRUCTIONS FOR LIFE

 1. Give people more than they expect and do it cheerfully.
 2. Memorize your favorite poem.
 3. Don't believe all you hear, spend all you have or sleep all you want.
 4. When you say, "I love you", mean it.
 5. Be engaged at least six months before you get married.
 6. Believe in love at first sight.
 7. Never laugh at anyone's dreams.
 8. Love deeply and passionately. You might get hurt but it's the only way to live life completely.
 9. Don't judge people by their relatives.
10. When someone asks you a question you don't want to answer, smile and ask, "Why do you want to know?"
11. Remember that great love and great achievements involve great risk.
12. Call your mom.
13. When you lose, don't lose the lesson.
14. Remember the three R's: Respect for self; Respect for others; Responsibility for all your actions.
15. Don't let a little dispute injure a great friendship.
16. When you realize you've made a mistake, take immediate steps to correct it.
17. Smile when picking up the phone. The caller will hear it in your voice.
18. Marry a person you love to talk to. As you get older, their conversational skills will be as important as any other.
19. Spend some time alone.
20. Open your arms to change, but don't let go of your values.
21. Remember that silence is sometimes the best answer.
22. Read more books and watch less TV.
23. Live a good, honorable life. Then when you get older and think back, you'll get to enjoy it a second time.
24. Trust in God but lock your car.
25. In disagreements with loved ones, deal with the current situation. Don't bring up the past.
26. Read between the lines.
27. Share your knowledge. It's a way to achieve immortality.
28. Be gentle with the earth.
29. Pray — there's immeasurable power in it.
30. Once a year, go someplace you've never been before.
31. If you make a lot of money, put it to use helping others while you are living. That is wealth's greatest satisfaction.

From Myrna's album, the visit of Nonong Pedero 3 years ago. *L to R:* Nonong, Lisa, Danny, Myrna, Mario, Oids, Malu, Manny, Offie, Ken. Nonong was on his way back to Manila from NY on a business trip, and dropped in to especially say hello to Malu, Berryl Silva, and others of their CAFA signing group from way back in the late '60s.

32. Remember that not getting what you want is sometimes a stroke of luck.
33. Remember that the best relationship is one where your love for each other is greater than your need for each other.
34. Judge your success by what you had to give up in order to get it.
35. Remember that your character is your destiny.
36. Approach love and cooking with reckless abandon.

Responses showed some doubts about Gani. From LME (Liliosa "Baby" Mangosing Evangelista):

Are you the same **Isagani Cruz** I know? You sound different this time.

The same ol' Gani came out fighting:

I just learned a great lesson from Liliosa: never, never to pass off as my own (even unwittingly by pressing "forward" on my computer) someone else's wise thoughts. No one will ever believe I could either originate or approve of such thoughts! And no, those thoughts were not mine. If I had thought up a quarter of those, I would really be not me!!! (How's that for self-knowledge?).

More needling from Liliosa:

Ay, sayang! I thought you had turned into a gentler, kinder guy. Ah, well.

JOng's last say on the matter:

Hi, Baby. Isagani has been accused of many things in his life, but gentleness is not one of them. But he's trying his best, and taking lessons from Erap Estrada.

Johnny's response to his unsuccessful political career was very much more dramatic:

Hi Guys!

Just to let you know that I have decided to leave my employer (Pilipinas Shell) after 31 years of service, with potentially 5 more to go. My last day of work will be on 15 June. Then Mila and I will move to the U.S. with our twin youngest daughters and the dog, and I will try to find another job there.

Immediate reaction from Mercy:

Are you one of those who are abandoning ship because Erap is the new captain? Now, I will call you *abandonados*. What is your timetable like? We must get together before you go. *Yung bang tipong maglalasingan.*

Well, it really went through. Johnny immigrated to the US June 20, but not before a small party was hosted, as reported by JOng. No mention was made about the lasingan aspect:

Johnny hosted a bon voyage for **Johnny**. Joining him, **Mila** and one daughter for dinner at Dad's Makati last June 11 were **Lino** and **Maureen**, **Ping** and **Merle**, **Mon** and **Mimi**, **Melvyn** and **Susan**, **Ting** and me, etc.

Send your articles, pictures, jokes, anecdotes, stories, opinions, or whatever. We need interesting material for publication.

The ill-fated Batangas excursion. It was circa mid 70's and about a dozen families embarked on a trip to what **Mon Pasicolan** swore was "the last unspoiled beach within a few hours drive from Manila". So we all convoyed following him. We got lost; the roads were terrible; and finally after getting there way past noon, we found the sea full of jellyfish, and woe were those brave ones who ventured into the water. Only due to **Fredie**'s inflatable dinghy were the children able to enjoy the water, by riding above it. By the time we had finished eating, it was time to go home. But it didn't turn out that simple. **Lino**'s car got stuck in the sand, and as the wheels spun, it dug itself

deeper, and the chassis got impaled on a bamboo stump. It took Fredie's ingenuity with a jack, a deflated tire, and lots of muscle power (including **Maureen**'s) to finally get the car out. And hours later, by the time we got to Muntinglupa, the South Superhighway was a parking lot, jammed solid with traffic. It took years for Mon to regain his credibility as a good tour guide!

This is from the album of **Tony**. Now, can anybody identify those back facing people. Obviously, there's Fredie and **Mercy** sitting against the Volks. Who else went to that picnic? What year was it? I remember we brought along **Nina Los Baños**, and used her car. - *Danny*

Now that our prolific correspondent, Johnny, isn't Philippine-based anymore, we'll publish this travelogue he made for Christie:

I haven't had a chance to get out into the bush for years, so what I am about to suggest to you will all be second-hand and limited to the usual tourist traps. The only jungles I know are the urban and concrete ones. Batangas City used to be wooded a few years ago, but is now heavily overcrowded.

Your world-traveller friends could visit Boracay Beach and see (microscopic) wild life. It is supposed to be one of the best beaches in the world, but the waters are infested with e. coli at the moment, because of overbuilding without proper drainage. They even built a golf course on the pristine island. Your friends could also visit Dakak Beach in Zamboanga—another great site—but unfortunately they can't view the pedophile who used to roam wild in the area, because he is currently in captivity and is confined in a zoo (Muntinlupa).

Wait a minute! When it comes to beaches, you should be consulting not me but Susan Po-Rufino (Poruf@aol.com) who owns a substantial proportion of Boracay, or Rory Abrera (Canikiisle@aol.com) who owns a whole island called Caniki.

Next on the list is Pagsanjan Falls. There are also a lot of (Caucasian) pedophiles in this area, so your friends should be careful not to fraternize too much with the local children. Taal Volcano is still worth visiting. Your friends could take a boat to the island from Balete or Tanauan in Batangas, and explore the crater on foot.

Mayon Volcano tops them all,

but it's a long drive from Manila over not-so-good roads. I guess it's better to fly round-trip to Legaspi. Your friends should also see the Banawe Rice Terraces before these are closed for good (The caretakers have become overseas contract workers in Japan and the Middle East). Banawe is only about six hours away from Manila via Nueva Vizcaya, but more than twelve hours away from Baguio, which is less than a hundred kilometers away from it. This Baguio-Banawe connection is always a challenge to our expat friends in Tabangao Refinery, but I have never done it myself. You need a four-wheel-drive vehicle to do it, and you always risk being cut off by landslides from both Baguio and Banawe, particularly during the rainy season.

I guess the best wildlife are in Palawan, and although I have never been there myself, I heard that the Underground River near Puerto Princesa is interesting. Come to think of it, we no longer have any real forests in the Philippines (I mean those with trees) except the one in Subic.

Closer to Batangas is Mindoro Island. Ferries run between Batangas City Harbor and Calapan (or Puerto Galera) every few hours, and the fast catamarans do the crossing in less than half an hour. There are also nice beaches in Puerto Galera, as well as coral areas. If they are lucky, your friends might see a sunken galleon. On the other hand, if

they wish to see real-live pirates they don't have to go farther than Manila Bay after dark.

Finally, if they are interested in seeing a wasteland full of lahar and desert beggars, they should visit the areas of Tarlac and Pampanga near Mt. Pinatubo, which as you know nobody thought was a volcano until it suddenly erupted after 600 years. (Makiling might be next.)

Exploring the crater of Taal volcano circa mid 70's: Danny, Jess, Jong, Tony and Ping. Jimmy was the cameraman. I took the next picture where all were lined up facing the other way, relieving themselves! - *Danny*

Note that travelling around the Philippines is costly and prohibitive to the locals, so there really are no such things as "tourist areas that only Filipinos patronize." It's much cheaper to go to Hongkong and back. As far as safety is concerned, I guess the only places your friends should avoid at the moment are Basilan, Jolo, Tukuran, Cotabato, etc.

I hope the above travelogue, by someone who hasn't been there, was useful.

Best regards. Johnny

THE "LOOP". *Undoubtedly, this term has often arisen, and to those who may still be confused, it's a group of Upscans in cyberspace:*

". . . listed below are the email addresses and identities of all those in the Loop. As explained in *earlier Newletters and in various email exchanges*, here are the guidelines:

1. The Loop is a group of Upscans and/or friends of Upscans who knew each other back in UP during the '60s, and who wish to continue being in touch via the Internet.
2. The Loop is broken down into three categories: Category 1, 2 & 3.
3. Category 2 are those who wish being on the mailing list for jokes, commentary, trivia, and other entertaining communications of good taste, with the end in view of keeping up the camaraderie and fellowship. Bear in mind that some of these communications may be published in the on-again off-again UPSCA Newsletter.
4. Category 1 members are a subset of Category 2 who are more daring, naughty and liberal, and are willing to hear more risque jokes, or even throw a few bantering barbs at each other (just like old times??) while the rest of the audience cheers on, gives their comments, or joins in the fray.
5. Category 3 members are those familiar names whose addresses have come to our attention but have not responded to the invitation to be part of the mailing list, or have elected not to be contacted. In other words, we know you're there, but will contact you only on the one-to-one basis.
6. Anybody can upgrade or downgrade to any category by merely circularizing an email to Category 2.
7. Members are enjoined to turn in addresses of other Upscans whom they feel might be interested to join.

Here is the list, compliments of Johnny Reyes, who arranged them in such manner as to make it easy to "cut and paste" the various categories into your address lists....."

This list is too long to publish in this issue, but the Mailing List on the last page shows most of the email addresses of the members, sans categories. For those with email who are interested, then email us.

Accretion of the Loop can come about in many different ways. Some samples:

From Arthur Adiarte: I was in a PSGM gathering last week and got in touch with **Boy de la Cruz**. He's planning to do a 6-month teaching stint in U.P. Diliman at the Electrical Engineering department and he's interested in *joining the loop*. His e-mail address is maczedam@aol.com According to Boy, "maczedam" is a permutation of his children's names! He works as a principal engineer in Rosemount Inc. in Chanhassen, Minnesota.

-o-o-o-o-

JOng relayed this message he got from **Jimmy Valera**. *Excerpts:*

"Hi JONG! I got your e-mail address from the KilosPinoysaMundo (NormMadrid@aol.com) manifesto sent through the e-mail. Some of our friends signed up and sent their own messages of protest. Anyway, how are you and everyone we know? Perhaps, I will visit ERAP's Philippines sometime. Regards to everyone. - JEMZ"

Hi, Jemz. Good to hear from you — but your message is tantalizingly short on details! Tell me more. In case you're interested, there is a fairly active e-mail loop of UPSCAns of our generation plus a few who are slightly more ancient. I'm alerting a few (Mercy Abad, Tigi, Tony Estrera, Susan Po, Isagani, Danny Gil) through the cc:, and you may hear from them soon. Stay in touch. - JOng

Needless to say, after a few more exchanges, Jong said " . . again, welcome to the loop, old friend."

-o-o-o-o-

From Liliosa: Eureka! **Lennie Abellera Blair** has been found, thanks to Arthur Adiarte's efforts, and she has given me permission to have her attached message sent to the rest of the Loop. She also wants to join the Loop, so pass the word (and the usual caveats?). Jun and Cynthia (Reyes) Calejesan are in town, but we are having a heck of a time trying to connect. We hope to see each other somewhere in this city sometime today.....

"Hi there, Baby! I'm sure this comes as a surprise to you, but maybe not - in the midst of this wonderful invention called e-mail!!! I got your e-mail address third hand from my brother Benjie, who keeps in touch with Art Adiarte from whom your e-mail address came from, get it?! I truly think that the e-mail must be the invention of the century, best thing since sliced bread!"
                    Lennie

Now for a change, some non-ancient pictures from last Christmas:

The Arambulos in Maryland: Lindus (Carreon), Kitty, Kathy & Primo. Lindus recently came back from the Philippines wherein she graced an exhibit of her unique artwork.

-o-o-o-o-o-

The Adiartes in Minnesota: Arthur and Cherrie up front, with sons Alex and Eric.

-o-o-o-o-o-

The Gatchalians in Manila: Pepito and May (Miñosa) with the grandkids.

Typeset by Danny Gil in Los Angeles from unwitting sources in the Internet, but only when in the mood. 19002 Horst, Artesia, CA 90701, fax (562) 402-1890

Street address, email and telelephone numbers (where present) have been erased from original printed hard copy.

Jimmy & Mercy (Rivera) Abad
Antipolo, Philippines

Rory Abrera
Dallas, TX 75380

Arthur & Cherrie Adiarte
St Paul, MN?55105

Ofie (Peñaflorida) & Ken Aid
Lakewood, CA 90715

Letty (Ramirez) Ajodah
Queens Village, NY 11428

Ely & Sonia (Alday) Alampay
Diliman,QC, Philippines

José Alzona
Long Beach, CA 90814

Nanette (Gadi) & Boy Angeles
Monroeville, PA

Lolly Aquino
Los Angeles, CA 90042

Myrna Aquitania
Camarillo, CA 93012

Primo & Lindus (Carreon) Arambulo
Rockville, MD 20852

Noli Arong
Arleta, CA 91331

Sisoy Arong
Houston, TX 77036

Divsy Astraquillo
Shorewood, WI 53211

Johnny & Alda Balaoing
Los Angeles, CA 90065

Nina Los Baños
Las Vegas, NV 89108

Tigi & Nora Barcelona
Quezon City, Philippines

Olga (Cruz) Barrios
Williamsville, NY

Enteng & Mely Batas
Lancaster, CA 93535

Jun & Cynthia (Reyes) Calejesan
Monaca, PA 15061

Ramon O. Casas
Strasbourge, France

Manny Castillo
Brea, CA 92621

Delfin Castro
Bowie, MD 20715

Remy & Anching Chica
Northridge, CA 90242

Tessie Chua Chiaco
North Hollywood, CA 91605

Isagani & Medy Cruz
Malate, Manila, Philippines

Nancy (Cruz) & Gerry Dienel
Little Rock, AR 72212

Bing (Ferrer) & Anthony Dubitsky
Riverdale, MD 20737

Cir & Rose (Lacebal)?Engay
Los Angeles, CA 90065

Georgina (Reyes) & Mervyn Encanto
Quezon City, Philippines

Manny & Lee Espejo
Saugus, CA 91350

Deo & Aleli Estacio
Altadena, CA 91001

Tony & Josie (Angeles) Estrera
Cerritos, CA 90701

Liliosa (Mangosing) & Gene Evangelista
Fairfax, VA 22309

Lino & Maureen (Holazo) Faelnar
Las Piñas 1751, Philippines

Susan (Rodriguez) & Dick Fagan
New York, NY

Dette Feliciano
Los Angeles, CA 90020

Temy (Dapilos) Gamboa
Patchogue, NY 11772

Malu (Barrios) & Oids Garcia
Cerritos, CA 90701

Pepito & May (Miñosa) Gatchalian
Quezon City, Philippines

Danny & Lisa (Señeris) Gil
Artesia, CA 90701

Erwin & Alita Gomez
Valparaiso, IN 46383

Ruben & Maria Habito
Sakyo-ku, Kyoto 606, Japan

Effie (Sta Romana) Hall
Bettendorf, IA 52722

Chit Inciong
Flushing, NY 11354
(718) 359-7737

Jessica Infante
Los Angeles, CA 90065

Jess & Jessie (Quinto) Javelona
Muntinglupa, Philippines

Nanette (Ortega) & Benny Jongco
South Orange, NJ 07079

Godofredo Juliano
Philippines

Christie (Borromeo) & Don Kawal
Albuquerque, NM 87122

Lallie Lacaba
Pateros, Metro Manila, Philippines

Clara (Reyes) & Bart Lapus
San Juan, Philippines

Raquel (Celera) & Ric Lejano
Torrance, CA 90503

Loida (Nicolas) Lewis
New York, NY 10019

Cheche (Lim) & Delfin Lazaro
Philippines

Eddie & Josie Magtoto
Parañaque, Phils

Mario & Myrna Manansala
La Palma, CA 90623

Romy & Edna (Zapanta) Manlapaz
Quezon City, Phils

Melvyn & Susan (Paulin) Martin
Ayala Alabang, Muntinglupa, Phils

Bernie (de Castro) & Jurg Muller
Geneva, Switzerland

Clemencia Natividad
Toronto, Ontario, Canada

Tony Nievera
Douglaston, NY 11362

Bong & Beth (Arcellana) Nuqui
Diliman, Quezon City, Phil

Jimmy & Ting Ong
Bo Kapitolyo, Pasig, Phils

Ernie & Jessie (Raqueño) Pangilinan
Mission Hills, CA 91345

Ramon & Mimi Pasicolan
Ayala Hts, Quezon City, Philippines

Lina (Soliman) Plantilla
Brooklyn, NY 11229

Priscilla (Bautista) Perez
Bronx, NY 10467

Sonia (Valenzuela) & Dietrich Quast
Sao Pablo, Brazil

Amelia (Bascon) Rasalan
Bayside, NY 11364

Hermie (Manoto) & Jess Rabe
Cerritos, CA 90701

Johnny & Mila (Garcia) Reyes
Belle Mead, NJ 08502

Ruben & Naida (Uy) Rivera
Quezon City, Philippines

Susan (Po) & Guilly Rufino
San Francisco, CA 94132

Maya (Arroyo) Santiano
Quezon City, Philippines

Greg Santillan
San Gabriel, CA 91775

Angel & Stella Sta Maria
Pasadena, CA 91103

Zeny (Roxas) & Sixto Ramirez
Los Angeles, CA 90041

Nel Reformina
Nanuet, NY 10954

Bing Pascual-Santos
Whittier, CA 90601

Alex & Miren (Dumlao) Santos
UP?Campus, QC, Philippines

Miren (Dumlao) Santos
Bethesda, Md 20817

Berryl Silva
Long Beach, CA 90808

Noel & Angge (Alday) Soriano
West Triangle Homes, QC, Phils

cont'd on page 6

14 April 1998

Dear Danny, Lisa,

Greetings!

We are getting the renovated **Delaney Hall** ready to be blessed on December 20, 1998. The repairs have started. We want the Hall to reflect our continued love and esteem of the man of cloth who helped us build the Chapel of the Holy Sacrifice now called the U.P. Parish of the Holy Sacrifice.

A bust of Fr. John P. Delaney will be cast in bronze by National Artist Napoleon "Billy" Abueva who made the huge Crucifix inside the Church. This bust will remind us of how the *"priest of fire and steel"* (Fr. F. Gough) and who died 40 years ago looked like.

We now appeal for your support. Your donations will help us finish the project for the December 20th blessing. You may forward your donations to Parish of the Holy Sacrifice, Diliman, Quezon City or you may call us at telephone numbers 926-9496 and 926-1592 for further information.

Thank you very much.

Yours with the Holy Sacrifice,

FR. ROBERTO P. REYES
Parish Priest

wordult

I was requested by
Selma Gonzales-Cortes
and Cora Rodrin to
pass this on to as
many vissctors and
Delaney friends as possible.
Please do the same.
Thanks! Peggie
Soriano
Tel 374-2170

UPSCA *ALUMNI ASSOCIATION, USA*

NEWSLETTER NEWSLETTER NEWSLETTER

A M D G | Vol 1, Num 7 (3rd quarter, 1998) | Published by UPSCA Alumni Association, USA

A TALE OF TWO PARTIES

Makati, July 25. Excerpts from May Gatchalian's e-mail: We've just come back from the mass for Gerry and the sumptuous dinner that followed. Enjoying the food and the company of "long-time-no-see UPSCANS" were the likes of **Angge Soriano, Tigi Barcelona** and wife, **Che-Che Lazaro, Gina Encanto, Jimmy Ong, Cornelia Braid, Ed Magtoto** and wife, **Lino** and **Maureen Faelnar**, and other nice people whose names escape us at the moment. Kindly convey our greetings to **Enteng Batas, Johnny Balaoing**, and other UPSCANs there who might remember us and the good times we had together - either at the Delaney Hall, the chapel basement, and the other nooks and crannies of the chapel which will forever remain etched in our mind's eye. And, of course, many thanks once again for the warm welcome you gave us when we dropped by your house last year. With all best wishes, **a.m.d.g.**, and all that.

A mass and dinner was held at the Gil residence in Makati on the occasion of the 3rd death anniversary of Gerry Gil July 26th. Guests were Upsca friends and members of the board of the GG Foundation, which aims to promote journalistic excellence through contests and awards. First contest is in December.

Los Angeles, July 12. Excerpts from Liliosa's letter: My recent California visit was quite a scorcher (literally & otherwise), thanks to you and the lovely reunion in your home. Thank you so much for your wonderful hospitality and for gathering a gaggle of old friends from the far-flung corners of L.A. for a memorable afternoon of music, dancing & food. But I have to confess that the best part was the galloping *chismis* session before the party finally broke up. It made me realize that I missed a lot of "action" during our college years, most likely due to my "age of minority". I would love to see the pictures in the newsletter - of **Jessie** [Raqueño] **Pangilinan** playing so well at the piano, **Johnny Balaoing** crooning, **Malu** [Barrios-Garcia] and I dancing *pandango* sans *ilaw* and *tinikling* for dummies! And the food, glorious food! **Lindus** & **Miren** & I will get together this Saturday, and they want to hear all about it. I hope to see you again soon. Perhaps there will be another reunion in the East coast?

Other crooner (without mike) is Manny Castillo. Another party is scheduled Aug 30 at **Oids** and **Malu's** house for visiting guests **Ping** & **Merle Tan**. Call Malu (562) 404-1195 for details.

Notice the framed prints on the back wall: the Chapel and the Carillon tower.

Contrary to what might be gleaned, there is no attempted parallelism between this issue and Charles Dicken's "A Tale of Two Cities" with it's juxtaposed dichotomy of "it was the best of times, it was the worst of times. . "

The somber tone of the above left-side picture may belie the fact, but as reported by Tigi, the Makati party was lively and freewheeling:

We had a Mass at 5 p.m. and afterwards an early dinner, the food was excellent. The rest of the evening was a wonderful session of discussions, debates, political tidbits, complaints about the government, etc, etc. The old house rang with the laughter and voices of Gerry's old friends and he was probably there in spirit. *Sabi ko nga kung nandoon si* Gerry the discussions would not have been so serious. Anyway Erap's government is not even warm in their seats and already they have generated so much controversy and heat. One of the chief topics of conversation was the courtesy resignations required by Danding's [Cojuangco] management of everyone from president to vice president level. Jimmy Ong and Mon Pasicolan are Senior VPs.

Jimmy and Mercy Abad came to the party directly from the airport after a trip from Colombo, Sri Lanka. We all had a merry time finding your house since the old entrance of Palma street has been closed and we all had to go down to JP Rizal and find the other end of Palma along the river to get to your place. Anyway we all got there. I was privately wondering if anything momentous would happen since, remember, Martial Law was declared while we were having dinner there in 1972, and again EDSA happened when we were again having dinner there in 1986. *Wala namang nangyari kagabi. Salamat sa Diyos.* We also discussed Oscar Evangelista's picture in the newsletter. His identity has finally been established among the people present last night. Gani could never have grown such a bushy moustache anyway. We all reluctantly said goodbye at about midnight and wended our separate ways home.

(Aside: when martial law was declared in 1972, Noel Soriano was on the pick-up list, and he actually hid away at our house for a couple of days. Though Gerry was not on the pick-up list, a year or so later he was picked up and esconched in Manila Hotel and was forcibly made to ghost-write a speech for Imelda on population control, as he was Popcon director then. I'm sure it was not in that speech where his famous pronouncement on the condom was created: "the condom was the perfect symbol of the Marcos regime, for it stopped production, created inflation, and gave you a false sense of security while you were being screwed").

JOng emailed an additional report:

Tigi left out of the report the most luscious tidbit of all: Jimmy Abad came to the get-together in slippers and with a noticeable limp. Mercy reveals that during their trip to Greece last month, Jimmy stared at the women so lustfully — it was summer, and a good many of them were scantily clad — that he must have offended the gods, and Poseidon caused Jimmy to twist his ankle badly, compelling him to stay on the bus and read while the rest of the tourists walked and admired the scenery. Up to now Jimmy's ankle hurts so badly that he cannot drive. But you mustn't blame Jimmy. Ting and I were there last year, and were truly overwhelmed at the classic beauty of their women. I was also struck at how openly pornography is sold on the sidewalks; but considering how gorgeous the models are, you have to concede that none has a better right to display their bodies. The question "Is this the face that launched a thousand ships?" was no fluke. I've already told my boy David that when it's time for him to seek a mate, I'm shipping him off to Athens."

-o-o-o-o-

On the other hand, the Los Angeles party was much more informal. The food, as usual, was potluck, and although Liliosa spoke glowingly about it, we must now admit that most of the better food was brought by the guys. We say better food not because the men are better cooks, but because we are such bad cooks that it's more expedient to buy the courses at the numerous Filipino *turo-turo* shops in the area. But for the home cooked dishies made by the ladies, ah, the best.
          Enteng Batas left a phoned message ruing his inability to attend the party, as he had to pick up his wife at work (and he lives way out 60 miles north). Greg Santillan emailed later that he would have wanted to attend, especially to meet his old buddy Dante Liban, but he was out of town then. Mario Manansala was up north in Monterey. And Tessie Chua-Chaco was having a concert at that time.

-o-o-o-o-

The Los Angeles party. First names only except those who appear for the first time. *L-R 1st row*: Manny, Ernie, Dante Liban, Oids, Danny, Johnny. *2nd row:* Rose, Alda, Jessie, Julz Tocong, Liliosa, Malu, Lisa, Tony.

Picture gallery at the Makati party, with candid shots compliments of Tigi Barcelona.

Josie Magtoto, Mrs Gil, Maureen Faelnar, Susan Martin & Nora Barcelona.

Melvyn Martin, Mon Pasicolan and Bong Nuqui. Mercy at the background.

Mercy Abad and Angge Soriano

Lino Faelnar and Jimmy Abad

-o-o-o-o-

Anecdote: Tigi was remembered to often sport a camera, and always clicking away. After one of those sumptious parties at his San Juan house, Upsca applicant Helen Ybañez confided to Lisa *"Ang ganda pala ng bahay ng Upsca Photographer!"*

Mercy emailed a cryptic note that Jimmy was coming to Wisconsin by the end of August, presumably for a short teaching stint. Wisconsin may not be like Greece, but just the same, we should all pray that he does not sprain his other ankle!

-o-o-o-o-

The DH fund drive still is in full swing. On Aug 12 we sent checks totalling a little over a thousand dollars. For those who wish to donate for the renovation of the Delaney Hall and the casting of a bronze bust of Fr Delaney, please make checks to "Parish of the Holy Sacrifice" and mail to address in editorial box.

In one of the previous issues, we promised some anecdotes about cars. So here goes, first from Johnny Reyes:

More about the blue Packard: In San Juan, there is a road going up to the back of the hilltop Pinaglabanan Church called Kalbaryo which has a grade of nearly 45 degrees. When I had the car and had new friends along, I would drive down this road and pretend that I had suddenly lost my brakes. (I think Isagani must have been along on one occasion when I did this.). In those days, old cars didn't have the benefit of today's dual brake cylinder systems/self-adjusting disc brakes/computerized brake balancing/anti-lock mechanisms/etc — and DID suddenly lose their brakes from time to time. I shudder and get goose bumps (the feeling you get when you meet a snake with rabies) whenever I think back to those stunts, but I guess I survived — because I'm still here (bad grass, etc). I think Isagani survived also.

The fuel tank had a dipstick, necessary because the gas level was always below the minimum range of the fuel gauge—I never carried more gasoline in the tank than absolutely necessary, because I didn't believe in tying up funds in working capital when it could be used for more productive purposes elsewhere. Also, I didn't want to return the car to my older brother with excess fuel, because chances were I would not recover it again.

Among the many defects of the blue Packard — aside from the dents on the right side — was that it often overheated; and whenever that happened, it would not start. For this reason, I always parked the car on a downhill slope, so it didn't have to be pushed to start if I needed it before the engine had a chance to cool down. (It was ideal if there was also a wall along the downhill road.)

On one occasion, I was driving along Highway 54 to U.P. (with four liters in my tank) when — luck upon luck!— I saw my future wife waiting for a jeepney in front of the Mercury Drug Store at the corner of K-10! (At this time, she was not my future wife yet by any stroke of the imagination, but merely the — not interested — girl of my dreams.) With her was **Elsa Payumo**, the former Miss Caltex who was taking a course at the U.P. Conservatory of Music. Of course I stopped to pick them up, and I guess I must have even gotten off and walked around to the other side to open the door for them (the one with the dents, unfortunately). Having stowed my valuable passengers safely aboard, I swaggered back on air to the driver's side — my arms swinging — and at this point the engine died.

I guess I was about 1-1/2 inches small while I unsuccessfully tried to restart the car — it wasn't a downhill slope — until the battery finally died, and

they had to get off again and transfer to a jeepney which had just arrived.

[Intermission: I am suddenly reminded of a classic incident at Tabangao Refinery many years later, when an employee sick with appendicitis had to be taken by an old hard-starting company ambulance to downtown Batangas where the hospital was. Halfway to the destination the engine died, and the patient had no choice but to get out and help push the ambulance to start it again.]

Isagani: No, Johnny, I was not with you in any of your drives where you lost control of your car. I was with you in one of those drives where you lost control of your *wits*, just because your future wife (then already suspecting that you wanted her to be your future wife) was also in the car. At that time, no one in the gang was even contemplating marriage (except perhaps **Melvyn**, or do I get my chronology wrong?). In fact, didn't **Fredie** plan to bring a *laughing gizmo* to your wedding?

The car accident I remember happened when I was out with **Ping Tan**, who was driving a car that was a lot better than Johnny's. We were on what is now Palanca street in Quiapo and the car suddenly spinned around like crazy, and we ended up on the sidewalk (funny, there were no ditches then for some reason, or perhaps the road was one big sidewalk). I was so mad with Ping I decided right there and then that I would be his compadre if or when we both got married (that explains why we are now compadres!).

After Johnny's Tales of his Packard Adventures, the Loop exchanged more car lore:

Tony: And talking about UPSCA girls in their cars, what about the Studebaker girl, she was the BA chapter chairman, Mon, I guess you might remember her name? **Rory Abrera** in her "push button" transmission Plymouth is of course with us already *[the Loop]*.

Danny: Tony, I think the Cadillac girl you were referring to was **Carol Vera**. And the Biz Ad Chairman with the Studebaker was **Cora Enriquez**.

Tony: No, I remember Carol Vera, in fact she was our neighbor near Roces Ave. Remember that Cadillac with those big fins at the back. I think that was a 1959 model when all cars had different shapes of fins at the back. I remember she also took foreign service and she was a good friend of **Bernie de Castro, Mon Casas**, etc. Don't forget your own Nash auto Danny, it was wide and spacious inside which we used for many of our "expeditions". Then there's **Dette Feliciano** in her 2 door Triumph,

Eleanor Laya in her maroon Mercedes 190D, . . . anymore cars you remember guys ???

Danny: Dette Feliciano is here in LA. The last time I saw her was at the 1995 camping trip at Azusa [LA mountains an hours drive away].

Christie to Tony: It's amazing that you remembered the "ladies with cars"! How about us poor ones who just rode the jeepneys and buses...hope we are remembered, as well.

Tony: Hi **Christie**, the reason I remember all those cars was because at that time I was busy taking the CIL members to their different assignments in the campus including Cruz na Ligas and I had to rely on the generosity of these girls who willingly lend their cars to us. Otherwise I still remember all of you.

-o-o-o-o-

I guess that even now, when some of us see certain models of old cars, we immediately think of people who used to drive or own similar types. Remember the Chevy of **Noel Soriano** which was named "Vergie". I don't know if it finally was retired after Noel fell asleep at the wheel and caused it to crash into a post, thus propelling **Tet Gambito**'s head through the windshield while occupants **Enteng Batas**, and other *chapel bugs* clamored about.

But it is with other *objects* that I find "associative recall" so fascinating. For instance, who else associates a *beret cap on a shaved head* with **Henry Tejada**. Henry was not an Upscan but often hung around DH playing the piano. He ran around with the "Filipinos" crowd. Then there was **Pinoc Baizas** with his *limbo stick*, and he could limbo so, so low. He belonged to the "Aztecs" group. These guys were mainly Manileños from classier high schools with the likes of **Ato Isidro, Mundy Gonzales, Gil Moreno**, and **Dodoy Villareal.**

And by the way, this brings to mind an interesting observation. In an early email of **Christie**, she mused about Upscans who might be in the *corridors of power* Well, Dodoy Villareal was Capiz governor some years back, and his older sister, **Fely Villareal**, was also an Upscan and a recruit of **Fr Gough** into the Cenacle order. She has since left and now is reputedly high in **Gloria Macapagal**'s staff. Their younger brother **Gabby** is UP law, a congressman, sits on the SMC board, and is **Cojuangco**'s son-in-law. An Upscan, we don't know.

And of course there presently is Cong **Dante Liban**, while in past administrations, there was **Noel Soriano, Ben de Leon, Poch Macaranas**, etc. And surely there are many more.

-o-o-o-o-

Then there were sets of people who invariably were associated with one another. Most of us remember lanky **Eddie Manlapig**, who always was where **Romy Manlapaz** would be. Since we couldn't very call them Mutt & Jeff, as Romy was just as tall, we settled for *Manlapaz* and *Manlapis!* A couple of years later, I met Eddie on a bus in Quiapo. He said he finished in UE and had a peace corps girl friend.

-o-o-o-o-

Looking back, it's funny that in those student days, the prospect of remaining footloose and free was an avowed end in itself. During the 1961(?) Upsca Baguio Conference, a group of us formed *"The Madhatters Club"*, with **Mon Casas, Jess Javelona, Gerry Gil, Tony Estrera, Fredie Santiano, Kit Santos**, etc, and I as core members. If I recall right, that name came from the straw hats all of us bought at the famous Baguio market, coupled with our crazy antics along the Lewis Carol classic. As misogamists — marriage haters, as opposed to misogynists, woman haters — we even proposed contributing a yearly amount into a pot which would go to the last one who "succumbed" and got married.

As the years went on, the last holdouts were Jimmy Ong and Gerry Gil. When finally it was only Gerry left, **Mon Pasicolan** quipped that *"pag-asa na lang kay Gerry ay kulam"*.

Despite my sanctimonious statements of "transcending mundane desires...", I apparently was the *first turncoat*, as I got married in 1967. I believe **Lino** and **Tigi** were ahead by a year, but then, they weren't Madhatters.

Informatively, Mon Casas is in France and married to a French-Greek. And in a letter I found in Gerry's computer files, he woefully expressed a lost Korean love during his Stanford days, so apparently he was a one-woman man. As for Kit Santos, I haven't heard about him for ages, save that he is somewhere in the Chicago area. So he'd be one more name included in the "whatever happened to" list. Anybody knows?

-o-o-o-o-

In an earlier issue, we ran a contest for creating a short story revolving around the picture at left. Only two entries were submitted, both of which are too long to reproduce. But **Johnny**'s entry was replete with references to such disparate topics as Captain Bligh of the Bounty, tetra-ethyl lead additives to gasoline, death by torture, body-

transference, and stealing story lines. He ended it with: "The photograph on page 5 of the last UPSCA Alumni Newsletter shows Tom Smithson inside *Ferdinand Hill*'s body. This is the reason I labeled my little story in part 1 above 'not original.' "

Johnny posted it on the Category 2 mailing list and this prompted a series of exchanges. Excerpts:

Johnny: By the way, Stephen King is also guilty of stealing concepts, and he does not even acknowledge it. His two best and most scary novels, "Salem's Lot" and "Pet Sematary," are adaptations of Bram Stoker's "Dracula" and the short story "The Monkey's Paw," respectively.

JOng: Hi, Johnny. Everyone steals concepts, so your *Pitcairn Island* tale is in good company. It's an old and honorable and eminently successful practice. The Greek dramatists did it. Shakespeare did it. Senatorial candidates, campaigning in teams, steal each other's jokes and oratorical flourishes. Sergio Leone's spaghetti Western "For a Fistful of Dollars," which started Clint Eastwood on the road to fame, is a remake of Kurosawa's "Yojimbo." Kurosawa did a bit of stealing in his time — his "Throne of Blood" and "Ran" are "Macbeth" and "King Lear" in samurai costume. As those of you who have wooed and won more than once well know, the trick is not to be original, but to be convincing. Let's have more of your remakes.

Danny: Okay, here's a remake below. This is one of Gerry's 43 non-de-plumes, in a letter to the editor poking fun at one of his favorite whipping boys, Larry Henares. Obviously, it's a remake of Poe's *The Raven*. I gather that at one point in time Henares wanted the job of Ongpin.

16 May 1986

Mr & Mrs Special Edition
DVA Box 327
Makati, Metro Manila

In reporting the mythical declamation contest at Xavier School (*Special Edition*, May 16) Larry Hernares (in burst of uncharacteristic modesty) omitted the sixth contestant who was Larry himself.

Let's look at how Larry handled the latter part of "The Raven."

He has just discovered that the bird is a messenger from above; he has asked for "respite and nepenthe" and the bird says, "Nevermore"; he has asked whether there is "balm in Gilead" and again, the bird says "Nevermore"; and now, Larry poses the final question:

"Prophet," said I, "thing of evil,
    prophet still if bird or devil,
By the heaven that bends above us,
    by that God we both adore,
Tell this soul if foul perdition
    Fells Ongpin, does this condition,
Make me heir to his position,
    which I've salivated for."

And the bird spat, "Nevermore."

Juan P. Antillon
San Antonio Village

-o-o-o-o-

NEWS, NEWS, NEWS for a change!

In the last get-together July 12, the group overwhelmingly railroaded **Malu Garcia** to be UPSCA Alumni Association USA president, with hubby **Oids** as vice. Congratulations, Malu. Now, **Tony & Josie Estrera** can retire.

-o-o-o-o-

As we go to press, an email came in from **Gus de Leon**, Upsca president prior to Noel Soriano. He was given a newslet at Saturday's (Aug 15) fund raising meeting at DH and we quote excerpts: ". .We enjoyed reading and getting news from other UPSCANs. The meeting with Fr. Reyes was most informative specially for UPSCANs of the fifties. We did not realize how complex the demands and administration of the U.P. Chapel community has become. Since the U.P. Chapel was converted into a Parish, it has to operate as one to serve a much wider community than the U.P. faculty and students. Today Fr. Reyes says there are five other catholic student organizations.

The Delaney Hall a facility that served as the brain center and network center of UPSCA and the community is now considered a space where everyone competes for its use. The U.P. Parish and Parish based organizations , the various student organizations in the University competes with UPSCANs for its use. The need for a renewal of lease from the University of the Chapel site by the year 2005 further can further complicate the administration of the facilities.

It will seem that for the future generation of UPSCANs to keep their priority claim for the use of Delaney Hall Fr. Reyes is on the right track in involving UPSCA alumni to rehabilitate the facilities and memorialize the Hall for Fr. Delaney.

Surprising also is how much history has been lost between the time of UPSCA in its early days in Diliman and today.

Hope these gives you with an idea of how important your newsletter is in bridging between the past with the present so that the vision of the future can be made in better perspective."

Gus De Leon
99 Mother Ignacia Ave.
Quezon City, Metro Manila
adlassoc@i-manila.com.ph

Action & Reaction!!!

Letters, faxes, e-mail, anecdotes, conversations....

This is a temporary title for this new column. Send us your suggestions.

José Alzona left a message about two items that came to his attention in a recent newsletter, which he wanted to address:

TD's Haunted House: The confusion about this should evaporize once you realate that some of us actually strive to emulate Hedy Lamarr[1] and did in fact live lives outside of UPSCA. Sometimes these alternate lives interlived (IRC, for instance, transvected my physics, chess, and Accelerated English circles in addition to UPSCA). Sometimes they dissolved as expected, right on schedule (e.g., my Mortar Battery/Model Platoon career). And sometimes they had undulating, impalmable bondaries (e.g. LG, V2, and others in my "Ripe for Jerry Springer" group).[2]

On the night in question, I sharply remember a count of exactly three guys roaming TD's haunts (or haunting TD's rooms) with me, crawling into crawl spaces, laddering up ladders, and cacchinating dementively while smashing pill bottles and Erlenmeyer flasks from TD's dusty shelves onto the floor. And I remember wrestling the other three for the single flashlight in our possession, the better to out-heeby-jeeby them all by uplighting my carefully contorted face. There was (1) me, (2) IRC, (3) VE, and a shadowy (4th) who was probably ABP (logical—he completes our surf-rock band quartet), but who could've been JemzV, RU *("Ilong")* or even JMRJr. I'm certain that San Tiano was elsewhere and not with us.[3] Furthermore, our nocturnal exploration was entirely interior—none of this bootless hide-and-seek amongst the flowers and candles outside.[4] Lastly, I'm certain I haunted there once and never returned. The conclusion is inevitaperonable: your sources are confusing two separate and orthogonal TD excursions involving two different but possibly overlapping groups. May I recommend gingko biloba?

The Irritating Me: There is similarly a very simple explanation for this image of me. In another concurrent literary life, I was called Huséng Banlág[5], or José Palacá, or Joseng Quoqac, sobriquets derived from my beautiful naturally crossed eyes, which presumably reminded the other group members of the decoupled oculomotorization of a frog.[6] Because of this physical attribute, people would see me at Delaney Hall and think that I was looking at them, then get irritated when I failed to respond or acknowledge their smile, greeting, bow, genuflection, or self–exposure. So let me make it perfectly clear: I WAS NOT LOOKING AT THEM, OK?!! I was looking at DC, who, alas, was flapping *pilik-mata* at someone else and never knew till long after the time of cholera. So, as Ms. Swan would say, *you guys need to take a chill pill! Casta laeng ti biag, muchachos.*

[1] Between acting and performing unspeakable acts on her co-stars under her table at Ciro's, Hedy patented a torpedo guidance system in 1942 whose idea is still used today in cell phones and military satellites. Her 1933 nude scene in *Ecstasy* (the first ever?) is no longer available, but *Samson and Delilah* should be out on video. Hedy's spirit represents the dogged exploration of all your karmic possibilities.

[2] Some agglomerations still make me scratch my head and go, "Huh?" My nebulous Boni Salamanca group included the genial hulk MV, who to my surprise assumed unbidden the post of personal bodyguard to me; and SM, who introduced me to *basi* and other forbidden ineluscenti at the Itneg Hellfire Club in Baguio (as Voltaire said, "Once, a philosopher; more than once, a perv.") I never saw these guys again after sophomore year. I think JOng also lived in this circle for a few weeks.

[3] Yes, I know pundits insist that bilocation is a perk of canonization, but knowing just as well San Tiano's trickster character and his proclivacious mischievity, he undoubtedly would've chosen to thumb nose at the pundits by opting to be in NO place at the same time instead.

[4] I guess even then we sensed what my kali master would later confirm: cemeteries are a waste of time for hunters of power, which, in a very real sense, was what our outing was all about. Ironically, he neglected to include his house in his enumeration of alternatives; it should've topped the list! My hair still stands on end when I remember those late-night training vigils in his yard. And that's why, testimony to the contrary notwithstanding, I'm convinced that what we visited was not so much TD's house, but TD's abandoned hospital, clinic, ward, or lab. Imagine the fierce emotions that soaked into its walls over years of operation!

[5] Lest the AMA and my prissy doctor cousin squawk, let me state here that yes, the proper clinical term for the syndrome is *duling,* not *banlág.*

[6] I suppose I was still marginally better off than our grossly maloccluded member Edding Pating, so christened because his huge upper teeth sloped perilously down and back into a steeply receding chin that gave him his unmistakable elasmobranchitic profile.

-o-o-o-o-

An email from JOng about Fredie:

Here's one about that son of Belial, Fredie Santiano, whose taste in elaborate hoaxes was legend at Delaney Hall even before I joined UPSCA, i.e., when he had Bernie de Castro and the rest of the CIL aghast and fuming for weeks over his supposed secret marriage. Years later, when Fredie really did get married, he got even with me for all the anguish I'd caused by teasing him about BN: he delivered the wedding invitations in person (which of course ensured that we would all be present at the great event), and, at the bottom of the card, scrawled his request that I show up in coat and tie. Which I did, totally unaware that mine was the only invitation that bore this innocuous request. And so this excresence gets married at the height of summer, cool and comfortable in a barong like everyone else in the chapel except me, suited up and sweltering and sweating like I was in a steam bath.

I was one of those involved in that elaborate hoax. There was that rock outcropping in the center of the lawn in front of DH which Fredie used to sit on while pensively smoking a pipe. So we both agreed that he'd spend much more time there, even assuming the posture of Rodin's The Thinker, so it would arouse the curiosity of the CIL girls, and then we'd spread the rumor that Fredie had a problem: he was secretly married, not by choice, but by having had to, and his problem was how to reconcile this status with his position of vice-president of Upsca. He even started going home early, rather than spend time hanging around DH. To hasten the spread of the rumor, we whispered it into the ear of Mila Abad, knowing that it wouldn't remain a secret for long, but surprise of surprises, Mila didn't say a word! Anyway, the news eventually leaked out, and there was heated debate in the Central Council, spearheaded by the CIL girls, about impeaching Fredie! Of course, they got even more mad when they found it a hoax.

-o-o-o-o-

Houston, TX
August 4, 1998

Dear Danny,

Attached is my $100 check donation to the Chapel of the Holy Sacrifice renovation. I'm also enclosing our family photo taken about one and a half years ago that I wish to be printed in the newsletter. I was motivated to send this picture after I saw **Mon** and **Eva de Veyra**'s family photo in the newsletter's previous issue. While it is always nice to see how we looked like, thirty or forty years ago, it is — at least to me, equally fascinating to get a glimpse of how the next generation looks like. I read somewhere that we achieve some sort of immortality through our genes.

Lino and **Maureen Faelnar** recently wrote me a long letter (the last time I saw Lino was in 1973) describing how their family has been doing lately. Although I was happy to hear from an old friend, I wish they could have included their family picture so I could see the faces of their kids — the next generation of Faelnars — who will be carrying the torch after their parents. I'm still curious to know whether Lino's kids look like him or Maureen. Anyway, I hope this will encourage our fellow Upscans whom we have not seen for thirty or forty years to send in their family photos so they could share with us an important part of their lives.

A message to Mon de Vera . . . I thought you were pulling my legs when you asked me in that Christmas card if I still remember you. How can I forget you, Mon (Alzheimer's or not), when you were our trusted confidante of our several childhood crushes during our Upsca days? Whatever happened to the old basement standby's in the late '50s such as **Ernie Santos, Gene Abril, Manny Ramos, Migs**(?) etc? Through our Pinoy pipeline, I heard that **Manoy Ray Cedeño** was here in the States lately. The last time I saw Eve was around 1962 when I was assigned in Iloilo with the old Bureau of Mines.

It must been 1967 or 1968 (I cannot remember which) that I saw you and **Lisa** when you dropped by that old house in Mandaue on your way to the airport with **Noel Soriano.** I think you were on your honeymoon at that time. I can't believe that was thirty years ago. Keep in touch.

Fondly,

Sisoy Arong

Encaptioned at back: Steve (22), Melina-Ann (15), Vincent (24), Cecille (?) and yours truly (18?). Only the girl is with us now at home. No grandchildren yet!

Yes, it was in Cebu way back in 1967 when we saw each other last, and Lisa and I were on our way back from Tanjay after a weeks visit, after our honeymoon which had been in La Union.

Anecdote: Sisoy was one the Arong brothers who spearheaded the "Filipino" group of Visayans in UP. Coming from a prominent Cebu clan with various businesses including a tailoring shop, Gerry would tease them by advertising "you can't go wrong in a barong by Arong". Their oldest, Joe, belongs to the Oblate order, and already was a priest when in Stanford as JOng's and Gerry's contemporary. They inveigled him into a girlie show in Palo Alto as a practical joke.

-o-o-o-o-

Excerpts from Sonia (Valenzuela) Quast's email:

Dear Christie,

Well, like you, Dietrich and I got married in 1969. We met at MIT when I was in the midst of the preparations for the doctoral exams and he was just finishing his MS. Then he returned to Brazil while I continued with my studies. He returned to MIT for his Sc.D. in Food Engineering and we got married soon after his return. When we moved t[~] S.P., I did a bit of teachin at the University of Sã Paulo as a visiting prof, bu I didn't care much for th environment, so I decided t go into English teaching. had a language school fo awhile but after 8 years, decided that was not reall what I wanted to do wit my life, so I sold my shar to my partner and gave up

on that. I am working as a volunteer at our parish - as a catechist, as a coordinator of a senior citizen's group, and last year, also as a volunteer visitor to women prisoners. I guarantee you I feel much better being busy with these activities than with any of the other things I had tried in my over 20 years here in São Paulo. Diego [son] has graduated from Mech Eng and is now working in the northeast, about 3000 km from here; Ernesto is studying Food Engineering in the south, about 700 km from here. So you see, we are all scattered here in Brazil . . .

Dear Danny,

I am just glad that the thing with Erap and Marcos seems to be over for the time being. Imagine, I had no idea who Erap was until May when I was on the plane to Geneve - I was reading an article about the then coming presidential elections in the Philippines and only then did I find out who Erap was. I thought he was a comics strip character because those jokes about him are really - well, comic . . .

-o-o-o-o-

Excerpts from Tigi Barcelona's email:

Dear Danny,

In reply to several queries about my grandfather's role in the Revolution, I'm copying you this for all that it's worth, *Centennial naman ngayon.*

I'm flattered by your interest in my ancestors, but yes my grandfather was Aguinaldo's personal physician during the revolution. I read his diary several times and it was tiring, they seemed to have walked all over northern Luzon during their campaigns against the Americans. They were finally captured in Palanan, Isabella and brought to Manila aboard the battleship Vicksburg and confined in Malacañang.

I interrogated my father closely about this years ago and my Dad said that Lolo was very impressed by how the Americans treated them. They always dressed for dinner, and when they sat down, the Governor General sat opposite Aguinaldo, the Military Commander sat opposite Col Simeon Villa, and the Surgeon General sat opposite my grandfather.

There is a very interesting exhibit on going right now in Unimart in Greenhills put up by the Ortigas Companies as their participation in the Centennial. They blocked off a whole section of the supermarket complex and built it up capturing the ambiance of 19th Century Philippines.

My sister, several years ago, went to the National Archives in Washington D.C. and looked up my Lolo. They were listed under the "Philippine Insurrection" not under any thing called the "Philippine American War"; no such war exists in the American Archives.

By all means pass this info to the History buffs you know.

-o-o-o-o-

At 1961 birthday party of Tessie Chua-Chiaco (standing) flanked by Rory Abrera, Johnny Ramos, Johnny Reyes, Cynthia Reyes, 1_?, 2_?, Mila Abad, 3_? (partly cut off) and Ping Tan.

1961 Corregidor cruise: *with faces seen L-R are* Tony Estrera, Johnny Reyes, Tigi Barcelona, Fredie Santiano, and Erwin Gomez. Others are unrecognizable except Ramon Pasicolan with salakot on back.

PICTURE GALLERY from the ARCHIVES of JOHNNY REYES and MALU (BARRIOS) GARCIA, spanning from early '60s to late '60s. Except last.

Ramon Casas, Mila Abad, Jess Javelona at 1961 Baguio conference.

Baguio conference: Arthur Adiarte, Jimmy Lapus, Mila Abad, Johnny Reyes, Gerry Gil, Kit Santos (partly covered), Liliosa Mangosing. Note straw hat of Kit, the basis for being a Madhatter.

Rector Yabes, Jimmy Abad, Jimmy Lapus, Mila Abad, Tessie Chua-Chiaco, Johnny Reyes. At Baguio conference.

At Pagsanjan Falls outing: Merle Tan, Vyva Aguirre, Susan Po, Jemz Valera, Malu Barrios, Oids Garcia, Peng San Buenaventura. All part of the ELPS group, meaning Eat, Laugh, Pray and Sing.

Seeing off Bing at MIA: Poch Macaranas, Vyva Aguirre, Malu Barrios, Bing Ferrer, Emily Bacaltos, 4_?, and Susan Po.

As a reply to Sisoy's request to "see the kids", here's a 1992 shot of some of the kids of the barkada. Poser: whose is which?

Roster of Names on Mailing List (emails erased)

Jimmy & Mercy (Rivera) Abad
Antipolo, Philippines

Rory Abrera
Dallas, TX

Arthur & Cherrie Adiarte
St Paul, MN
t

Ofie (Peñaflorida) & Ken Aid
Lakewood, CA

Letty (Ramirez) Ajodah
Queens Village, NY

Ely & Sonia (Alday) Alampay
Quezon City, Philippines

José Alzona
Long Beach, CA

Nanette (Gadi) & Boy Angeles
Monroeville, PA

Lolly Aquino
Los Angeles, CA

Myrna Aquitania
Camarillo, CA

Primo & Lindus (Carreon) Arambulo
Rockville, MD

Noli Arong
Arleta, CA

Sisoy Arong
Houston, TX

Divsy Astraquillo
Shorewood, WI

Johnny & Alda Balaoing
Los Angeles, CA

Nina Los Baños
Las Vegas, NV

Tigi & Nora Barcelona
Quezon City, Philippines

Olga (Cruz) Barrios
Williamsville, NY

Enteng & Mely Batas
Lancaster, CA

Lennie (Abellera) & John Blair
Libertyville, IL

Jun & Cynthia (Reyes) Calejesan
Monaca, PA

Ramon O. Casas
Strasbourg, France

Manny Castillo
Brea, CA

Delfin Castro
Bowie, MD

Remy & Anching Chica
Northridge, CA

Tessie Chua Chiaco
North Hollywood, CA

Isagani & Medy Cruz
Malate,Philippines

Nilo Cruz
Makati, Philippines, (temp)
San Francisco, CA

Boy dela Cruz
Quezon City, Philippines (temp)
Cottage Grove, MN

Nancy (Cruz) & Gerry Dienel
Little Rock, AR

Bing (Ferrer) & Anthony Dubitsky
Riverdale, MD

Cir & Rose (Lacebal) Engay
Los Angeles, CA

Georgina (Reyes) & Mervyn Encanto
Quezon City, Philippines

Manny & Lee Espejo
Saugus, CA

Deo & Aleli Estacio
Altadena, CA

Tony & Josie (Angeles) Estrera
Cerritos, CA

Liliosa (Mangosing) & Gene
   Evangelista
Fairfax, VA

Lino & Maureen (Holazo) Faelnar
Las Piñas, Philippines

Susan (Rodriguez) & Dick Fagan
New York, NY

Dette Feliciano
Los Angeles, CA

Temy (Dapilos) Gamboa
Patchogue, NY

Malu (Barrios) & Oids Garcia
Cerritos, CA

Pepito & May (Miñosa) Gatchalian
Quezon City, Philippines

Danny & Lisa (Señeris) Gil
Artesia, CA

Erwin & Alita Gomez
Valparaiso, IN

Ruben & Maria Habito
Kyoto, Japan (temp)
Dallas, TX

Effie (Sta Romana) Hall
Bettendorf, IA

Chit Inciong
Flushing, NY

Jessica Infante
Los Angeles, CA

Jess & Jessie (Quinto) Javelona
Muntinglupa, Philippines

Nanette (Ortega) & Benny Jongco
South Orange, NJ

Godofredo Juliano
Philippines

Christie (Borromeo) & Don Kawal
Albuquerque, NM

Lallie (de Vera) Lacaba
Pateros, Philippines

Clara (Reyes) & Bart Lapus
San Juan, Philippines

Raquel (Celera) & Ric Lejano
Torrance, CA

Gus & Toti (Yuson) de Leon
Quezon City, Philippines

Loida (Nicolas) Lewis
New York, NY

Cheche (Lim) & Delfin Lazaro
Philippines

Dante & Baby V. Liban
Quezon City, Philippines

Eddie & Josie Magtoto
Parañaque, Philippines

Mario & Myrna Manansala
La Palma, CA

Romy & Edna (Zapanta) Manlapaz
Quezon City, Philippines

Melvyn & Susan (Paulin) Martin
Alabang, Philippines

Jess Martinez
Freeport, IL

Bernie (de Castro) & Jurg Muller
Geneva, Switzerland

Clemencia Natividad
Toronto, Canada

Tony Nievera
Douglaston, NY

Bong & Beth (Arcellana) Nuqui
Quezon City, Philippines

Jimmy & Ting Ong
Pasig, Philippines

Ernie & Jessie (Raqueño) Pangilinan
Mission Hills, CA 91345

Ramon & Mimi Pasicolan
Quezon City, Philippines

Lina (Soliman) Plantilla
Brooklyn, NY

Priscilla (Bautista) Perez
Bronx, NY

Susan Po
San Francisco, CA

Sonia (Valenzuela) & Dietrich Quast

Sao Pablo, Brazil

Amelia (Bascon) Rasalan
Bayside, NY

Hermie (Manoto) & Jess Rabe
Cerritos, CA
Johnny & Mila (Garcia) Reyes
Belle Mead, NJ

Ruben & Naida (Uy) Rivera
Quezon City, Philippines

Maya (Arroyo) Santiano

Greg Santillan
San Gabriel, CA

Angel & Stella Sta Maria
Pasadena, CA

Zeny (Roxas) & Sixto Ramirez
Los Angeles, CA

Nel Reformina
Nanuet, NY

Nem & Bing (Pascual) Santos
Whittier, CA 90601

Alex & Miren (Dumlao) Santos
Quezon City, Philippines

Miren (Dumlao) Santos
Bethesda, MD (temp)

Berryl Silva
Long Beach, CA

Noel & Angge (Alday) Soriano
Quezon City,Philippines

Ping & Merle (Custodio) Tan
Quezon City, Philippines

Bernie (Abrera) Tjarks
Dallas, TX

Dell & Julz Tocong
Bellflower, CA

Girlie (Alzona) & Tito Valbuena
Astoria, NY

Sari Valenzuela
Brooklyn, NY

Jimmy & Nora Valera
Ontario, Canada
valeraj@iname.com

Mon & Eva (Singson) de Veyra

EDITORIAL BOX

Published in Los Angeles by nostalgic members of the UPSCA Alumni Association USA, from materials mainly culled from email amongst Upscans in cyberspace. Photos, letters, faxes, etc are most welcome. Send them in to Danny Gil, 19002 Horst Ave, Artesia, CA 90701, fax (562) 402-1890, ferngil@aol.com.

Join the fray! Send in your two cents worth. Suggested topics:
1. Can you identify those unidentified people in photos?
2. Other Aztec members? Filipinos Group ? Chapel Bugs?
3. Whatever happened to those names Sisoy mused about?
4. Initials in Joe Alzona's letter? E.g. IRC is Gani Cruz.
5. Other Upscans who walked in the corridors of power?
6. Name chronologically the Upsca presidents?
   etc, etc.

UPSCA ALUMNI ASSOCIATION, USA

NEWSLETTER   NEWSLETTER   NEWSLETTER

A M D G | Vol 1, Num 8   (4th quarter, 1998)   Published by UPSCA Alumni Association, USA

WORDSMITH BOOK WINS AWARD!

SM MEGAMALL, SEPT 12, 1998

JOng & Wordsmith made it! Ring the bells, toast Jimmy, and do say a prayer for Gerry.

Jimmy received the award, an 18-inch piece of sculptured bronze created & donated by the national artist Napoleon Abueva, who did the Crucified Christ at the UP Chapel.

Jimmy made a short after-award "speech" & Gani Cruz, emcee & president of the Manila Critic Circle that sponsors the annual competition, replied with "If Gerry were alive, he'd have said more!"

From Gani Cruz:

Gerry's book won the National Book Award for Journalism, given by the Manila Critics Circle, at ceremonies held on 12 Sept at the Philippine Bookfair (an annual book fair) in SM Megamall in Metro Manila. Jimmy Ong and Mrs. Gil accepted the award. The prize was a trophy designed by National Artist Napoleon Abueva. The ceremonies were covered by ABC and RPN, as well as by newspapers.

I head the Circle, but during the voting, I did not have to say a single word for the book. Everybody immediately chose it above the other finalists (which were heavyweights themselves). Some of the judges even quoted from memory from the book!

Meanwhile, the book is available at the Bookfair in the De La Salle University Press booths (I'm publisher). The Press has a website (though I am not sure Gerry's book is already on it), and the book can be — or eventually will be — available through credit card purchase from the webpage.

Here is the citation read at the awarding ceremonies of the National Book Awards for Gerry's book. It was written by Doreen G. Fernandez (chair of the Department of Communication of Ateneo de Manila University):

"Our world has come to depend much on the work of journalists. From them we expect information, enlightenment, guidance, insight, contemporary history, the truth. And all this we wish them to deliver to us lucidly, wisely, and gracefully — in memorable language. All those who knew the late Gerry Gil will remember that he did all that as a newspaperman, columnist, writer of letters to the editor, writer of

editorials, writer. His erudition and wide reading, his insight and his humor, his passion for accuracy and his fearlessness, and especially his clear and graceful language — all are found in the book put together by his friends, impelled by Gerry's spirit."

The Manila Critics Circle presents the National Book Award for Journalism to this book that will provide models for writing classes, historical data for contemporary researchers, and a class memory for journalists past and future.

Informatively, the National Book Award is the highest publishing award in the Philippines. It's now on its 17th year, and like the Academy Awards, there are nominees and the winner is announced during the awarding ceremonies.

-o-o-o-o-o-o-o-

ON-GOING FUND DRIVE FOR DH:

We have remitted about $2,200 (with about $300 still enroute). Gus de Leon reports that they have collected $2,950 and P103,000 so far. So apparently, many U.S. donors are remitting directly. We are glad to have been of help in this drive which was started mid year when Angge Soriano sent a request for us to pass the word along, which we did via email and newslet.

Here are excerpts from the message of Narita Gonzales, one of the members of the Delaney Memorial Committee:

Fr. Robert Reyes and the Delaney Memorial Committee wish to thank the US UPSCANS for their generous donations for the Delaney Projects.

About the Delaney Hall: we have to thank Fr. Robert for initiating the Movement to honor the memory of Fr. John P. Delaney, SJ. He had started the renovation of DH, where many of you have fond memories.

The first meeting of the Delaney Memorial Committee which also served a reunion of Delaney friends was held last August 15, 1998 at the partly renovated DH. Glass sidings now prevent the rains from coming in and/or flooding the floors. They also shut of the noise of other activities going around.

About the Delaney Bust: The bust will remind the new UPSCANS, the young UP Community and the hundreds of Sunday church-goers (nine Sunday masses are scheduled, three daily, on weekdays) how this beloved man of the cloth looked like.

And about the Library: When there's enough money left, a Delaney library cum museum will be built at the right side of the mortuary. Already Angge Soriano has donated several precious albums filled with pictures of UPSCA happenings. We will try to trace the whereabouts of the chalices, wine and water cruets, the bells, the elevator altar etc. We believe that when the library has been set up, these *recuerdos* of Fr. Delaney's days will be donated to the collection and, thus, find a proper place of repository.

About the Delaney Book. A book is being prepared also about this Grand Old Man of the UP Chapel of the Holy Sacrifice. Anyone who has an anecdote to share is welcome to contribute.

About the UPSCA Spirit: Do keep up the UPSCA spirit here in America. There is nothing like old friends bonded together with common spiritual values and genuine friendships.

The members of the Delaney Memorial Committee are: Angge Soriano, Gus de Leon, Maurie Borromeo, and all these "oldies" who are members of the Parish of the Holy Sacrifice and knew Fr. Delaney quite well: Nanay Teresa Ortigas, Tessy Daza, Florinda Lesaca and Narita M. Gonzales.

I close with the AMDG.

FR. NERI'S 25th ANNIVERSARY:

Excerpts from various correspondents:

Bobby Neri celebrated the 25th Anniversary of his priesthood on Sunday, September 6, 1998 at the Ateneo High School covered courts. The majority of the Jesuit Community was present. Leading them was **Fr. Ben Nebres**, the president of Ateneo de Manila and Jimmy Ong's schoolmate in Stanford. Present from our crowd were **Mercy Abad**, **Jimmy Ong**, **Ping** and **Merle Tan** (who walked in straight from the airport), **Mon Pasicolan**, etc. Bobby gave a speech about his career as a priest and how he came to decide upon the priesthood.

reported by Tigi

To Tigi's report on Bobby Neri's 25th anniversary, you may wish to add Bobby's own reminiscence of how he found his vocation.

Bobby said that he first felt the stirrings of a call to the priesthood when he was in first year high and a daily mass server at the Ateneo. He enjoyed everything that seemed to be associated with the priests' life: waking up early, the mass itself, even the scent of breakfast cooking.

As we all know, he went to UP for his engineering studies; but sometime in his third year or so he began thinking more seriously about the priesthood.

One day he went to see **Fr. Ben Villote** and asked, "How do I find out if I have a vocation?" Fr. Ben's answer: "You apply."

So one day Bobby skipped classes and went all the way to I forget where (Novaliches? La Ignaciana?), to knock on the door and express his interest in applying. It was opened by **Fr. Benigno Mayo**, SJ (who would later become the Jesuit Provincial), who welcomed him saying, "Come in, Bobby. We have been waiting for you a long time."

reported by JOng

-o-o-o-o-o-o-o-

NEWSBITS & TIDBITS:

NVM & Narita Gonzales are in Los Angeles for a short teaching stint by NVM in UCLA. From her email:

We received Gerry's book. Thank you loads. NVM has been chuckling as he read on. "What we need is another Gerry Gil," he said.

NVM will give a public lecture on November 16, Monday 4:00 pm at the UCLA Faculty Center. Please come and bring along some UPSCANS. The talk is sponsored by the Asian-American Studies of UCLA.

A documentary is being finished by Jerome Academia and Russell Leong. This is a second docu. The first one was sponsored by U.P. Department of English and the NCCA (National Commission on Culture and the Arts). It has footages done in Mindoro, setting up most of NVM's works. Jerome and Russell visited

Romblon, birth place of NVM. When this second documentary is finally finished, it will be distributed throughout the country.

The NVM's will spend Christmas in San Mateo with [children] **Lakshmi**, **Myke** and **Ibarra** (no longer an SJ). All grew up in the U.P. and are UPSCANS too. **Selma** is left in good old U.P. teaching and writing workbooks in Arts and Crafts.

-o-o-o-o-o-o-o-

*Ping & Merle Tan were feted at a party in Oid's & Malu's place in Cerritos, LA, August 30. They already had spent 2-3 weeks in the southwest and east coast where they met Upscans **Erwin Gomez** and **Jess Martinez**, among others. Ping's digital camera made instant*

recordings of various happenings, such as shown above. I sent this picture electronically to Johnny in NJ. The exchange:

A good rule to follow is NOT to put mirrors in the background when taking group pictures. - *Johnny*

That's precisely why I choose that picture taken by Ping which had mirrors in the background, to make it appear that there were more of us, and also to confuse you. Then again, I could have asked you to imbibe some spirits so you'd see two of everything. - *Danny*

-o-o-o-o-o-o-o-

Myrna Aquitania joins the Music Theatre of Southern California as a Board of Director. It is a professional non-profit company, entering it's 15th season. Congratulations, Myrna. We probably will be able to see more shows now.

-o-o-o-o-o-o-o-

*Johnny Balaoing has been made the chairmain of the ad hoc committee for the West Coast chapter of the **Bayanihan Cooperative Venture Inc.** with **Dr. Manny Castillo** as treasurer. This is a movement started by **Dr. Ting Tiongco** in the Philippines, and has been gaining notice worldwide. It is described in his excellent book "Child of the Sun Returning". The movement makes health-care more affordable, especially in third world countries. For a very reasonable amount, we could join the cooperative and let our folks in the Philippines avail of coverage. For more info, contact Johnny or Dr. Gene Pulmano in NJ.*

OBITUARY:

Gal Miñoza passed away. His sister May Miñoza-Gatchalian emails more data. Excerpts:

I just arrived from the airport about an hour ago. The first thing I did was to call up Angge Soriano, who in turn was in touch with Mian Chanco-Sison and with Bel Olivarez-Cunanan and other local UPSCANs. This is all about a very sad news, my youngest brother Gal Miñoza, also an UPSCAn, died of complications due to lung cancer October 10 in Denver, Colorado. This was draining both emotionally and financially. Gal, wife Amanda and daughter Jenny had just migrated to the USA two years ago in their search for a better life for the family. They were only starting there and then this. Their two sons are still in the Philippines. Gal requested that all his friends be told to "stop smoking at once, it can surely kill". He was very active in "Couples for Christ" when they were still in the Philippines. Please inform our network about Gal's death. We ask for prayers and other moral support to help the whole family through.

Gal was one of the on-campus Upscans whose group included Abay Lesaca, Nasi (?), and a few others, and whose folks were mainly UP Professors. Years ago, Gal's wedding was a celebrated televised event because he met his wife on a TV dating game, and they were first couple to make it to the altar on that show.

-o-o-o-o-o-o-o-

COMMENTS ON LAST ISSUE:

"Thanks to Malu; my children didn't recognize me in that very clear picture." *Jemz Valera, on seeing a very crisp mid '60s picture of him and the ELPS group, from Malu's picture archives.*

"I received the newslet in the mail over the weekend and couldn't believe how you were able to match perfectly the caption with picture, which at that point, I hadn't seen yet." - *Liliosa, on seeing how the caption for the group song & dance picture was a verbatim quote from her earlier email.*

"And the pictures of the Baguio conference brought back fun memories, but also of getting so sick on the bus trip home, I think I threw up on JMR who happened to be sitting next to me (with Mila Abad on his other side, watching him like a hawk)!"-- *Liliosa, referring to the '60s Baguio conference pictures.*

"I believe the girl above Ping Tan's head (rightmost edge of the picture) is Cora Reyes (no relation). By copy to Tessie: Hi, and thanks for inviting me to your 16th birthday party" - *Johnny, commenting on the identities of a 1960 picture during Tessie Chua-Chiaco's party.*

IMPRESSIONS OF 2 NEWCOMERS TO THE LAND OF PROMISE:

Jimmy Abad is presently in Wisconsin on a 4 month teaching assignment, so he'll be back in the Philippines before the height of winter. Of course, he comes and goes pretty often, and spent a number of years here eons ago during post-graduate studies.

Johnny Reyes also comes and goes, but now is the latest Expatriado*, having immigrated here with wife Mila, 2 younger twin daughters, and a Maltese mutt.

Excerpts from Jimmy's letter to Tony, and to JOng:

Dear Tony, thanks for calling - you just rescued me from that decadent practice of TV watching! Gads, I should be doing something more civilized. My e-mail address will now appear here (I suppose!). I have classes every day, 11-12 and 1-2; two subjects: Intro. to Lit. (25 students) and Philippine Culture and Society (9 students; also an introductory course - I'm on exile here, doing a lot of reading, reading, so I can learn with my students a little more about our country and people). I should very much like to be in touch again with Joe Alzona. Try and find out from Danny if Joe has an e-mail address. Thanks. Truly,
Jimmy

Dear JOng, CONGRATS [for winning the book Award]. And our friend Gerry Gil must just be grinning ear to ear up there - and I think I hear him crack some celestial joke, in all the tongues of the world. He was truly one who knew language - had a deep sense for it, and great joy in using it: which is why he's delightful to read. All you say about English - and about our books in the Philippines - nothing is truer. But sometimes, I have dark thoughts. Maybe, all our high tech visual media nowadays may be spelling the doom of reading and writing. At least, I get a vague sense of that with my students here in America and in our country. Just this morning, we took up "Araby" - you remember James Joyce's story. It was impossible - or else, I just don't know how - to make them appreciate the language of the story. So, how can they even enter into the spirit, the heart, of the story itself? They seem too literal minded; they are not able to produce images (*nasanay na sa pre-fabricated images*); irony is beyond them! Their sense of language is just ordinary communication; no expression. It may be language is slowly dying - at least, the kind of beauty and power in language that we used to know. I'm glad I got included in that e-mail circuit. Regards to all.
Jimmy

From Johnny:

Hi, Jimmy! Good to hear you are in Wisconsin for four months. But although we are located inside the same country, we might as well be in different continents, considering the distances around here. When I was in the Philippines, I used to think the Filipinos in the U.S. were probably all having a grand time getting together every week-end. Now I realize they hardly see each other once a year, even if they happen to be in the same state! Everyone seems so busy around here, and as I already said earlier, the distances are much longer than they look on the map.

Moreover, the distances here are in miles, not kilometers, so consequently the towns and cities are spaced farther apart (by a factor of 1.6) than in countries using the metric system!

I just realized that for us to drop by in order to see you would require a mini-*Lakbayan '98. Anyway, don't watch too much TV.
Johnny

---

* Footnote: Johnny early on coined some very interesting terms, such as *Loyalistas - those Upscans who stayed on in the Philippines through thick and thin; Expatriados - those who immigrated to the US; Resurrectos - those who were out of touch for a long time and finally came back to the fold,* etc. The term *Lakbayan* was the planned cross country journey by a convoy of visiting Loyalistas and Expatriados, which fizzled out after the Asian crises, so it became the *Walakbayan.*

-o-o-o-o-o-o-o-

SOCIETY PAGE and FICTION(?):

Johnny Reyes wrote:
By the way, the Virginia/Maryland girls are planning a major UPSCA ladies-only reunion sometime week-end after next.

JOng added:
Pardon my denseness, but what is the point of an UPSCA ladies-only reunion? UPSCA reunions invariably undergo a division akin to cell mitosis, and separate into a ladies-only table at one end of the room, and a gentlemen-only table at the other end of the room. Whether the Virginia/Maryland girls congregate by themselves or bring their hubbies along, they will still end up in a ladies-only cluster within an hour or shortly after dessert. It's inevitable.

Johnny followed up a few weeks later:
Yesterday, **Liliosa Mangosing-Evangelista** and **Lindus Carreon-Arambulo** hosted a farewell luncheon in Falls Church, Virginia, for **Miren Dumlao-Santos** who is due to return to the Philippines after a three-year stint with the National Health Institute in Washington DC. I understand she has been involved in DNA cloning experiments with the NHI. (The first human they cloned lived only for a few days--but I guess the technology should improve with time.) Lili and Lindus' luncheon also celebrated our arrival here, so the entire U.S. branch of the **Reyes** Family were invited, including **Mila**'s sister **Trining Garcia-Bonifacio** who knew Miren in college. The party was held at the Malibu Grill, a Brazilian barbecue restaurant with authentic gauchos fresh from the Pampas serving the meat. (Falls Church is just outside Washington DC, on the southwest side.) The food was so good we all over-ate, and we overstayed until we were ejected from the restaurant to give way to the early evening diners. On the way home, I took the circumferential road clockwise to avoid having to go through DC, but because of the beer I must have dozed off and I missed the turnoff which should have taken me out of the loop, back north to New Jersey. I drowsily ignored the warning signs which kept coming up about "delays in entering Virginia," thinking happily, Lucky I'm

The Virginia/Maryland girls: Lindus, Liliosa, Trining (guest), Miren, Mila (guest).

going in the opposite direction - away from the bottleneck - those dumb highway control engineers must have placed the warning signs the wrong way. I thought I must already be getting close to Baltimore when all of a sudden, I was surprised to see the Potomac River and the skyline of Washington DC again, and the orientation of the Capitol and the Washington Monument was such that I could only be southeast of them! This means I must have followed the circumferential road 270 degrees! Lost an hour there.

Johnny hastily added again:

It seems I got the clone story all wrong - Miren just sent me a note correcting what I had said in my earlier messages to you all. The first adult human she cloned as part of a U.S. National Health Institute experiment was actually a female. During the dark and stormy night in question, lightning struck the NHI laboratory building in Washington DC, ripping open the French windows and letting the rain in. Since the lab was unattended at the time, nobody saw the three-day-old adult human clone break free of her life-support tubes and walk out of the building. It was a gloomy and horrible night and no one was in the streets of the nation's capital, so again no one noticed her walking around the Georgetown area, not far from the spot where the Jesuit priest Fr. Karras in the seventies had fallen out of a third-story window into the pavement below. The clone was known to have superhuman strength, but there is no solid evidence connecting her with two bodies discovered the following day in the area, both show-ing the effects of a violent struggle. She must have wandered around for some time, because subsequent investigation revealed that she had gotten as far as Pennsylvania Avenue near the White House, quite a

Could this be the clone that Johnny describes so tantalizingly in his nocturnal report?

distance from Georgetown. Miren says the security of this building must have been very lax at the time, because the creature managed to get into the hall connecting with the Oval Office. What happened after this is not so clear, because the information was suppressed by the Secret Service (to cover up their laxity?), but I am told that the details are now available elsewhere on the Internet.

Johnny's yarn-spinning abilities was again demonstrated in a travelogue about NJ which was posted on the Loop. It is too long to reproduce in this issue but prompted literary heavyweight Jimmy to

comment thus: "you're such a story-teller - a natural! I read your travelogue about Hoboken. If only you'd set your hand to writing a novel (it can all be experimental, just your own natural style, without need for any definite plot!)."

-o-o-o-o-o-o-o-

JOKE TIME!

In a previous issues, we got complaints from some quarters regarding the "inappropriate" content of one of the jokes published. So, this time, we will warn you in advance: this probably is inappropriate, but considering that it came from such an august and scholastic source in Japan, then it probably isn't. You be the judge:

A team of archaeologists was excavating in Israel when they came upon a cave. Written on the wall of the cave were the following symbols in order of appearance.
  1. A tomato
  2. A donkey
  3. A shovel
  4. A fish
  5. A Star of David
They decided that this was a unique find and the writings were at least more than three thousand years old. They chopped out the piece of stone and had it brought to the museum where archeologists from all over the world came to study the ancient symbols.

They held a huge meeting after months of conferences to discuss what they could agree was the meaning of the markings. The President of their Society stood up and pointed at the first drawing and said, "This looks like a tomato. We can judge that this was a highly intelligent race as they knew how to grow things to eat. To prove this statement you can see that the next symbol resembles a donkey, so, they were even smart enough to have animals help them till the soil. The next drawing looks like a shovel of some sort, which means they even had tools to help them.

Even further proof of their high intelligence is the fish which means that that they had a famine that hit the earth whereby the food didn't grow, they would take to the sea for food. The last symbol appears to be the Star of David which means they were evidently Hebrews."

The audience applauded enthusiastically and the President smiled and said,

"I'm glad to see that you are all in full agreement with our interpretations."

Suddenly a little old Jewish man stood up in the back of the room and said, "I object to every word. The explanation of what the writings say is quite simple.

First of all, everyone knows that Hebrews don't read from left to right, but from right to left. Now, look again. It now says: HOLY MACKEREL, DIG THE ASS ON THAT TOMATO."

SAMPLE ARTWORK

Lioliosa sent pictures of the unique artwork of Lindus. She hand tools aluminum sheets into beautiful pictures and images. Shown here is a partial picture of sample measuring about 9" x 11". Contact Lindus at her address/phone if interested in placing orders, or email Liliosa.

-o-o-o-o-o-o-o-

HISTORY of UPSCA from the '30s to '56

In the 1979 Souvenir Program for the 2nd Anniversary of the Inauguration of the UP Chapel to be that of a Parish, there appeared an excellent article written by Fely Zafra-Reyes. Herein below is the first half of an abridged version.

No learning would be complete without religion. So it was that Catholic students of the State University in the mid 30's found themselves in the old St. Rita's Hall, the Knights of Columbus Clubhouse for lectures on Catholic philosophy with Masses and communion at the nearby Ateneo chapel. The late *Fr. George William, S.J.*, who had always been identified with the Knights of Columbus patterned these meetings after his original group of the young peoples arm of the Knights of Columbus - the Junior Daughters of Isabella and the Columbian Squires.

Up towards the start of World War II, Catholic students of the University partici-pated only in a small way commensurate with the sparsity of their group. *Lolito Arrastio-Santillan* recalls now that aside from the masses either at the Ateneo or at the CWL Headquarters located on Calle Florida, they were enjoined to attend the Monthly Socials to "serve as examples that good decent fun could be had within university circles." Most Filipino middle-class families referred to the U.P. as a "Godless University." This was not at all surprising for at that time the popular trends were towards Masonry, secularism and indifferentism. For one, there was a provision in the University Code barring priests from speaking in the campus.

There was also the founding of the Scholastic Philosophy Club in the College of Liberal Arts under the advisorship of *Prof. Nicolas Zafra*. Regular Sunday meetings were also held and active partici-pation in various religious activities were undertaken, such as the Eucharistic Congress and the annual Christ the King procession which was traditionally an all-male procession.

At this point, *Fr. James McCarthy*, an Irish Columban priest who had enrolled at the U.P., succeeded in organizing the simple beginnings of what eventually was recognized as a chapter of the University of the Philippines, a member of the Manila Archdiocesan Students' Catholic Action under the late Rev. Michael O'Dougherty, the then Archbishop of Manila. Responsible faculty members agreed to take on the position of adviser of the different chapters within the university. Thus the U.P. Students' Catholic Action came into being.

Due to the number of units represented in the Manila SCA, the U.P. Chapter was able to get the most positions in the annual election of officers as it had so many units represented. Three past presidents of the early Manila SCA were member's of the UPSCA - a *Mr. Hervas, Dr. Lopez, and Atty. Joaquin Gonzales*.

The UPSCANS and their activities drew continuous tirades from the secularists - and the anti-Catholics who charged that certain provisions of the U.P. code prevented even the existence of UPSCA itself. There was a time when permission given earlier to UPSCA to meet within the campus was withdrawn. After asserting their rights of assembly and religion, however, they were allowed to "exist unofficially" under the direct responsibility of the President of the university.

Former post advisers had *Prof. Nicolas Zafra* for the Liberal Arts unit, *Prof. Juan Canave* for the Education unit, *Prof. Justo Arrastia* for the Engineering unit ably assisted by *Prof. Angel Martinez*, and *Prof. Mariano Ocampo* for the Medicine unit. A Pharmacy unit was also founded.

Immediately after World War II, UPSCA was the first to organize among the Manila SCA groups. With the University having shrunk in physical size, and the onslaught of war providing a levelling status in human society, the post-war years showed tentative groupings towards more unified and concerted action. What else but the attendance at Mass and Communion at the Ateneo or the CWL Headquarters? Familiar names surface. *Nori Acosta-Sison* was President at one time. Her officers and members included *Marie Delicia Unson, Generoso Almeda-Lopez, Dolores Arrastia, Vicente San Juan, S.J.* (before the S.J. came about). *Patsy Acosta-Sison* come in later. So did *Cesar Majul*.

By the time Prof. Arrastia introduced Fr. *John P. Delaney, S.J.* to the UPSCA at a Communion-Breakfast in 1946, the UPSCA President was *Jose Espinosa* of the College of Law. Prof. Arrastia who had been particularly close to the UPSCA became ill shortly after and died. The unenviable task of reviving UPSCA fell to *Prof. Angel Martinez,* a close friend and colleague.

The 1946-47 UPSCA started out with 23 active members who were determined to take advantage of the more liberal attitude shown by Catholic Action organizations. Among the year's activities: Third Sunday Mass-Communion-breakfasts (often held at the Ateneo Cafeteria after Mass at the Ateneo chapel), study clubs, lectures where the still famous Love, Courtship, and Marriage series were first introduced. A choir was also formed through the initiative of *Vicente Paterno*, with *Prof. Antonio Molina* in patient attendance. Socials were started too. These were quite apart from the Women's Clubs well known Monthly Socials which earned credits in Euthenics at semester's end. The UPSCA social always had a catchy name attached and was the guide-stick by which future socials were measured. These socials were unique in the sense that these socials started very early indeed. The students prepared the hall together, decorated it together themselves, cooked the party fare almost together. This was all to support Fr. Delaney's theory that going to a party need not necessarily mean that the party goer could not go to communion the next morning due to a disturbed conscience. Although this meant a reduction in the phonograph's supply of "slow drag" dance music and no furtive sneaking in of unauthorized booze, this made for a great deal more fun and laughter and camaraderie and served as the basic ground for the cementing of "Delaney Marriages" which still survive, happily enough, these twenty-five-thirty years later.

Rene Dawis, son of a Los-Baños man responsible for the planting of all the stately acacias trees lining the avenues of the Diliman campus today, was elected president for 1947-48. Activities were expanded to include Christmas Package Drives, catechetical instruction at Welfareville and the printing of the ACTION newsmagazine, UPSCA's official paper which went off the press on September 1948. By the end of this year UPSCA had reached to 300-youths.

In 1948-49, Rene Dawis was re-elected President of UPSCA. Here came the "final evolution of the basic organizational pattern of the post-war UPSCA." The first UPSCA Constitution drafted and then approved by the University Council Committee on Student Organizations and Activities (UCCSOA) as well as by the Archdiocese at Manila. With 500 members, UPSCA become both a mandated Church organization and an officially recognized University group at last. This was a period of expansion for UPSCA. Chapters were organized in practically all the colleges of the University as for as Los Baños and even Iloilo. Its first committees were the Catechetical Instruction League, Social Work and Library and Posters. The Glee Club was regularly giving concerts and the UPSCA socials were getting to be a byword in university social circles as affairs where one could have a ripping good time - economical too, with a warm unselfconsciously friendly atmosphere.

Late in 1948 the University of the Philippines under *President Bienvenido Gonzales* transferred its main campus from the cramped and pockmarked Padre Faura buildings to the wide and spacious grounds in Diliman with its two mirror-image concrete buildings and a plethora of sawaii huts and army pre-fab units in varying shapes and sizes. Transportation was definitely a problem with only a few buses at first venturing out into the dark wilderness that was Diliman. España through to East Avenue was the only route going to U.P. The local folk were still shooting flocks of *tikling* where Araneta Coliseum now stands. Most parents were filled with trepidation of early independence for their children who would need to take up residence within the campus itself. How healthy would the environment be, emotionally as well as physically, for their children? The season was indeed ripe for the invasion of a true Christian way of life for the average student by the UPSCA.

It was within this stark pioneering environment that the so called "Delaney era" evolved from 1950-56.

*To be **continued** in next issue . . . .*

*To be **continued** in next issue . . . .*

Where are they now? *We all know of the Zafras, Profs. Molina, Canave, Majul and other UP Campus names.* ***Past presidents*** *Rene Dawis is in Minnesota connected with the University while a Joe Espino is listed in the UPSCA webpage roster in Manila, and recently gave some memorabilia to the Committee according to Gus de Leon, but he may be not the Joe Espinosa, as cited. An email of May Gatchalian gives more interesting lore on past presidents: " . . like Atty. Jose Espinosa, Fenny Hechanova, Vicente Paterno, Ric Feliciano, the former Nawasa Head who also promoted CFM (I forgot his name at the moment; he married his Upsca Secretary), then Brick Pascual, etc." More lore, anyone?*

Typeset by Danny Gil in Los Angeles supposedly every quarter, but more so based on mood, and material as culled from unwitting Upscans in cyberspace (well, not really, as we do seek permission first from some of the authors). Email, snailmail, fax, or call in news, pictures, trivia, etc., to either 19002 Horst Ave, Artesia, CA 90701, ferngil@aol.com, (562) 402-5098 or (562) 402-1890

Printing costs and postage have sometimes been spontaneously underwritten by readers such as Nancy, Rory, Malu and others. Mercy is always the Philippine postmaster. This issue is compliments of Tony & Josie. Thank you to all.

Action & Reaction ! ! !

Letters, faxes, e-mail, anecdotes, conversations....

José Alzona's piece in the previous issue provoked some lively discussions. Excerpts:

Liliosa:

The newslet was great. But somewhere, I lost J. Alzona. His article sounded like alien-speak.

Danny:

It actually took me a few re-reads to comprehend his piece. Firstly, he abbreviated all name references (TD for Tess Daffon, IRC for Isagani R. Cruz, JemZ for Jimmy Valera, JOng of course is Jimmy Ong). I think RU is Roger Umali, VE is Vic Espinosa. Johnny M. Reyes says JMRJr can't be him because he is not a Junior, and V2 might be Vic Vitug. San Tiano is recognizably Fredie Santiano. I don't know the identity of LG, ABP, SM, MV or DC. When I asked Joe, he said it's up to us to guess.

Then he created words which coalesce the thought trends of the sentence (evaporize, for evaporate & realize), (realate, for relate & realize), (transvected, for transpose & vectored), etc. These are just my conjectures, and it's anybody's guess.

His footnotes expounded on the themes. Note 1 for instance showed how Hedy Lamarr's life bridged so disparate a field, similar to some of our UP activities. Though a dumb-blonde type Hollywood sexpot, Lamarr was at one time married to a European physicist. Together with another Hollywood producer, she patented a discriminating system which found first use in torpedo guidance, and whose theory now is used in cells phones and the like. But I like Joe's footnote 3 best, about San Tiano's non-bilocation.

Anyway, the first section of his article deals with a visit to Tess Daffon's Makati residence, which at that time was an old abandoned hospital beside the cemetery and reputedly haunted. Joe insists that my recollection of the event was different from his because he had gone there on another occasion, with a different set of people, hence he suggested *gingo biloba*, a herbal medicine for enhancing memory.

The second section explains his side regarding JOng's observation that like Gani, he could irritate people by just look-ing at them. In fact, he was looking at somebody else, but his look was unrequited. Perhaps his statement about "age of cholera" refers to the popular South American author Gabriel Garcia Marquez whose book bears a similar theme. And his last sentence is an Ilocano phrase meaning roughly *c'est la vie.*

Jimmy:

I think your exposition on Joe's narrative should be in the next Newslet. It helped me appreciate what Joe was doing. Now I can think of Joe's text as a remarkable experiment, even if difficult reading.

I told Joe in my letter to him, I found it delightful (for the exotic vocabulary and their sounds). I suppose from time to time we should have our revenge on the English language.

-o-o-o-o-o-

Obviously, many in the Loop chat during office hours, and there can be problems:

Liliosa emailed her problem: "We have been put on notice about a new policy in my office about using Email. Because of a very serious case of abuse that is being prosecuted here, all staff have been alerted to the nightly random scanning and examina-tion of all eMails . . ."

So I sent an email to all, captioned "STOP LILIOSA from Prosecution" *which explained about no email to her henceforth. She answered* "Danny, what a silly SUBJECT. But thanks." *But Johnny sent her this email anyway, with this short intro:*

To update evangeli@who.org on current events, I sent the following message — disguised to penetrate the WHO barrier against personal e-mail messages. Waiting to see if she breaks the simple code. Johnny.

Subj: Message for the World Health Organization
         (c/o Mrs. Evangelista)
From: Juanmreyes
To: evangeli@who.org

I represent a company recently incorporated in Isagani (capital of the Republic of the Congo) and in Vera Cruz (Mexico). We believe that nothing but persistence wins the world-wide war against epidemic disease, and that half-way measures can never be justified. More than a million lives are at stake, and the cost in dollar or pound or peso terms is nothing compared to winning the ultimate prize - victory against pestilence and disease. Efforts spent for achieving this objective will pay huge dividends. Writing off the mistakes of others in the past is needed, and Musical Chairs (my company's name) are prepared to help you play this game of tremendous stakes. The human race is entitled to this and nothing less. Call 1-800-and then seven sevens.

A week or so passed, then Liliosa appeared with a new email address, with this message: "Johnny ALREADY sent a nutty message to my WHO email address. Tell him it was posted on the cafeteria bulletin board for all the World-Health-Organization to read!"

And I answered: "To decipher the code, read the last word of each line. Isagani won half a mil."

Actually, Gani alluded to his prize in an earlier email from Paris which expounded on **tax pesos**: "Dante Liban and I are together in the Philippine government's delegation to the UNESCO World Conference on Higher Education being held here in Paris (5-9 October). Now a Congressman, Dante (entered UPSCA in 1966 under Fr. Perez and chaired the Mass Servers Committee) heads the House Committee on Education. I am here to repre-sent the National Commission for Culture and the Arts. Dante is in our loop ("liban@pacific.net.ph"). By the way, is anybody on the loop in Paris? I still have two days here and can look you up. (The conference is an absolute bore and will achieve absolutely nothing, like all such conferences. The only thing that makes staying here worthwhile is Medy is with me. I spent my **prize money** from the Centennial Literary Contest on her ticket. Dante and I, and a dozen others, are spending your **taxpayer's money** on our tickets.)"

JOng's earlier email to Johnny was more specific: "Ani won third prize in the Sarswela category for 'Pito-Pito.' I also sent him a query about his plans and his loot, but since he's returning Oct 14, I don't suppose I'll get an answer till then."

-o-o-o-o-o-

Loop Accretion: as more people get into the internet, finding old friends can be serendipidious.

Bong Nuqui emailed:

Some of the email I have been receiving in the loop mention a **Vyva Aguirre**, but it was only today when I realized she is not in the email loop. Here is her address: VYVA@claw.upd.edu.ph. When I was at Quezon Hall in charge of STFAP (Socialized Tuition and Financial Assistance Program) I would meet her at meetings because she was a legal officer of the Student Disciplinary Tribunal (SDT) in Diliman. I also met her when we were trying to set up a LEXIS-type database for the College of Law. I gave her your address and gave her a general rundown of the categories. If she doesn't get you first, perhaps you can write her.

I forwarded Bong's email to Malu, a dear friend of Vyva, then realized that Vyva already contacted me:

I just heard from Bong Nuqui that he reads about me from the UPSCA Newsletter. I sure would want to be in the mailing list! Can you also send me back issues?

Malu's reply was almost instantaneous:

Wow — this is really phenomenal!!!! Finally, after all these years I am about to connect with a long lost friend. Listen, Vyva was not a bridesmaid — she was my maid-of-honor at our wedding officiated by Bishop Felix Perez. How wonderful to know that Vyva will be in our Loop! Somehow, we lost touch with each other after she entered the lay order — Notre Dame de Vie — while Oids and I started a family and went on our careers.

-o-o-o-o-o-o-o-

*Another source of Upsca names is the **Upsca Web Site**. As described in an earlier email:*

Maybe some of you guys are already aware of this, but I just found an amazing URL, an UPSCA webpage made way back in 1997. Log on *http://www.geocities.com/heartland/prairie/7876/* and then you will see what I mean. There is also a registration section, and only 107 have posted their names so far. I recognize only 2 names: **Vic Vitug** and **Art Intengan**; most of the others are of much later vintage. Vic is in NY, while Fr. Art of course is in Ateneo. If that website is too much a mouthful, then go to your search engine and enter UPSCA and that site should be linked up to eventually.

*So we got **Vic Vitug** into the Loop, and he emailed us:*

How are you guys doing? Has anybody been put out to pasture yet? It always gives me a shock whenever I do the arithmetic and realize that those UPSCA days were some thirty years ago. I am currently what you would call a techie. I handle networks and Oracle databases for a large non-profit association with branches all over the country. I used to do a lot of traveling doing the same stuff for my previous employer but happily, not for this one. I think I recognize some of the e-mail addresses but I do need to jog my memory a bit and there are some that totally do not mean anything to me. I can't wait to get the list [email] you mentioned.

-o-o-o-o-o-o-o-

Dr. Gene Pulmano in NY got be a cyber pal after an exchange of email on the no-to-Marcos-burial initiative. Turns out he is an Upscan. Excerpts:

I got the two issues of the UPSCA newsletter you sent me. Many, many thanks. I definitely was not "in" at that time. Why, I missed all the fun that people were talking about in the newsletter. Nevertheless, I enjoyed reading it. One person I recognized was **Johnny Balaoing** (wasn't he CE?) who was a good friend of my brother **Victor** (himself a CE, '60). Johnny was senior eng'g, I think, when I entered U.P. in 1960. I was rather at the periphery of UPSCA life at that time because, for one thing, I was awfully shy. For another, when I got to Diliman, my brother put me up at

the quonset huts (barracks, I call them) rather than at one of the classy dorms; that wasn't the bad part. The bad part was, I didn't have much interaction with my peers; all my roommates were seniors, one was senior eng'g (**Boy dela Cruz**, who treated me nicely), one was senior law, one was senior English and another senior eng'g. Normally, except for Boy, they didn't have much to do with me. Who would have bothered with a freshman like me. Anyhow, it was when I joined UPSCA that I got some kind of social life in Diliman, but just when I was beginning to enjoy the campus life in Diliman -- I had to leave for the College of Medicine in Herran, Manila. And that is another story.

-o-o-o-o-o-o-o-

*Another MD's email, **Benny & Nanette (Ortega) Jongco**:*

Thanks for the acknowledgment [donation for the fund drive]. Have been enjoying the exchanges in the LOOP, glad you included us in it.

*Plus the handwritten note of **Nanette**:*

I am one of those rare illiterate folks [on email] and have to depend on my husband or son. Finally, here I am doing it the old fashioned way - actually writing my note to you!

I was with UPSCA - Arts & Sciences '60-'63 and medicine '63-'68. I have very happy memories of Delaney Hall. It's fun to read news about familiar people from all over - **Jimmy** and **Mercy, Selma, Baby Mangosing** (who coached us in a debate), **Lindus** (who happens to be my cousin), etc.

We've been in NJ since 1971 - and remember seeing only **Sari Valenzuela** and **Nancy Cruz**. Perhaps it's time to plan a reunion.

We go home every year to visit family and join Medical Mission. Next time, we'll make an effort to visit Diliman and Delaney Hall.

*Yes, Nanette, why don't all of you Upscans in the East coast set up a re-union. Just look at the address list and you'll see quite a crowd. A new-comer to the list, as I understand it, is one of the Delaney stalwarts, **Flora Libay** in NY, who also may have a wider list of earlier Upscans. And on your next trip home, do try visiting Fr. Ben Villote at his QC halfway house for migrant youths. You will find it an interesting and worthwhile project.*

-o-o-o-o-o-o-o-

Still another MD's email:

My name is **Beth Zaraspe Yoo** from Los Angeles. I was the Chairperson of the UPSCA College of Arts and Sciences Chapter in 1965 - 66 and was the College of Medicine Chapter president later. I'm also the younger sister of **Raquel Zaraspe Ordonez**. Thank you for sending the UPSCA Newsletter. We came from a meeting with some of the UP College of Medicine alumni who hosted the Dean of the College before he leaves back for Manila. We arrived at 12:30 am and looked at the mail and saw the newsletter. I could not stop reading it. Memories began to pile up one on top of another as I look at those young faces. How are all of you?

-o-o-o-o-o-o-o-

*And another MD's mail, **Lina (Soliman) Plantilla**:*

Enclosed is a small gift for the Delaney Hall renovation. Thank you for the newsletters. I am still a practicing dermatologist in NYC; my husband - Eduardo Plantilla, Ateneo pre-med '63 and UP med '68 - is a practicing surgeon in NYC as well. Here is a picture of my family with children Edward Jr. and Maria Teresa.

One of the two '60s photos of the Choir Program emailed by Vic Vitug. Seems as if those extra hands belonged to someone too slow in posing. Vic's caption read: "Randy David is in one of the photos." Is he in this photo? Can you identify more of them? Where are they now? As far as we can recall:

4. Imelda Palumbarit (?)
5. Tercy (nee Mortola) Villaruz, Phils
6. Ed Celeste (?)
7. Roly Mesa (?)
8. Benny Lim (?)
9. Vic Vitug, NY
10. Tinoy Desamito, Phils
12. Manny Espejo, Los Angeles
13. Rex Baquiran (+)
15. Roger Hipol

After UP, Rex Baquiran went to PMA and from what we heard, was one of those victims during the dirty war between the military and the NPA. Is older brother Rodney still in Manila?

Taken in 1980 at the UP President's Residence (Noel Soriano was then UP President) on 25th death anniversary of Fr. Delaney. *Sitting, L-R:* unidentified, Fredie Santiano, Eli Lademora, Jimmy Ong, Fr. Manny, Tigi Barcelona, Oscar Evangelista, Jimmy Abad, Danny Gil, Jun Abao. *Standing, L-R:* unidentified, Gerry Gil, Fr. Mat Sanchez, Lita Belmonte, unidentified, Lolly Aquino, Lisa Gil, Angge Soriano, Cardinal Sin, Lina Valcarcel, Nina Los Baños, Maya Santiano, Mercy Abad, Nora Barcelona and unidentified priest.

Fr. Ortiz (+)   Fr. Gough (+)   Fr. O'Brien   All together: Frs. Sanchez, Neri, Arevalo, Clarke(?), Pedrosa, O'Brien and Gough. These pictures are from Lolly's album, taken at the 1977 Inauguration of the UP Parish. Inset is a picture of Fr. Delaney at DH in 1980. Anecdotes we've heard (true or not, we can't say): Fr. O'Brien was a New York taxi driver before joining the order, and woe to the car that was lent to him to drive in Manila. Fr. Gough's hand was crippled by a war wound and he had to get special dispensation prior to being ordained. Fr. Ortiz at one time was the father confessor of Pres. Quezon, and had more of his share of political influence.

OCTOBER 24 party, just after grace was said, and before attacking the food. As identified and expounded further: *1 & 2* - **Noli & Rosita Arong**. *3 & 4* guests of honor **NVM & Narita Gonzales**. *5* - **Johnny Balaoing** (wife **Alda** couldn't make it). *6* - **Lisa**, whose other half **Danny** took the picture. *7 & 8* - newcomers **Tita (Tueño) & Lito Balucan**. Tita and Johnny hadn't seen each other for years and both remember the UPSCA Corregidor excursion 38 years ago where they were part of the group of about two dozen who got inadvertently left behind when the ship lifted anchor. It was **Fr. Ortiz** who pulled strings at the Phil Navy and had a fast cutter dispatched to pick up the stragglers after midnight. And small world indeed, Lito and Noli found that they had many friends in common, having both come from CIT in Cebu. *9 & 10* - **Ken & Ofie (Peñaflorida) Aid**. 11 & 12 & 13 - **Josie, Tony** and **daughter Lisa Estrera**. *14* - **Malu (Barrios) Garcia**, new president of the group with hubby **Oids** unseen, manning the other camera.

15 & 16 - **Rose (Lacebal) & Cir Engay**, old faithful to most parties. *17* - another newcomer **Lolly Aquino**,"perennial" sacristene since the late '60s until she left the UP campus in the early '80s, and known to most of all of the priests and Catholic community leaders from the Zafra's to the NVM's to Angge Soriano and more. Other stragglers came in later: **Mario Manasala, Manny Castillo**, and **Dell & Julz Tocong** with their guitar. Old faithful **Ernie & Jessie (Raqueño) Pangilinan** couldn't make it this time, so no one could play *ouido* on the piano to accompany the eager singers. But Del took the slack with his guitar, and we all had a rip-roaring fun time. It wasn't all food, song nor dance, though. We did have a serious meeting about the state of affairs in UP, fundraising, the Medical Cooperative movement of which Johnny is involved, and the like, which although cut into part of Manny's joke-telling sessions, was well worth it.

DETAILED MAILING LIST - DELETED

UPSCA ALUMNI ASSOCIATION, USA

NEWSLETTER   NEWSLETTER   NEWSLETTER

A M D G | Vol 1, Num 9 (1st quarter, 1999) | Published by UPSCA Alumni Association, USA

EMAIL LOOP LINKS UP AND DOWN!

UPSCAN NETWORK EXPANDING

The popularity of the Loop and the Newslet got a further boost when more UPSCANs got into the mailing list and linked up with each other via email.

Excerpts :

From Danny to Oca Palabyab:

You probably won't remember me, but I'm one of the earlier Upscans. Well, we maintain close camaraderie with a circle of Upscans of our vintage, via email and a newslet. One of the group, Mercy Abad, mentioned in an email, and I quote: "Yesterday, at Marilou Quinto's party, I met her UPSCA generation who want to link to the loop that we already have. There was Oscar Palabyab who will be the contact person for the group. I am sending him a copy of the newsletters to route to his gang."

So I'm taking the liberty of pasting below some of the stuff we recently circulated. You might find it interesting and we'd be happy if you could throw in more stuff.
Danny

His reply:

Thanks very much for the mails. I probably represent the transition from the post-Delaney era through the turbulent days in the campus. I have seen how the ideological tug of war almost cut UPSCA way down the middle. I was able to see UPSCA survive even during the martial law years and after and its rapid decline as the U.P. parish developed and put UPSCA on the sidelines. Since I come from the law school, I have realized how strong the fraternity system works in our society and how I wish we could also develop the kind of network that fraternities have and how they support each other. Let's see where we go from here. There are other batches after mine who maintain their contacts and get together from time to time. With the advent of the e-mail era, I suppose we can establish a wide network we never dreamed of. Even in the US where three of my brothers live (two of whom are UPSCANS) in California, we have a group there that meets from time to time. I just have to collect their e-mail addresses. Anyway, thanks indeed for including me in the "loop." I will get more UPSCANs to join. Regards
Oca Palabyab - AB '68, LLB '72

The idea of an ever-growing network of email participants has, of course, it's pluses and minuses. For one, it can get quite unwieldy. On the other hand, the more the merrier, and the network can maintain it's viability by keeping loops within loops, as broached by Gani.

From Gani Cruz:

Okay, let's make another loop that consists of the group that physically gets together in Manila every other month or so. There is no need to dismantle the existing groups, although admittedly, Danny has to work double. Just getting the other — older and younger — UPSCANs involved was quite a feat, and is worth continuing. We want to avoid any kind of elitism or separatism or schism or whatever, especially since it appears that our UPSCA network is *truly a world organization, which could lead to world domination* and other games adults play. In any case, I am all for having a tiny circle of origs, where *we can truly insult each other* without having to worry about who is the person with that funny email address or whatever.
Gani.

(The Loop started about 3 years ago with a couple of close pals who traded jokes and friendly insults.)

Another alternative way to continue maintaining this connectivity is for all (who are now on the present Loop) to register in the UPSCA Website (www.geocities.com/Heartland/Prairie/7876) presently being maintained by a set of 90's UPSCANs, then actively participate in the Bulletin Board posting, etc. Suggestions, ideas, anyone?

-o-o-o-o-o-

FUNDRAISING RESULTS

In the financial statement dated January 4, 1999 for the Delaney Memorial Fund released by Tessie Daza, a total of P174,090 and $4,175 was collected from a total of 61 and 44 contributors, respectively. The sale of the book "The Jesuit Meddler" brought in another P6,500.

About P206,000 went to the Delaney bust, plaques and pedestal. Printing costs and other miscellaneous expenses and supplies took up another P34,000.

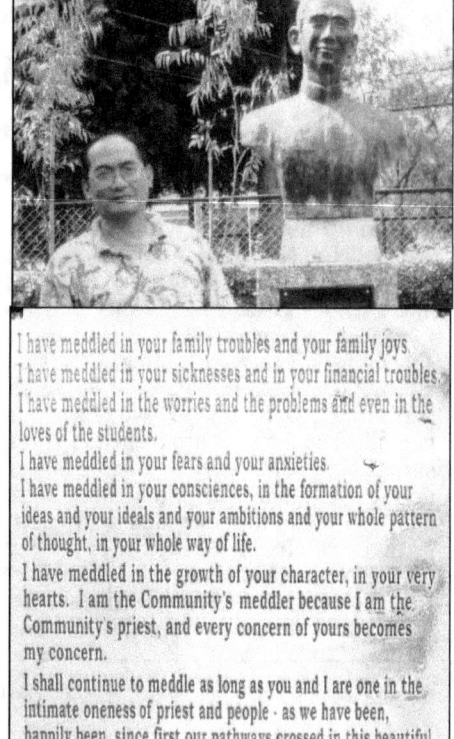

I have meddled in your family troubles and your family joys.
I have meddled in your sicknesses and in your financial troubles.
I have meddled in the worries and the problems and even in the loves of the students.
I have meddled in your fears and your anxieties.
I have meddled in your consciences, in the formation of your ideas and your ideals and your ambitions and your whole pattern of thought, in your whole way of life.
I have meddled in the growth of your character, in your very hearts. I am the Community's meddler because I am the Community's priest, and every concern of yours becomes my concern.
I shall continue to meddle as long as you and I are one in the intimate oneness of priest and people - as we have been, happily been, since first our pathways crossed in this beautiful experiment in Community living which is our Diliman.

The bronze bust of Fr. Delaney is shown above. Straggler is in photo to give a sense of proportionality. Each side of the pedestal has a plaque. Shown also is a blowup of the plaque of his famous reply to the charge of meddling.

The Delaney Hall's rehabilitation is almost complete. In addition to contributions collected from other fund drives, Fr. Reyes got Diocese funds for Chapel and building upkeep. And as the picture below may barely show, DH is all glassed in, painted and spruced up, back rooms air-conditioned, with mural on wall, etc.

So after all the accounting, there is a balance of about $2900 in the Memorial Fund, earmarked for other projects.

THE DELANEY BOOKS

Liliosa sent an email which was relayed to the others in the loop with the catchy title **Lili's Challenge:**

All these flashbacks make such interesting chapters for a book on UPSCA history or investigative journalism. Fr. Delaney would of course be a focal point, but what is remarkable is that even before he arrived, there was already fertile ground for his efforts. Credit goes to those now-retired/departed faculty members and students who went out of their way to start small exchanges of ideas, plans, projects, etc. How about it, prize-winning authors of the loop? Do you think that these eMail exchanges could serve as building blocks for a serious treatise on whether or not UPSCA made a real difference in our college years and later lives, or was it merely a fun time to be remembered, and nothing more? Or would you think that having a religious organization in campus was actually a liability, holding back pursuit of academic freedom, etc.?

More from Lili:

Whew! My yahoo mail nearly exploded with all the messages I saw this morning. All these after going on leave for only 2 working days! Danny, don't worry about the mis-sent messages. I was delighted with all the responses, but I hope you are not *asking me to do the writing* [of the book]. Who, me? Why, between the kitchen sink, my number-crunching desk, and the unfinished cross-stitch projects, I could never even get started! And I have been away from everybody for soooo long. Besides, there are so many more capable historian-journalists-writers in the loop who would do justice to this cause. I was glad to contribute by *setting the challenge*, as you call it, and would be happy to send in a few more recollections and reflections.

It was nice to hear from the ladies! *Malu Barrios-Garcia, Susan Po, Rory Abrera, Beth Arcellana-Nuqui, Nanette Ortega-Jongco,* thanks for sharing your wonderful thoughts.

When *Miren Dumlao Santos* was here, I was surprised to realize that she and *Lindus [Carreon-Arambulo]* didn't really know each other. So over the phone, I gave them both instructions to meet at the subway station, trusting that they would get along. Well, they did and both of them said later on that it seemed like they have always known each other. Miren later on referred to it as the "UPSCA spirit". In retrospect, that may have been a trusting spirit, a certain kind of caring (despite our corny jokes, teasing episodes, frustrations and disappointments, etc.) that we all tried to share with each other as special friends. And for good reason. In a university setting where we were supposed

to meet head-on with "life as it really is", a circle of friends such us ours made it possible for us not to lose our bearings.

Excerpts of responses to Lili:

From Susan Po:

UPSCA was the only organization I was involved with during my college years. And I should say that it cushioned the transition from a sheltered colegiala's life to life out in the jungle. And I still go back to my UPSCA network to sustain me.

It must be those weeks (or was it months) of cleaning the chapel windows, standing on DH chairs, as an UPSCA applicant; grovelling before UPSCA members to get their signature to fill up my applicant's form; answering *Mon Pasicolan's* charge about our UPSCA clique (our singing group with *M'lu Barrios, Oids Garcia, Nonong Pedero, Ping Tan, Bess Silva, Jess Martinez, Manny Castillo, Ruben Habito, Jemz Valera, Poch Macaranas,* etc.) to be less - well - "cliquish" and more inclusive; fending off attacks from those misogynists led by *JOng*; straining to rebuild my self-image after being nicknamed "Monster" by *Tigi Barcelona* who would not stop at yelling out this "pet name" from his Mercedes over to me in my proletarian VW Bug, etc., etc.

From Mon Pasicolan:

Hooray to *Susan Po* for her great and gritty recollections of her Upsca days and her pesky "tormentors". She took after her great and beloved father *Don Joaquin Po* — "un gran hombre"

From Malu (Barrios) and Oids Garcia:

I know it made a difference in our lives 'cuz *Oids* and I met in UPSCA, were in the same chapter, clique, and attended the same functions and later married by *Bishop Perez.* It's a good idea to come up with a book with us as authors as there are quite a few loopers who write alá-author.

From Beth Arcellana-Nuqui:

This is a great idea, and I hope we start this project ASAP. My fondest memories of college, and even of 4th year high school, are of Upsca and the Upscans. Some of my most vivid recollections as a child are about Fr. John Patrick Delaney, S.J. One of these days, I will sit down and write about it.

From Rory Abrera:

UPSCA during our time was a great way to make friends with very down to earth people. I'm not sure if all of us were that religious, but I think we all had a conscience and really wanted to do good for everybody around us. I remember how the frats and sororities at the time had a rather tainted reputation for hazing, etc. which didn't make any sense at all.

Delaney Hall was a fun place to meet. I always felt welcome and was almost sure to find someone to talk to and/or hang out with. Chapter meetings were always taking place at one time or another. I just remember it was usually buzzing with one kind of activity or another. Besides you being there, I could almost expect to see *Jimmy Abad, Merci Rivera, Freddie Santiano, Danny Dequito, Mon Pasicolan, Gerry (your brother), Lili Mangosing, Lino Faelnar, Maureen Holazo, Tigi Barcelona, Willie Abrera (my cousin), the Gordon sisters, Tessie Chua, Melvin Martin, or Susan Paulin* there when I dropped by. I was there a lot particularly because of practice with the Drama Guild with *Kit Santos.* Real fun days!

I heard a lot of discussions on politics and government, theology, etc. among the guys and gals - it was a just a great forum for an exchange of ideas. What a great way for young people to start off and build their lives with - the ability to talk about all kinds of issues. In UPSCA we had a social consciousness and a world view. We were the dreamers for a better future. And I believe we enjoyed doing it. I'm not sure that young people these days are anything like we were. It's just a different time!

Then Gus wrote that in the course of collecting the memorabilia of Fr. Delaney, the committee-in-charge would include some of the writeups.

From Gus:

The book publication project is making progress. Book One will be the compilation of the Chapel Chismis (originally Chapel Chatter), plus the writings of Fr. Delaney about the mass. Book Two is the History of UPSCA and the chapel. Materials are from the Action. We have materials up to 1952. We are still looking for Action issues after 1952. We are also looking for materials on Love Courtship and Marriage. *The recollection of history (Dawis paper), write ups of Upscans, their recollections of Upsca days and Fr. Delaney will be in this book. The response of Upscans to Lili* will be included in this book on the chapter "40 to 50 years after."

We have commissioned a ward of *Fr. Ben Villote* to type out on Pagemaker [a desktop publishing software] the Chapel Chismis, and the articles for the manuscript.

-o-o-o-o-o-

Published by Danny Gil in Los Angeles supposedly every quarter. Material is culled from unwitting Upscans in cyberspace. Email, snailmail, fax, or call in news, pictures, trivia, etc. to either 19002 Horst Ave, Artesia, CA 90701, ferngil@aol.com, (562) 402-5098 or (562) 402-1890

HISTORY OF UPSCA from the '30s to '56 (second part), continued from last issue. Taken from an article written by Fely Zafra-Reyes in a 1979 Souvenir Program

It was within this stark pioneering environment that the so-called "Delaney era" evolved from 1950-56. Because of the very apparent need to help one another in a necessarily spartan existence, a sense of community developed, not only among the faculty members who had heeded President *Gonzales*' call to Diliman but also among the students, now living in boarding houses and dorms - rickety row-houses that were previously occupied by soldiers of the US Army Signal Corps.

It was not only the faculty and the students which made the trek to Diliman. Fr. Delaney followed his UPSCANs there. A ramshackle *sawali* structure with a vague suspicion of pseudo-spires where the present School for Social Work now stands had served as a nondenominational chapel for the soldiers. For some years after, this chapel was used for the some purpose also. After Sunday Mass, the altar would be stripped and the Protestants would come in and use the place. The Aglipayans, too.

After Fr. Delaney had accepted the challenge of celebrating Mass daily for the UPSCANs in Diliman, he commuted to and from Ateneo, Padre Faura with much difficulty. Only 6' x 6' army trucks went back and forth from Diliman to Quiapo and certainly not in time for early morning mass. The Liturgical Taxi, Ltd. was formed as a result. Every morning at 4:30, Fr. Delaney was picked up in front of the Ateneo Cafeteria by *Guilly San Juan*, and brought to Diliman for Mass. After breakfast at one of the faculty members' houses (rotation by schedule fixed by *Miss Presentacion Perez*), he was brought back to Ateneo by *Mrs. Luz Zafra's* car after dropping her off at FEU. More than a year of commuting passed before his Jesuit superiors decided to release him from his duties as teacher and guidance counselor at the Ateneo High School. Finally, he came to UP, no longer as commuter but as a bona fide resident.

A small space behind the altar was earmarked for Fr. Delaney's use, big enough for a camp bed that was hardly longer than his 6-ft-plus frame, a table and chair, and a bookcase. Yet it was from this *sawali* house of worship that the UPSCANs learned to understand and love the Mass, learned to value the meaning of friendship and self-sacrifice, infusing in them the buoyant, militant spirit of Catholic Action. It was here too where the Lecture series on Love, Courtship and Marriage came into full flower, where Fr. Delaney rallied the UPSCANs to propagate "simple living" as a way of life, where purity and chastity became more than mere abstract virtues and blank words.

Here also was the dignity of work demonstrated - where nobody waited for somebody else to do the dirty job - one just went ahead and did it! Nobody ever said No to hard work. The Sacristennes are indeed a good example of work done, no matter what. Counting out the hosts for the Chalice may be a glamorous job but sweeping out the chapel, dusting the pews and throwing out smelly wilting flowers, and washing the vases certainly will never hit the society page. Yet *Prof. Samson Lucero* of Cebu says today that he met his wife in UPSCA and wooed her after waiting for her to finish her chores in the chapel every afternoon. He was not alone in the waiting. Many UPSCA marriages started out the some way.

The Engineers as a working team is another example. The grounds around the chapel were always soggy. Somebody had to dig the drainage ditches. The bamboo walls were riddled with *anay*. Somebody had to replace them. Switches, bulbs and rough uncemented patches had to be repaired. A long line of engineers have left their mark in this chapel - *Louie Paterno, Domi Lee, Sito Sison, Gasty, Vic and Ruel Ortigas, Mon Ordoveza, Mel Alincastre, Ben Catane, Joe de Castro, Noel Soriano, Jess Ignacio, Chito Quitans, Arthur Uichanco, Ernie Fabriga, Nonoy Saddul, Jess Perias, Noy Hamoy,* the list stretches on and on.

Rene Dawis embarked on his third term as President of the UPSCA for the year 1949-50. At this time, UPSCA had a membership of 500. The following years saw an increase in activities, both spiritual and temporal. Expansion also came in the form of marriages among the UPSCANS themselves. Many of these marriages were truly a part of the constancy and fidelity, the love and the spirit of self-sacrifice which Fr. Delaney demanded of each and every UPSCAN and which he was expected to carry over into his own marriage.

Social work had been efficiently organized; a Dramatic Guild was formed; catechetical instructions were being given at the U.P. Elementary School as well as in Cruz na Ligas; Mass servers, adult and children both, were on a definite daily schedule; finally too, the ACTION actually came out every month for several months at a time.

Best of all, there grew a definite Oneness in the growing record-breaking attendance of both students and faculty members alike at daily Mass and Communion. This culminated in the building and completion of a new chapel for Catholic students in time for the Christmas celebrations of 1955 - the Chapel of the Holy Sacrifice - the fruit of all the sacrifice, big and small, financial and otherwise, of students, teachers and non-academic workers of the University community. Many an UPSCAN will remember the dress for the

Junior Prom gladly sacrificed with the corresponding cost added to the Chapel fund. And how many will count the number of times they went without their customary coke and *halo-halo* in order to give the money saved over for the new Chapel? And the cigarettes unsmoked, the movies unseen? And the Holy Thousand - those who wanted to give more - the gift of themselves in daily Mass and Communion for the success and completion of the chapel - their names enshrined forever within the cornerstone of the Chapel.

The One-ness also grew in student-faculty relations. Early in the school-year, a simple ceremony introduced incoming Freshmen to upperclassmen UPSCANS and to a number of faculty members who were assigned as unofficial *ninongs* and *ninangs*, opening their homes and their hearts to these greenhorns in the campus. The *Salcedos*, the *Zafras*, the *Valenzuelas*, to name a few have warm memories of their charges and the tearfully emotional problems they were wont to collect as normal adolescents. Some problems though were complicated by tragically painful conflicts with their parents. Not a few of the faculty foster parents served as mediator and/or referee between parent and child. Another facet of faculty-student relationships were the famous Faculty Follies, full-length extravaganzas in all-to-true living and breathing color. These were joint faculty-student productions to augment the ongoing Chapel fund.

The year 1950-51 found *Luis Paterno* at the helm; *Luis V. Sison* in 1951-52; *Constantino Nieva* in 1952-53 and *Tony Santos-Ocampo* in 1953-54. By this time, UPSCA had grown into a virtual power center in the University. They turned their attention to campus centering on the venalities of the socially prestigious Greek-letter societies, as well as pinpointing the brutality of fraternity initiations. Many an UPSCAN at this time fought a painful battle with themselves in making decisions as to where their true loyalties lay. And in the midst of all the conflict engendered by the UPSCANS tilting their idealistic lances at the offended established fraternities, Fr. John P. Delaney wearily took himself off to Baguio after the festivities of inaugurating a new chapel. Only a handful of UPSCANS came to the Zafra cottage to say good-bye to him. These were the students who could not afford to go home to their families for the holidays and had been invited to stay the while with their faculty ninongs.

He died quietly on Mirador Hill, home again in the bosom of his Jesuit brothers, away from his beloved students, away from his warring and non-warring couples.

On January 14, 1956, the new chapel was the scene of another sacrifice. Fr. Delaney lay in state and was later buried at

Sacred Heart Novitiate, Novaliches. His funeral cortege was one of the longest ever seen in the Philippines to that day. It was made up not only of the students with whom he had lived but of the many other people he had helped in his lifetime.

Life went on. *Fr. Pacifico Ortiz, SJ* was appointed the next chaplain of UPSCA by his Jesuit superiors. Soon after he had come to take up his post, Fr. Ortiz said wryly that coming to UPSCA was like marrying a window who has not yet forgotten her first husband. But the very basic groundwork had been laid; the positive virtues had been implanted. And the U.P. student had come to a realization that Christ was here and now and that life could be truly worthwhile if we followed in His footsteps.

-o-o-o-o-o-

To buttress these Upsca history writeups, here's a list of Upsca presidents from the postwar period onward to the '70s, though it may not be 100 percent accurate. Accompanying the list are pictures of some of the presidents, with approximate year when picture was taken.

Name	Year(s)	Where now
Joe Espinosa	45-46	Phils
Telesforo Ramos	46-47	?
Rene Dawis	47-50	US
Ting Paterno	50-51	?
Luis Sison	51-52	?
Constantino Nieva	52-53	?
Tony Santos-Ocampo	53-54	?
Gasty Ortigas	54-55	(+)
Brick Pascual	55-56	?
Ric Feliciano	56-57	Guam
Gus de Leon	57-58	Phils
Jimmy Cruz	58-59	US
Noel Soriano	59-60	Phils
Johnny Ramos	60-62	Phils
Jimmy Abad	62-63	Phils
Melvyn Martin	63-64	Phils
Jimmy Ong	64-65	Phils
Mon Pasicolan	65	Phils
Benny Lim	66	Phils
Jimmy Salazar	66-67	Phils
Ely Lademora	67	Phils
Douglas Villanueva	68	?
Ed Valencia	68-69	?
Oca Palabyab	69-71	Phils
Ronnie Reyes	72-73	Phils

So, what are they doing now? Jimmy Abad, Melvyn Martin, Mon Pasicolan, and Jimmy (JOng) Ong are all part of the Loop. Jimmy is with UP. Mon and JOng recently retired from San Miguel, Melvyn runs his PR firm in Makati. Johnny Ramos is with the UP Conservatory of Music, and Noel Soriano is recuperating from a stroke. He had been UP President during Marcos's time, and was in high government positions during Cory's and Ramos' tenures. Oca Palabyab and Ronnie Reyes are practicing attorneys. Jimmy Salazar is a judge. May Gatchalian

Oca Palabyab - '80　Eli Lademora - '80

Johnny Ramos - '61　Jimmy Abad - '99

Gus de Leon - '99　Jimmy Ong - '99

Melvyn Martin - '99　Mon Pasicolan - '99

Noel Soriano - '91　Jimmy Salazar - '80

reports that Atty. Joe Espinosa was a former neighbor, and is now bedridden. Gus de Leon runs a consultancy and is very active in various Foundations. Gus reports that Jimmy Cruz is somewhere in the US, and Ric Feliciano is in Guam. Regarding earlier president Rene Dawis, Gus writes:

Rene Dawis, I recall is a tall lean man with a crew cut. He was much our senior when I was in Diliman. Fr. Delaney spoke so highly of him so it is as if those in our generation knew him well.

We managed to connect up to Rene, and he sent in an email which gave a whole lot more insight of the early Upsca.

From Rene:

Thanks for the copy of the UPSCA newsletter. It is interesting to read about the many, many people who have been UPSCAns during their UP student days and are now doing well in the world. I'm a bit frustrated, however, by my not recognizing most of the names. But why should I expect otherwise, when it is 50 years since I was an UPSCAn and first met Father Delaney.

I joined UPSCA at the beginning of the 1946-47 school year. At that time, UP was located in Padre Faura, primarily in the Cancer Institute, 2 floors of Villamor Hall (partially destroyed), and PGH. UPSCA president at the time was *Telesforo Ramos. Vicente Paterno, Yoly Tambuatco*, and (I think) *Nali Arvisu* were the other officers. The president before "Puring" Ramos was *Jose Espinosa* (College of Law; not to be confused with *Jose Espino*, College of Engineering). I don't know who were officers with Joe Espinosa. After "Puring" Ramos, I was president for 3 years (1947-50), with Ting Paterno, Mitos Sison, Nali Arvisu, and *Yoly Sebastian* serving as officers.

Father Delaney became UPSCA's adviser in 1946. I think the LCM (Love, Courtship, and Marriage) series was also inaugurated that year. We had a monthly Mass, and annual retreat (absolute silence; initially, one day; then, in Diliman, three days). We also had several lecture series (of which LCM was repeated annually and had the biggest attendance). We had a choir — conducted by *Prof. Antonio Molina*, with *Mitos Sison, Nali Arvisu*, and *Reli Estanislao* as soloists — that gave several performances. (I remember the Mass by Vitadini, which we sang at the US Army Chapel at Christmas time, and also at the Ateneo Chapel.) Father Delaney was "sintonado," so I can remember only one Mass that he "sang" (sic) with us.

We had a basketball league (the UPSCA Inter-Color League, with teams like the Reds, Blues, Greens, Purples, etc.) complete with their own cheering sections. *Mel Panlasigui, Bob Charnetsky*, and I started an UPSCA newsletter, which with the help of others (*Nick Balderrama, Iquing Bonto, Joe Espino*, et al.) became the ACTION ("published occasionally by the grace of God"), first in mimeograph (Gestetner) form, later printed. Father Delaney lent us the facilities of his office (at the time he was Dean of Students at Ateneo), which we used to take over after office hours.

We wrote a constitution and organized the college memberships into chapters, led by chapter chairmen. We had "socials" (dances that we strove to make inexpensive and enjoyable, fun! I remember a group of boys whose "assignment" was to see to it that there were no "wall flowers", that every girl got to dance — (we were "boys" and "girls" in that era.) We had excursions (to Tagaytay, Los Baños, etc.). We had Christmas Package Drives for the less fortunate.

We had catechetical groups, the most famous (notorious?) of which was the group led by *Luis Paterno* and the (mostly) Engineering boys (*Gasty Ortigas, Pins Peña*, et al.) who gave religious instruction to the juvenile inmates of Welfareville in Mandaluyong. (Several juveniles escaped once, which the rest of us attributed to diligent instruction by the Welfareville crew.) We even rented and showed movies, to foster the idea of decency in film-viewing. We also said the Rosary together at the Ateneo Chapel during the month of October, and participated as a group in various religious events (Christ the King processions, Eucharistic Congresses, etc.).

During our Padre Faura days, Father Delaney was our priest (for our Masses) and our lecturer (ANY lecture he gave, on ANY topic, was always "full house" or "SRO"). The only other activities in which he participated were the annual basketball game between UPSCA students and faculty, Father playing with the faculty, and once he wrote a radio script about St. Paul (our UPSCA patron, I think) that UPSCA produced under his direction. I remember hearing rebroadcasts of it (it was that good) but I don't remember which station did it.

When UP moved to Diliman in January, 1949, Father's role changed. He continued as UPSCA's spiritual adviser, of course, doing what he used to do for us in Padre Faura. But now there was a Catholic community in the (at the time) "boondocks" of Diliman. Students and faculty lived on campus, but the nearest church was in Kamuning. So Father became the de facto chaplain (parish priest, really) of the community. When we first moved to Diliman, a large number of volunteers cleaned up the old Army chapel (which had actually been used as a stable by nearby farmers when the US Army left the premises but before the UP took over). We shared the chapel with the Protestant student group and Protestant faculty. During the first months, Father would come (from Ateneo) early Sunday morning, about 5:30 to hear confessions before Mass, which he celebrated at 6:00. Then he would say a second Mass at 7:30 or 8:00. The Protestants would hold their worship service at 10:00 or 11:00.

When the confession lines grew longer and longer, Father decided he had to come to Diliman on Saturday afternoon and stay overnight. So, with his own financing, he got a contractor friend to refurbish the chapel, with a new sanctuary, new altar with communion rail, and offices and sleeping quarters in the back (I think he even finagled the Ateneo chapel's old pews). Then Father started to come

Saturday afternoons, staying over to Sunday morning. His meals were taken care of by the community, Father rotating from one family to another. During special times, like Easter or Christmas, he brought other priests to help him, usually *Fr. Gough*. The two priests would conduct 3-hour Seven Last Words services on Good Friday that were unforgettable. They would also conduct 1-day, later 3-day, closed retreats that were spiritual high points for UPSCA. UPSCA continued its many activities, but now with the Mass and the chapel at its center. UPSCA activities blended with Catholic community activities, and Father Delaney was our leader, our "meddler-in-chief".

When Father was relieved of his post as Dean of Students, he was not given any new assignment right away, so he took advantage of the hiatus to live in Diliman and offer Mass every day. We finally had a resident priest! We quickly became a de facto parish. Father even obtained permission for baptisms and (in the beginning) 12 marriages (later increased to 20). These were the Delaney couples.

In 1950, *Luis Paterno* became UPSCA president. In 1951, I married *Lydia Villareal* and started teaching at UP (Psychology). I don't remember who succeeded Louie Paterno; could have been *Gasty Ortigas*. (I remember *Fenny Hechanova* as Liberal Arts chapter chairman, among many others). My family and I left for the US in mid-1953 for me to do graduate studies in psychology at the University of Minnesota. We heard once or twice from Father — describing his plans for a new chapel with a radical round design. We received his invitation to attend the Inaugural Mass a few days after he died. Mother Donahue of the Cenacle Sisters, Father's good and old friend (from childhood) who was here in Minneapolis, broke the sad news to us.

We returned to the Philippines that same year (1956). *Father Ortiz* was the new UPSCA adviser and UP chaplain. *Gus de Leon* was UPSCA president, assisted ably by *Fely Villareal*. The Chapel of the Holy Sacrifice had been built. But Father Delaney was not there. Late the following year, September 1957, we left for the US and stayed here for good. With a growing family (four kids by then, seven all told) and no household help, we lost contact with UPSCA.

Rene V. Dawis, Professor Emeritus, Department of Psychology, University of Minnesota.

-o-o-o-o-o-

May Minoza-Gatchalian writes about Gus de Leon:

Gus, who had his high school in UP Diliman and had, therefore, been with Fr. Delaney since that time is one among the few fortunates who practically grew up with Fr. Delaney. Gus was the moving spirit of UPSCA at UP High and he later

became UPSCA President when he went to College (Business Administration). He graduated just a year or two ahead of me and missed Gerry by just a few years. But he must have totally missed you and your batch. But considering that *Tigi* and *Enteng Batas* spanned through several generations, we feel that us older folks are also virtually linked with all of you in the younger generation. Besides, with *Noel* and *Angge Soriano* and *Sonia* and *Ely Alampay* around, we all feel that the cement that binds UPSCA from the Delaney time and onwards can remain strong, provided that the new generation can continue to feel his influence and even his presence for a long time.

Gus kind of wraps it up:

Only each UPSCAN can judge for himself if Upsca made a difference. For me I am content that as we write each other by e-mail today, this would not be without Upsca. When I think of *Gasty Ortigas* , when I see *Ed Olaguer*, when I meet those who joined the religious order and those who left for their own reasons, I still see and feel the influence of Upsca.

One of my involvement is with ERDA Foundation for street children. We are supporting 26,000 children to be in school instead of roaming the streets. We have a tuklasan house where children who work in the streets can be provided with shelter, food, and a chance to be rehabilitated.

We have a livelihood project in Smoky Mountain. We have a vocational high school with now 800 students so street children who make it to high school can have a chance to learn skills that can give them a chance to change the course of their lives. Guess who are the Loyalists of ERDA: *Susan Villareal* (Pharmacy) and *Fely Marzan* (Law), Upscans of our generation.

Gus de Leon is second from right. Wife Toti is at left. Taken at the Tigi's "Centennial" party January 3 at his San Juan house. Katipunero is Ely Alampay. Others are Nora Barcelona, Sonia Alampay, Angge Soriano and Tigi.

Action & Reaction ! ! !

Letters, faxes, e-mail, anecdotes, conversations....

From a card of Clemencia "Babynats" Natividad in Canada:

My brother's son got married, and Mama and I flew back home. It was a happy reunion with 2 brothers and 2 sisters, nephews and nieces. **Georgina Reyes** saw me in Greenhills and arranged an impromptu get-together with **JOng** and **Elmar Perez**. Alas, 2 hours was not enough to catch up on sights and sounds, the wonder and feelings that have popped our way. To date, I do not have a personal computer at home; at work, a memo has been sent warning employees personal use of e-mail is subject to discipline. No loss at all, I'm no fan of e-mail nor computers (though I've taken courses galore). The Y2K bug, heard of it? The Canadian Army is embarked on a 14 month preparation to handle looting and rioting due to the predicted breakdown in electricity, water and food distribution, loss of heating, communication failure, etc. The Canadian navy will position ships to serve as power generators, field hospitals and soup kitchens.

From an email exchange:

Johnny wrote: **Mercy Abad** started a grammatical error by calling me an "abandonado" for leaving the Philippines "just because Erap became President." I just received a letter from **Lindus Carreon-Arambulo**, and she has picked up Mercy's error and perpetuated it by calling me the same name. Granting for the sake of argument but without conceding that I have indeed forsaken the home country for the moment, the correct term should be "abandonista," or better yet, "abandonero."

Danny chimed in: How about "abandonador"? (Rhymes with aparador!)

From Lili to Johnny after his trip to Washington, DC from NJ:

Just a bit of warning to anyone who ventures into the Washington, D.C. area. The city and its environs developed out of a plan that started with the colonial group of George Washington et al., hence the streets, avenues, and circumferential by-ways (back here it's called the Beltway) are not arranged in the grid formation of most cities. This was intended to confuse the enemies of the revolution (i.e., the redcoats). Unfortunately, they also confuse the friends of the revolution, particularly those who like to hang out in taverns and imbibe an extra dose of Virginia ale. Mila and Johnny, glad to know you made it back safely!

Johnny's reply to Tony's commiseration:

Yes, thanks, Tony. Just wish to clarify that — (a) I wasn't going in the opposite direction. I was following the ring road the correct way but missed the turnoff and overshot, inadvertently continuing full circle. (b) The lost hour wasn't for trying to make a U-turn on the freeway, but the actual time spent travelling the unnecessary distance along the ring road and then catching up the lost distance (via a more direct radial route) after I had realized my error. (The circumferential road of Washington DC is a bit bigger than say the ring road of Paris, which is so compact you can see the Eiffel tower from almost any point on it.)

Sonia Valenzuela-Quast's revelation that Brazil has more than 100 Filipinos:

. . . then in September, we went to the Pantanal - this is somewhat like the Everglades of Florida - to visit some experiment stations of EMBRAPA, govt organ for agro-industrial research and development. Early in December we went to Brasilia to visit some other experiment stations . . . Last Sunday, Dec 20th, we had the **annual Filipino get-together in Vale Verde**. There must have been somewhere near **100 participants**. It was lots of fun, there were plenty of games as well as food and the usual singing.

Excerpts from Malu's writeup of the January 6 party they held for visiting New Yorkers Vic Vitug and wife:

It was a party of five. **Vic** and his charming bedimpled wife **Vicky** Potenciano Vitug, **Tony Estrera**, **Oids** and myself. As planned our house was the meeting place. Lost no time and questioned them about how they met, etc. over chili-ed pistachio nuts while Oids insisted on picking oranges from our backyard to give the couple from NY a sampling of our Winter harvest. So Oids packed them a box of *calamansi, suha, cherimoya* (*atis* counterpart), and oranges to go. Had I not stopped Oids we would have waited "forever" for him as he was on a rampage. Tony had been coaxing me about trying this new Pinoy place in Bellflower — *Handaan sa Nayon* — so there we went. The special for the night was "*Niladlad na Manok*" which I thought was already a catchy enticement for the palate. The Pinoy dialect descriptors by themselves were conversation starters, I say. We had *kinilaw na tanguigui* and squid as appetizers, then we had this beef ribs (the name escapes me at this time of writing — Tony, *ano na ba nga ang tawag nung maitim-itim na karne na yun* that Oids was insisting we save the bones for our... hmmmmm... chihuahuas at home????), *kare-kare, pancit, garlic rice*, etc. It was really *masarrrrap*. I thought si **Manny Castillo** lang ang connoisseur *sa pagkain*. The best part wasn't the food. One could sing on a *karaoke* machine with a list of songs one could choose and request to sing him/herself. There was this DJ-singer named **Alex** who can switch voice to sound like **Alexandra**! We thought at first he was lipsynching a "she". To qualm everybody's queries, just shared my thought — bisexual voice, I whispered. Alex did have a voice range that is remarkably soprano to bass! The best part wasn't Alex of course. It was these two singers from New York who each sang "*Bulaklak*" and "*Araw-araw, Gabi-gabi*" — none other than *Vic* and *Vicky*. Of course the agreement after that was that we weren't leaving the "scene" unless everyone in the party of five would have a rendition. So Oids sang an old favorite, "*Greenfields*" and I sang "*Tell Me*" - a *Joey Albert Pinoy* song, and as to **Tony**, he refused to sing and "threatened" us that he was the one holding the car keys and rationalized that he does not even sing in the privacy of his shower room! We attempted to write Tony's name in a piece of paper and hand it to the DJ. But by that time, there were more brave people who had turned in their little white paper requests to the DJ. Tony must have been praying so hard! He got away with not singing! We had dessert at home and sat around munching on fried *dilis* and *adobong* peanuts over *calamansi* juice till Vic and Vicky said their time zone had gone off. So, there, Ferngil. Got too carried away with my story, huh? Tell Johnny — the loop isn't dead. You're back! How was RP? Your turn.

Susan Po's rejoinder:

So next time you visit S.F. - bring me some *cherimoyas* and *guavas*! I only pig out on exotic fruits. . . but that "Handaan" restaurant sounds like a place where NOT to bring **Manny Castillo** - puhleeze! Hello to everybody - I might just pop up there for the UPSCA reunion on the 30th of January - if you promise to produce **J.E. Alzona**. (I'm still searching for the music sheet he wrote for me entitled "Samba da Susana".)

From Gani Cruz:

Pls send my birthday greetings to **J E Alzona**. When is he going to have an e-mail address? (Or is he already on the loop?).

From a letter from Nim Gonzalez in Santa Clara, CA:

Now about the Institute: The basic insight of the ICTS (Institute of Communications, Technology and Spirituality) is this. There has been, still on-going, a communication revolution brought about by technological developments: from personal computers in the 1980s to the internet five years ago. The evolution in technology and subsequently in communication is exponentially growing. What is happening to the human spirit? Is it also changing? If it is, in what direction? Is it "growing" positively or negatively. Tielhard de Chardin predicted as early as 1955, through his writings, that the world is evolving from a biosphere (life), to a noosphere (mind/knowledge), and to a Christosphere (moral/spiritual). ICTS is investigating if indeed there is a growth in the Christosphere . . brought about by the internet. The VCR machines in the early 80s proliferated because of the x-rated tapes. So did the growth of cable. The internet has its own x-rated webs. But more things are going on there these days. Is there a direction in the growth of the internet? Is the email short-circuiting communication so that the dichotomy between form and content is disappearing. These are some of the issues ICTS is mulling over. We offer seminars on this topic and invite people who are interested on these issues to dialogue with us. Take care and give my regards to all.

From an email of Pete Tandoc in Chicago:

It's nice to hear from old friends. I did go to Thailand on scholarship in 1966, went back to the Philippines in 1968, got married in 1970, begot 3 kids with **Merle** (Guillermo), a nurse from PGH, and came here to the U.S. in 1973. We begot another daughter here in 1981. All my 3 older kids are done and on their own. Two are getting married this coming year, and the youngest will be entering college. My wife, my youngest daughter, and I, are members of a covenant community here in Michigan, the *Bukas Loob Sa Diyos Covenant Community*, which was our cause for spiritual renewal and a constant source of spiritual strength. **Jimmy Valera**, from Toronto, who gave me your number, is also a member of the same community. Anyway, nice to hear from you. I will keep in touch. Merry Christmas again, and God Bless All of You. A.M.D.G.

Email from Danny Uy of the mid 70's:

Thanks for the Newsletter. It was a wonderful read and reminded me a lot of the days at UP with my friends at UPSCA. I noticed that the LOOP uses CC to get their email to everybody. Ever think about setting up a mailing list? I can set it up for you if you want. I look forward to seeing you and the rest on Jan 30. I'll bring some old pictures.

From Mercy Abad in Manila:

We have to keep NVM in our prayers. They are going to do a probe on his brain tumor which is acting up again. He has not started dialysis yet but it looks like this is the way to go. Despite his physical problems NVM is a cheerful sight, always with a bright and happy word for all. I like his spirit.

(Note: NVM Gonzalez was in UCLA for a semester. He and Narita met a number of LA Upscans at his lectures, parties in his honor, and film exhibit. He returned to the Philippines mid December.)

Most of the younger set of Upscans never knew Fr. Delaney. And many of them got to love and revere later-day chaplains. Here is a write up from Malu Barrios-Garcia:

While rummaging through a heap of photos I chanced upon a photo that brings back memories of a person whom many an UPSCAN remembers, knew, and loved — **Bishop Felix Perez**, circa late-60's to early 70's. I remember him as Father Pea, who in UPSCA days, was rumored to be a Monsignor. No one ever really thought the title mattered - at least not to me, while I was still in my teenage years; it didn't mean like I had to kiss a ring or anything like that or be reminded of his status. A red monsignor "cap" he didn't don. To me, he was plainly - chaplain of UP Chapel of the Holy Sacrifice - the priest to consult whenever my proverbial Catholic (school) guilt came back to haunt me as I set foot on this nonsectarian (whatever that meant) university called UP.

I fondly called him Father Pea or FP for short, even after he became bishop. I remember the day I copied others as they kissed his blood-colored stone-ring that was perhaps worn only once – on the day that he got installed at the Manila Cathedral, as Bishop of Imus, Cavite. FP had several traits I admired but what was most remarkable about FP was his piety, humility and his sense of simplicity. It was the era that most of us contemplated on — whether or not we had the "calling" to the priestly or religious life — so to frequent the Chapel, the rectory, the library and the Delaney Hall was the thing to do for "discernment"…eat, laugh, pray and sing and hang around with the ELPS clique. In the meantime also hanging around FP's office by the library was a Mass Server named **Eddie Garcia** (who later was given a new *bansag* by UPSCAN, **Girlie Alzona Valbuena** – Oidee as in cartoon Popeye language, or **Oids**, for short). FP took no time in matching me, a sacristeen, to a Mass server — naming Oids as his "candidato". Every other contender was a thumbs down by FP. Oids and I did go steady and every question I had was consulted with FP's spiritual direction. It was an up close and personal relationship between him and us which revealed to us a man who had compassion for the poor with he himself living a life that was to the bare essentials. Oids and I, through five years of going steady, saw in FP, a true servant of God, wearing a pair of overworn shoes, that, if not for the holes, he would not think of replacing. Our years of guidance and consultation through love, courtship and marriage allowed us to gift him with a total of two pairs of shoes. FP did marry us and even while Cavite became his residence, he and his faithful driver, Joaquin, drove this old beat-up VW and took the time to visit with us whenever he was in Manila. (Note: Joaquin died of a broken heart one week after FP's demise.) Oids and I kept our connection with him through joyous and sad occasions, trekking the highways to Imus, Cavite, to have our children baptized, or visiting with him and letting him be the third party over unsettled conflicts we might have had. Always, FP had one resounding advice, to make that "leap in the dark" whenever we had major decisions in meeting life's crisis. I used to argue against him on this because I said one had always to make a leap in the light and not in the dark.

In '82, Oids and I, with our three children, left the Philippines and migrated to the U.S. A couple of months later, I got my first job at Neiman Marcus with UPSCAN, **Susan Po**. I came home from work one evening and got a message that FP was in SF. Apparently he had been looking for Oids and me but was leaving that evening to return to Manila. There was no time to wait for Oids who was out on his sales job; so I bravely took a cab and paged FP at the SF airport. There he was at the waiting area. How precious to have had a chance to visit and consult with him again.

In December of 1990, I was in the thick of preparing for my masteral comprehensive exams when I heard FP's familiar voice on the phone. Could Oids and I pick him up at this place where he was staying? He said he wanted to say Mass at our house and visit with the family. I asked UPSCAN (whom we consider as family) **Ofie Peñaflorida Aid**, and her husband, **Ken**, who lived not too far away, to bring the wine for the Mass. How comforting that FP was there on my own father's death anniversary to say Mass at our house!

I was aware that FP has had a history of heart disease and yet I wanted to prepare him a meal fit for a bishop. So I made this complete pochero dish which FP ate with such gusto, that made me feel guilty afterwards.

I knew he had undergone a heart surgery and asked about his pacemaker. He said that when the time comes when the battery runs out, that would be his final call. He had a distant gaze. This was the last visit he was going to make, he said. Two months later, we got word from Manila. Bishop Felix Perez had passed away on February 29th, 1991 on a leap day! I thought about him. I thought about his words. LEAP in the DARK, Malu. Tearfully, I finally understood what he meant all along. FP, you mean, LEAP of FAITH, didn't you? (Oids and I request the reader to say a prayer for Bishop Felix Perez on his eighth death anniversary on February 29th).

From Vic Vitug:

I am attaching another UPSCA picture. This one has Father Jess in it (Sorry, don't have a date for you).

Do you remember Efren Bautista? He was in the other Choir picture I sent to you. He is in New York too and just had a spinal operation some two weeks ago. He had problems with his lower spine and the surgeons had to support some vertebra with titanium devices. I can't recall what they call the procedure. Anyway, my wife and I brought copies of the newsletter last week and he was very happy to receive them. He said he had quite a few Upsca pictures which could be used and he said he would write some of the guys. I told him I could send e-letters for him if he wanted.

Errata to the 1960 picture in the previous issue: #13 was Rodney Baquiran, not the younger brother Rex. #7 was Randy David, and not Roly Mesa. Johnny Reyes says #11 could be Manny Pornillos.

Volunteered by José Alzona, literally "before" & "after" shots. At left is a 1980 picture of Baby Natividad, an unidentified friend, her sis Menchu, Bing Ferrer and Joe. Taken at Joe's apartment in Maryland. On right is Joe, in a 1998 pose at Danny's house, looking like The Great Gatsby.

In an earlier email, Sonia Valenzuela-Quast mentioned about a picture of us in a tree. She continues: I have just found the picture. It is very faded. I am sending it to you anyway. See if you can do anything about it. It was taken on Oct 1, 1961, in Parañaque, an acquaintance party of the Engineering chapter. I am sending you another picture which I find very funny: Lenny Abellera seems to be giving (I forgot his name) a scolding. It was taken on the grounds of the Delaney Hall. There must have been a game or something. My cousin Charito (Sari) is on the picture as well as Edna Rodrigues and me, of course. I like looking at these old pictures every now and then - sign of age, I know. *I sent a copy of the picture to Nim Gonzalez in SF to verify if it was him who was being scolded. His reply:* The profile is definitely like me. But one thing that I was not sure of is the watch on the left hand. I usually wear my watch on my right hand. That may really be Lennie Abellera, but from the scanned picture (the original could be clearer) it also looks like Lina Soliman Plantilla from NY.

Tigi's Centennial Party, in the forewarning words of Mercy:

Well, as it happened, Tigi went berserk why we were not too keen on his centennial photographic event i.e., everyone come in some Filipino attire (preferably centennial) to which occasion he would ask a professional Kodaker friend to make a pictorial for each family and for the entire group. I forget the name of this friend but it sounded like we could not afford his services if we contracted him professionally. Since there were not too many free days left for everyone, we decided that the January 3 affair [party for Danny] coincide with Tigi's brainchild. So Danny, I am warning you. Come as Basilio or as an insurrecto whatever. Actually, some of the guys do not like the idea but Tigi says "*Batukan yung mga umu-ungol-ungol*" (which means JOng, the loudest). Most of the girls like it though. So this means we will have the affair at Tigi's place from early afternoon to *sawa*. We would have wanted from lunch up to night but nobody wants to go out at noon dressed up like that. Besides, they say it is not a good time for photography.

Danny's rejoinder after the fact:

Anyway, all I can say is that it was a fun party. I took this group picture since the photographer was late and Tigi was scared people would start leaving (or the makeup would start melting?). Let me identify just the "matrons", not the daughters. *Front row L-R:* Jessie Javellona, Mimi Pasicolan, Nora Barcelona, Susan Martin. *Back row:* Merle Tan, Angge Soriano, Naida Rivera, Toti de Leon, Sonia Alampay, Bernie Muller, Medy Cruz and Mercy Abad.

DETAILED MAILING LIST - deleted

UPSCA *Alumni Association Newsletter*

Staleletters   Nobrainers   Portrayals

A M D G   Vol 2, Num 10   2nd quarter, 1999

THE TRIBE INCREASES AS OLD MEETS YOUNG

No, this is not about the Woodstock Anniversary. It's about the latest Upsca party January 30 at Malu's house, as described first by Danny then corrected by Malu in an email exchange:

It was like "*the old meeting the young*". There was this group of guys who were younger brothers of those in our generation: **Jemz Valera**, **Nilo Cruz** and **Lallie de Vera**. It was another in their group, **Danny Uy**, who gave me their addresses, and so I had mailed off to them early December the flyer for the party. Anyway, **Fred Valera**, **Rene Cruz**, **Joe de Vera** and **Danny Uy** all came together.

In the flyer, I had asked for old pictures. Indeed, many brought old pictures, mementos, etc. **Susan Po**, who flew all the way from San Francisco, brought her Upsca scrapbook. But unfortunately, the scanner at **Oids** and **Malu**'s computer conked out and we couldn't record any of them, except for the pictures that **Ernie** had: we slipped off to our house 3 miles away and scanned them, and printed blowups. Only then did we realize that in one of those early pictures, **Elizabeth Zaraspe-Yoo** was shown grinning. Even she herself didn't realize it when she saw Ernie's original pic.

Anyway, the food was good and plentiful. One of the rarer treats was specially made "laing" from Bicol, compliments of **Nina Los Baños** (unknowingly). When I went home last month, Nina asked her folks to prepare a whole styropor box of frozen "laing", which I brought back, then split with Nina when she came over from Las Vegas 2 weeks ago. Since the party was potluck, and Lisa and I were running out of time to prepare some dish, we just steamed our cache of the delicacy.

Johnny Balaoing as usual led in the singing. **Julz** accompanied on the guitar and his son complimented it further on the organ. Later on, **Angel** and **Stella Sta Maria** led the group in line dancing, cha-cha, etc. There even was a ladies choice dance, to coach those shy guys unto the floor.

When we started singing "An Army of Youth", Malu printed out the wording from that recent email exchange wherein **Liliosa** had asked for the words. Surprisingly, an older brother of Lisa, visiting from NJ (whom we picked up at

From Danny Uy's digital camera, *L to R:* Upscans Danny, Johnny Balaoing, Beth Zaraspe-Yoo, Lisa Señeris-Gil and *sitting*, her brother Ramon (guest). At Malu's January 30 party.

the airport an hour earlier and brought over with us), knew the song. He had been in UP for a year during Delaney's time.

The newslet [num 9] deals a lot about Fr. Delaney. I just mailed out copies to about half the US locals, and I should complete the rest by tomorrow. As for those in the Philippines, **Ofie** and **Ken Aid** are leaving for Manila Thursday, and they probably can bring over the sets, for **Mercy** to distribute. A funny thing was that in the newslet, I had included a roster of Upsca presidents, with pictures accompanying some of the names. I had an '80s picture (I got from **Lolly Aquino**) of a homecoming party group, one of whom looked like **Oca Palabyab**, but I wasn't too sure. But I scanned it anyway and captioned it as him. Only when the younger ones verified that indeed it was Oca, did I breathe easier. Otherwise, another erratum on the next issue.

Now, all of us are looking forward for the next LA Upsca "happening". So what say you? Shall we have a camping or picnic come warmer weather, or another party perhaps mid April or so? Is any Eastcoaster coming this way? Perhaps we should coordinate.   *Danny*

-o-o-o-o-

Malu quickly added:

Erratum: Julz Tocong's (UP Los Baños) hubby, **Del**, was the one playing the guitar. (**Jessie Pangilinan** AKA, Ms. Conservative, got to rest this time from playing the piano to give way to Del and Julz son, **DJ**, senior high schooler). Noteworthy are new UPSCA "singers" who joined in — **Lisa Filler** of the Cathechists Committee (under Chairman **Josie Angeles**, UPSCA Pres **Jimmy Salazar**'s era) had a couple of UPSCA ditties to share besides "An army of youth" — such as a chant like "I've got the Upsca spirit deep in my head, I've got it, etc." and another one I forget at time of writing. **Bing Pascual Santos** too joined in, and Beth Zaraspe Yoo. Of course the usual old time singers joining lead singer **Johnny B** were **Manny Castillo** and moi (Malu) singing our tonsils out. It made Manny sweat big drops of sweat which made some of us laugh. Didn't know singing is equivalent to a workout, Manny! Danny, while you and **Lisa** were at the airport, you missed the little game we played which was — that each one had to come up to someone he/she didn't know in the party and learn at least five things about the other person

The newcomers, *L-R*: Rene Cruz, Joe de Vera, and Fred Valera.

At January 30 party in Malu's place: Bing Pascual-Santos, Rose Lacebal-Engay, guest Randy Perry and another newcomer Lisa Filler.

so this made everyone feel relaxed and meet someone from a different batch. I think I can still remember at least four things about **Joe de Vera** . . he's UPSCA batch 65, graduated in 69, was a Mass Server and also was in the Productions Committee! Danny, you were smart to have thought of making sure I provide each one with a nametag. It served its purpose coz *the tribe has increased* and my having to write each name on each tag made me remember each person's name.

We had nominated **Angel Santa Maria** to be the D. I. D. (Dance Instructor Daw) and beauteous wife **Estela** and they did a dance exhibition of swing and the tango. **Bing** Pascual too was another Tango partner to Angel and boy, the double dipping dips made everyone cheer and swoon. One thing we forgot though was to take a photo of all those present. We made sure that we took a good shot of the array of food. **Ken Aid**, **Ofie**'s hubby, commented that this is the most varied of all the potlucks — international cuisine.

We had Korean, American, Filipino, and Chinese food. A basket of home-grown guavas brought by Angel and Estela were hidden from the camera and from eyesight specially from **Susan** who had asked if I could still find her some guavas like the ones I gave her in November. Not in January, I told her! **Ernie P**, as per your concern about having to coordinate what food to bring, turned out great despite no attempts by me at coordinating. The pancit you brought from your Chinese "neighborhood restaurant" was deeelicious and it matched every dish on the table, don't you think?

Danny, I already asked Ofie about taking the newsletters to Manila. Last but not the least thanks to **Manny Castillo** who donated $50 to sponsor the newletters' production and mailing cost. And of course to you, Danny, who painstakingly put the newslet together for everyone's reading enjoyment. I know that you pushed yourself into finishing the newslet in time for the party. *Mainit pa* when you brought them over. A million thanks!

Malu

Reactions from the younger ones:

It is only now I can reply to last Saturday's Reunion! Anyway, to go with the flow, $10 for gas, $10 for the potluck we brought but being with UPSCANS again was PRICELESS!!!!!!!!!!!!

We hope we can also get some of our generation in the next Reunion!!!!

Fred Valera

First, thanks for that wonderful experience last night. It brings back old memories that are always pleasant. The pictures that I took with my digital camera are ready. Each is 120K to 160K in size. I can email them one at a time to you or I can set up a web page where all pictures can be accessed by every one with an Internet connection. Let me know if you prefer email but I think I'll go ahead and set up that web page. Regards.

Danny Uy

A few days later:

As Danny Gil's previous email mentioned, I've prepared a web page that for now has the pictures I took during the party at Malu's place. Please visit it at **http://www.aceja.com/upsca**.

Danny Uy

So all you cyberfreaks, log on, enter cyberspace and see more of Upscans in action at above site.

–o–o–o–o–

NEWS FROM MANILA

Re the Delaney Archives, Gus de Leon's email prompted this report to all:

Hello everybody, here's excerpts from Gus's email. Bottom line is that:

1) if you have anything to donate for the Delaney archives, you can do that now and be assured that there is a ready repository, and

2) submission of writeups for the forthcoming book is end of April.

Gus' email excerpts:

We had a good meeting this morning at the residence of **Tessie Daza**. The good news, Tessie Daza was able to get **Sally Arlante**, the archivist of the U.P. Library on board our projects. In general terms she will be willing to receive the memorabilla of Fr. Delaney in the U.P. Library under a deed of donation for the documents to U.P. She will organize, index for reference, file and safekeep the documents in the archives of the U.P. Library. There will be no specific Delaney section in the archive, instead the materials will be filled under existing classifications like Era of President Tan. So the Fr Delaney papers during that period will be with this file.

So as not to create any confusion, we have asked her to write down the terms, conditions, procedures she requires for the donation and to outline to use the way they propose to handle the materials donated to them.

Then he emailed a picture, shown below, of Fr. Delaney's bust, now all surrounded

by a pond and rock garden. This calls to mind an earlier exchange:

From Vyva Aguirre:
You might be interested to know that the Delaney bust is now surrounded by a small lagoon and what could pass for a rock garden. It's really nice and I enjoy looking at it each time I pass the Chapel.

Danny to Vyva:
When I took pics January, I stepped right up to the pedestal. Now, one would have to be able to walk on water to do that! Reminds me of the joke about Jesus at the tempest: He told the disciples "Oh ye men of little feet."

*Out of the blue, an email appeared with the screaming heading: LAZARUS RESURRECTED. It was **Ramon Casas** in France, our good ol' buddy and fellow **Madhatter**. So I passed it on to the others which of course prompted a whole slew of replies. Trouble is, after the initial hoopla, he disappeared. No reply as yet. Here is his email en toto and some excerpted exchanges:*

Dear dear Lisa and Danny,

First of all my E mail or rather my son Alexis' E mail (he understands computers a lot more than me; after all computers are not part of my culture!)

alexis@cybercable.tm.fr

Well anyway, thanks for the last Newsletter (got it right now and I'm indeed determined to answer *tout de suite*) and for the previous ones that really were heartwarming.

Last spring I got a letter from **Joe Alzona** and I got to talk to him by phone. He was in CANNES for the festival and I think he was hunting for a producer who would hire him for his next film. *Il va être très connu.*

It's been eons and eons since I last saw or heard of the **Madhatters** and the other more normal UPSCANS.

I felt bad for **Gerry** and **Fredie** (anyway when I think of him I cannot help saying to myself *babatukan at duduraan kita*, such expression having been patented as my best contribution for the enrichment of Tagalog)

As for me, I'm about to retire for good (In fact I started retiring since I first left Manila).

In my splendid isolation I will definitely have more time to write for the News letter. So in a years time the screens of all the other Upscans will be bombarded regularly *avec la culture française qui reste une des plus supérieures!* You still remember, I'm sure, of my CULTO Doctrine. I pester my French friends with my insisting that human beings are not worth such qualification if they remain INCULTO.

I last talked to Lisa and was able to give you my new address. Please take note of the right spelling: 27 Quai Zorn, 67000 STRASBOURG, FRANCE. My

phone: area code: 03.88 number: 35.49.54. We in France do not aggregate numbers as it seems Americans do. We sort of prefer splitting things (very Cartesian style of *raisonnement*). Split, analyze and come to a new conclusion which should immediately by questioned and so on.

I'm sending you pictures Christmas '98 vintage. You'll get a glimpse of Marie-Christine (who met Gerry in 1982, you were gone years before), Alexis (20 years) and Ghislain (13 years) They enjoyed the food back in Manila last August 98. I think they are convinced of one Filipino value: take a cab or rent a car even if your destination is fifty yards away (air conditioned of course).

Barong Tagalog is not really fitted for wintry weather, so I experienced!

The fourth picture was taken at the Blue Mountains (1 hour drive from Sydney). I insisted visiting my Australian buddy who was so glad to see again his kin.

This is all by now (good for you because my brain is going to pieces, judging from what I'm writing).

Bons baiser to all of you.

Mon CASAS

-o-o-o-o-

Immediate reactions:

From Lennie Abellera Blair:
Indeed, it's like rising from the "what?" Welcome to the LOOP! After sooooo many years, it is such joy to connect again! Mon, you might remember that every time you came to our house in Baguio, my mother would sit you down at the piano and have you play "Un Suspiro." Great, fond memories. Hope your kids got those genes for music!
Take care and God bless.

Rory Abrera:
What a NEAT surprise to hear from Mon Casas! So glad to know he is living in Strasbourg, France, something that doesn't surprise me at all. I remember how he loved French and spoke it to near perfection in college. Is there a way we can see those pictures he mentions? Welcome to the loop, Mon!

Tony Estrera:
Mon, your CULTO is certainly welcome and enjoy the best insults you can possibly get from the loop.

JOng (first touché?):
Hi, Danny, Mon Casas looks wonderfully preserved. He's kept his hair, his complexion, his emaciation.

This exchange brings to mind more about Mon. How he'd irritate the romantic in us by playing Chopin's Etude in E Flat (No Other Love) first in one key then he'd

transpose it to the next higher key for the second stanza, and so on. Or how, as also a Spanish speaker, he bandied about a fictitious person by the name of Dolores Fuertes de Barriga. And as Tigi loves to relate, Mon and two of his other brothers got standing ovations when each graduated from UST as summa cum laudes, all at the same time. That was before he came to UP for yet another degree.

-o-o-o-o-

This account is about another Resurrecto, not spontaneous. Malu was searching for some old friends. Danny to Malu:
I, too have no clue about **Emily Bacaltos**, except that her sis Gwen passed away in Florida some years back. Here's 2 addresses I got from a web search in Florida. No emails, just tel numbers. You might want to call as a shot in the dark. The other year when **Tigi** was here, he traced some of his friends in a similar manner: I searched, got the tel numbers, and he started calling one by one.

Her reply:
This is unbelievable! From the 2 addresses and phone numbers you had sent me, I picked **Charito Bacaltos** because I sorta recall that name and sure enough, Charito is Emily's sister! I am still in a daze! **Emily Bacaltos Popp** has been a widow (with no child) since 1992, and is into mind/body (institute) like that of Deepak. Her email address is: visaka@worldnet.att.net We are completing the circle of "ELPS." Emily writes so she could be a contributor to our newslet.

Danny to Malu:
Give me a list [ELPS] of those you've made contact with already, and those still missing. Good article for the newslet.

Malu to Danny:
Jemz Valera, Jess Martinez, Vyva Aguirre, Girlie Alzona Valbuena, Emily Bacaltos — found or first heard from them thru the net. Then there are **Ruben Habito, Sue Po Rufino, Jemz Valera, Manny Castillo, Nonong Pedero, Ping Tan** who either have communicated by phone, email or by coming to America to visit. Then there are the incommunicado elps — **Tiny Anden, Cora Nievera, Bing Ferrer, Alex Cuejillo, Benny Mendoza, Benjie Vitasa, Beryl Silva, Vangie de Castro.** And **Gwen Bacaltos** who had passed away. And **Rudy Suaco**, who tendered his resignation from the ELPS, putting it down in writing, which we found ridiculously funny that he would "resign". This is really making me feel nostalgic. Girlie Alzona Valbuena emailed me and was so thrilled. I may be missing somebody on our list. **JOng** used to hang around with us especially when we'd go to Ma Mon Luk and other restaurants. Remember the "e" in the acronym "elps" stands for "eat" (tee-hee).

Ramon Casas in splendid isolation, France.

FICTION SECTION

Meeting Erap, *by Johnny Reyes, the master storyteller.*

When I read in the Philippine Daily Inquirer last Sunday that Erap was flying to Poughkeepsie, NY, to attend the funeral of his older brother, I said to Mila, why don't we go there too, so we can see our President. It would be a pity to miss this opportunity, when the place is within striking distance of our house.

But it's too far away, Mila said.

With a flourish I pulled out my brand-new $4.57 Rand McNally Atlas (purchased at Wal-Mart at $6.42 off the normal price) and showed Mila the route we had driven to Montreal last year. See, this is Route 87 which goes up through New York State all the way to the Canadian border. Poughkeepsie is at the bottom end of this highway, just above the New York/New Jersey border (well, give or take a few miles), and it is only a bit farther away than West Point. (I didn't tell Mila the total distance from our house to Poughkeepsie was more than a hundred miles.)

We don't know their address, Mila pointed out. (I had already looked for the name Emilio Ejercito on Switchboard.com, but he was not listed.)

Don't worry, I said, Poughkeepsie is not a big city. As you can see, it's just a blip on the map. We'll find Erap.

There's a snowstorm warning for this evening, Mila said.

As far as I know, the snow won't come until midnight. It's just past 2 p.m. now. We'll be back home at Belle Mead in plenty of time before the snow starts.

All right, Mila said, let's go!

By 3 p.m., Mila had packed a picnic supper, we had put on formal clothes, and we were ready to go. Just before leaving, Mila called up one of her sisters, who had lived in Upstate New York sometime in the past, to ask about the route to Poughkeepsie. This particular sister does not use maps when she drives, but relies on landmarks. She said, just take 287 all the way, then when you pass a big bridge, you're in Poughkeepsie. But as usual, I had already planned our route in detail. Route 287 all the way until the New York border, and then it will change to Route 87. At Newburgh, turn right into Route 84, then left into Route 9, and then we should hit our target. (I could not help thinking, Route 9 passes within 20 miles of our house. In theory, we could just get on it here in New Jersey and it would take us all the way to our destination. But then, it would probably take two days, with all the traffic lights along that busy route.) Anyway, we were on our way. There was a steady drizzle, but it was pure water, not snow. No problem — rain, I can handle.

The traffic on Sunday afternoon was unusually light. Toll on Route 87. Soon we were at the famous bridge, which turned out to be on Route 84 and also had a toll. Immediately after the crossing, I saw directions to turn left on "Route 9D." This was too early, I thought — the map showed a few more miles before the turning. But I followed the sign anyway and turned left. I soon learned that 9D was not the same as 9, just a parallel route to it — but no harm done, because eventually it merged with Route 9 anyway.

Soon we saw commercial signboards indicating we were in Poughkeepsie. The city was not as small as I had imagined. We decided to head for the Business District ("Centrum" in Dutch), to look for Police Headquarters. Mila's sister had suggested that we inquire there. It was a sleepy, rainy Sunday afternoon, and there was only a desk sergeant on duty. I said we were from out of town, and we were looking for the house of Dr. Emilio Ejercito, who had just died and who was the brother of the Philippine President. The policeman didn't know.

Mila said did he have a telephone directory, and he brightened up. We went through the white pages but could not find any Emilio Ejercito. Then Mila remembered that the news item in the Inquirer had mentioned Dr. Ejercito being the head of a department in a hospital. So we looked up the list of physicians and surgeons in the yellow pages, and lo and behold! Dr. Emilio Ejercito! But the address listed was just the hospital, so we called up St. Francis from a pay phone at the Police Station to ask for his home address.

The lady who answered said Dr. Ejercito had just passed away, but sorry, she could not give out the information I wanted — might she know who she was speaking with? I replied that we were friends of the family, and would like to pay our respects. Well, she could give me the address of the church where the services would be held the following morning, or the address of the funeral home in Wappinger Falls where there would be a viewing from 7 to 9 that night. She said we just missed the 2 to 4 schedule. Why don't we get something to eat first, and then we would just be in time (It was 5:30 p.m. on my watch). Here's how to get there . . We said goodbye to the desk sergeant, who looked very happy that we had found what we wanted.

Back in the car, Mila and I reassessed our strategy. Our original plan was to just drop in at the house and then leave right away, so we could avoid the snowstorm, just in case it came earlier than predicted. We still didn't know where the house was. But then we realized that houses in the U.S., unlike in the Philippines, are not designed to accommodate hordes of visitors. Therefore, we were probably better off paying our respects at the funeral home. But we would have to follow the viewing schedule, and that would delay us by another hour and a half. Oh, what the heck. It was still raining water, not snow, and the route home was all freeway, which is the first thing the highway engineers clear when there is a snow storm. We didn't come all the way here to give up now. So we waited for 7 p.m.

When the Roberts & Straub funeral home opened to visitors, we were among the first to enter, and we queued to pray at the coffin, which was closed. There were plenty of photographs, though, around the coffin. I remembered that during an interview in Manila right after Erap was elected President, his mother had said that Erap was not her handsomest son — the older one who lived in the U.S. was handsomer. We could not help being curious, therefore. Next step was to offer our condolences to the American wife of the late doctor, to three of his four daughters who were present, and to his only son, who were standing in a line and who all looked pure American. But no sign of Erap.

To pass the time, Mila chatted with some of the other Filipino visitors, who turned out to be U.P. graduates. But sooner or later we had to go.

Just as we were about to leave, in walked Erap, in a black Chicago-style overcoat, with his wife and two of his sisters.

oOo

When we left the parking lot of the funeral home just past eight o'clock, there was already a minor traffic jam in the neighborhood. We noticed that a few snow flakes were starting to fall. Don't worry, I said to Mila, we'll be home before the snow storm.

Along our way, the snow drifted down continuously, but melted as it hit the ground (too warm). Traffic on the freeway was now getting very thin. By the time we got to the New Jersey border, the snowfall was so thick it felt like we were slicing through spaghetti (without tomato sauce). I never thought visibility could be reduced that much. But at least the snow was still not accumulating excessively on the road.

This started to change when we passed Morristown. Now the highway had a thick white coating except for twin grooves made by the few cars ahead of us. But since the snow was fresh and dry, the flakes were not slippery – yet.

After we left the freeway and entered Route 206 (my territory), the slush was already thick on the road. The snow plows were not yet out. We learned from the radio that the snow storm was actually coming from the southwest, so we were heading into it, and it was a few hours earlier than predicted. Our worry was that by now our driveway might be buried in snow, and we could not get into the garage. Then I noticed that whenever I braked, the car started to slide in strange directions. The lone car following me must have noticed it too, because after that happened to me a few times he maintained a respectful distance behind me – 30 car lengths!

Finally – home! We wrestled through eight inches of snow on the driveway, and finally ended up with the car in the garage – all covered with snow except for the windshield, but otherwise unscathed. I said to Mila, did you notice how scared I was earlier? I could sense Mila was dying to say I told you so, but she didn't say a word – at least until we were out of the car.

The funny thing about New Jersey weather is that two days later, the temperatures were in the fifties and the thick layer of snow on the ground was melting fast. We are beginning to miss winter already.

We also missed Erap's eulogy delivered at the funeral the following day (a working day).

-o-o-o-o-

Responses, responses:

Johnny is indeed a master storyteller. I would highly recommend that he write a book on any topic of his choice, maybe his memoirs(?) :-)
I wish I had his driving abilities during snow conditions. Fortunately, New Mexico does not get too much snow and due to our ever present sunny weather and high altitude (5000 ft above sea level), the snow melts fast and never stays too long on the ground.
Happy Spring to all!
Christie Kawal

Dear all [Beta Ep brods], I thought I should share this with you all, and might find it interesting and also *medyo may suspense pa, parang isang episode sa* TV. Cheers!
Alex Santos

What a narrative! Shades of Jack London or maybe even early Hemingway. But the best thing of all was that it was from Johnny Reyes. Thanks for sharing the narrative. I look forward to more of it. Definitely truth is more interesting than fiction, although this is not exactly the way the saying goes.
Erwin Gomez

As expected, the more irreverent of the Loop, i.e. Category 1, started the friendly insults:

Last Wednesday the Inquirer reported that Pilipinas Shell earned P1.6 B after losing P1.5 B the previous year. Must be some connection between this dramatic turnaround, and the retirement of this Shell executive who risks being frozen or rear-ended in a snowstorm, just to see Erap in a Chicago-style overcoat.
JOng

Wait a minute, wait a minute. Don't miscalculate the time frames. The turnaround happened during business year 1998 (Jan-Dec). Retirement date was actually not until end June. Therefore the last desperate efforts of this particular executive during his final six months to rehabilitate Shell and safeguard his niche in its company history must have been extremely effective.
Johnny

-o-o-o-o-

JOng cc'd us an email to a Manila Times staffer, which started a run of email exchanges:

Mr Ermin Garcia
The Manila Times

Dear Ermin,

Your friends at the Gerry Gil Foundation extend felicitations and best wishes on the occasion of President Erap Estrada's libel suit vs you and the rest of your crew.

If Gerry were alive, he'd be having a wicked time as usual, skewering Erap, Ronny Zamora, Jerry Barican and other lawyers and former journalists in Malacañang, though he may have had a few pithy comments as well on the Times' handling of the IMPSA-Napocor story.

All things considered, this retaliatory action by a man who is both the nation's chief executive and its principal joke should be regarded as a badge of honor. It will serve as a call to arms by the Fourth Estate, while providing entertainment to readers for months to come. Salud and give 'em hell!

Mon Pasicolan and Jimmy Ong

What was Erap's suit all about?
Christie

Hi, Christie.
Erap's suit is all about a P16 B power generation project of the National Power Corp, involving the rehab of three power plants in Caliraya, Botocan and Kalayaan and construction of a new power plant and spillway. The project was the subject of a spirited contest between a company owned by Eugenio Lopez Jr, with John Gokongwei as a minor participant, and the eventual winner, CBK Power, which is 40% owned by an Argentine firm called IMPSA. Big bucks, big controversy, big decision-makers involved, from FVR's time to Erap's.

The Manila Times reported that there were all sorts of backroom negotiations to revise this or that provision in the contract, and named Erap's executive secretary Ronny Zamora as one of the key brokers, and Erap himself as unwitting godfather.

What the Times failed to mention was that publisher Robina Gokongwei's father had a vested interest in torpedoing the IMPSA contract. Erap was pissed; he called Gokongwei "Intsik," (which he is), and said he didn't mind being called "bobo" (which he is), so long as you didn't call him a crook (which he ... well, never mind). Gokongwei, mindful that presidential ire can be hazardous to one's economic health, tried to apologize, but Erap ignored him and sued everyone in the Times. Zamora says he will do the same. Among those sued is Ermin Garcia Jr, who helped the Gerry Gil Foundation obtain Phil Press Institute administrative support for an editorial award in Gerry's name.
JOng

JOng, really appreciate the info on Eraps's lawsuit. It's amazing how contracts are negotiated and to what extent people will go through to win one, especially those that involve big bucks. Of course these situations exist everywhere including in our "Land of Enchantment", New Mexico!
Christie

Then, the punsters (aka cornballs) took over:

Can anybody help me. JOng wrote two emails in quick succession and I quote: "this Shell executive who risks being frozen or rear-ended in a snowstorm, just to see Erap in a Chicago-style overcoat" and again "Erap's suit is all about a P16 B power generation project."
My question: Is Erap's overcoat the same as his suit?
Duh-knee

Hi, Duh-knee, suits me, but Erap may claim he was miscoated.
JOng

The suit was filed because he was thin-skinned. The overcoat was skin-tight.
Johnny

-o-o-o-o-

*The Gerry Gil Foundation is a group of Gerry's friends headed by **Mon Pasicolan** who are promoting excellence in newspaper journalism by sponsoring writing contests.*

FUNNY CORNER

In an earlier email, **Sari Valenzuela** suggested a Tagalog Section. Since no one has volunteered or submitted anything so far, here's an item pulled out from cyberspace, sent by none other than **Ruben Habito** in Japan. As he warned, it may be a bit raw:

Tagalog Section (and humor)

SA MGA MIYEMBRO NG "UHAW"

UHAW - Union of Husbands Afraid of Wives

The foreign chapters of the fraternity of husbands composed of YUKUZA (Yuko sa Asawa), SANSUI (Isang Sutsot, Uwi) and U _ _ _ (Unyon ng mga Tatay na Inaapi ng mga Nanay)

When you say: "Ako ang tigas sa amin." You really mean: "Ako ang tigas-saing ng kanin, tigas-sampay ng labada at tigas-sundo sa eskuwela ng mga bata."

When you say: "Gagawin ko kahit ayaw ng misis ko." You really mean: "Gagawin kong maghugas ng pinggan kung ayaw niya, gagawin kong maglaba kung ayaw niya."

When you say: "Kapag sinabi kong hiwalay, HIWALAY!" You really mean: "Hiniwalay ko na ang puti sa de-kolor at baka kumupas ang labada."

When you say: "Lahat ng utos ko ay pasigaw." You really mean: "Hoy bilisan mo naman iyang kape at giniginaw na ako dito sa labahan!"

When you say: "Ako ang laging nasusunod!" You really mean: "Oo, dear susunod na ako sa iyo sa palengke."

When you say: "Nakukuha ko siya sa isang salita!" You really mean: "Honey, huwag mo na akong batukan at masakit!"

When you say: "Inaabot siya sa akin ng mura!" You really mean: "'Ling naman, mura lang naman iyong sapatos na bibilhin ko!"

When you say: "Nakukuha ko siya sa isang tingin!" You really mean: "Hon, patingin naman ng periodiko pagkatapos mong basahin."

When you say: "Kaya ko siyang paluhurin!" You really mean: "Paluhod niyang sinabing 'Hoy duwag, lumabas ka riyan sa ilalim ng kama kungdi tatamaan ka sa akin!'"

When you say: "Hindi niya ako kayang paglabahin!" You really mean: "Hindi puede kasi hindi pa ako tapos mamalantsa."

-o-o-o-o-o-

And about the Y2K bug:

"Y-to-K" PROJECT STATUS.

Our staff has completed the 18 months of work on time and on budget. We have gone through every line of code in every program in every system.

We have analyzed all databases, all data files, including backups and historic archives, and modified all data to reflect the change. We are proud to report that we have completed the "Y-to-K" date change mission, and have now implemented all changes to all programs and all data to reflect your new standards:

Januark, Februark, March, April, Mak, June, Julk, August, September, October, November and December.

As well as: Sundak, Mondak, Tuesdak, Wednesdak, Thursdak, Fridak, and Saturdak.

I trust that this is satisfactory, because to be honest, none of this "Y-to-K" problem has made any sense to me. But I understand it is a global problem, and our team is glad to help in any way possible.

And what does the year 2000 have to do with it? Speaking of which, what do you think we ought to do next year when the two digit year rolls over from 99 to 00? We await your direction.

-o-o-o-o-o-

Before Gus emailed the solution on the problem of archives, the Loop had some spirited discussions:

From Lili Mangosing Evangelista:
By the way, I respectfully nominate Tigi Barcelona as the Chief Archivist of the group. Tigi has the rare combination of artistic and technical skills, as well as a unique historical perspective of the Organization, from which we all could really benefit. I would love to help if I were there on vacation. If someone seconds the motion, and Tigi agrees, I suggest we send our artifacts to him through Danny.

From Lennie Abellera Blair:
Of course — he'd be a great choice for archivist. I remember sitting in Delaney Hall or during any given UPSCA party — listening to Tigi as he'd go into details of chronology, comings and goings of UPSCA personalities, events and highlights, etc. Seemed like he was always there from the beginning of time!

From Ramon Pasicolan:
Since we have now a legitimate archivist, the better role for Tigi is to be the THE ARCHIVE itself . . and a talking one at that . . .

BACK TO BEING SERIOUS

From Cynthia:
I'm reporting from the Phil. Talked to **Jimmy Ong** already. Would have seen him at the memorial service for Mom but he forgot the date. Will see him some other time. Did see **Oca Evangelista** and wife, **Susan.** Also got to meet the "running priest", **Fr. Reyes**, who led the "Prayer Walk with Erlinda" (he said it is "with" rather than "for" because she is indeed always with us) around the U.P. Lagoon area. I mentioned to him my UPSCA Stateside ties.

Guess what I found while my brother and I were clearing out things in Mom's house ? A little card containing "The UPSCAN's Rule of Life". A little while ago someone was asking about the **UPSCA Pin** so some might be interested in this as well. It says:

I have many high ideals.
I will never abandon any of them come what may!
They will be with me in the battle, and they will be an armor plate of encouragement and hope.
I would be TRUE, for there are those who trust me;
I would be PURE, for there are those who care;
I would be STRONG, for there is much to suffer;
I would be BRAVE, for there is much to dare;
Never let me forget these three — GOD, my SOUL & ETERNITY!

Idealistic indeed, but surely values worth keeping. I thought this went hand in hand with the UPSCA "Army of Youth" song.

Happy Easter to all!

Jun and Cynthia Calejesan

-o-o-o-o-o-

This was the email about the Pin:
And while we are on the subject of the Upsca Pin, can anybody volunteer some info on when it first came out and who designed it? I call especially on the reps of the earlier generations: Gus de Leon, May Gatchalian, Rene Dawis, etc.

Typeset by Danny Gil in Los Angeles supposedly every quarter. Assisted by others (via electronic transfer) who insist on anonymity, perhaps for libel protection. Much material is culled from unwitting Upscans in cyberspace. Email, snailmail, fax, or call in your pictures, trivia, jokes, manifestos, etc, to either 19002 Horst Ave., Artesia, CA 90701, ferngil@aol.com, (562) 402-1890, or (562) 402-5890.

Action & Reaction!!!

Letters, faxes, e-mail, anecdotes, conversations . .

Following the previous issues' writeups on Upsca history and the rejoinders from some members, I had asked Oca Palabyab, Upsca president 69-71, to contribute. His reply:

Dear Danny,

I joined UPSCA at a time when student activism was about to take a new form. The kind of unrest that swept France at that time (Sorbonne?) and the anti war protest (Vietnam) fever in the US mainland found its way in the Philippines. U.P. was at the forefront of all these developments. I would say that this is the period of transition from the post Delaney era to the period of "middle revolution." Before the first quarter storm. I became President, the resistance against the Marcos pre-martial law regime was intensifying.

After many years of "good and easy life" at the DH grounds, UPSCA ventured into this highly political field. It was my policy to make UPSCA relevant during those days and we took part in whatever issue we thought was really important. It was our initiation into the volatile world of ideological ferment. Those days were days of "isms".

Because traditionally, UPSCA had been identified with the Church, the progressive elements in the campus felt uneasy about UPSCA's being active in the campus. For one thing, we had the number and we ventured into campus politics by fielding candidates in the college councils and the university council, all the way to the level of the Vice Chairman when we fielded TJ Jayme running with Mon Paterno in 1969. Before that, we tried first with the A.S. Council by fielding TJ Jayme, Ms. Abrera (I forgot her first name, the sister of Thetis) and guess who - Ericson Baculinao. That was the famous "JAB".

The following year we supported Mon Paterno's party with TJ running for Vice Chairman. After several years, UPSCA was back in the political arena and the more progressive elements in the campus looked at UPSCA with some disdain. By 1970-1971 or during my second term, we were allied with the so called moderate group in the campus, as against the more radical elements who toe the "Maoist" political line.

It was a terrible time in the campus and UPSCA was not spared. A number of our younger members were attracted by the romanticism of the revolutionary spirit of the national democratic front, thanks and no thanks to the ever increasing intransigence of the Marcos government. We still believed that UPSCA mst show some moderation in campus and take a sober approach while the rest are in some kind of a frenzy to bring down the system.

UPSCA survived but some of our very active leaders moved to the "other side". What I can say is that the UPSCANs who joined their ranks added credibility to the cause espoused by the radicals. We became part of the big league in campus and a force to reckon with. I recall that I was welcomed by the fraternity leaders who influenced the political landscape in U.P. in recognition of UPSCA's influence in campus. That is one of the reasons why I was drafted to run with Manny Ortega in 1971. Manny won as Chairman of the Student Council and I was the Vice-Chairman. We were able to defeat the powerful SM (Sandigang Makabansa) which is the party of the National Democratic Front in U.P. While UPSCA did not support us officially, the support was there and a core group worked quietly and their deep involvement in the election campaign won the admiration of fratmen with whom we had an alliance.

In addition, I remember that we were supportive of any rally that the UP Student Council endorsed and I encouraged UPSCANs to join such rallies and demos. We managed to have our own delegation in such rallies. Then came the U.P. barricades when Pastor Mesina was shot. He happens to be the younger brother of Art Mesina, an UPSCAN and a close friend. Then there were those violent demos where some UPSCAns witnessed some bloodshedding due to pillbox explosions.

These had some cathartic effect on the UPSCAns. The great ideological debate on what line to follow almost ripped us apart. There was a common enemy, the government of Marcos but there was a question of how to confront such an enemy. The Natdems seemed to have all the answers at that time. But through all these, our good old UPSCA SPIRIT kept us together, knowing the value of good clean fun, of working together and not forgetting how to smile, laugh and sing. This is in contrast with the tense demeanor of those who were rabidly anti establishment, young people who lost the smiles on their faces and who suddenly became revolutionaries. It was some experience and I feel that it was truly a challenge to be the president of UPSCA during those turbulent days.

It has been a long time and there are still tons of memories to unload. For the time being, I certainly hope that I have been able to satisfy your curiosity.

You know, sometimes I regret that I did not join any fraternity, seeing how fratmen keep their contacts for life. UPSCANs of the Delaney era I'm sure have so many things in common and they can identify themselves and keep ties for a lifetime but the other generations do not have that same bond.

I wonder if we can rekindle the UPSCA spirit among these different generations of UPSCA. That we shared the DH grounds should be enough, as far as I am concerned. All that is necessary is to keep the network alive and I'm glad with modern technology at hand, we must might be able to enlarge our circle.

I admire your group and I truly hope that I can whip up enough interest among UPSCANs of my time era to keep that UPSCA spirit ALIVE!

Regards.

Oca Palabyab

-o-o-o-o-

Another email:

Thank you for the copy of UPSCA Alumni Association, USA Newsletter which you sent us (**Arlene Vallesteros** and **Arsenio "Noye" Alfiler**). Noye and I enjoyed reading it and started reminiscing about our UPSCA days. We did not realize that a number of our UPSCA friends are abroad. What is interesting is that we may even be able to link up with our cousins whose addresses are in your mailing list, i.e., **Ernie Pangilinan, Lindus Carreon Arambulo** and **Nanette Ortega Jongco**. Actually it was Arlene-Alfiler Vallesteros, my sister in-law, who first contacted you. We were quite excited when we got Num 9 of the Newsletter. We eagerly went over the mailing list just to know where our UPSCA friends are.

In fact, we may be able to get another UPSCA president (**Douglas Villanueva**) to link up with you. Douglas resides in our village. We shall pass on a copy of the newsletter to him. He may yet add to the interesting pictures of UPSCA presidents and perhaps give his account of UPSCA in 1968. There are other UPSCANS whom we know who may be interested in being part of the loop and in getting copies of the Newsletter. **Mila Abad-Reforma**, for instance is a faculty member in the UP National College of Public Administration and Governance, where I also teach. Thank you once again for the Newsletter. Please include us in your mailing list. *Noye and Maricon Alfiler & Arlene Alfiler Vallesteros (Upsca batch '62).*

A dinner honoring Christie Borromeo Kawal on her 1998 visit. *L - R,* Christie, Ping Tan (standing), Medy Cruz, Rolly Mesa and wife Josie, Gani Cruz, Merle Tan, Mercy Abad, Jimmy Ong. Not shown in this photo sent by Mon, but present at the party were Lino & Maureen Faelnar, and Tigi & Nora Barcelona. As Mon's caption said, since they were all AMDG's (*ang mga demonyong gutom*), they repaired to Tigi's house for more snacks.

Before and after shots. Rightmost, Ernie Pangilinan in 1999. Then again in an early '60s group picture with Beth Zaraspe and possibly Celia Morales at extreme left. Godo Juliano mentioned that he met Celia and Dante Morales in NY during his visit last year.

Del Tocong, Malu Garcia, and Manny Castillo belting it out with song while Del also strums his guitar as son DJ plays on the organ.

At Malu's dancing party: Susan Po, and dance maestro Angel Sta Maria and wife Estela. Susan flew in from SF for the party.

From another old album, as identified by Ernie, is Emma Narvaez, from the Pharmacy Chapter. Eddie Cailao is seen in the background. Eddie probably was still in UP High then. He eventually married Reggie Cruz and has been in the airline industry since.

HAPPENINGS

On May 8, Saturday, starting 6:00 pm at Danny & Lisa's place, the LA Upscans will have a potluck party. Special guests are the **Palabyab**'s from Manila. We hope more new faces appear, especially among the younger set. All are invited.

On May 24, in Anaheim, **May Miñoza-Gatchalian** will receive the prestigious E. Jack Lancaster Award for 1998 for creating quality awareness in the Pacific Rim countries. She says "much of what I am today is Upsca based!!!"

The UPAAA (UP Alumni Association of America) headquartered in the East Coast, will hold a general meeting in Las Vegas Oct 15 to 17. Pres **Menchee Fulgado** invited Upscans to attend singly or as a group. For those interested, call (718) 568-1999. The Colorado chapter is headed by Upscan **Linda Rojas-Santos**, who wrote about her UP days in their newslet. She reiterated Menchee's invitation. I mentioned to her that we really aren't an official organization — no bylaws, no fees, no elections; our newslet is more of a hobby for fun. Maybe some of us could plan going to Vegas come fall. In the meantime, isn't there still time for a summer camping perhaps?

UPSCA'S D'JOLLY MINSTRELS back in 1963. Photo and caption sent in by Myrna Aquitania. *From left:* Victor Carreon, Niza Castañeda, Conchita Guerrero, Mildred Acayan, Consuelo Orillo, Emmie Acuña, Jess Martinez, Myrna Aquitania, Ermine Bautista, Bing Fragante, Fe Balmaceda and Rosby Teopaco. Not in photo: Cary Abeleda, Grace Abela, Vicky Bustamante, Cora Liamzon, Cora Nievera, Manny Matoto, Ben Paras, Ave Flamenco, Maggie Revilla and Zeny Tamondong. If you know where some of them are now, contact Myrna.

From Ernie's album: Godo Juliano, Danny Gil, Thelma de Ausen, Tessie Chua-Chiaco, and Ernie Pangilinan. At the Chapel grounds, 1961. Anybody knows Thelma's whereabouts?

Montage: Christie Borromeo at an excursion, with Johnny Ramos obstructing the view. Cynthia Reyes with Fredie Santiano in the background. Dates and places unknown. Anybody's guess?

Identities, anyone? Many look familiar, but only name I remember is Delfin Castro (now an attorney in Bowie, MD) shown near center, posing like James Dean. And possibly, Tom Aquino at lower left.

MAILING LIST

Jimmy & Mercy (Rivera) Abad,
Antipolo, Philippines

Rory Abrera
Dallas, TX 75380

Arthur & Cherrie Adiarte
St Paul, MN

Ofie (Peñaflorida) & Ken Aid
Lakewood, CA

Vyva Aguirre
Quezon City, Philippines

Letty (Ramirez) Ajodah
Queens Village, NY

Ely & Sonia (Alday) Alampay
Quezon City, Philippines

Noye & Maricon Alfiler
Quezon City, Philippines

Rico Alfiler
McLane, VA

José Alzona
Glendale, CA

Nanette (Gadi) & Boy Angeles
Monroeville, PA

Myrna Aquitania
Camarillo, CA

Lolly Aquino
Los Angeles, CA

Primo & Lindus (Carreon) Arambulo
Rockville, MD

Noli & Rosita Arong
Arleta, CA

Sisoy & Cecile Arong
Houston, TX
arong1@hotmail.com

Fr Lito Arong, OMI
Oakland, CA

Johnny & Alda Balaoing
Los Angeles, CA

Nina Los Baños
Las Vegas, NV

Tigi & Nora Barcelona
San Juan, Philippines

Olga (Cruz) Barrios
Williamsville, NY

George Bartolome
Vallejo, CA

Enteng & Mely Batas
Lancaster, CA

Lito & Tita (Teaño) Balucano
Cerritos, CA 90703

Lennie (Abellera) & John Blair
Libertyville, IL

Reggie & Eddie Cailao
Marikina, Philippines

Jun & Cynthia (Reyes) Calejesan
Monaca, PA
calejj@ch.etn.com

Ramon Casas
Strasbourg, France

Manny Castillo
Brea, CA

Delfin Castro
Bowie, MD

Remy & Anching Chica
Northridge, CA

Tessie Chua Chiaco
North Hollywood, CA

Isagani & Medy Cruz
Manila, Philippines

Nilo Cruz
Makati, Philippines

Rene Cruz
Diamond Bar, CA

Boy dela Cruz
Cottage Grove, MN

Rene & Lydia Dawis
Minneapolis, MN

Nancy (Cruz) & Gerry Dienel
Little Rock, AR
t

Josie (Canicosa) Dimatulac
Philippines

Bing (Ferrer) & Anthony Dubitsky
Riverdale, MD

Cir & Rose (Lacebal) Engay
Los Angeles, CA

Georgina (Reyes) & Mervyn Encanto
Quezon City, Philippines

Manny & Lee Espejo
Saugus, CA

Joe Espinosa
Manila, Philippines

Deo & Aleli Estacio
Altadena, CA

Tony & Josie (Angeles) Estrera
Cerritos, CA

Oscar & Susan Evangelista
Quezon City, Philippines

Lili (Mangosing) & Gene Evangelista
Fairfax, VA
l

Lino & Maureen (Holazo) Faelnar
Las Piñas, Philippines

Susan (Rodriguez) & Dick Fagan
New York, NY

Dette Feliciano
Los Angeles, CA

Temy (Dapilos) Gamboa
Patchogue, NY

Malu (Barrios) & Oids Garcia
Cerritos, CA

Pepito & May (Miñosa) Gatchalian
Quezon City, Philippines

Divsy (Astraquillo) & Ken Geoge
Shorewood, WI

Danny & Lisa (Señeris) Gil
Artesia, CA

Erwin & Alita Gomez
Valparaiso, IN

NVM & Narita Gonzalez
Quezon City, Philippines

Ibarra Gonzalez
San Jose, CA

Ruben & Maria Habito
Kyoto, Japan

Effie (Sta Romana) Hall
Bettendorf, IA

Chit Inciong
Flushing, NY

Jessica Infante
Los Angeles, CA

Jess & Jessie (Quinto) Javelona
Muntinglupa, Philippines

Nanette (Ortega) & Benny Jongco
South Orange, NJ

Godofredo Juliano
Alabang, Philippines

Christie (Borromeo) & Don Kawal
Albuquerque, NM

Lallie (de Vera) Lacaba
Pateros, Philippines

Clara (Reyes) & Bart Lapus
San Juan, Philippines

Raquel (Celera) & Ric Lejano
Torrance, CA

Loida (Nicolas) Lewis
New York, NY

Cheche (Lim) & Delfin Lazaro
Philippines

Gus & Toti (Yuson) de Leon
Quezon City, Philppines

Dante & Baby Liban
Quezon City, Philippines

Flora Libay
New York, NY

Eddie & Josie Magtoto
Parañaque, Philippines

Mario & Myrna Manansala
La Palma, CA

Romy & Edna (Zapanta) Manlapaz
Quezon City, Philippines

Melvyn & Susan (Paulin) Martin
Muntinglupa, Philippines

Jess Martinez
Freeport, IL

Bernie (de Castro) & Jurg Muller
Geneva, Switzerland

Clemencia Natividad
Toronto, Canada

Tony & Bernadette Nievera
Douglaston, NY

Beth (Arcellana) & Bong Nuqui
Quezon City, Philippines

Jimmy & Ting Ong
Pasig, Philippines

Rachel (Zarespe) Ordonez
New York, NY

Oca Palabyab
Makati, Philippines

Ernie & Jessie (Raqueño) Pangilinan
Mission Hills, CA

Ramon & Mimi Pasicolan
Quezon City, Philippines

Lina (Soliman) Plantilla
Brooklyn, NY

Priscilla (Bautista) Perez
Bronx, NY

Susan Po
San Francisco, CA

Gene Pulmano
Roseland, NJ

Sonia (Valenzuela) & Dietrich Quast
Sao Pablo, Brazil

Amelia (Bascon) Rasalan
Bayside, NY

Hermie (Manoto) & Jess Rabe
Cerritos, CA

Zeny (Roxas) & Sixto Ramirez
Los Angeles, CA

Nel Reformina
Nanuet, NY

Johnny & Mila (Garcia) Reyes
Belle Mead, NJ

Ruben & Naida (Uy) Rivera
Quezon City, Philippines

Portia Salvacion
Los Angeles, CA

Maya (Arroyo) Santiano
Quezon City, Philippines

Greg Santillan
San Gabriel, CA

Angel & Stella Sta Maria
Pasadena, CA

Linda (Rojas) Santos
Denver, CO

Bing (Pascual) & Nem Santos
Whittier, CA

Miren (Dumlao) & Alex Santos
Quezon City, Philippines

Berryl Silva
Long Beach, CA

Noel & Angge (Alday) Soriano
Quezon City, Philippines

Susan Sulit
Manila, Philippines

Ping & Merle (Custodio) Tan
Quezon City, Philippines

Pete & & Merle Tandoc
Canton, MI

Dell & Julz Tocong
Bellflower, CA

Bernie (Abrera) Tjarks
Dallas, TX

Danny Uy
Northridge, CA

Girlie (Alzona) & Tito Valbuena
Astoria, NY

Sari Valenzuela
Brooklyn, NY

Jemz & Nora Valera
North York, Ontario, Canada

Fred Valera
Chatsworth, CA

Arlene Vallesteros
Makati, Philippines
t

Jose de Vera
Granada Hills, CA

Chit de Vera
Vorhees, NJ

Mon & Eva (Singson) de Veyra
Marikina, Philippines

Vic & Vickie Vitug
Richmond Hill, NY

Priscilla (Javier) Weber
Manhattan Beach, CA
t

Elizabeth (Zarespe) Yoo
Los Angeles, CA

UPSCA *Alumni Association Newsletter*

Staleletters   Nobrainers   Portrayals

A M D G   Vol 2, Num 11   3nd quarter, 1999

THE LOOP GOES TO HIGHER TECH PLANE

This headline is not only ambiguous, but also old hat, but as the sub heading says something about staleletters, then this stale news is apropos.

The Upsca Alumni Association has a website, not just one of those freebie things that any crackerjack webmaster can cobble together under his/her ISP provider with the typical kilometric URL address (example:http://www2.jps.net/~enriqueb/ or http://www.geocities.com/Heartland/ Prairie /7876/) but rather, Upsca has a domain name! Called UPSCA (of course), with the extension .ORG, meaning organization, and not anything else.

Best to reproduce excerpts of the email exchanges on how this came about:

Hello Fellow Upscans, as you probably know, our "Loop" of Upscans with email has been growing steadily, so now we number about 80 or so. Our supposed quarterly Newsletter carries the complete list. This list of Upscans in cyberspace will undoubtedly continue to grow, as we keep networking with more Upscans in different generations, and more come on board the cyberspace wagon. Consequently, as suggested by one of the more savvy members, Danny Uy, we should streamline the system by consolidating an address list.

Danny Gil

It might be a good idea to register a domain for Upsca. I'll be willing to handle the paperwork and the annual cost.

I need to submit a request for the domain name to the *Internic*. It takes anywhere from a few days to 2 weeks and then they email a confirmation that the domain name is registered. After that, they mail an invoice which will cover the first 2 years. I think it's $100 for that.

Registration requires the following information. This is what I'll be using:
   Domain name: upsca.org
   Organization name: upsca loop
   Organization address: (my address or some other)
I'll be the contact person with the Internic.

The .ORG domain is mainly used by civic and non-profit organizations. The NET domain is normally used by entities other than those that usually go into the .ORG domain and who have large computer networks. Personally, I prefer .ORG as it immediately identifies a non-profit organization.

We have the option to register upsca.com and upsca.net but I believe this will cost another $70 (not $100) each.
Let me know if this is acceptable.

Danny Uy

Great! Let's go. I think we need only to register as one name. We'll chip in. What does it take and what else is needed? I'm cc'ing some of the others so they can put their two cents worth.

Danny Gil

Good news to all. The registration process seems to have been very much improved. The domain UPSCA.ORG has been registered. We'll be able to use it very soon.

Danny Uy

Bottom line, now that it is in use:

1. *When sending an email message to all the 80 plus upscans (so far), you need only to address it to* **upsca@aceja.com**, *instead of listing the 80 plus individual names.*
2. *If you want to see the latest Upsca postings, then go to the site:*
       http://www.upsca.org
and you'll see something like this:

UNIVERSITY OF THE PHILIPPINES STUDENT CATHOLIC ACTION
NEW The Jesuit Meddler (extracts) A portrait of Fr. Delaney is also available
Send your picture
Jokes Galore
Let us know if you have UPSCA-related events
Your quarterly source of information
Is your friend in the list?
Upsca pin scanned by Lennie Abellera-Blair
This page has been viewed 1,000,000 times!

However, we caution that prudence be taken in sending email to the *upsca@aceja.com* address. Generally, we discourage chain letters, dirty or corny jokes, or virus warnings (which generally are hoaxes). Should any message be forwarded, we suggest the body of the message be cut and pasted to a new outgoing email, so all the excess baggage and markings are stripped off. This goes also for replies to incoming email.

For a complete listing, send an mail to *majordomo@aceja.com*, with the message *get upsca upsca.list,* and then wait for the emailed reply.

-o-o-o-o-o-

SOCIETY NEWS
by Malu Barrios-Garcia
To those UPSCANS who missed the May 8th party — you REALLY missed a fun-filled get-together at **Danny** and **Lisa Gil**'s home — the biggest crowd so far. We're getting to be a "forward-looking" bunch — oops, I mean a bunch that looks forward to every UPSCA-Alumni party. I heard someone ask, "When's the next

Honoree Oca Palayab and perennials Johnny, Jessie, Lisa and Malu, singing their lungs out.

one? And how often do we get together?" And I say, if it isn't post-Christmastime, whenever an UPSCAN from out-of-town-or-country passes through LA, we try to make it a good excuse to call for a gathering — meaning we think we are feting the of-of-towner, when in fact we really are doing it for ourselves. I mean, how can anyone pass excellent food, good wine and genuine San Miguel beer, a chance to sing and dance and tell/listen to jokes of every variety, exchange stories down memory lane, and go home all aglow with the joy of having relived one's youth, all senses satisfied? It's almost surreal!

But seriously, this was a night to remember. I don't think there was any UPSCAN or guest there at the party who felt left out. Even some of the UPSCAN's children who were there had fun posing before **Danny Uy**'s so called Ilocano camera — De-jay-tal camera. Everyone found his/her niche . . . be at the kitchen, the living room, the reception area, the den, the dining room, the driveway, the back yard. There was always a buzz, buzz here and a buzz-buzz there. Everyone was plain Dick and plain Jane happy!!!!

Late'60s UPSCA pressy, **Oca Palabyab**, and his cute wife **Tatish** and sons of course were the honorees, but all else who had special occasions which were celebrated within that week, were also honored. Danny and Lisa just had their 32nd wedding anniversary, yehey or yahoo!!!!! **Nonie** and **Milna** (nee Arevalo) **Vales** opted to celebrate their 28th wedding anniversary right there that same evening, good for you guys!!!! Then **Oids Garcia** (yours truly's hubby) had his b'day too the day before, announcing that he just turned thirty two, ya right, Oids!!!!

So it was waltz time for the celebrants, dim lights of course, but no dirty dancing, mind you. UPSCANS never do dirty dancing, right, **Angel Sta Maria**? The only couple, by the way, who is allowed to do dirty dancing or should we say labada or lambada (whichever!) is none other than dance king and queen, Angel and **Estela Sta Maria**. It made a lot of us jealous not to be able to dance so beautifully "dirty" or dirtily beautiful, like this couple. Just kidding!

Bing Pascual Santos, another ballroom aficionada didn't come with her prince, but did her routine on the dance floor, along with **Lisa Filler**, who was great at line dancing and getting there at Todo-Todo.

Overheard Physics-ists, **Ernie Pangilinan** and **Greg Santillan** exchange their scientific jargon to impress each other that they still remember who's who between them. That is, who's the instructor and who's the student? It goes this way— Ernie was Greg's instructor at UP and Greg's now a professor at Cal State, LA.

Rose Lacebal-Engay is one who would not miss an UPSCA party for the world. Although she and hubby Cir, are quite still involved with their grown-up children, they are often the first to show up in any UPSCA get-together. Rose can identify people by their names and faces as long ago as 1964. This remarkable memory is due to the fact that *Philippinensian* matches its graduates' pictures with corresponding names. The thing though about Rose is that she does remember these graduates even before she reads the labels! Yes, old Philippinensians usually find their way in our parties too. We had at least 4 old issues.

Ofie (Peñaflorida) and **Kenneth Aid** are another early bird couple. Ofie donned her UP-logo sweatshirt which

motivated **Jessie Pangilinan** on the piano, for the group to start singing the Alma Mater song, *UP Beloved*. **Johnny Balaoing**'s tenor voice, outstandingly led the entire crowd, followed by the UPSCA song, and *Bayan Ko*. Hey, but the girls

were mesmerized when **Oca Palabyab** joined in with his bedroom voice and rendered his songs. Rico Puno's voice pales to Oca's rendition of *Gaano Kita Kamahal*. Wow! Thanks to **Rene Cruz**, who had given us the inside information about Oca's visit, or, we would have been robbed of listening to Oca's "malamig na boses" (says Jessie P.) And in one corner, by the cheese and baguette, we spot Joe. Hey, did anyone know that **Joe de Vera** is really the Boy de Vera that we knew of Productions Committee in the mid 60's?

Party animals, we may seem to be, but the 8th of May, also showed the serious side of us. In between the merriment, Danny and Johnny took the mike and explained about **Gus de Leon**'s Manila ERDA project. There was verbal approval on a proposal to participate in supporting five "poorest of the poor" students in RP for a monthly $25, which we individually could sponsor. Danny promised to email/snailmail more details on the mechanics involved. Also discussed was the UPAAA general meeting in Vegas on Oct 17, and the Medical cooperative movement which Johnny is active in. Oca gave a response in which he said UPSCA, among other things, is not only social, but also impressively solid. Somebody yelled, "It's the food!" Remember what AMDG stands for?

Tony Estrera came without his significant other, so we missed Josie's singing voice, as well as **Manny Castillo**'s, who is in Boston on a conference. No wonder the singers lacked the pizzazz. **Enteng Batas** couldn't have possibly made it since his eldest son got married that afternoon. **Nina Los Baños** had called a week earlier to say that if it weren't for her European tour, she'd come over from Vegas. The flyer for the party called for Upscans and friends, and indeed many friends of ours came: there were engineering guys **David Unson**, **Gene Eugenio** and **Toti Kasilag** and their beauteous wives. Not surprisingly, they knew a lot of the others through other associations.

There were newcomers **Portia Salvacion**, and **Emiliana "Milna" Arevalo-Vales** who showed her keen memory by recalling so many details about many of us. Milna offered her place in Yorba Linda for the next reunion.

Most of those with cameras kept snapping away on candid shots only, so there doesn't seem to have been a general group picture, but the headcount at it's peak must have been about 45 or more.

So everybody, take heed when the next flyer comes for another get-together.

Better take heed soon. Here's a email exchange about a forthcoming party:

From Malu:

Hi Poch! Manny Castillo emailed me and told me of your forthcoming visit in September. Let us know of your itinerary coz the UPSCANS here in LA are wanting to have a reason to have another get together. Someone had already volunteered to host, would you believe. So pray thee tell, when are you passing thru LA and when are you available to be feted by us? How are things out there?

From Poch:

How nice of you guys to host me at an UPSCA reunion! I will definitely inform you of the exact dates of my trip — siempre itatapat ko on a weekend so madali for all to drive around. I don't have specific dates kasi I do not know if my vacation will indeed be for a whole month dahil sa new developments in our New York City office.

A backgrounder. Malu was looking for other members of their mid 60s "cliche" called the ELPS (Eat, Laugh, Pray, Sing)

From Malu:

Forgot to mention that Poch Macaranas was/is an " elps". We had three pianists in the group — Nonong Pedero, Jess Martinez and Poch Macaranas. They took care of the "s"ongs accompaniment and arrangement. JOng, d'you know Poch's email? How come he is not in the loop?

From Jong:

It's taken a while — 6 wks since you wrote — but I finally tracked down Poch Macaranas. You can write him at fmm@bworldonline.com

After serving in the Cory and FVR administrations, his last post being Undersec for Foreign Affairs, Poch is now president of Clemente Holdings (Asia) Ltd and chairman of Strategic & Integrative Studies Center, Inc.

Met him last night; we're involved, in differing capacities, in the 1999 Philippine Quality Awards. Told him there is this e-mail loop of UPSCANs; 80 names in four continents last time I looked; though of course no one knows everyone and so there are subloops within loops. In behalf of everyone, Poch, welcome.

LATEST NEWS

ERDA fund raising:

Melvyn Martin in Manila helped Gus de Leon create a website for ERDA: http://fastfreewebs.com/top/prworkshop/index.htm

Excerpts from the website:

<u>A priest started it</u>

ERDA Foundation was organized by Fr. Tritz S.J. He was one of the Jesuit missionaries expelled by China in 1948. They stayed in Chabannel Hall, a makeshift evacuation camp located where the Ortigas Center is now. The legendary Fr. Delaney asked for their assistance when Diliman needed an extra priest. Most of the Jesuits in Chabannel Hall eventually organized the Xavier School for Chinese children.

Then, Fr. Tritz started to look for his new missionary work in the Philippines. His research led him to know that street children come from the poorest among the poor families. They are unable to pay the threshold cost to avail of the free educational system. These include minimal school fees and contribution expected from parents of students, school clothes, pencil, paper, school bag, rubber slippers.

His idea was simple: help the children to go and stay in school and they will not be begging in the streets.

<u>What the Foundation is doing</u>

Most of the street children come from the families of the poor who cannot afford the basic cost to send their children to school. ERDA Foundation provides for this. Cost Pesos 2,000 (roughly US$53) per student per year. This includes cost of social workers who work in the area to identify these children and arrange a covenant with the parents not to send their children to the streets to earn a livelihood for the family.

We also started a pre-schooling program whereby pre-school age children are organized for 'classes' in the squatters area where they live. We find that getting them before age 5 is one way to influence their 'values' and to be able to reach out to their parents. The children learn the value of time as they look forward to doing something interesting at fix and schedule time during the week.

The teacher is able to point out that 'stealing' is wrong even if they see adults do it everyday in their community. We are able to advise the parents of the ill effects of verbal and physical abuse against the children. We are able to point out that it is wrong for men to physically abuse their mother. Cost of each class for 30 to 35 students is Pesos 35,000 (roughly US$921).

In Smoky Mountain at the North Harbor, we find that even helping out the children get back to school is not possible unless we do something for the families of the scavengers. We have a project there we call SABANA, which integrates livelihood alternatives.

Under this Foundation we also have a program to pick up children from the street and try to rehabilitate them. This is the TUKLASan program. We have a house for these children, provide a surrogate father and mother, food and shelter , counseling. We try to reunite them with their parents if possible. Those who stay we also help to go to school. Retention rate is very low at twenty percent.

Children who had worked in the street find it hard to adjust to another kind of life that is more disciplined. Cost is Pesos 35,000 (less than US$1,000) per child.

VOLUNTEER WORK IS ALWAYS A BLESSING!

<u>Want to know how you can help?</u>

***

Some of us Upscans have already pledged/donated at least a year's worth of support at $25 a month. We already gave a lump sum for the first 6 month's donation. For those others who would like to join, it would be easier to maintain a monthly amount. Luckily, Susan Po, as one of the directors of Philippine International Aid (PIA) has offered to make the outfit available as a conduit for the donations to ERDA from the U.S. so that the donors will be able to take advantage of IRS tax deduction.

Here's the tax ID # of Philippine International Aid: 94-3 0 0 8 3 8 3

PIA issues receipts for donations of $250 or more (as mandated by law). Otherwise, your cancelled check is your receipt. Mail donation to ERDA, with address at:

Philippine International Aid
c/o Filipinas Magazine
363 El Camino Real, Suite 100
South San Francisco, CA 94080

-o-o-o-o-o-

UPAAA Las Vegas Reunion:

Some of us Upscans are attending the October 15, 16 & 17 UPAAA affair. As lifted from their Mission Statement:

"Founded in 1981 in New Jersey, the UPAAA exists for the purpose of providing its membership an alumni network and linkage with their beloved Alma Mater. True to its purpose in assisting UP in fulfilling its mission as an academic institution, the UPAAA is launching its fundraising activity for the UPAAA scholarship Fund at the General Assembly and Reunion Oct 15-17, 1999 in Las Vegas, NV".

For those interested, a package deal $175 ticket ($100 for the spouse/guest) will bring 5 meal tickets which include the Friday reception, Saturday luncheon, Saturday dinner-dance, Sunday brunch, etc. And a discounted $50/day room rate at the Excalibur hotel. Contact UPAAA President and Upscan Menchee Fulgado at CQFPHD@aol.com or (718) 658-1999, for particulars. Individual event tickets are available at $15 for the Friday night reception, $35 for the Saturday luncheon, $50 for the dinner-dance, and $10 for the Sunday brunch. It actually is more cost effective to get the package deal.

-o-o-o-o-o-

UP is about midway in Academic excellence among Asia's institutions:

The 1999 Asiaweek survey placed UP as 32nd out of the 79 Best Schools in Asia

Criteria / Score / Perfect Score / UP Rank			
Academic Reputation	14.87	20	24
Student selectivity	20.49	25	8
Faculty resources	13.68	25	58
Research output	2.62	20	52
Financial resources	2.14	10	64
Overall score	53.80	100	**32**

Ateneo ranking was 71, DLSU was 76, Sto. Tomas was 78.

UP prof annual salary is $25,000 (i.e., purchasing power) vs that of Tohoku U's $84,500/yr. (Using direct conversion, UP comes out closer to $8,500/yr).

UP is way down in research output of teachers. In number of kilobytes per second in Internet bandwidths per student, UP is 0.01 kbps as against Sun Yat-Sen U's 29.39 kbps.

***

Rejoinders:

The numbers are very telling. We see the after effects of the devastation of our economy by the Marcos regime, other unscrupulous politicians and national leaders, and by their lack of vision.

I visited the college of engineering last year and you could hardly see any faculty member in any department. They were all, nearly all, moonlighting. They have to survive. They have families to feed, to shelter and to educate.

And unless our economy significantly improves, U.P. will remain the same no matter how smart the professors are and how many, assuming many would stay.

Again, unless we get our economy going and robust, we will just see our beloved U.P. continue to fade in the shadows of other universities in Asia.

Dr Gene Pulmano

I am suggesting that in the next rating of universities, US universities including, one measure should be research output per $1,000 of salary. We'll see how everybody will compare using this measure!

More UP data. On a per-student basis, UP spends about P40,000 or $1,000 per student. This factors only "cash expenditures", i.e. does not include the cost of land or buildings although it does include cost of most equipment and library books. It is no surprise of course that richer countries can afford to spend more than that for the students in their state universities. The important question is to relate the per-student spending to GNP per capita.

Malaysia, which has a GNP per capita about 3.5 times higher than the Philippines, spends about $5,000 in its best universities or 5 times more than the Philippines.

In terms of the tuition fees contributed by students, UP students are some of the luckiest in the world. Even the children of millionaires pay only P12,000 per year in UP — which covers only 30% of cash expenditures. The other 70% is subsidized by taxes. Ateneo and La Salle obviously have better physical plants (i.e. newly painted buildings, more air conditioned classrooms, newer books in the library, etc.). I estimate that Ateneo charges in the neighborhood of P60,000 per year and that La Salle charges P 80,000 per year. In spite of this, I don't think either institution is making any money.

In spite of all these, there must be something about the air in the UP campus which keeps us from straying too far. . . .
Prof Bong Nuqui, Math dept

-o-o-o-o-o-

COMBINED HUMOR / POLITICS / TAGALOG / RELIGIOUS SECTION:

The Gospel according to Erap

In the beginning, Jose Marcelo Ejercito studied at the Ateneo de Manila. And that school was filled with darkness and chaos because of him, so they expelled him.

Finding himself in the cinema, he said, "Let there be LIGHTS, CAMERA, ACTION!" And he regaled the masa with his grade-B action movies,and they loved him, and he, them, so Erap was born. And it was so, in the evenings and mornings of his second decade.

And Erap said, "Let there be stars (and starlets) to fill my nights, celestial bodies to fill my bed, with beauty queens and actresses of all shapes and sizes." And it was so. Erap blessed his stars and said, "Increase and multiply! Fill the Philippines with my name! In my name shall, ye fill the earth and subdue it. And the starlets begat him children, JV, JR, and other illegitimate children too numerous to mention, and he saw all that he did and said that it was good, very good. And it was so, in the evenings and mornings of his third decade.

Then he saw the Ilokano 'god' and the Waray 'goddess' on the face of the earth, and he knelt and kissed their feet and hands (and asses) and said, "Let me be mayor of San Juan and I will pledge undying loyalty to thee and thine own. Whether thou goes, I go, whatever thou doest, I do." And so when Martial Law was

declared, Erap set an example. He imprisoned those who opposed him, threatened the townsfolk of San Juan with violence if they did not comply. He did all the things that were right in his eyes, and no one opposed as god (Da Apo) was on his side. He ruled like a lord in his fief, and saw that it was good, very good. And it was so, on the mornings and evenings of his fourth decade.

And during the past few decades, Erap said, "Let there be wine, smoke and jueteng. Let sabong and jai-alai entertain the masses. Let me be a shining example of all these vices. Let me eat, drink, smoke, gamble and be merry for tomorrow I will do it again." And it was so.

But 13 years ago, Erap was ousted by the Yellow Brigade, because his god went to Hawaii. He was unrepentant in his loyalty to Da Apo. And Da Apo died in Hawaii, kept as a popsicle in a giant freezer, where his widow, Imeldific, insists on a hero's burial at the Libingan ng mga Bayani to this day. Erap was distraught, his god died, and he was fired by the canaries. And he raised his fist and shook it against the Yellow President and her cronies and said, "BULLET DAY I WILL GIANT YOU! (Balang araw, ako ay maghihiganti!) I WILL BE PRESIDENT ONE DAY! (no translation needed)" And the earth trembled at his oath.

And for a time there was some progress in the Philippines after Cory, but when the elections came, Erap said to the huddled, bleeding and ignorant masses, "IBOTO NINYO AKO AT TULUNGAN KO KAYO! AKO AY PARA SA MAHI-RAP!" And the masses, like sheep to the slaughter, did so, and Erap said, "Let there be a LANDSCAPE (landslide, in proper English) VICTORY, to show the world that I am the president the masses love!" And it was so, and there was weeping and gnashing of teeth among the educated and the enlightened, for they knew that darkness and chaos had come not only in Ateneo, but the whole archipelago. But the masses cheered their hero, who was really Macoy loyalist all the way.

And Erap wanted his Ilokano 'god' buried with honors at the Libingan ng Bayani, but the people would not let him, and he relented. Then all the cronies, all the kamag-anaks, kabits and 'toma'-dachis were appointed. People with questionable backgrounds went to the offices of ministers, assistant ministers, secretaries of state. The 'bebble gam' king became minister of defense. The son of 'god' became the governor of Ilocos Norte, his widow, Imeldific a senator, while the daughter of 'god' became congresswoman. Loyalty before principles was the order of the day.

And Erap pursueth his enemies without mercy. The first to feel his wrath were James Gordon of Subic, followed by Manoling Morato (alias Ling-Ling) of the Board of Censors. Next in line were Lito

Lapid and Rey Malonzo, mayors both, for winning in public office but for running in the opposition party. Joey Marquez was next. Those whom Erap perceiveth his enemies were persecuted and harassed with unpaid tax charges and fiscal anomalies. He bullied that small newspaper, the Manila Times and its publishers, the Gokongwei clan with lawsuits and spurious charges of tax evasion. And the Gokongweis apologized and withdrew the article, and Erap smiled that crooked smile, and walked that crooked walk, and said, "I won again!"

And Erap sought but failed to have some laws passed, but failed. The SAL (statement of assets and liabilities to track down possible candidates for kidnap or blackmail?), the warrantless arrest (shades of martial law) encouraged by his right hand man, Ping Lacson (ala General Fabian Ver), the abolition of English as a second language (I don't know about you, but the way RP is experiencing a brain drain these days, it might just work), legalizing gambling as a form of revenue (jueteng, jai-alai, sabong, masiao, betting on horse races).

And these were the scandals galore that doggeth Erap in the office of Malacañang: the textbook scandal at DECS, the pyramid scam by Reli German's ex-wife, Baby; the 'JR' scandal (a beauty queen who claimeth parentage with Erap); the Romy Jalusjos fiasco (see the Jacuzzi, the air-con, the hamburger stand, the tennis courts at Muntinlupa prisons? That is punishment!); the counter investigation of FVR about the Expo Filipino funds; the Imelda Marcos 'pardon'; the 'Loot'-cio Tan tax suit; the vcr tape of Erap gambling in a casino with a drug lord; releasing the sons of Freddie Webb (Hubert Webb for the Visconde massacre) and Dolphy's son for arson and homicide (for burning down Mina Aragon's house with her mother and children in it) just because their fathers are Erap's buddies.

And the righteous crieth out,"Where is justice?"

In a little while, after 6 years, you may see it. Then again, you may not.

And the misdeeds of Erap, his eraptions and his shenanigans, are they not recorded, and are still being recorded in the book of ACTS? (for actors, silly).

Thus endeth this gospel (for now).

———

Typeset in Los Angeles supposedly every quarter, but mainly when in the mood. Most material culled from unwitting Upsca emailers. Email, snailmail, fax or call in your pictures, trivia, jokes, manifestos, etc, to either 19002 Horst Ave, Artesia, CA 90701, ferngil@jps.net, ferngil@aol.com, (562) 402-5098 or (562) 402-1890. Or send to dau@aceja.com.

MORE NEWS

Upsca East Coast Reunion, as reported by Johnny Reyes. Here are excerpts.

You may be interested to know that we recently had a grand reunion on the East Coast.

Nope, there was no singing of the UPSCA Song. But an unusual aspect of this reunion was that not all of the guests saw each other, and not all of the guests saw the host.

Nope, it was not held in total darkness in the old Usher house, and the host was not an elusive and eccentric recluse. Instead, it was held in our little townhome, and the host was only me. Two of the three guests, Cynthia and Jun Calejesan, came on the week-end of 23 July, after they visited other friends on the East Coast.

The third guest, Liliosa Evangelista, came on the week-end of 30 July, after she visited her brothers in North Jersey.

The original objective was to synchronize, but because of scheduling problems, one week apart was the closest orbital encounter achievable in the end. Cynthia and Jun drove all the way from Western Pennsylvania to Belle Mead, taking a brief detour via Vermont and New York.

They were planning to stay over with us Friday night, culminating their trip with a reunion elsewhere in New Jersey the following day among friends from their Puerto Rico sojourn. Unfortunately, the morning of the day they were supposed to have dinner with us brought sad news from Pittsburgh — a very close comadre of Cynthia had passed away suddenly in the night. As a consequence, the couple had to take an unwanted course of action — abort their trip and head back for home immediately. But since Belle Mead was on their route home from New York, they made it a point to drop by along the way. Mila prepared a quick lunch.

It turned out that Cynthia had never met Mila before. Jun knew Mila from their UP Chemical Society days, but didn't know she was my wife. (Mila, on the other hand, remembers everyone who was in UP during our time, by face and name.) The lunch was an enjoyable one, and our own little adopted Maltese was an active participant.

The only one missing was me, because I had a work assignment in Pleasantville NJ ninety miles south of Belle Mead, and was not due back until the evening!

Next Friday, the third visitor came in the early afternoon and stayed over with us until noon on Saturday. After an early [Saturday] lunch, Mila and I drove Liliosa to the Greyhound station in Mt. Laurel NJ, where she took a bus for Washington DC and home to Maryland, four hours away.

If anybody else wants to join the East Coast Reunion, it is still open.

FICTION becoming HISTORY's deja vu?

The media oftentimes carries news items about incursions of fishing and/or gunboats by China at the Mischief Reef, which is part of the Spratly Islands some hundreds of miles west of Palawan, claimed by a host of nearby countries, reputedly because of a vast oil reserve potential. One can recall that more than 30 years ago, a Pinoy sailed there and declared independence, or something to that effect.

I was going over some of Gerry's computer files and found this unfinished editorial, which would probably have been published in the Manila Standard Sunday magazine:

gerry gil
methinks ... 26 September 1993

Field of battle

Imagine a situation where President Corazon Aquino served for eight years (two four-year terms), Mt. Pinatubo did not erupt, and the United States did not quit its military bases until June 12, 1994.

Also, imagine that Mrs. Aquino's successor had come into power by cobbling together a coalition with the National Democratic Front and the Moro National Liberation Movement — with the result that he had two vice presidents, one from either group, and that the government had become a federal system, with Mindanao as a "commonwealth."

Imagine further that the Philippine military is not exactly weak. True, the navy is composed of 40-year-old frigates, corvettes, radar picket ships and sub-chasers, but it has helicopter gunships carrying short-range laser-guided anti-ship missiles. The air force is strong enough to base in Puerto Princesa, Palawan a small squadron of F-4E fighter bombers and F-5R day fighters.

This is the unlikely world that is the setting for Dale Brown's novel Sky Masters, which came out in paperback last year but has hit the local newsstands only recently. Brown is a retired US Air Force captain, who serves as a navigator on B-52 bombers and FB-111 fighter-bombers.

In this unlikely world Brown portrays, the oil-rich Spratly Islands are the reason for a war between China and, believe it or not, the Philippines. The Chinese navy attacks an oil barge of the "National Oil Co., . . a Philippine company run by a relative of the new Philippine president . . , financed by and operated mostly by rich Texas oil drillers."

The Philippine navy and air force inflict such losses on the small Chinese fleet in the Spratlys that the Chinese admiral decides to use a tactical nuclear weapon. "My fleet is surrounded, we are under attack, we are in danger of losing the Spratly Islands and indeed most of the South China Sea to the Filipinos," the Chinese admiral explains.

If you find this incredible, what comes next is even more incredible. The Filipino vice president affiliated with the National Democratic Front welcomes the Chinese admiral as the liberator of the Philippines.

The Americans intervene at the invitation of the other Filipino vice president (the one associated with the Moro National Liberation Front) — and the big battle of the war takes place on Oct. 10, 1994, when the Chinese try to capture Davao.

Among the Americans who fight in the Philippines are Lt. Col. Patrick McLanahan and Lt. Gen. Brad Elliot, the heroes of Brown's first book, The Flight of the Old Dog. This first novel was very well received — and the two appear in Day of the Cheetah, Brown's third novel, and Hammerheads, his fourth. Sky Masters is his fifth novel.

Brown does not know much about the Philippines (and Asia). He cannot even give the Chinese and Filipino characters plausible names. But Brown — who, according to the book reviewers, is extremely good at depicting modern sea-air combat — really doesn't care.

It seems to me that all he really cares about is telling a good story that involves the use of a state-of-the-art B-2 bomber and almost everything else in the American arsenal (plus a few weapons that don't exist).

For example, one of the B-1B Excaliburs that participated in the fight for Davao took "an incredible array" of weapons into battle — eight SLAMs [Standoff Land Attack Missiles], eight Mk 65 QUICKSTRIKE mines (shallow-water high-explosive anti-ship mi

The text ends right there. Being curious on how the novel ends, I tried to get hold of the book locally, but failed. Even with most of Gerry's books having been distributed or donated, I managed to trace and borrow back the book which had landed with Tigi. However, I could barely finish it, as it wasn't my type of reading, but if I recall right, the plot thickens with the second veep murdering the other, and the Chinese communists overrun Davao, then Manila, but just like a fairy tale, the good finally triumph over evil and they live happily ever after, etc. Simple story-telling ending, ha?

I wish it were that way, too, in real time. Would Erap come into the picture?

Action & Reaction!!!

Letters, faxes, e-mail, anecdotes, conversations . .

Email Exchanges

Here are some interesting tidbits culled from cyberspace:

Between Cynthia Reyes Calejesan and Johnny M Reyes on Biblical (Voltage) Difference, after CRC emailed JMR this observation.

You do know what would have happened if it had been three wise WOMEN instead of men, don't you?

They would have asked for directions, arrived on time, helped deliver the baby, cleaned the stable, made a casserole, and brought practical gifts.

JMR: Then the baby would have developed into a well-balanced stable person and might not have felt the urge to change the world.

CRC: Are you saying He was an unbalanced person born in a stable and that's why He felt a compulsion to change the world? Just wondering.

JMR: Unbalanced only in the sense of having a greater voltage difference between one's poles. The driving force to do radical things is diminished if you are born into a contented well-to-do household, in which case getting up to carry out a difficult task would have become doubly difficult.

CRC: Hm-m-m. This compels me to look at each of our children to determine their peculiar poles and voltages. Thanks for the positive spin on some advantages to being unbalanced. Hadn't thought lately of the correlation between contentment and the propulsion towards achievement.

CRC: Just wanted to report the results of my informal, non-scientific study. Our kids seem fairly contented, but since we have three in college, I think it's safe to say we're far from well-to-do. Not that we want the children doing anything radical (in the negative sense of the word, that is), but we pray that they never fall prey to complacency either. Interesting theory, that.

JMR: [Note to Ferngil: Careful here. I don't want to be branded as a heretic and a blasphemer.]

-o-o-o-o-o-

A joke circulated by Johnny M Reyes:

In a recent issue of "First Class" Magazine (publication of the International Airline Passengers Association), I noticed a letter to the editor by a certain Isagani R. Cruz describing his amusing experience aboard a Lufthansa flight from Europe back to Manila. (I don't know whether it is OUR Isagani R. Cruz, considering there are more than one of them floating around the journalistic world at the moment.)

I can't remember the details of the letter exactly — as you know, I have a bad memory — but I believe it went something like this: It seems Mr. Cruz had one too many aboard the aircraft and was badgering the stewardess for still another drink, but she told him he had had enough and Mr. Cruz became belligerent. The Chief Steward — a Mr. Offenbach — said, "Gott in Himmel! I vill call the Polizei!" To which Mr. Cruz replied, "Ha ha ha, that won't work. You know very well we are 32,000 feet up in the air and the Police can't reach us here." And he continued harassing the stewardess. After 15 minutes, the German Police walked in and hauled Mr. Cruz away, who was heard muttering, "Curses! Foiled again! How was I to know our flight was delayed?"

Another joke as posted by Jemz Valera:

I would like to share a pressing issue. Cheers!   JEMZ

DRESS OF LOVE:

An old woman went to visit her daughter and she found her naked, waiting for her husband.

The mother asks the daughter, "What are you doing naked?" The daughter responds, "This is the dress of love."

When the mother returns home, she strips naked and waits for her husband.

When her husband arrives, he asks her, "What are you doing naked?"

She responds, "This is the dress of love."

"Well," he says to her, "go iron it."

***

Dear whoever sent the "dress of love":

Greetings from the Philippines! I enjoyed that joke very much. It made me wonder which parts should be ironed first? Sincerely,

May Miñoza-Gatchalian

***

Maybe the feet. Old ladies' feet are the most tired parts, having worn them out by a lifetime of shuffling from task to task. I, too, enjoyed this joke, and so did Lindus Carreon Arambulo.

One of the best from the loop!

Liliosa Mangosing-Evangelista

-o-o-o-o-o-

During the campaign for the UP presidency, we had some exchanges with Dr Amador Muriel, our physics professor from way back, who has established quite a reputation in turbulence theory. He was throwing his hat in the ring.

Danny to Amador:

Whether serious or tongue-in-cheek, here's an excerpt from an email of a mutual friend, Mercy Rivera-Abad: "I do not think Muriel will survive the UP culture which is far different from what he grew up in. Besides, the Presidency is becoming more like a circus with such names as Escudero, Alba, Sha-shahani, Sicat and others interested in it. Tell Muriel if he wants to live longer, do not attempt to run for the UP Presidency."

Amador:

Too late, my name is in already. Good advice though, that's what I want to do, get the circus part out.

Here's how the campaign is conducted: at the BOR level, initial weeding out, at the campus level, straw polls, interviews, forums, etc., back to BOR for short list, after the short list, Malacañang. Supposedly favored by Malacañang are Nemenzo and Shahani, by the candidates' accounts. I'm supported by Espiritu and Loida Lewis at the Malacañang level, campaign for Estrada's attention has begun. We will send you clippings and webpage access.

Danny:

I'm all for you to get it. In my reply to Mercy, I told her you're most likely to get the most funding for UP. And indeed, the circus is a fun place! Cheers.

I misread his comment about the circus. Thought he liked it. Anyway, UP oldtimer and long-time campus resident Dodong Nemenzo got the job. Many newspapers didn't fail to mention his left-leaning "Marxist" views in his earlier years.

Incidentally, his wife is a mid '50s Upscan, Princess Ronquillo.

*From new comer **Renan Pineda**:*

I found out about the Upsca loop via a forwarded email from my fraternity brother in Beta Epsilon, **Rozel Santos**. We also have an email group for our fraternity. The heading from his email had the Upsca address on it which caught my eye since I was very active in Upsca for two years in '79 and '80 and have many close friends from those years. When I moved to NYC in '85, I found four other Upscans in the area and we even had a small party when "Derps" (**Fr. Manny Gabriel**) visited NY on his way to Rome. I now live in central New Jersey although I still work in Manhattan.

*From Danny to **Mart Martell**:*

I'm one of Malu's friends and she cc'd me some of the exchanges you had on Gus' activities re Fr Delaney. Malu and I belong to a much later era, mid '60s and missed Fr Delaney entirely, but not his legacy.

We have a very active "Loop" of cybernet Upscans spanning from the early '50s to the late '60s, a quarterly newslet (two recent issues reprinted a history of Upsca written by Fely Zafra), and recently, a website (www.upsca.org) different from that '90s group you mentioned.

*From **Mart**:*

Ave, Danny! I greet you in Latin because it was one of the things I remember about Father Delaney, he made see how beautiful the Latin Mass can be. It's wonderful to see all the effort going on for ole John P. I can imagine him looking down at all of us, through those bushy eyebrows of his, with that ever-quizzical smile on his narrow face, as if to ask, "What's all the fuss about?"

At right is snapshot of the painting by Cheloy Dans of Fr. John P Delaney.

*From **Sisoy Arong** to Danny:*

I'm interested in getting a copy each of the UPSCA book "The Jesuit Meddler" and Gerry's book "Wordsmith With A Slingshot". The first is for my eldest son Vincent, who recently called us from Sophia University in Japan (where he just finished his post-grad work in Asian Studies) that he is seriously considering joining the Jesuits there. **Father Delaney** has snared one more Arong again to the vocation!

*From **Vic & Vickie Vitug** to Malu, Oids & Tony:*

Vicky and I would like to express our gratitude and appreciation for the kindness and hospitality you have shown us. It was great seeing you guys again after quite a few years. That restaurant you took us to was a very good one. The food was great notwithstanding the super fancy names like *nagbabagang tadyang ng baka and naliliyab na ___ ng dagat* or something like that.

*From **Girlie Alzona-Valbuena** to Malu:*

I keep up-to-date with everything that's going on over there by reading the newsletter. It's nice to know that you get to see each other on a regular basis there. Nakakainggit kayo. Maybe we'll relocate to the West Coast since masyadong malamig dito sa New York!

*From **Danny** to **Gene**, after Gene mused about the political turmoil at home, and how we should sometimes just relax with some good poetry which he shared:*

Hi Gene, that was pretty good. They remind me of Grey's Elegy. The transience of life, the "sayangness" of unused potential, viz, such as in the later stanzas:

> Full many a gem of purest ray serene
> The dark unfathomed caves of ocean bear
> Full many a flower is born to blush unseen
> And waste it's sweetness on the desert air

But the Puck in me always brings out the Philippine parody, just as appropriate:

> Full many a tin of purest gasoline
> The dark unfathomed tanks of jeepney's bear
> Full many a tire is born to burst unseen
> And waste it's pressure on the dusty air

-o-o-o-o-o-

SIGHTINGS & TIDBITS & WHO'S WHO

We enjoin readers to send in clippings from books, magazines, or other publications which make mention of Upscans we knew back in college. Who knows, maybe these people aren't aware that they're mentioned in those particular publications. Samples:

From the **PinoYork** book published by Filipino American National Historical Society of Metro NY, for the 1998 Centennial:

Atty Loida Nicolas-Lewis - used to publish the Ningas Cogon Newsmagazine (which under the pen of activist Nelson Navarro, stood up against the Marcos dictatorship); first Asian to pass the NY state bar exam; and richest Filipino entrepraneur as CEO of Beatriz corporation.

Dr Gene Pulmano - first Filipino president of the medical-dental staff of Jersey City Medical Center. Also, together with spouse Violeta, are active devotees of the Barangay of the Virgin.

Drs Benny & Nanette Jongco - one of the many successful MD specialists practicing in the NJ area and leaders of a bible study group.

RN Jane Orendain - active in the La Liga Filipina providing educational, cultural and social opportunities and encounters in the beauty and culture of Filipino heritage.

From the **Filipinas Magazine** recent issues:

Randy David - TV host gives his views on the working service class Pinoys in Europe during his visit there a few years back.

Jennifer Romero-Llaguno - mentioned as being the chairperson of some foundation helping abused women overseas contract workers, or something to that effect (can't find particular issue).

From the Business section of the **Philippine Inquirer**:

Tara (Tessie) Daffon - being promoted to a top slot in one of the broadcast media companies in Manila.

Of course, many Upscans are always in the news. They have columns (*Gani Cruz*), or are/were in public service (*Poch Macaranas, Dante Liban*, etc.), or are on TV (*Boots Anson-Roa*) so we all hear about them, for better or for worse. Case in point as reported by Mercy Abad "Do you know that this crazy Ombudsman (*Desierto*) who has been clearing out the Marcoses and cronies was an UPSCAN during the Delaney days? Djahe talaga." I guess this is a classic case of "famous or imfamous, just as known as well".

-o-o-o-o-o-

FLASH: As we go to press, we got the news that late '60s Upsca president **Atty Benny Lim, Jr** passed away. Poch Macaranas emailed the sad news, and mentioned that he had seen Benny a few days earlier at the Makati rally. We understand that Benny had had a stroke sometime much earlier, and was not in the best of health. Let us offer prayers and condolence to the family.

-o-o-o-o-o-

NOTICE: WE ARE BUYING AN AD IN THE UP ALUMNI ASSOCIATION AMERICA (UPAAA) SOUVENIR PROGRAM FOR THE OCT 15, 16 & 17 GRAND REUNION. IN LIEU OF THE MAILING LIST, THE AD IS REPRODUCED ON THE BACK PAGE. IF YOU WISH TO CONTRIBUTE A FEW DOLLARS FOR THIS AND FOR THE WEB SITE, PLEASE ENDORSE TO MARIA LOURDES GARCIA.

Before & after shots . . . . ?

Kneeling, L - R: Mon Casas, Lennie Abellera, Lallie de Vera. *Standing:* Fr Pat, ??, ??, Romy Ong, ??, ??, ??, Fredie Santiano, Erwin Gomez, Melvyn Martin, Maureen Holazo, Cynthia Reyes, ??, ??

Pictures compliments of Mon Casas. Taken during the 1962 Baguio conference.

Reaching for the stars. Among others: Romy Ong, Ruben Rivera, Mon Casas, Fredie Santiano with Jimmy Abad taking center stage.

Mon Casas and possibly Ruben Rivera. Can you name more?

These above pictures are on the Upsca website, but with incomplete captions. Identify the unidentified, and send in your guesses. Mon Casas will give a prize.

A party at the Faelnar residence last year, for the September-born. *Sitting:* Nora & Tigi Barcelona, Mon Pasicolan, Melvyn Martin, Mercy Rivera-Abad, Lino Faelnar, Ping Tan, Jess Javellona. *Back row:* Ting Ong, Susan Paulin-Martin, Ed & Josie Magtoto, Bernie de Castro-Muller, Jimmy Ong, Merle Custodio-Tan, Mimi Pasicolan, Maureen Holazo-Faelnar, Jessie Quinto-Javellona. Caption on back: "Big, beautiful faces? Jess' remark - hindi na tayo makatayo, may mga arthritis na!" Bernie is based in Switzerland.

Page 9 had been languishing for lack of picture fillers, then the loop exploded with reminiscings after Tigi's piece. Here are portions, edited for brevity:

Dear Guys,

Seems to be the time for reminiscing about our old haunts in the Manila of our days. May I share some memories with you?

Many was the day when I got tired of driving my heap, that old dark blue 1948 Chrysler which I loved like a mistress. I would park it in the Chapel and take a bus to Manila for whatever venture I had that day. It could be a movie, buying books, shopping etc etc.

Our favorites were those huge new Halili Transit Buses the 1001 and the 1002 which many of us called the "Turbine Buses" because of the high class whine it gave forth when it travelled.

In Quiapo common destinations were the Times or Boulevard Theatres for a movie or the Forrester bookstore near Times Theatre.

Other destinations were Raon with its myriad electronic shops which I frequented to buy parts for my attempts at making a ham radio. Plus its record stores and toy stores. The walk would eventually lead one to Rizal Avenue or Avenida Rizal and the 15c and Up store for the latest plastic model airplane kits, or Ideal Theatre, and Ever and Avenue and later Galaxy and Odeon for the latest movies.

All along Rizal Avenue were the hole-in-the-wall eateries where one could get excellent ham sandwiches made with good Chinese ham and you were always alert to ask the person making the slices to please "May taba ho lang."

On affluent days usually with your gang the ultimate destination, especially during the Christmas season, was "Rice Bowl" on T. Pinpin which was just a short walk from Avenida Rizal. There the gang could order fried rice, sweet sour pork, vegetables, and century eggs on a communal basis where the cost was shared by all, and of course a Chinese meal, comida china, was most efficiently and economically eaten by a large group. This was the treat of treats.

Escolta was still the main shopping drag. There were no malls yet. Escolta had Botica Boie for wonderful snacks, American Hardware near the Pasig had the most wonderful toys but only one or two of each. There was Berg's department store and Walk Over, and Syapp's, but these were only visited in the company of parents and for very serious purposes like buying a pair of shoes or a belt for graduation.

Tigi Barcelona

I used to pass by Quiapo Market too, to buy pancit palabok for 10 centavos and it was wrapped in banana leaves - have not tasted anything better. There was also that panciteria WA NAM just behind Quiapo Church that had the best pancit Canton.

Tony Estrera

Hi, Tony.

Was Wa Nam the place about which there was this rumor of a cook who committed suicide by jumping into his own oven? If it was, I think it was closer to Sta Cruz Church than Quiapo Church.

Not to be confused with Cho Nam, maybe 5 minutes walk away from Quiapo Church, and on the same street, Quezon Blvd; or Nam Wah, and Sun Hwa, neighbors on F Torres St near the Republic Theatre.

In the early 60's the latter two panciterias were among the favorites of the Collegian staff on press nights every Tuesday. The most junior reporters were usually assigned to look for restaurants that served the cheapest and biggest platters of pancit canton, as we had to stretch the meal allowance of P15 to feed as many as 10 editors and reporters. Even then, the price of canton was way beyond the 10c palabok of your memory; you must be talking of your high school days.

Jimmy Ong

Dear Tigi, what a thoroughly enjoyable account! Some places are familiar from frequenting them with my Mom on her shopping forays in Escolta and Divisoria. I wish she were here to read this reminiscence. Surely she would have added the regular trips to the USIS with my brothers and sister in tow to promote a reading habit and, on the way home, a stop at Kim Chong Tin to buy some steaming hot hopia and ampao or, if time were not a factor, going to Quiapo Market for halo-halo (although I always thought Pasay's was much better). Such fond memories! Thanks for rekindling them.

Cynthia Reyes-Calejesan

Wasn't there a restaurant called "Dencia" on Escolta? Or was it just in my imagination? Tigi would know! It served the best Pancit Luglog I have ever tasted in my life. I have been relishing the exchanges on the net. Hi to y'all!!!

Nancy Cruz-Dienel

Hi Tigi, your email reminds me of many more places in Manila, including: the surplus store in Quezon Boulevard where one can buy leggings, circa WW1 or WW2 for ROTC use. If you have more moolah, second hand combat boots, canteen, ammo belt are all for the taking.

- Raon street was where electronic enthusiasts can get all the parts for building amplifiers and other electronic gadgets. For the music lovers this was Manila's Tin Pan Alley.

- On the same street you have several choices for meriendas, corn beef sandwich or giniling sandwich for 15 centavos on the corner of Ronquilo and Raon or lumpia, with extra crushed peanuts, for 30 centavos(?) on the staircase of the Globe theater building.

- Quiapo Market's sontanghon with "Aling Simang" is the best, while the sales pitch at Central Market "Food Court" is unparalleled anywhere, if your arms don't get pulled out of your body.

- Near the corner of Azcarraga and Quezon Boulevard beside the Old Bilibid at 4:00 p.m the lard and oil factory brings out their Chicharon Bituka. You burn your tongue literally when you eat them.

- Somewhere here is Mon Pasicolan's Dad's bookstore.

- While in Doroteo Jose is Susan Po's Dad's Bookstore "Po"pular Bookstore, get the pun?

- On this street one can read comics for 3 pcs for 5 centavos. You can extend the reading by passing your read materials to your friend and vice versa, so long as the watcher doesn't see you.

- On Doroteo Jose, if you are tired of reading you can play "Foot ball" aka Fuzzball for 5 centavos per game.

- On the corner of Avenida Rizal and Doroteo Jose, you have two choices of entertainment places, Galaxy on the right, where "Ten Commandments" was showing for about ten years and on the left, you have "Opera House", with daily live stage shows. Further towards Azcaragga, you can drink beer, for 35 centavos, with live music entertainment at Alex.

Can somebody start an article about CUBAO. We can talk about A&E, the first drive in shop; Embers, Ma Mon Luk, D&E, a place for many debuts and parties, Little Quiapo, Araneta Coliseum, New Frontier and Matsuzakaya.

So long, it is fun to walk through memory lane.

Tony Nievera

I recall Wa Nam to be right behind Quiapo Church, in fact, it was on the same block as the church. They served the most delicious Nido soup I ever had. Nam Wa was across Quezon Boulevard towards the Quezon bridge where they had great lugao, it was right next to a second/third run theater (25 centavos) whose name I could not remember. Speaking of halo-halo, do you guys remember the old Little Quiapo in Diliman, right across where they built the co-op? That was very good too.

Vic Vitug

Wa Nam was in Sta Cruz. In Quiapo, near Raon Street. On Quezon Boulevard was Ma Mon Luk with the life size picture of the proprietor watching all the clients slurping on their extra soup. A common question asked by those enjoying the gastronomic treat is why there are no cats or mice on the premises. Maybe because of the siopao.

Tony Estrera

Tigi, how does one love a 1948 Chevy like a mistress? Please explain.

Sgd. Ms Naive (AKA Malu Barrios-Garcia)

to be continued in next issue . . . .

GREETINGS to the UPAAA !

UPSCA *Alumni Association*
"We've kept in touch, through all these years"

Jimmy & Mercy (Rivera) Abad,
Antipolo, Philippines

Rory Abrera
Dallas, TX

Arthur & Cherrie Adiarte
St Paul, MN

Ofie (Peñaflorida) & Ken Aid
Lakewood, CA

Tomas Africa
Manila, Philippines

Vyva Aguirre
Quezon City, Philippines

Letty (Ramirez) Ajodah
Queens Village, NY

Ely & Sonia (Alday) Alampay
Quezon City, Philippines

Noye & Maricon Alfiler
Quezon City, Philippines

Rico Alfiler
McLane, VA

José Alzona
Glendale, CA

Nanette (Gadi) & Boy Angeles
Monroeville, PA

Myrna Aquitania
Camarillo, CA

Lolly Aquino
Los Angeles, CA

Primo & Lindus (Carreon) Arambulo
Rockville, MD

Noli & Rosita Arong
Arleta, CA

Sisoy & Cecile Arong
Houston, TX

Fr Lito Arong, OMI
Oakland, CA

Johnny & Alda Balaoing
Los Angeles, CA

Nina Los Baños
Las Vegas, NV

Tigi & Nora Barcelona
San Juan, Philippines

Olga (Cruz) Barrios
Williamsville, NY

George Bartolome
Vallejo, CA

Enteng & Mely Batas
Lancaster, CA

Lito & Tita (Teaño) Balucano
Cerritos, CA 90703

Lennie (Abellera) & John Blair
Libertyville, IL

Reggie & Eddie Cailao
Marikina, Philippines

Jun & Cynthia (Reyes) Calejesan
Monaca, PA

Ramon Casas
Strasbourg, France

Manny Castillo
Brea, CA

Delfin Castro
Bowie, MD

Remy & Anching Chica
Northridge, CA

Tessie Chua Chiaco
North Hollywood, CA

Isagani & Medy Cruz
Manila, Philippines

Nilo Cruz
Makati, Philippines

Rene Cruz
Diamond Bar, CA

Boy dela Cruz
Cottage Grove, MN

Enedina (Garcia) de Guzman
Chesnut Ridge, NY

Rene & Lydia Dawis
Minneapolis, MN

Nancy (Cruz) & Gerry Dienel
Little Rock, AR

Josie (Canicosa) Dimatulac
Philippines

Bing (Ferrer) & Anthony Dubitsky
Riverdale, MD

Cir & Rose (Lacebal) Engay
Los Angeles, CA

Georgina (Reyes) & Mervyn Encanto
Quezon City, Philippines

Manny & Lee Espejo
Saugus, CA

Joe Espinosa
Manila, Philippines

Deo & Aleli Estacio
Altadena, CA

Tony & Josie (Angeles) Estrera
Cerritos, CA

Oscar & Susan Evangelista
Quezon City, Philippines

Lili (Mangosing) & Gene Evangelista
Fairfax, VA

Lino & Maureen (Holazo) Faelnar
Las Piñas, Philippines

Susan (Rodriguez) & Dick Fagan
New York, NY

Dette Feliciano
Los Angeles, CA

Temy (Dapilos) Gamboa
Patchogue, NY

Malu (Barrios) & Oids Garcia
Cerritos, CA

Pepito & May (Miñosa) Gatchalian
Quezon City, Philippines

Divsy (Astraquillo) & Ken Geoge
Shorewood, WI

Danny & Lisa (Señeris) Gil
Artesia, CA

Erwin & Alita Gomez
Valparaiso, IN

Ibarra Gonzalez
San Jose, CA

Ruben & Maria Habito
Kyoto, Japan

Effie (Sta Romana) Hall
Bettendorf, IA

Chit Inciong
Flushing, NY

Jessica Infante
Los Angeles, CA

Jess & Jessie (Quinto) Javelona
Muntinglupa, Philippines

Nanette (Ortega) & Benny Jongco
South Orange, NJ

Godofredo Juliano
Alabang, Philippines

Christie (Borromeo) & Don Kawal
Albuquerque, NM

Lallie (de Vera) Lacaba
Pateros, Philippines

Clara (Reyes) & Bart Lapus
San Juan, Philippines

Raquel (Celera) & Ric Lejano
Torrance, CA

Loida (Nicolas) Lewis
New York, NY

Cheche (Lim) & Delfin Lazaro
Philippines

Gus & Toti (Yuson) de Leon
Quezon City, Philppines

Dante & Baby Liban
Quezon City, Philippines

Flora Libay
New York, NY

Poch Macaranas
Makati, Philipines

Eddie & Josie Magtoto
Parañaque, Philippines

Mario & Myrna Manansala
La Palma, CA

Romy & Edna (Zapanta) Manlapaz
Quezon City, Philippines

Mart Martell
Jersey City, NJ

Melvyn & Susan (Paulin) Martin
Muntinglupa, Philippines

Jess Martinez
Freeport, IL

Bernie (de Castro) & Jurg Muller
Geneva, Switzerland

Clemencia Natividad
Toronto, Canada

Tony & Bernadette Nievera
Douglaston, NY

Beth (Arcellana) & Bong Nuqui
Quezon City, Philippines

Jimmy & Ting Ong
Pasig, Philippines

Rachel (Zarespe) Ordonez
New York, NY

Oca & Tatish Palabyab
Makati, Philippines

Ernie & Jessie (Raqueño) Pangilinan
Mission Hills, CA

Ramon & Mimi Pasicolan
Quezon City, Philippines

Lina (Soliman) Plantilla
Brooklyn, NY

Priscilla (Bautista) Perez
Bronx, NY

Renan Pineda
North Plainfield, NJ

Susan Po
San Francisco, CA

Emily (Bacaltos) Popp
Miami Beach, FL

Gene Pulmano
Roseland, NJ

Sonia (Valenzuela) & Dietrich Quast
Sao Pablo, Brazil

Amelia (Bascon) Rasalan
Bayside, NY

Hermie (Manoto) & Jess Rabe
Cerritos, CA

Zeny (Roxas) & Sixto Ramirez
Los Angeles, CA

Nel Reformina
Nanuet, NY

Johnny & Mila (Garcia) Reyes
Belle Mead, NJ

Ruben & Naida (Uy) Rivera
Quezon City, Philippines

Portia Salvacion
Los Angeles, CA

Maya (Arroyo) Santiano
Quezon City, Philippines

Greg Santillan
San Gabriel, CA

Angel & Stella Sta Maria
Pasadena, CA

Linda (Rojas) Santos
Denver, CO

Bing (Pascual) & Nem Santos
Whittier, CA

Miren (Dumlao) & Alex Santos
Quezon City, Philippines

Berryl Silva
Long Beach, CA

Noel & Angge (Alday) Soriano
Quezon City, Philippines

Susan Sulit
Manila, Philippines

Ping & Merle (Custodio) Tan
Quezon City, Philippines

Pete & & Merle Tandoc
Canton, MI

Dell & Julz Tocong
Bellflower, CA

Bernie (Abrera) Tjarks
Dallas, TX

Danny Uy
Northridge, CA

Girlie (Alzona) & Tito Valbuena
Astoria, NY

Sari Valenzuela
Brooklyn, NY

Jemz & Nora Valera
North York, Ontario, Canada

Fred Valera
Chatsworth, CA

Milna (Arevalo) Vales
Yorba Linda, CA

Arlene Vallesteros
Makati, Philippines

Jose de Vera
Granada Hills, CA

Chit de Vera
Vorhees, NJ

Mon & Eva (Singson) de Veyra
Marikina, Philippines

Vic & Vickie Vitug
Richmond Hill, NY

Priscilla (Javier) Weber
Manhattan Beach, CA

Elizabeth (Zarespe) Yoo
Los Angeles, CA

For more information on how to join, contact either one of these past/present "informal" presidents:
Malu Barrios-Garcia, tel (562) 404-1195, email malu@juno.com
Tony Estrera, tel (562) 809-3342, email tonest@aol.com
Danny Gil, tel (562) 402-5098, email ferngil@jps.net

UPSCA
Alumni Association Newsletter

Staleletters   Nobrainers   Portrayals

A M D G   Vol 3, Num 12   4th quarter, 1999 & 1st half 2000

BOOK ON FR. DELANEY COMES OUT

The "*Chapel Chismis*" on **Fr. Delaney** came out three months ago.

See the writeup of Gani Cruz on page 4.

It seems as if we LA Upscans are luckier in that we already have some copies. The first batch was brought over by a friend of **Ofie (Peñaflorida) Aid** for the six people who had placed orders beforehand. A few weeks later, during the March 18 get-together, **Gus de Leon** brought another set.

Upscan **Erlinda** Rojas-Santos in Colorado had her daughter reserve a set in Diliman, but missed the book launching. "I do wish I could have my reserved copy for the Chapel Chismis come faster through your conduit. I had made the reservation through **May** [Miñoza] and **Susan** [Sulit] but my daughter's birthday party coincided with that Diliman book launching. Could you get it for me here in Denver?"

For those interested, contact **Susan Sulit** and/or **Gus de Leon**. See their addresses on page 10.

-o-o-o-o-o-

An Upsca get-together is scheduled for June 25, Sunday, late lunch, about 1:30 pm at Danny & Lisa's place in Artesia. The occasion is to host East Coast Upscan **Rory Abrera**, and hopefully some others, as this excerpted email indicates:

"Yes, I am expecting to be at the UPSCA gathering in your home on Sunday, June 25. My sister **Bernie** [from Dallas] will be joining me, and hopefully **Priscilla Bautista-Perez** and **Amelia Bascon-Rasalan as well**. My daughter **Sandra** will probably join us from Arizona. Amelia is the comptroller of Career Blazers in New York City."

-o-o-o-o-o-

The last get together March 18 came out very well. As reported to the loop:

The party last night held at our place was somewhat similar to the party hosted by **Johnny Reyes** last year at his Belle Mede residence: the guests came and went at different time frames. But while his event was over a period of 7 days, yesterday's party was over a period of 7 hours.

The first guests started coming in at 6:30 pm. One of the first was also a first timer to the group, **Thelma Ibañez-Teves**, BSBA 1968. She first heard about the Upsca LA group at last year's UPAAA

March 18 get-together. Special guests were Gus de Leon, seated, second from right, and to his left, Ed Valencia, both from the Philippines. More guests came later. Guess the others!

meeting in Las Vegas when she saw the ad we had placed at the souvenir program.

Good ol' regulars **Malu & Oids**, **Angel & Stella**, **Ofie** came in shortly after. But many other regulars had prior engagements, and some of them did promise they'd come in later. Ernie & Jessie were entertaining a guest, and so was Manny Castillo. Johnny Balaoing was at a wedding.

In any event, we had a pleasant surprise: two past Upsca presidents attended, just out of the blue. **Gus de Leon** (pres 1957-58) called an hour before to say he flew into town with his son yesterday for a month's business trip and that they'd be coming over. **Ed Valencia** (pres 1968-69) came along with with **Danny Uy**, **Fred Valera**, & **Joe de Vera**. Later on, I found out that Ed Valencia is the younger brother of **Juliet Valencia**, who was more of our contemporary with CILer's **Bernie de Castro**, **Lennie Abellera**, etc. Like Bernie, Juliet is married to a Swiss and resides there. Ed is Philippine based, but comes and goes very often to the US.

Dette Feliciano brought her friend Lily (who told us that though she was from PWU, two of her sisters were from UP and she felt at much at home in the crowd).

The food was a oddity at first. As the favorite dishes brought in by the guests were laid out on the table, all of them were fish dishes: smoked salmon, kippered herring, broiled catfish, fried tilapia, baked cod, a ton of dilis, etc. We started joking that either all of us mistook the day for a Friday, or we all were health freaks.

Then more dishes appeared: chicken barbeque, and baked potatoes, vegetables, etc. Ah, here was more diversity.

Gus said grace, and we all started enjoying the food. The crowd was predominantly from the late 60's vintage, and the group was riotous in their conversations about mutual friends from way back. Despite all the name tags we had given to everyone, it took some time for **Thelma** and **Dette** to realize that they had known each other some 3 decades earlier.

Then they started a game, some sort of charade: one would state a name, and then each would try to recall all the details of the person: the looks, the walk, etc., and of course punctuated by bursts of laughter by all.

At about 9:00, more people came: **Mario Manansala**, and **Manny Castillo**. At about that time, Dette and her guests had to go because they had another party to attend. Gus and company were all set to go, too, when Johnny called to say he wouldn't be able to make it, but when I told him that Gus de Leon was here, he changed his mind and told Gus to wait, wait. **Lisa Filler** also called to ask if it wasn't too late, and I said of course not, so she and Randy appeared shortly.

Then came the grand entrance of **Ernie & Jessie**. Frankly, we were all waiting for Jessie to play the piano so we could sing. No one seemed to be in the mood to dance, despite the cajoling we made to expert dancers Angel & Stella to lead.

Also, neither did anybody seem interested in the multi-award winning Jose Rizal movie that was set up and playing on VHS at the next room . . .

Last guest left at 1:30 am, 7 hours after the first guest came.

-o-o-o-o-o-

SOCIETY NEWS
Reported by Johnny Reyes

Last week-end, **Mila** and **I** were honored to attend [Apr 8] a party wherein we met well-heeled Filipinos from Long Island in New York and also from our own state of New Jersey. The address was 126 Ogden Nash Street, Jersey City, and the hosts were Danny Gil's smart and pretty daughter, her handsome and enterprising husband from the Caribbean paradise of Belize, and their 6-year old son who is a dead ringer for Elian Gonzalez.

Danny Gil (who was visiting with **Lisa** from Los Angeles) had advised us guests to use Palisade Avenue in Jersey City as a starting line to find Ogden Nash Street parallel to it, "located along a bluff overlooking Hoboken." From Danny's description, Palisade was supposed to be the crossbar of an H, with the approach roads to the Lincoln Tunnel and the Holland Tunnel forming the legs of the H.

But in the actual situation the crossbar turned out to be on a different plane from the legs, passing underneath them without any access ramps, so you could not turn directly into it. As a result, those of us who were unfamiliar with Jersey City overshot Palisade. (Danny's excuse for the bad directions was that "he wuz not from dese parts.") At this point, there must have been about eight rows of cars battling each other bumper-to-bumper to get into the few lanes of the Holland Tunnel (just like the entrance to the South Luzon Tollway at the Nichols area on a Friday evening).

To avoid getting sucked into Manhattan and incurring at least another 30-minute delay (plus a $4 toll for using the tunnel), I turned left last chance I got before the tunnel entrance (fortunately I was near the leftmost lane) and ended up in Hoboken. No sign of Palisade Avenue here, of course. Not having a detailed street map of the area, I had to rely on Danny's clue: "a bluff overlooking Hoboken," so the idea was to go uphill and away from New York City. To make a long story short, we eventually got to the house on Ogden Nash Street, albeit a bit late.

Three Filipino MD's from New Jersey were present at the party: Lisa's brother, Lisa's first cousin, and **Gene Pulmano**, internist. Remember Gene -- the man who quotes Matthew Arnold's "Dover Beach" ("where innocent armies clash by night"), and recommended Marilou Diaz-Abaya's "Jose Rizal"? Also present was another poet -- the Haiku Master himself, **Chit Inciong**! And surprise, someone who actually worked with **Fr. Delaney** as a student -- **Flora Libay**!

She told us a lot of interesting stories about her dealings with the famous priest, but we who never had the pleasure of meeting him asked Flora, What do you think was so unique and special about Fr.

Party at Jersey City: Danny, Norman, Mila, Lisa, Sandy, Flora, Johnny and Chit. Norman felt so at home he doffed his shoes. Tony & Bernie left early. Gene was called on emergency, not surprising for a doctor. Flora, recently retired from the UN, used to be the UP Engineering librarian back in the early '60s. Norman, now an economist, is an active figure in his "loop" of Betan engineers, and is spearheading one the movements to draw investment to the Philippines. Flora, Gene and Norman have known each other for years in the East Coast.

Delaney? What differentiated him from other expat Irish-American priests assigned to the Philippines? Flora thought long and hard, and then replied that it was probably Fr. Delaney's homilies (which unfortunately were not recorded, and therefore could not be included in the "Chapel Chismis" reprints) and his "Love, Courtship, and Marriage" talks which really made him great.

Soon two more couples arrived, **Tony** and **Bernie Nievera** and **Norman** and **Sandy Madrid**. These two families and Chit Inciong all hail from the affluent areas of Long Island in New York State, where the town names are *Jericho, The Hamptons, Kings Point, Douglaston, Hicksville, Flushing, Hicktown*, etc.

Tony recently rejoined his old company IBM, located in the Big Apple, which he referred to as "that giant money-making machine out there," pointing to the lights of Manhattan in the distance.

Norman, a 1962 graduate of the U.P. College of Engineering, kept the group entertained with his original and unconventional ideas, and the way he kept calling Chit "Tigi." He also spoke about his venture capital enterprise, named Manila Tiger Das Kapital or something.

The food and the wine were good. But unfortunately, half of those present were "designated drivers," so we had to take it easy on the booze.

Remember, we still had to find our way out of Jersey City.

-o-o-o-o-o-

Surprise Birthday Party in LA
Reported by Malu

April 1. A birthday party was thrown in honor of Johnny Balaoing.

I was under the impression that if one attends a surprise birthday party that age becomes public information...well, not in the case of our beloved Johnny Balaoing! We were all buzzing curiously about Johnny's age...last April 1st at the *Bahay Kubo* restaurant on Temple St. in L.A., wondering how old the man was. You know how it is, the more you keep the truth under wraps, the more we get "curious-er and curious-er!"

There was no way my UPSCAn hubby, **Oids**, and I would miss this special occasion. Johnny is such a special person! The UPSCA table consisted of **Remy Baluyot** (UPSCA mid-60's), **Cir** and **Rose (Lacebal) Engay**, **Manny** and **Lee Espejo** and their two children, **Rosemarie** and **John Paul**; **Angel** and **Estela Sta. Maria**, **Ernie** and **Jessie Pangilinan**, Oids and myself...

We were a happy and contented lot! Food was delicious and a-plenty, the company was in high and giddy-spirited mode, singing UP songs, *UP Beloved* and *Push on, UP*, drowned our nostalgia... Hey, it was one great party! Johnny was teary-eyed of course -- being surrounded by caring people, especially with beauteous wife, **Alda**, and their children, **Michael** and **Arlene** greeting Johnny on April Fools' Day! (Johnny was a ham at looking surprised, I say!)

The highlight of the party was the personal appearance of famous rock star of the 50's and 60's, Elvis Pelvis Presley-look-n-sound-alike. He was unbelievably mesmerizing us UPSCA baby boomers into screaming fans alá teenagers. Oids yelled, "Elvis is alive!" Then Estela got her paper napkin to wipe the rock idol's forehead like the impersonator was the real Mc Coy! But like all good things, the celebration had to come to a halt. It was past the party animals' bedtime and *Bahay Kubo* didn't want to take responsibility for us being still out there late in the night without our parents! 10 PM curfew. No fooling !

-o-o-o-o-o-

Late 1999 and early 2000 seemed to be travel time and quality time for so many Upscans. Some were unplanned, as they lead to obits.

From Liliosa to Tigi:

Our condolences to you on your father's passing away. I met your father only once, and it was during a visit to your house for carolling one Christmas, many years ago. **Jimmy** and **Mercy** were with the group then, **Danny** and **Gerry Gil**, **Rory Abrera**, **Melvyn Martin**, and others whom I can't remember too well.

What made the visit rather hilarious was that **Lindus** somehow ended up as the *conductora* (given her musical background). The only problem was that every time she raised her arms to swing the baton(?), her Jackie Kennedy-styled blouse also went up to reveal her torso. And then everyone would start to laugh and have a hard time getting started to sing! But your mom and dad were so gracious and appreciative of our lackluster singing, and in fact fed us very well!

May all your Christmas carols be touched with the fond memories of your dad.

From Lennie Abellera-Blair:

Hi there everyone! This Christmas, the whole, entire **Abellera** clan will have a grand reunion in Baguio. My sister **Helen** and her hubby and two girls, and my brother, **Benjie** and his wife, **Vicky** Guerrero, will be going too. The six **Blairs** will be traveling at different days:

I have contacted **Mercy Abad** and asked that she corral some ole (now - really getting old?!?) friends of yore (Delaney Hall mob) for a nice get together and it looks like it might be a lunch somewhere between Quezon City and Makati - hmmm - that's really being specific, huh? But no matter - *basta lang* we get together, right? Am looking forward to this. Would also like to hear about the NVM funeral and all.

Lennie and company did meet with some of the ol' Upscans for dinner somewhere between QC and Makati because the bonus was coffee and sweets at Tigi's ancestral house in San Juan.

From Danny:

Upon hearing a message from my mother that "Pa has died, but is alive again" and then talking to her on the phone a hour later, Lisa and I decided to fly home to Manila pronto. Thus began the saga of an unplanned balikbayan.

As it turned out, we stayed two weeks, then came back. But 3 days later, Pa passed away, and just I and my brother went home for the funeral. This was the reason why the Jan 29 LA get-together was cancelled, and was moved to Mar 18.

Comments on the previous issues:

From Lindus Carreon-Arambulo:

She called to say that in the 1962(?) Bagiuo picture showing Fr. Pat flanked by a dozen or so partly identified Upscans, she was the girl with a straw hat!

From webmaster Danny Uy:

Number 9, page 7, column 1, you have "Email from Danny Uy of the mid 70's". I just wish I was 10 years younger but I actually graduated in 1970.

Also, in the picture shown on page 8 with **Fr. Jess**, I recognize **Tim Faustino** (standing 3rd from left) and **Tony Ganal** (middle front). Since the picture came from **Vic Vitug**, did he also send the names of the people in the picture?

Number 10: In the picture on page 9, bottom right: I believe that is **George Bartolome** in the stripe shirt in front.

-o-o-o-o-o-

OUTSTANDING GREETINGS:

Dear Jong,

Belated happy 5xth birthday! Time does go by rather quickly when one is rushing through the beat of the everyday workworld — which of course you have already excused yourself from unlike unluckier mortals like us. I am sure you have reflected carefully on the millennial aspects of existence, and all those sort of philosophical meanderings retired execs are wont to do. Are you back in the "quality" groove and group? Maybe I'll see you once again one of these days in a similar meeting as last year's.

Best regards, Poch [Macaranas]

-o-o-o-o-o-

Hello Everyone!

Although I haven't been communicating for a while I have been reading all your messages. I have enjoyed hearing from everybody and all that is going on in your lives. Thank you for your generosity of thought and spirit and sharing your lives with your old friends like me. Life certainly is so much richer and more meaningful when we have friends and relations with whom we can share memories and experiences.

May this new year bring us all good health, peace, prosperity and happiness. May we continue to have many more opportunities to write, to meet again and to make more happy memories!

Love, Rory Abrera

-o-o-o-o-o-

Other New Year Wishes:
From Johnny Reyes to Mercy Rivera-Abad:

What do I want to happen in June? Heh, hehe. Kaunti lang naman --
1. A new president in office (puede ba, somebody other than Gloria?);
2. A Philippine growth rate competitive with our neighbors;
3. The peso appreciating;
4. The MRT completed from Caloocan to Baclaran;
5. The LRT 2 completed from Divisoria to Masinag/LARGO;
6. The Skyway extended to Binan;
7. The South Expressway completed to Batangas City;
8. New railway systems between Manila and Batangas City, Matnog, Clark, Subic, and Damortis; between Davao and Zamboanga City, and from Iloilo back to Iloilo along the circumference of Panay;
9. A new freeway along the east coast of Luzon from Aparri to Lucena;
10. Bridges between Batangas and Puerto Galera; between Matnog and Samar; between Leyte and Surigao; between Iloilo and Bacolod; and between Cebu City, Dumaguete and Tagbilaran;
11. A navigable canal connecting Infanta with Manila via Laguna de Bay;
12. A causeway connecting Calamba with Jalajala via Talim Island;
13. Universities and factories prohibited within Metro Manila, to disperse the population (Not that Great Britain and the Philippines have roughly the same area and population, but theirs is evenly distributed while ours is all in Metro Manila. A couple of hundred of kilometers away, Mindoro is so sparsely populated that if your plane crash-lands it will take weeks to find you.);
14. Policemen penalizing traffic singiteros instead of encouraging them;
15. The Pasig River with crystal-clear water;
16. Drivers obeying stop signs and traffic lights at night even without policemen or other cars on the road;
17. Loud music prohibited in restaurants and fast-food joints;
18. Concrete (roads, plazas, basketball courts, waiting sheds, etc.) outlawed in the country;
19. The Manila International Airport relocated to Clark, and it's old site converted to a park (without concrete structures);
20. Cutting down of trees and changing of street names declared heinous crimes punishable by death;
21. Customer service ladies in department store public address systems sating "Please come to ....." instead of "Please proceed to......."

Seriously though ... etc.

-o-o-o-o-o-

Action & Reaction!!!

Letters, faxes, e-mail, anecdotes, conversations . .

Herein is a writeup of Gani Cruz lifted off his column from The Philippine Star, April 20:

Delaney's Chismis

"Holy Thursday is a day of joy in spite of the fact that it is so close to Good Friday and the commemoration of the Passion. It is the Feast of the Institution of the Holy Eucharist and the Ordination of the Apostles at the Last Supper."

That is how Fr. John P. Delaney, S.J., described Holy Thursday in his parish newsletter to Catholics in the University of the Philippines in 1951. That kind of surprising yet accurate reading of Catholic tradition came week after week in Delaney's homemade publication. (This was long before desktop publishing, photocopiers, and even personal computers! Publishing anything in those days was, forgive the word, hell.)

I never met Delaney. He was dead by the time I joined the University of the Philippines Student Catholic Action (UPSCA) in the early sixties. I knew the name Delaney from "Delaney Hall," the home of UPSCA on the Diliman campus. I knew the person's spirit, however, because everybody older I met then was still under his spell. He had built not just the chapel, but the community, at a time when agnosticism was fashionable in U.P. and to be a Catholic was considered hopelessly conservative. (The anti-Catholic attitude turned out, of course, to be limited to only a few philosophers and administrators, because UPSCA would win the Student Council elections regularly, trouncing fraternities handily.)

With the publication of two volumes of collected (actually, selected, since not everything could be retrieved) Chapel Chatter and Chapel Chismis newsletters, done by Delaney from July 1949 to December 1955, I am now able to know the good priest much more intimately. Now, I am more sorry than ever that I was born too late to have met him.

I learned from the book that Delaney was not one to honor tradition if it contradicted common sense. For instance, he did not hold the Seven Last Words at noon. In 1950, he wrote, "The Seven Last Words, the Siete Palabras, or the Three Hours Agony, will be from six to nine in the evening. Why at that time? The main reason is that these hours should be much cooler than the hours from noon to three o'clock."

He was always eager to look for the logic behind Catholic traditions. For instance, in 1951, he explained the lack of a Mass on Good Friday: "In commemoration of the death of Our Lord on the Cross, the Mass is suspended. Why? Perhaps in early times it seemed unfitting that a human representative of Christ should dare to offer the Holy Sacrifice on the very day on which Christ Himself had offered Himself."

But he was always willing to honor Filipino traditions, such as the one of children jumping on Holy Saturday: "I don't know if the children are sure to grow during the year if they jump when the bells are rung at the Holy Saturday Gloria. Just for the sake of peace in the Church, I suggest that all the children save their jumping until after the Mass. As soon as they come out of the Chapel after Mass, I'll ring the bells all over again and they can jump to their hearts' content all over the lawn."

He wanted his parishioners to be as intelligent about their faith as they were about their academic pursuits. For instance, he asked for "very faithful and intelligent attendance at all the ceremonies of the last three days of Holy Week. By intelligent attendance, I mean that you read over the ceremonies ahead of time with your family, so that you'll all understand what is going on and be more ready to enter into the full spirit of them. By intelligent I

also mean that you follow the ceremonies in your booklets during the ceremonies themselves."

Delaney liked to describe himself as "Irish by descent, English by birth, American by nationality but Filipino by choice." He died less than a month after completing the chapel that now stands in UP Diliman, a chapel that was designed by young artists then still unknown (Leandro Locsin, Vicente Manansala, Arturo Luz, and Napoleon Abueva, now National Artists), financed by thousands of students, and honored as both an architectural and a religious landmark in our country's history.

Perhaps one of the most striking phrases in the whole two volumes of Chapel Chismis (Fr. J. P. Delaney Memorial Committee, 2000) is the simple, inspiring sentence Delaney wrote on Easter Sunday, 1951: "A community united in prayer is irresistible." Today, these words are as powerful as ever. May these words help us reflect during these four holy days (not holidays) on the passion, death, and resurrection of our Lord.

Happy Easter, everyone!

-o-o-o-o-o-

Master story-teller Johnny has been clipping electronically interesting editorials from Philippine Newspapers and posting them on the Loop. Here are excerpts from one such posting and the resulting rejoinders:

From the column of historian Ambeth Ocampo:

Seeing the droves of people swimming in polluted Manila Bay over the Holy Week made me ask if it would ever be possible to swim safely in the Pasig again. Then I dug up references to bathing in early travel accounts of the Philippines.

Many of the foreigners observed that Filipinos took a bath daily, which was quite strange for many Europeans who did not have to endure so much heat. Even Jose Rizal, when he was living in Europe, once bragged to his horrified family that he had not taken a bath in a month!

One of the earliest accounts of the Philippines is by the Jesuit Pedro Chirino. "Relacion de las islas Filipinas" was published in Rome in 1604 and he mentioned that the Filipinos:

"From the time when they are born.they.are brought up in the water. Consequently, both men and women swim like fishes, even from childhood and have no need of bridges to pass over rivers. They bathe themselves at all hours, for cleanliness and recreation . . .

"Bathing, an indispensable activity, is done every day, not only by Indios, but also by whoever enjoys the advantage of living near a river, that is to say, almost everybody. On holidays, men, women and children jump into the water pell-mell, but half-dressed. The women with their thick hair display ravishing grace. The tapis covers their bodies, and the men decently keep their pants on...The rivers of Marikina and San Mateo, whose limpid waters are supposed to be very healthful, are much frequented in summer, and baths taken in their water mixed with water from the chorillo de Marikina are a great help for gastric ailments."

The above seems to be historical trivia, but then history can be useful particularly to people marketing beauty products, especially shampoo. While the 21st century Filipino uses a shower rather than a river and doesn't worry about crocodiles lurking in the bath water, his concern for cleanliness and shiny black hair remains. I have always wondered why there are so many shampoo ads in print and TV showing hair with lather, scented hair and even shampoos that, unlike gogo, do not irritate the eyes and can be used on children. Modern Filipinos do not use coconut shells when bathing, but still use a tabo made of plastic.

Comments by JMR:

I don't know how true it is, but I've heard it said that the British take fewer baths per capita than Americans, while the northern continental Europeans (including the Dutch) take fewer baths than the British. [The reason appears to be practicality: Showers in Holland are so narrow it is difficult to even turn inside them. One wonders how the tall Dutch manage.] And the southern Europeans (including the French and the Spaniards) use perfume instead.

I've also heard it said that although Filipinos -- unlike Westerners -- are untidy with our surroundings (disposing of trash into the streets, garbage into rivers, and spittle onto sidewalks), we -- unlike Westerners -- are meticulously clean with our bodies. We take baths every day and never allow ourselves to stink. We also use tabo, not paper. Am I correct?

Magrespond naman kayo diyan!

From Danny:

Well said, Johnny. Re the Dutch, I agree. When I was a kid, my Pa was working at Standard Vacuum Oil Company and there were lots of expatriates. Once, we were at a company excursion and this Dutch expat, already in his swimming trunks, lifted his arm, and I caught a sniff of his terrible KO! As to the *tabo* vs paper, how about stones, as used by some of the middle eastern nomads? And I guess you all know about the well-worn joke on how a bus ticket can be used for TP!

From Liliosa:

I read somewhere that the Spanish missionaries in the Philippines were so appalled by the natives' custom of daily baths, and they actually considered bathing by the river a mortal sin. What could be so sinful about keeping clean? It must be that the indios were having such fun and frolic, that bathing became an "occasion for sin" which, in the old catechism, merits the same punishment as mortal sin. Boy, did those old friars miss a lot. Or did they?

From Vic Vitug:

When I was working with PRC, late '60s (Philippine Refining Company, a UNILEVER company), I received a British Health Habits survey form which I was supposed to use as a model in designing a Philippine version of the survey form.

One of the items that really surprised me was the way the form differentiated between baths and showers. As a Filipino, I thought of baths as *dutsa* or *tabo* type bathing. After some research (I asked an Englishman) I found out that baths were when you soak in a tub or what ever, (the operational word being soak) while showers were dutsa or tabo type bathing. (Swimming was not even considered).

With this new found knowledge, I re-examined the survey form and a sample of their results (in Britain) and found that the expected frequency of baths was from once a week to once every 6 months and even once a year. Showers for them were expected to be more frequent - once every two days, etc, etc. (There was also a provision for "Never" for baths and showers).

After designing and implementing the Philippine version of the survey, I sent a copy of the report to the Unilever Headquarters in England and promptly received a missive from them demanding a re-examination of the survey methodology and results because the numbers were "ridiculous".

My report indicated that a large segment of the Filipinos took "showers" twice a day, with some even three times a day. The bulk of the population took "showers" once a day and that we hardly took a "bath" (soaking). I was using their definitions. It took some convincing before they would reluctantly accept the results.

But eventually, they did.

-o-o-o-o-o-o-

WAXING NOSTALGIC

Walking down Memory Lane

Tigi started it all when he wrote a couple of long treatises about old Manila, and we mean the Manila of his time, as "old" can be so relative. Abridged excerpts:

Dear Guys,

A couple of mornings ago I picked up the phone and a familiar voice said: "Hoy Tigs, BER na?"

The sound of the familiar voice, my balikbayan cousin Bobby, and the words made wave after wave of dejá-vu wash over me. BER, the BER months: September, October, November, and December.

My thoughts winged back to those distant days here in San Juan when we were little boys growing up. . . .

Going to my grandmother's house we would pass through Sta. Mesa, Legarda, Azcarraga, Governor Forbes, crossing Avenida Rizal, into Tayuman and then a right into Ipil Street, to Lola's house.

I always prefer to call it "Avenida Rizal" instead of Rizal Avenue.

In my youth it was the street for all things.

Let us begin our meanderings from the end nearest Plaza Sta Cruz, nearest the Ideal Theatre. If we stood there what I remember the most was the Classy Spanish Store "Freixas."

I visited Freixas only three times in my life and it was as a young boy accompanying his mother and Lola.

My impressions were strong; it was a small store, it was air-conditioned. It was very simply appointed but had an elegant simplicity about it. Dark wood walls with some black panels all around. The glass "estantes" were full of Spanish goods. Most prominent were fans, and then to the delight of my masculine heart one "estante" displayed some very elegant Spanish wallets. These were of an odd size and I noted the compartments were quite different from the American style wallets we were used to.

I gawked at these things while Lola and Mama chose and purchased something for someone.

Walking out of Freixas we go along Avenida Rizal towards Monumento or basically North East.

Prominent on the left is the Ideal Theatre, home of MGM pictures. This is where pictures such as "The Three Musketeers" with Gene Kelly and June Alyson, "Scaramouche" with Stewart Granger, "The Prisoner of Zenda" again with Stewart Granger and Deborah Kerr, and a lot of musicals starring Judy Garland, Eleanor Powell, etc. delighted our whole generation of kids.

Right after Ideal was the "Good Earth Emporium". Good Earth was famous for having a sale perpetually and for having prices ending one centavo short of the next peso, P 4.99, P 14.99, P 8.99, etc.

Now looking to the right opposite Good Earth was the "15 Cents and Up Department Store." I think this as an attempt to emulate the American concept of the five and dime store. We often remarked with amusement that most of the things sold there were mostly "Up" and hardly "15 Cents"

Moving on we come to the "State Theatre", home of 20th Century Fox movies. Here we saw "The Mark of Zorro" with Tyrone Power, "The Black Swan" again with Tyrone Power, "Gunfight at O.K. Corral" with Henry Fonda in black and white, not the later one with Kirk Douglas as Doc Holiday.

Look to the left and we see the corner of Bustos. At this corner was a store called "Fongs", which specialized in belts. Past Fongs began a lot of small stores in between which were the small hole-in-the-wall eateries where one can get an excellent sandwich of Chinese ham with all the "*taba*" you want. It was also in this block that there was a fellow with meztiso or Caucasian features dressed as a US sailor peddling a watch to a Filipino-looking guy as a come-on to the passers by. They would keep this act on all day. Do you guys remember this ?

To the left and we see the Rialto Theatre. This was a first class movie house that showed first run double feature B-Movies. Later on Rialto would be torn down and replaced by a larger theatre, "Ever."

"Ever" was notable for being the first movie to show Cinemascope wide screen movies in Manila. What was the first movie? "Prince Valiant" starring Robert Wagner as Prince Valiant, Sterling Hayden as Sir Gawaine, Janet Leigh as Aleta, and Debra Paget in a blonde wig as Ilene.

Next we come to Raon St. and at the corner of Raon on the second floor of the building on the side towards Azcarraga was an institution beloved of many UP bugs, the Center Billiard Hall. I went there once with a friend but not being a pool afficianodo I was not too interested but I was surprised at the number of familiar faces playing billiards there whom I knew should be in class at that moment.

Further on, on the same side of Avenida was "Alemars". These bookstores figured prominently in our lives because of our perennial quest for text books.

Then we come to "Azcarraga" now "C.M. Recto."

The street right after Azcarraga is Doroteo Jose, where "Mapua Institute of Technology" and "P and P" Popular bookstore was located, a vital source of textbooks for UP students.

Right after Doroteo Jose, the second building after the corner is the "Manila Grand Opera House", a rather misleading name since it was the home of vaudeville and stage shows rather than Opera.

Curious, I went there once and it was a real treat. Bayani Casimiro did a tap dance, Katy de la Cruz did a song and dance number in tights, and for the fun part we had Pugo and Tugo for comedy relief. Could you ask for more within the Philippine context?

We go on and come to Mayhaligue. At the corner of Avenida Rizal and Mayhaligue is "Mayon Trading", a place of wonder and fun. It sold mainly magic tricks, toys, and baby things. Model airplanes were also sold if there were any available. These were the days of import control and we were made to understand that toys and such things as model airplanes were not essential to life.

Further along we come to an old theatre the "Alegria", Tagalog movies, old movies, and sometimes a double feature.

Then comes Tayuman and we turn here past Camarines Street, to go to my Lola's house on Ipil Street.

Tigi apparently wrote his reminiscences late at night which prompted Johnny to say:

Another enjoyable masterpiece! More!! More!! We should always keep Tigi awake at 2:30 in the morning, because this appears to be his most productive time.

Susan Po added:

But really Tigi, you'll be giving Nick Joaquin a run for his money! I read that Quijano de Manila just published a coffee table book on Manila. Well, here are all your editors and critics ready to help you deliver YOUR book. We are also your captive market. What else do you want?

Liliosa said:

Tigi, you have the memory of a pachyderm! Wouldn't it be nice if you could compile all these mental meanderings along the streets of old Manila, together with the responses of the loop, and publish a book! I have already forgotten many of these places you mention, but something of the atmostphere and character of the time and place lingers. Remember the house of Ramon Casas in San Miguel (or Quiapo)? What a grand relic of residential Spanish style architecture it was! Jess Javelona said that when he stayed over at Mon's house one night, he couldn't sleep because the bed, an intricately-carved mahogany piece, was too ornate for his taste.

-o-o-o-o-o-

JOKE TIME

Hi everybody, to spice up your weekend from an otherwise uneventful Category 2 Loop, here's a politically incorrect something from Johnny.

Island (Ach! Not original)

There is a beautiful deserted island in the middle of nowhere where the following groups of people are stranded:

2 Italian men and 1 Italian woman
2 French men and 1 French woman
2 German men and 1 German woman
2 Greek men and 1 Greek woman
2 Bulgarian men and 1 Bulgarian woman
2 Irish men and 1 Irish woman
2 American men and 1 American woman
2 Indian men and 1 Indian woman

One month later on this absolutely stunning deserted island in the middle of nowhere, the following has occurred:

One Italian man killed the other Italian man for the Italian woman.

The two Frenchmen and the Frenchwoman are living happily together in a "menage a trois."

The two German men have a strict weekly schedule of when they alternate with the German woman.

The two Greek men are sleeping with each other and the Greek woman is cleaning and cooking for them.

The Bulgarian men took a long look at the endless ocean and one look at the Bulgarian woman and they started swimming.

The Irish began by dividing up their island, Northside and Southside, and by setting up a distillery. They do not remember if sex is in the picture because it gets sort of foggy after the first few liters of coconut whiskey, but at least the English are not getting any.

The two American men are contemplating the virtues of suicide while the American woman keeps on talking about her body being her own, the true nature of feminism, how she can do everything that they can do, about the necessity of fulfillment, the equal division of household chores, how her last boyfriend respected her opinion and treated her much nicer and how her relationship with her mother is improving. But at least the taxes are low and it is not raining.

....AND...

The 2 Indian men are still waiting for someone to introduce them to the Indian woman.

Commentary from Johnny:

The ending is a bit of a letdown. (The joke was probably written by an Americanized Indian -- you know, someone who migrated to the States more than two years ago and now looks condescendingly on his compatriots from the old country and their quaint customs.) It could be altered so that the statement says instead, "The two Indian men are still waiting for someone to arrange their marriage to the Indian woman." Or a Filipino ending could be substituted -- **Isagani** is adept at this -- and the Indian thing dropped.

Isagani obliges:

Here is one possible Filipino ending, if we add 2 Filipino men and 1 Filipino woman to the original cast of characters.

The 2 Filipino men decide to have an election between the two of them on who should have the Filipino woman. The results: The First Filipino Man = 1 vote, the Second Filipino Man = 78 votes. The First Filipino Man protests to no avail, since this is a democracy and Johnny Reyes did not run (it's an island, remember?) as he was expected to.

The Second Filipino Man, therefore, takes in the Filipino woman to be his domestic helper, negotiates successfully with all the other men still left on the island and takes in all the other women as his *queridas*, giving the other remaining men shares of Philippine stocks (naturally involving a pyramid scheme), and lives happily ever after.

The First Filipino Man establishes a Filipino organization, publishes his own newspaper, lists his name in the Who's Who among Survivors, and starts a chain letter denouncing the sexist and chauvinist tactics of the Second Filipino Man. Meanwhile, the Filipino woman swims to Saudi Arabia, successfully wards off a rape attempt, returns to the island to become its wealthiest singer, and finances a film on her exploits.

Oh, the name of one of the Filipino men is J.E. (not Joseph Estrada, but Jose Emiliano, of course), but I won't tell you which one. (Apologies to grim and determined feminists on this list, but blame Danny Gil for getting me started on this one.)

Other comments:

Could it be the Indians referred to in the ending are people from the country of India rather than native Americans? Just a suggestion. Thanks for the laughs, Johnny.
Cynthia [Reyes-Calejesan]

Who ever said it was referring to Injuns rather than Indians?
Johnny.

-o-o-o-o-o-

FLASH: As we go to press, Gus de Leon emailed that they are preparing the third volume on the Fr Delaney series consisting of the recollections, biography, history of Upsca, the chapel, etc. One of the chapters will be entitles "The legacy of Fr Delaney lives on beyond his lifetime." Upscans are encouraged to contribute articles for this chapter. Narita Gonzalez will be doing the editing and will shortly be in town, where we can meet for further discussions.

Published in Los Angeles supposedly every quarter, but mainly when in the people behind it are in the mood. Most material is culled from unwitting Upscans in cyberspace. So other sources are most welcome. Please email, snailmail, fax, or call in your pictures, trivia, jokes, manifestos, etc, to either 19002 Horst Ave., Artesia, CA 90701, or ferngil@aol.com, or (562) 402-5890.

Picture gallery, from way back when.

1962 Baguio conference with Mon Casas, Melvyn Martin, Ruben Rivera, Cynthia Reyes, Digna Dacanay, Romy Ong, Fredie Santiano and Joe Alzona. From the archives of Ramon Casas, who sent it in from France.

Arthur Adiarte and Johnny Reyes trying "to do a Sebastian del Cano", as in their words. Date & place unknown.

THE DAILY MIRROR, WEDNESDAY,

Celia Maria Feliciano, who is leaving to take up her masters degree at the New York University School of Arts was honored with a despedida party by friends. Seated from left are Manya Ro- *driguez, Lynn Sunico, Miss Feliciano, Nore Raquel-Santos and Cora de Jesus. Standing are Rogel Rodriguez, Rene Sunico, Alexi Antonio and Chet Tan.*

A scan of news clipping from the album of Dette Feliciano. Seems as if the Daily Mirror is in error. We know of a Manya Alvendia who looks like the person captioned as Rodrigues. Though not Upscans all, can anybody tell us where they are now? Rogel and Rene are in Manila. Dette is in LA. Last we heard of Alexi was when he still was in UP telling us that his dad was a grafter, because he was a plastic surgeon.

Dette Feliciano, Thelma Ibañez-Teves and Danny Uy. March party in LA. Notice the identification name tags.

At the April NJ party. That's Gene Pulmano, Chit Inciong, and Norman Madrid, who was showing the cash-flow analysis of the Manila Tiger Investment Fund.

Both photos were taken January at the posh Stock Exchange Penthouse restaurant at the Ortigas area, as arranged for by Mercy, a frequent habitué. Men's photo shows (standing) Jess Javelona, Melvyn Martin, Ping Tan, Bong Nuqui, Godo Juliano, Nilo Cruz, Jimmy Abad, Mon Pasicolan. Sitting is Jimmy Ong and Danny Gil. Ladies in upper photo are (standing) Maureen Holazo-Faelnar, Susan Paulin-Martin, Mercy Rivera-Abad, Mimi Pasicolan, Deng Juliano, Jessie Quinto-Javelona, Beth Arcellana-Nuqui, Muni Cruz and Maya Santiano. Sitting are Anggé Alday-Soriano, Mrs Narita Gonzales and Lisa Señeris-Gil. The ladies complained that the super wide angle camera lens didn't do justice to their figures, especially those shown at the edges.

Above is Vic & Vickie Vitug, visiting from NY in 1998, and LA hosts Oids & Malu Garcia, and Tony Estrera. On right photo is Mon Pasicolan, Jimmy Abad, Mimi Pasicolan, Mrs. Avelina Gil, Maya Santiano, Mercy Abad and Tigi Barcelona, at Loyola.

Trying to look solemn: Ruben Rivera, Mon Pasicolan, Danny Gil, Jimmy Ong and Melvyn Martin at the wake of Danny's Pa, early February.

At the September UPAAA conference in Las Vegas, Helen Ybañez-Kluck, Nina Los Baños, and her sis Ditas.

At Noel & Angge Soriano's house, January 2000. Standing left to right to right are Angge, one of the nieces, Sonia Alday-Alampay, Lisa Seneris-Gil, Eva Singson-de Veyra, and Danny Gil. Part of Noel's therapy is painting, and he has had a number of exhibits. It was a weekday and Danny & Lisa were visiting. Soon after that, we went to a nearby restaurant in QC where Mon de Veyra met up and treated us to lunch. Mon is one of the three judges in the court of appeals, and after the lunch treat, he and Eva brought us over to his office near the QC Welcome rotunda to see how a judge operates. Very impressive.

While we were going through the delicious meal, who should pop in but Johnny Ramos. It was his birthday and he was being treated by his friend, the owner of the restaurant, among others. We hadn't seen Johnny in almost 10 years. Except for his greying hair and heavier set, it was the same 'ol Johnny as we remembered him years ago leading the choir as a conductor, in a similar smart barong with a pen clipped up front. Johnny still is Head of the UP Conservatory of Mucis. We had to dissuade him from adding our bill to his. Shown above are L-R: Sonia, Angge, Mon, Eva, Lisa and Johnny.

UPSCA Roster. The roster below originally was a mailing list. But as the "loop" of cyber Upscans kept increasing, more names appeared which didn't necessarily carry a postal address, nor a more definitive identity for incorporation to the Upsca database. So just before printing this issue, we emailed those in question. And while some did answer, others haven't as yet, hence only their name and email address appear below. Others have moved residence without any forwarding address, while still others prefer to keep their street and email address secret. We enjoin the readers to make updates and corrections, and to send in more names of their fellow Upscan friends whom they think may be intersted in receiving this newsletter or joining the cyber loop.

Jimmy & Mercy (Rivera) Abad Beverly Hills, Antipolo, Philippines	Nanette (Gadi) & Boy Angeles Monroeville, PA 15140	Olga (Cruz) Barrios Williamsville, NY	Delfin Castro Bowie, MD 20715	Nancy (Cruz) & Gerry Dienel Little Rock, AR 72212
Rory (Abrera) Somerstein Southlake, Texas 75092	Myrna Aquitania Camarillo, CA 93010	George Bartolome Vallejo, CA 94519	Rey Cendeño Industrial Valley, Marikina, Phils	Bing (Ferrer) & Anthony Dubitsky Riverdale, MD 20737
Arthur & Cherrie Adiarte St Paul, MN 55105	Lolly Aquino Los Angeles, CA 90042	Enteng & Mely Batas Cypress, CA	Remy & Anching Chica Northridge, CA 90242	Carmen Dungca Moorpark, CA 93021
Ofie (Peñaflorida) & Ken Aid Lakewood, CA 90715	Primo & Lindus (Carreon) Arambulo Rockville, MD 20852	Lito & Tita (Teaño) Balucan Cerritos, CA 90703	Tessie Chua Chiaco North Hollywood, CA 91605	Cir & Rose (Lacebal) Engay Los Angeles, CA 90065
Tomas Africa Philippines	Noli & Rosita Arong Arleta, CA 91331	Butch Bautista	Norma (Egay) Cornelio Marikina City 1801, Philippines	Georgina (Reyes) & Mervyn Encanto Quezon City, Philippines
Vyva Aguirre U.P. Campus, Quezon City, Phils	Sisoy & Cecile Arong Houston, TX 77036	Lennie (Abellera) & John Blair Libertyville, IL 60049	Ludy Corrales Basking Ridge, NJ 07920	Jose Enriga UP Campos, QC, Philippines ovppa@nicole.upd.edu.ph
Letty (Ramirez) Ajodah Queens Village, NY 11428	Fr Lito Arong, OMI Oakland, CA 94610	Maurie Borromeo Malapaya Village II Capitol Site, QC, Philippines	Isagani & Medy Cruz Malate, Manila 1004, Philippines	Manny & Lee Espejo Saugus, CA 91350
Ely & Sonia (Alday) Alampay Diliman, Quezon City, Philippines	Remy Baluyot Los Angeles, CA 90065	Reggie & Eddie Cailao Marikina, MM, Phils	Nilo Cruz Tordecillas St, Makati, Phils	Jose Espinosa Malate, Manila, Phils
Noye Alfiler North Susana Exec Village Diliman, QC, Philippines	Johnny & Alda Balaoing Los Angeles, CA 90065	Jun & Cynthia (Reyes) Calejesan Monaca, PA 15061	Rene Cruz Diamond Bar, CA 917665	Deo & Aleli Estacio Altadena, CA 91001
Rico Alfiler Maclane, VA 22101	Nina Los Baños Las Vegas, NV 89129	Ramon O. Casas 67000 Strasbourg, France	Boy dela Cruz Cottage Grove, MN 55016.	ALL STREET ADDRESSES AND EMAILS AND TEL NUMS HAVE BEEN ERASED.
José Alzona Glendale, CA 91206	Tigi & Nora Barcelona San Juan 1500, MM, Philippines	Manny Castillo Brea, CA 92621	Rene & Lydia Dawis Minneapolis, Minnesota 55414	

UPSCA

Alumni Association Newsletter

Staleletters   Nobrainers   Portrayals

A M D G   Vol 3, Num 13   Special Edition   1st half 2001

LAKBAYAN BECOMES A REALITY!

A little over three years ago, a group of Manila Upscans hatched a plan to troop over to the US and make a cross country drive, starting in LA and ending in NY, dragging along some of the locals, visiting as many Upscans along the way, and having party after party at each stop. The fervor was contagious, and pretty soon, US Upscans were roped into the plan, dates were set, the route was plotted out. A master spreadsheet was generated showing the daily route, vehicle rental and gasoline costs, lodging data, miles and time on the road, average speed, etc. There were to be two loops, starting together for the first week, with one going cross country to NY and lasting 3 weeks, and the other loop lasting two weeks, where they were to take off at Dallas and head to Yellowstone, then back to LA.

The planning was featured in at least two issues of the Newsletter, and spawned a number of unique terms: *Lakbayan* - obviously from Lakad Bayan, was easy to surmise. But etymologist and mystery writer Johnny Reyes coined other terms such as *Lakviajeros, Loyalistas, Expatriados, Resurrectados, Despalinjados*, etc.

Alas, the free fall of the peso in late 1997 derailed the Lakbayan. It was only after Johnny and family had immigrated to the US did the idea arise again. This, after a hiatus of almost 3 years.

By that time, San Miguel VPs Jimmy Ong and Mon Pasicolan were already in retirement and together with the Abads, they gave, out of the blue, a firm date when they'd come over: mid April, 2001. And can we US locals plan and make the arrangements?

And so we *Expatriados* did just that, scrambling to put a cohesive schedule together for the *Loyalistas* who were coming over, thus fusing into one group of *Lakviajeros.*

Firstly, we factored in the geriatric condition of most of us, and decided that a cross country drive was too strenuous. We even considered renting a recreational vehicle, but finally settled for a two-part adventure: a western and then an eastern cluster. The western cluster involving

April 14 party in LA after many of the engineering friends of Mercy had left. Shown with numbers are the western cluster Lakviajeros: Mercy & Jimmy Abad 1&2, Josie & Tony Estrera 3&4, Lisa & Danny Gil 5&6, Ting & Jimmy Ong 7&8, Ramon Pasicolan 9 (Mimi not shown) and Erwin Gomez 10 (son took picture) both of whom flew in from Indiana. Others are Upscans Tessie Chua-Chaco, Ernie & Jessie Pangilinan, and friends Toti & Gloria Kasilag and David Unson. The Gomez' later flew off from Las Vegas, while Christie Borromeo & Don Kawal and Nancy Cruz & Gerry Dienel joined the group in Sedona.

almost a weeks travel in a rented 15 passenger van to Las Vegas then Sedona, Arizona, and back to LA. Planners for this trip were Danny Gil and Tony Estrera. Then an eastern cluster starting with a red-eye flight to New Jersey for another week or so of travel, shopping and partying, planned and hosted by Jun Calejesan (based in Pittsburgh), Johnny Reyes (Belle Mead, NJ), Tony Nievera (NY) and Liliosa Mangosing-Evangelista (DC).

A good deal of the fun was in the flurry of email exchanges for the planning. Excerpted samples:

Mercy: We talked about the Lakbayan and only three couples are sure. April 15 plus or minus a few days is fine with the three couples. Ramon should be emailing you about the major limitations in planning the itinerary, namely, food and crankiness. When we were talking, the reality dawned on me that we are dealing with a group of geriatrics, whose hormones are fast fading away.

Ramon: Yes, cranky old men that's the best way to describe the guys, who will join the lakbayan safari. During last Sunday's get-together of the September-born at Ruben Rivera's new house, the consensus of JOng, Gani, Jimmy Abad and myself, the one and only unassailable assumption the engineers doing the itinerary planning should always consider is, and here

I quote JOng: . . and soon we will get into each others nerves, for we are all getting cranky. And Ani chimed in: . . I do not know whether we can trust the engineers, better leave the planning to the poets, that way, we are at least sure to get nowhere.

So here are some trade-offs, inverse relationships and any combinations thereof as guidelines:

1. The trade-off between time and crankiness.
2. The trade-off between distance and crankiness.
3. The trade-off between gall bladder capacity and crankiness.
4. The trade-off between the wive's patience and husbands' crankiness (remember the wives always rule).
5. The trade-off between and this the most important of all, FOOD and crankiness.

Reading Tony's recent suggestion of using a recreational vehicle which he claims gives comfort facilities and rotational privileges for couple's privacy, I was tempted to include as Trade-off No 6 Sex and crankiness.

But I have no empirical evidence that the presence or absence of sex leads to crankiness. So I suggest to the engineers to lay-off this issue and let the poets take it on.

The incipient danger is the Triple AAA syndrome - Aburido, Arthritis and Alzheimer's.

JOng: While rental costs for the RV should obviously be split evenly among participating couples, Ting suggests a modest premium for bedroom use. Frequent users pay more naturally; the rest can always cite budgetary constraints and waning passion.

Jun: How about a Broadway ? Anybody with good connections to get advance tickets to a fairly decent show?

Danny: Quite difficult, getting advance tickets to good shows. Best bet is to catch one of those last-minute ticket stalls in Times Square. Let's play it by ear.

Liliosa: We all must have very playful ears!

Ramon: AT OUR AGE, that's the only part of our organs we can play with!

Jun: Actually I have no problem so long as Mon keeps to his own.

Liliosa: If we don't watch out, this trip may turn out to be *Lakbawdy*.

-o-o-o-o-

Danny: How about driving to Puerto Nuevo, that famed exclusive lobster enclave in Mexico, 45 minutes south of Tijuana (the armpit of San Diego, 2 hours south of LA), and have Mexican lobster.

JOng: If I tell my students that I crossed the border into Tijuana, Mexico and touched nothing but lobster, and they believe me, I would die of shame.

Erwin: Any lobster sounds good. Mexican lobster is a different species, quite different from Homarus species (Maine lobster). Having a daughter study in Maine and now living in Martha's Vineyard, I can now deliver a lecture on lobsters. Mexican lobster, which I think is the same as the one we can get occasionally in my hometown (or at least used to), has its charms, but Maine lobster rules. Mon Pasicolan should have different expectations from Mexican lobster.

Mon: Aaah, Erwin, you just reconfirmed that Maine lobster has got to be it. But Danny's suggestion of the Mexican variety with tequila ought to be something else.

Jun: I believe you should try them all, Mexican, Maine, Baltimore, plus Philippines. Then let's hear Mon's report on the comparative merits - should be good for a few hundred miles of driving.

As it turns out, we didn't use an RV, never got to Tijuana or Baltimore or Maine for lobster, but had something better. Do read on to Johnny's Lakbayan Diary. Indeed, the Lakbayan was a smashing success.

More excerpts:

Nancy Cruz-Dienel: It was a good get-together at Oak Creek Canyon and Sedona. Really nice to see everyone after all these years (>30 years!) and meet new friends, Ting and Mimi.

Liliosa:

Natapos ang pista
Nabasag ang pinggan
Nabutas ang bulsa
Naubos ang handaan ....

Or something like that.

Hope you survived it all, and see you in Provençe, I mean, Pittsburgh!

Jun & Cynthia:

Actually, ang nabasag ay pitchel (now I have an excuse to get a better one). Methinks Lakbayan I was a resounding success; already look forward to the next one. Must say the planning of it was half the fun. It's a tribute to the group's flexibility that even though the plans continued to evolve up to the very last day, everyone kept their cool. Glad to note too that the much-warned danger against crabs were on the table and not around it. Thanks for the memories, guys - and gals!!!

Liliosa:

What delighted me was discovering new things about the lakabayanis, whom I thought I knew so well:
- that Jun Calejesan's sense of humor matches his extraordinary organizational skills; no wonder Cynthia is so serene.
- that earthy, worldly, portly Mon Pasicolan could be so enthralled by an ascetic, supernatural, and out-of-this world site such as the Franciscan Monastery, catacombs and gardens (they were beautiful!); must be Mimi's influence.
- that Jimmy Ong and I could still agree on certain things such as "We are incomplete and imperfect human beings, but our friends complete us", with Ting nodding in full approval.
- that Mercy Abad's hug is still strong and reassuring, and that Jimmy Abad's mind can be picked for deep thoughts even while he is picking at crabs.
- that Johnny Reyes never leads, never follows, doesn't like convoys, but can still be on time (well, almost); Mila must have a good sense of direction.
- that Danny Gil is such a romantic man; my favorite picture is that taken of him taking Lisa's picture somewhere in Georgetown; with the caption, "Mr and Mrs Gil" it could win a prize in a photo contest.
- that it is never too late to make new friends; Bing Ferrer Dubitsky and I hit it off so well, laughing so hard on our way to New York that we took the wrong exit somewhere in Philadelphia but lost about 15 minutes lang, oy!

- that Tony Estrera is new to the Washington DC area; you all should have stayed longer!
- that the Quisumbings make fine neighbors; are we adopting them?
- that Loida Nicolas-Lewis still remembers me; I must have done some pretty silly things back then.
- that Lindus and I could look so good on a cake!

I had a fabulous time with you all, even if I only had a few days to join, and was still recovering from some foreign bug. [*Lili recently came in from Europe*].

Jimmy: How Mercy and I wish we had more time! -- in Los Angeles and Las Vegas (oops! not too long in the latter place), Sedona and the Grand Canyon, New Jersey and Pittsburgh, New York and Washington, D.C.; more time for the traveling and sight-seeing, the shopping and the feasting, the museums, the Broadway show, the bookstores (ye gods!) -- but above all, more time for the company of truly great friends. After so long a time, it was wonderful to meet again Erwin Gomez and his son Victor who joined us in Los Angeles and the Western leg all the way from Indiana; later, we spent two idyllic days in Sedona with Christie (Borromeo) and Nancy (Cruz) with their American hubbies. In various parties and reunions too -- at Danny's, at Tony Nievera's, at Lili Evangelista's place -- we had such a congenial time with friends whom we had not seen since college days, like Primo and Lindus Arambulo and Raquel (Zaraspe), so wrapped with stories about each others lives, one could wish the time would not run. It was also an occasion for Mercy to meet some dear Eng'g friends whom she had not seen for more than 30 years like David Unson and Toti Kasilag . After all she will always be one of the boys. Mercy and I will always gratefully remember how Danny Gil and Tony Estrera took turns driving hundreds of miles during the entire "odyssey", perhaps the most relaxing drive in our lives not only because there were no potholes but largely because both are driver extraordinaire as Casas would put it (and not only that they also know which way to go); and how Johnny Reyes and Jun and Cynthia Calejesan also drove us to malls, factory outlets, and interesting places to see; how our friends' homes were open to us - Danny and Lisa, Babette and Ian, Johnny and Mila, Jun and Cynthia, Ed and Cely Quisumbing, Dodi and Becky Castillo; how Loida Nicholas Lewis threw a party for us -- oh, what giant lobsters! -- at her own beautifully appointed suite.

Truly, there is no sweeter gift from heaven than an enduring friendship.

Mercy: Cheers, and let us make the next trip happen before we are too old.

-o-o-o-o-o-

Lakbayan Diary
(complete and unexpurgated)
by Johnny Reyes

The trees of the Garden State were just budding with leaves after a long, cold winter when seven bleary-eyed survivors of the Lakbayan Western Cluster stepped out of the plane at Newark Airport on a fresh and sunny Saturday morning. The group had left Los Angeles close to midnight on Friday night and just when they were falling asleep after five hours, had to land at Detroit to catch the remaining hour-long connecting flight to EWR. Mercy (Rivera) Abad said their aircraft from LA had been overbooked and they were offered $400 each to take a later flight. Although sorely tempted to accept, they would never even think of disappointing those meeting them at Newark, so they insisted that the airline provide an extra plane. The result was that although the strategically-located airport of New Jersey is now said to be busier than JFK, on this particular morning the Lakviajeros were the only arriving passengers at the Northwest Airlines Terminal and the baggage carousel was nearly empty, except for the Lakbayan suitcases and two electric guitars which Jimmy Abad was taking home as presents for his twin sons. (For the guitars to be accepted as carry-on baggage, Jimmy needed to show that they were an essential part of his equipment as a travelling rock musician, so he had to dress and act the part.)

The rest of the arrivals were Mimi (Martirez) and Mon Pasicolan and Ting (Tejada) and Jimmy Ong, who joined Mila and myself in our minivan, and Tony Estrera, who teamed up with the Abads in Lisa (Señeris) and Danny Gil's rented Dodge Intrepid, currently the second most macho American-made stock sedan (after the Chrysler 300M). The Gils themselves had arrived from LA two hours earlier. Completing the Eastern Cluster cast of characters were Cynthia (Reyes) and Jun Calejesan, who were expected to join up with the Lakviajeros at the UPSCA Alumni grand reunion scheduled later in the day.

This grand reunion was set from 1:30 pm "until sawa" at Bernie (Jaramilla) and Tony Nievera's Long Island estate. After briefly freshening up at their hosts' townhouse in Belle Mead, NJ, the group braced for the torturous trip to Babylon, NY, which is twice as far to the east of Manhattan (through some of the US East Coast's most sluggish traffic) as Belle Mead is to the west of it. With all alternative routes to Long Island expected to be equally slow, we chose the scenic Belt Parkway route which at least features the beautiful Verrazano Suspension Bridge, with the longest single span in the world --

much longer than San Francisco's Golden Gate. Bumper-to-bumper traffic in Staten Island moved inch-by-inch towards the bridge for mile after endless mile, but we finally made it -- we were at the crossover point to Brooklyn at last. As the twin catenary cables stretched out in both directions toward the magnificent pylons of the Verrazano, blue in the afternoon sun, guess how many passengers were awake to enjoy the view?

The Nievera's huge house, though extremely difficult to get to, was not difficult to find, and it even had valet parking (Tony). Our minivan arrived promptly at 4:30 pm (Filipino time), and the Gils and the Calejesans checked in soon after. We were all thrilled to recognize faces we hadn't seen in more than 30 years. Aside from the Lakviajeros, present were (in roughly reverse-alphabetical order) --

Sari Valenzuela;
Amelia (Bascon) Rasalan;
Priscilla (Bautista) Perez;
Nel Reformina;
Violy (Sumulong) and Gene Pulmano;
Raquel (Zaraspe) Ordonez;
Norman Madrid;
Loida (Nicolas) Lewis;
Wilma (Jimenez) and Chit Inciong;
Susan (Rodriguez) and Richard Fagan;
Letty (Ramirez) Ajodah;
Vicky (Potenciano) and Vic Vitug; and
Glenda (Villajuan) and Ramon Gil.

Vic had brought his (1967) copy of the Philippinensian, and that was a big hit,

Danny, Tony, Sari Valenzuela and Priscilla Bautista-Perez looking at Philippinensian.

since most of us had lost our own copies long ago. I thought Vic was in gladiator costume, but he explained that his leather wristbands were for therapeutic purposes. As usual with potluck dinners, the food was overflowing. This must have been the first UPSCA Alumni reunion ever held on the US East Coast, and the 30-odd who attended were a good-sized crowd by local standards. By acclamation, Tony and Sari were appointed to coordinate future reunions, which would be held regularly from now on.

After an overnight stay at the Reyes townhome in Belle Mead, the plan was for the Lakviajeros to proceed next day in two identical Voyagers -- one green and the other white -- to Fairfax, VA, with a sightseeing stop at the US Naval Academy in Annapolis. The Reyes basement had been converted into a World War II-style air-raid shelter, with folding beds and sleeping bags borrowed from Mila's sisters, to accommodate all the nine Lakviajeros (excluding the Gils). Next day was a Sunday, and we started the day off early by shepherding the group to the St. Charles Borromeo Parish nearby for Mass. Along the way, the white Voyager driven by Jun Calejesan followed the wrong green minivan and disappeared. The rest of us suitably panicked because I had neglected to give Jun the address of our destination, and an all-points search was conducted among the streets of Belle Mead for a runaway white minivan. It turned out we had underestimated Jun's resourcefulness -- he stopped at the first Protestant church to inquire, and was promptly directed to the nearest Catholic church -- the only information they could not give him was the schedule of services. In the end, everyone found his/her way to St. Charles Borromeo and managed to attend a substantial portion of the Mass. (The final hymn was appropriately "Ode to Joy.") A skill I didn't have before was travelling in convoy -- whether leading or following -- but during the Lakbayan I learned how.

Before leaving the neighborhood, we made a quick visit to Princeton University. The campus is not big -- it looks like a bonsai version of Yale. After driving around the block one-and-a-half times, I announced that we had done Princeton. Next stop was the modest house of Albert Einstein at #112 Mercer Avenue nearby, which still belongs to the Princeton Institute for Advanced Study (where both Einstein and Tigi Barcelona worked), and is currently occupied by a genome scientist. (The exterior of the house was featured in the movie "IQ" starring Meg Ryan, Tim Robbins, and Walter Matthau as Einstein, but because the house is so small the interior shots had to be taken in another house.) Mon Pasicolan happily jumped out of the minivan and asked Jun Calejesan to take his pictures with Einstein's house in the background. After several well-choreographed shots by Jun, the rest of us suddenly realized Mon was posing in front of #110 -- wrong house! Take two.

On the way to Annapolis, the plan was to stop for lunch at our favorite place -- the "best Chinese buffet in New Jersey." To be more precise -- "the best (and only) Chinese buffet in the strip mall in the town of Brick, NJ." Jun misheard me and thought the restaurant was 15 minutes off the direct route between Princeton and Washington DC. Actually, what I had said was "50 miles off." During the hour-long trip there were a lot of frantic hand signals from the other minivan which we could not decipher, so we just waved back, but we eventually made it to the restaurant (which is only a few miles short of the Jersey shore) and enjoyed a hearty meal -- anything tastes good at 2:00 pm. Mila's sister Trining (Garcia) Bonifacio, who lives nearby, joined us at the buffet.

But a new problem had come up: We were expected at Liliosa (Mangosing) Evangelista's place for dinner at 6:00, and the time left for Annapolis was diminishing. Earlier, I had tried to bargain with Lili-O to allow us to come at 7:00 instead, arguing that at this time of year 6 o'clock was mid-afternoon. But her reply was that (a) the paella being prepared by Primo Arambulo was no good when cold and needed to be served promptly at 6:00; (b) the other guests had already been told; (c) the next day was a working day for these guests; etc. In the back of the minivan, JOng was heard muttering, What will happen if we don't arrive on time -- will she excommunicate us? But I felt I had no choice except to abort Annapolis, and the other minivan grudgingly agreed to abide with my decision. We made it to the Evangelista townhome at Fairfax before 6:30. Guess what time the paella arrived?

Also present at Liliosa's dinner party, aside from the Lakviajeros, were Lindus (Carreon) and Primo Arambulo, Liliosa's sister Nereida (Mangosing) Koeppen; Cely (Tayag) and Ed Quisumbing (an agriculturist and official of the World Bank); Bing (Ferrer) and Tony Dubitsky, who live nearby; and Mon Pasicolan's son Paolo, who works in Washington, D.C. Liliosa's surprise for the evening was a birthday cake for Lindus with a black-and-white UP Diliman-vintage photo of the two girls lasered into the icing. Those who were not looking closely probably didn't notice that the picture was a 3-D hologram, showing different points of view from different angles. The wonders of technology! Mon Pasicolan remarked that a similar cake featuring Primo and Tigi would look great. After the dinner, the Pasicolans, Ongs, and Calejesans were assigned to stay over at Liliosa's townhouse in Fairfax VA, while the rest (Abads, Gils, Tony Estrera, and Reyeses) stayed at the Vienna VA home of the Quisumbings, where a story-telling session lasted until early Monday morning. One of the anecdotes was about Ed's stay in Indonesia, where he learned that the local word for tooth was "gigi," with the g's hard. Toothpick was "tusuk-gigi."

When he asked for a toothpick at a crowded restaurant, the waiter bellowed at the top of his lungs to the kitchen while pointing at Ed, "TUSUK-GIGI!!"

The original program for the next day was a tour of Washington DC, the Basilica of the Immaculate Conception, the Franciscan Monastery, Mount Vernon, Shenandoah Valley, Skyline Drive, and the Luray Caverns. Since we had missed Annapolis the day before, we were also considering squeezing it into the schedule. If we had enough time left at the end of the day -- perhaps Richmond VA as well. The assumption was that we would get started at 3:00 am -- para makarame. But since we all woke up after 9:00 o'clock, it was decided to delete some of the items from the itinerary. The two minivans met at the Quisumbings, disagreed on the route to DC, met again at the WHO Headquarters downtown to pick up Lindus, then after driving around the Washington Monument block one-and-a-half times for the benefit of Tony Estrera who was a first-time visitor to the U.S. capital (We've done Washington DC!), proceeded to the Basilica for lunch in the cafeteria. Built in the 50's in the Romanesque style, the church is the sixth largest in the world. The group noted that one of the chapels in the church crypt is dedicated to the Virgin of Antipolo (Our Lady of Peace and Good Voyage). The

gorgeous floral landscape [see above] around the Basilica was conducive to photo sessions, but because of the size of the building it was impossible to get the colorful eggshell dome inside the same picture when taking shots of the group in front. The alternative was to move the subjects a few hundred yards forward, and then use the church as a distant background, but we didn't have time to scout around for the optimal lookout point, much less for the group to do much walking.

At this point, the two minivans split up again -- the white Voyager heading for the Franciscan Monastery, Mount Vernon,

Shenandoah Valley, and the rest of the tourist stops listed earlier, and the green taking Tony Estrera to the Smithsonian Aero-Space Museum for a one-stop but comprehensive visit. I dropped off my passengers and looked for a parking slot. When I rejoined them, I was expecting the girls (Mercy, Lisa, Mila) to be already climbing excitedly over the magnificent lunar landers, biplanes, and WWII bombers on display. Instead, I was surprised to find the group sitting forlornly on a bench in the middle of the crowd, patiently waiting for Tony to finish his inspection. Since for some reason the ladies didn't find the museum so hot, it was agreed to go to the art gallery across the mall and look at Monets, Van Goghs, Gauguins, and Cezannes instead.

Again it was a dinner appointment determining our schedule, because the plan was to meet at Capt. Pell's Maryland Crabhouse, highly recommended by the Quisumbings, at 7:00 that evening. Since we still had some quality time left before then, we agreed to make a quick visit to the hilly, leafy, and eerie Georgetown University campus -- Remember Fr. Karras' famous leap from an upper-story window down to the street below in "The Exorcist"? We didn't have time to look for that famous house (built specially for the movie), but with Danny Gil navigating

we found the fake-Gothic [see above] campus easily and did the usual photo op.

The task that faced us at the crabhouse can be appreciated best by viewing the before-and-after photos of the eight dozen male crabs which had to be attacked by hand, with only sledgehammers as weapons. (It is illegal to harvest female crabs.) Rice and vinegar were brought along by the area hosts. Those not equal to the task settled for prawns instead, which required less manual labor. Later, Cynthia Calejesan was to remark that it was good the crabs were on the table, not around it -- considering the pressures on the Philippine Lakviajeros of the two-week trip and the constantly-changing plans. After dinner, the Lakviajeros headed for their assigned lodgings, except for Tony Estrera and Mon Pasicolan who were shown "Washington DC By Night" by Bing and Tony Dubitsky in their car. The trade-off was that they missed the second joke session at the Quisumbings which lasted until early Tuesday morning.

Time to head for Pittsburgh, which Jun Calejesan explained is part of the East Coast. (Sige na nga!) This time the green Voyager and the white Intrepid agreed to follow Jun's lead, and we maintained a well-behaved convoy during the entire four-hour trip. We also gained Tony Estrera's cell phone, so we had high-tech wireless contact with the other vehicles - no more hand signals. The route was mountainous, and during the uphill laps my underpowered 2.4-liter/4-cylinder Voyager had its hands full keeping up with Jun's 3.3-liter/V-6 Voyager and Danny's Intrepid which was also a V-6. But the consolation was that I was doing 22 miles per gallon of regular gasoline, while they were probably doing only 17. The reshuffle had the Pasicolans and Ongs riding with the Calejesans, the Abads and Tony with us, and the Gils in the Intrepid. I noticed that our passengers were slowly dwindling -- possibly because of the continuous Golden Oldies music in my minivan. But Mon was the "ideal Filipino visitor." Everytime I tried to refuel, he would instantly appear beside the gas pump (even if he was riding in the other minivan) and pounce on the Hindu attendant to hand over the payment. "From the Bank," Mon would explain. (It seems the Lakviajeros had formed a cooperative, with Mon appointed as Treasurer.)

We stopped for a picnic lunch in the Ohiopyle Park, at a dramatic lookout point alongside the Ohio River, where the rocks in the shallows churned up the water and created white-water rafting conditions --

the Pagsanjan Rapids *[see above]* on a grand scale! No rafting for this group though, in view of the prevailing level of maturity, so efforts were focused on attacking the appetizing pizza and giant subs bought from a country store along the way.

The rushing river in the woods prefigured our next destination: the most famous house in modern history, Frank Lloyd Wright's "FallingWater," designed and built in the 1930's for the department store-owner Kaufman Family. Our group was given a very detailed tour inside the magical house by a knowledgeable and elderly guide, who said she has a Filipina daughter-in-law. This created a rapport with the Lakviajeros and generated so many questions that the only two Americans in our tour group, a guy couple, were completely left out. Our guide said that Lloyd Wright was commissioned by the Kaufmans to build them a summer retreat in their private woods, and they expected him to position the house facing the waterfall. Instead, he placed the house on top of the falls itself, making use of the available rock materials, the terrain, and the rushing water to create a living,

breathing house *[see above]* with natural ventilation, cooling, and sound effects. Lloyd Wright's masterpiece [Remember the photo in our Humanities 1 textbook?] set a trend for modern architecture, and the style of the house has been copied so much that whenever we see its features in other houses and buildings, we take them for granted. Even the AS and Engineering Buildings in UP Diliman were influenced by the Frank Lloyd Wright style, and seeing the original now was almost anticlimactic. The guide mentioned, though, that the distinctive cantilevered concrete slabs were now sagging and were currently undergoing a lengthy repair process. As a consequence, temporary scaffolding can be seen in our photos supporting the slabs.

Another short drive through the woods and across a dizzyingly high bridge, and finally we were at the Calejesan home in Monaca PA. Cynthia and her charming eldest daughter served dinner featuring Puerto Rican cuisine. Afterwards, the Lakviajeros gathered around the DVD player in the family room to watch The Three Tenors performing in Paris (with Dick Cheney conducting, disguised in a blonde wig), and then after drawing lots were distributed around the house, to get a good night's sleep in preparation for the next day's strenuous activities.

Early Wednesday morning, after a brief tour of downtown Pittsburgh in the two minivans, the girls split off, heading for the main event of the day: factory outlets in Grove City. The boys had no choice but to kill time at Best Buy and at the Half-Price Book and Video Store. Patiently enduring the long wait, Jimmy Abad and Jimmy Ong decided to pass the time by filling up a shopping cart -- might as well. After reuniting with the girls at Grove City, we drove back to Monaca for dinner again with the Calejesans, then watched another DVD video -- this time a Julie Andrews-emceed musical extravaganza. One of the numbers, performed by Heather Hedley, foreshadowed the Broadway musical we were going to see on Friday night.

The Lakviajeros got an opportunity for some social climbing when we were invited for Thursday night dinner at the Manhattan Upper East Side apartment of billionaire UPSCA businesswoman Loida Nicolas-Lewis, overlooking Central Park. The plan was to leave Monaca PA as early as possible, drive the six hours back to Belle Mead NJ, freshen up for a couple of hours, then drive another two hours through peak-hour traffic to get to New York City in time for Loida's 7:00 o'clock invitation. Once more it was a dinner appointment determining our schedule -- there go the side trips we had been planning to Cornell and West Point -- but the Upper East Side dinner was an event no one in the group wanted to miss. The long six-hour leg from Pittsburgh to New Jersey was uneventful -- since there is literally nothing along the way -- but we noted that after a week of Spring, the trees in New Jersey were now in full bloom at last. The Calejesans had the Pasicolans in their minivan, the Gils had the Abads, while we had the Ongs and Tony Estrera. The road stretched out level all the way -- no more mountains. I volunteered to be the pacer this time, to ensure that we got to Loida's on schedule, and Jun agreed -- but he set a condition that I must not exceed 70. Some pacer -- with tractor-trailer trucks cruising at 75-80!

We arrived at Loida's luxurious 9th floor apartment only 30 minutes late. The walls were covered with paintings from her late husband Reginald's extensive art collection. Loida was giving a guided tour, but I was at the back and managed to catch only the words "a rare pink Picasso" and "Joan Miro..." Some of the paintings were done by African-American artists, not so well known -- to me, anyway -- but equally gifted. Loida kicked off the dinner by asking how many of the guests agreed with the wisdom and the timing of the Philippine Government's decision earlier that day to place Joseph Estrada under arrest. The first reaction of the gung-ho Lakviajeros was, Good decision! About time! But when Loida pointed out the potential negative effects on the coming

The Lakviajeros in an after-dinner pose at the living room of Loida's NY 5th Ave residence.

elections should Estrada be made into a "martyr," some of the guests started to waver. [With the benefit of hindsight, though -- now that we know the outcome of the failed march on Malacañang -- it was probably still best for Gloria Macapagal-Arroyo to have jailed Erap when she did and brought things to a head.]

Liliosa Evangelista, Bing Dubitsky, and Liliosa's daughter Beatriz caught up with the group at this time, with Bing driving all the way from VA. Because they were a bit late, Liliosa got to sit at the head of the table with Loida, a St. Theresa schoolmate. The main course was lobsters! Some of us had never had this dish before, except with fillet stuffing, and never realized that almost all parts of the lobster contain edible meat. We didn't need to go to Maine, after all, to enjoy this delicacy. Afterwards, Loida introduced her Filipina chefs who had prepared the sumptuous dinner.

At this point, Liliosa bade the group, "See you in Provençe!" [There had been talk of holding a Lakbayan II in Southern France in two years' time, after everyone has had a chance to save some money. In my view, a driving tour of Great Britain would be more enjoyable and meaningful. All of Europe is saturated with history, but England is the most vicariously familiar area to us Filipinos, who have been exposed to nothing but English literature in our lives. For instance, a week's drive -- Mila and I did it over a three-day week-end -- through London, Cambridge, Sherwood Forest (Robin Hood!), York and the Yorkshire Moors (Heathcliff!), Edinburgh, Lancaster (War of the Roses!), the Lake District (Wordsworth!), Oxford, and then London again, with overnight

stops in isolated bed-and-breakfast cottages (the spookier the better - there are more ghosts recorded per square mile in England than in the rest of the world), is unbeatable. Also, together with the US, England is certainly the most civil and civilized country in the world -- you don't need to pay to get into a public rest room. And best of all, the natives can speak English! In contrast, what's familiar to us about French history and literature -- aside from Joan of Arc, Napoleon, and Les Miserables? Did we ever enjoy a French novel?]

Home again to Belle Mead NJ for an overnight stay, with some of the Lakviajeros spending the night instead at the Jersey City house of Danny and Lisa's daughter Babette and her husband Ian. The plan for Friday was to visit more factory outlets and then to end the day with a Broadway musical in the evening. Mila's original intention was to take the group to her favorite neighborhood outlets in Flemington NJ near Belle Mead, but this is a small and unassuming country-style shopping area which cannot compare with the Grove City factory outlets. To avoid a letdown, we decided to take the group instead to a huge new indoor shopping stadium Mila and I had never been to ourselves: the Jersey Garden factory outlets mall in the busy area of Elizabeth NJ. This was female territory, and the ladies were busy for the next 3-4 hours. Mon and Tony spotted a bargain -- Samsonite carry-on bags (with rollers) at only $59.99 each! -- and during the debriefing afterwards, the two proudly exhibited their trophies to the group. Ting Ong then shyly pulled out a similar carry-on bag (with rollers) she said she had just bought -- for $17. After about a minute, Ting added (to break the silence), "It's slightly smaller, of course."

Cynthia, Jun and Danny, meanwhile, had been busy lining up in Manhattan for Broadway tickets. When we met up with them at Babette and Ian's house, we learned that the musical they had selected was Loida's recommendation: Elton John's modern version of "Aida." Onward to the lights of Broadway! "Aida" was standing room only, but very cost-effective -- at $10! The lead role of a Nubian princess calls for an African-American actress-singer; obviously written with Heather Hedley in mind for this role, I guess the production cannot stand on its own if she is ever replaced by another star. During the intermission Mercy Abad commented, "This is music for the young!"

Afterwards, Mon Pasicolan led us to the Carnegie Deli on 7th Avenue for mammoth corned-beef-on-rye or pastrami-on-rye sandwiches. [Back during the Lakbayan planning period, Mon had e-mailed the Loop that he was "looking forward to leisurely enjoying a sub at the Carnegie." All the time I thought he meant the Carnegie Center.] We had a contest on who could finish an entire sandwich, but only Tony Estrera qualified. Not bad for $10.95 per sub. And the deli is very close to the only parking building I know of in this area (located between 7th and 8th and between 53rd and 54th) where you can park and lock your car yourself -- no obligatory valet parking.

[It is interesting to note that on the evening of May 10, only two weeks after the Lakbayan exercise, a Mafia hit team walked into the very same Carnegie Deli, climbed the stairs, entered an apartment on the second floor, and executed five individuals gangland-style (two survived). One of the victims was a lady dancer who had appeared in the movie "Dirty Dancing." Responding NYPD officers, who theorized that the killings were related to a drug deal gone bad, closed off the building for hours with customers still trapped inside the deli on the ground floor. A few of the stranded diners fumed, but like typical New Yorkers the majority relaxed and enjoyed their meals.]

After the corned beef dinner, we dropped our passengers off at the Jersey City home of Danny and Lisa's daughter, which they intended to use as a convenient base in the next few days to get to their respective take-off points (Newark Airport; NY Penn Central Railroad Station; etc.). Mila and I reluctantly left the Lakbayan East Coast Cluster at this time. It had been an enjoyable and exciting week for us, and we are already missing the Lakviajeros.

-o-o-o-o-o-

EDITORIAL BOX

The UPSCA Alumni Newsletter is published ill-frequently in Los Angeles. This issue is dedicated mainly to the recent Lakbayan trip. Written material herein has been generously supplied by the listed contributors. Pictures are taken from the digital cameras of Johnny Reyes, Ed Quisumbing, and the scanned photo prints of Danny Gil. Picture quality as been maximized as much as possible, but some sourcing has been deficient.

Recipients in the mailing list (especially the first timers), and the recent participants in the featured activities are enjoined to send in their pictures, comments, anecdotes and trivia to Danny Gil at 19002 Horst Ave, Artesia, CA 90701, tel/fax (562) 402-5098, e-mail ferngil@aol.com, so the next issue can be started. This will include the usual departments on Humor, Politics, News, Commentary, Fiction, etc.

This issue, as are the earlier 12 issues, will also be posted on the Upsca website (http://upsca.org) maintained by webmaster Danny Uy. More pictures of alumni activities are also available on the website for the loop members.

Other acknowledgements: thanks to Tony Estrera, Malu Garcia and Manny Castillo for helping out on the postage and other expenses for the last issue, and to Mercy Abad for same on the Manila end.

A MONTAGE OF PHOTOS

First row left shows the raffle during the LA Apr 14 party at the Gil's house wherein Mon gave out a couple of unique Manila-printed T-shirts with various motiffs. Seen in left are Ting Ong reading a winner, Rose (Lacebal) Engay bending over to get another ticket, Baby (delos Reyes) dela Cruz standing in center, Malu holding up a T-shirt she just won, Mon in the back enjoying it all, and on the right sitting is, Thelma (Ibañez) Teves.

First row right shows stragglers at the same party, sitting L-R, Angel Sta Maria, Jimmy Abad, Bing (Pascual) Santos, and standing, Mon, Elizabeth (Zaraspe) Woo, JOng, Erwin Gomez (note the T-shirt), Malu (Barrios) & Oids Garcia. Since this was a joint UPSCA and Engineering party, name tags were in order.

Second row left, at the NY party, with Chit Inciong at right, his wife Wilma on the left, and Letty (Ramirez) Ajodah between.

Second row right, taken at Sedona when the Lakviajeros just arrived that Monday night and met Christie (long braided hair) and Nancy (at end of table) and their hubbies Don and Gerry. They had been in the Sedona Cabins since Saturday.

Third row left to right, closeups of Rachel Zaraspe, Amy Bascon, Susan Rodriguez, and Nel Reformina, all from the east coast. On the right are west coast Upscans Baby delos Reyes, Lisa Filler and Evelyn Machan. Note that the ladies are all identified by their maiden names.

-o-o-o-o-o-

These three pictures capture the adventure in Capt Pell's Maryland Crabhouse. Having anticipated eating lobsters first in Tijuana, then Baltimore, and perhaps in Maine - and up to that point in time, all coming to naught, the group finally acceded to Ed Quisumbing's suggestion of pigging it out on crab instead. So there we were, twenty strong, from the Lakviajeros to the DC hosts, all ready to eat. For starters, we had eight dozen crabs, and a couple of baskets of shrimp, in addition to the three pots of rice, with vinegar, that we brought. *Upper left photo* shows Jun taking center stage as he takes a candid shot of the group, as Mon and Mimi show off their crabs, and Liliosa, oblivious to all, grabs for another, while DC host Cecy Quisumbing, Cynthia and Jimmy appear to be saying grace. *Top photo* shows JOng and Ting holding up their mallets, demanding their crabs, while Danny yawns. Finally, it's all over, as shown in *photo at left*, with Mercy grinning widely that she is full, full of crabs. Bing indicated that another DC resident, Delfin Castro, was supposed to have come, but may have gone to the wrong branch of the restaurant.

Photo on left: Liliosa's party also was a birthday party. Note the laser generated cake decor of an old 60's photo of Lindus & Liliosa.

Resurrectado Upscan Bing Ferrer-Dubitsky, and husband Tony. Liliosa's party.

Primo Arambulo and his much-anticipated Paella creation. It was great.

At Loida's 5th Ave NY residence, saying cheers over the giant sized lobster dinner. We accelerated our itinerary to make it that Thursday night. Barely distinguishable are, *on left*, Lisa, Jun and Mercy, while *on right*, are Liliosa's daughter Beatriz and Mon. Loida is at far end of table.

Jimmy Abad and Loida Nicolas-Lewis, taken at Tony & Bernie Nievera's Babylon residence in Long Island during the Apr 21 party. Further east would be another of Loida's residences in the Hamptons.

The "formal" UPSCA group picture taken at the Nievera party Apr 21. *Sitting, L-R:* Danny Gil, Amy Bascon-Rasalan, Cynthia Reyes-Calejesan, Mila Garcia-Reyes, Ting Tejada-Ong, Sari Valenzuela and Priscilla Bautista-Perez. *Standing, L-R:* Gene Pulmano, Nel Reformina, Vic Vitug, Jimmy Abad, Mercy Rivera-Abad, Jun Calejesan, guest Norman Madrid, Mon Pasicolan, Lisa Señeris-Gil, Chit Inciong, Susan Rodriguez-Fagan, Tony Nievera, Rachel Zaraspe-Ordoñez, Tony Estrera, Jimmy Ong, Letty Ramirez-Ajodah, Bernie Jaramilla-Nievera and Johnny Reyes. Loida Nicolas-Lewis already had left. Other guests were in the living room enjoying a show in the large high defintition TV.

Mailing List (complete address on database) - emails and tel numbers erased

Jimmy & Mercy (Rivera) Abad
Antipolo, Philippiness

Rory Abrera
Southlake, TX

Arthur & Cherrie Adiarte
St Paul, MN

Vyva Aguirre
U.P. Campus, QC, Philippiness

Ofie (Peñaflorida) & Ken Aid
Lakewood, CA

Letty (Ramirez) Ajodah
Queens Village, NY

Ely & Sonia (Alday) Alampay
Diliman, QC, Philippines

Arsenio & Maricon Alfiler, Jr
Diliman, QC, Philippines

Rico Alfiler
McLane, VA 22101

José Alzona
Glendale, CA 91206

Evelym (Machan) Andamo
Huntington Beach, CA

Nanette (Gadi) & Boy Angeles
Monroeville, PA

Lolly Aquino
Los Angeles, CA

Myrna Aquitania
Camarillo, CA

Primo & Lindus (Carreon)
    Arambulo
Rockville, MD

Fr Lito Arong, OMI
Oakland, CA
(

Noli & Rosita Arong
Arleta, CA

Sisoy & Cecile Arong
Houston, TX

Marylou Fermin Aurelio
San Nicolas, Ilocos Norte, Phils

Johnny & Alda Balaoing
Los Angeles, CA

Lito & Tita (Teaño) Balucano
Cerritos, CA

Remy Baluyot
Los Angeles, CA

Nina Los Baños
Las Vegas, NV

Tigi & Nora Barcelona
San Juan, Philippines

Olga (Cruz) Barrios
Williamsville, NY

George Bartolome
Vallejo, CA

Enteng & Mely Batas
Los Angeles, CA

Lennie (Abellera) & John Blair
Libertyville, IL

Reggie & Eddie Cailao
Marikina, Philippines

Jun & Cynthia (Reyes)
    Calejesan
Monaca, PA

Ramon O. Casas
Strasbourg, France

Manny Castillo
Brea, CA

Delfin Castro
Bowie, MD
(301) 464-5742

Tessie Chua Chiaco
North Hollywood, CA

Remy & Anching Chica
Northridge, CA
(818) 368-1709

Norma Cornelio
Marikina, Philippines

Celia (Morales) Cornelio
San Diego, CA

Ludy Corrales
Basking Ridge, NJ

Baby dela Cruz
Los Angeles, CA

Boy dela Cruz
Cottage Grove, MN.

Isagani & Medy Cruz
Malate, Philippines

Nilo & Muni Cruz
Las Vegas, NV

Rene Cruz
Diamond Bar, CA

Rene & Lydia Dawis
Minneapolis, MN

Enedina (Garcia) de Guzman
Chesnut Ridge, NJ

Nancy (Cruz) & Gerry Dienel
Little Rock, AR

Bing (Ferrer) & Anthony
    Dubitsky
Riverdale, MD

Carmen Dungca
Moorpark, CA

Georgina (Reyes) & Mervyn
    Encanto
Quezon City, Philippines

Cir & Rose (Lacebal) Engay
Los Angeles, CA

Manny & Lee Espejo
Saugus, CA

Jose Espinosa
NH del Pilar, Malate, Phils

Deo & Aleli Estacio
Altadena, CA

Tony & Josie (Angeles)
    Estrera
Cerritos, CA

Oscar Evangelista
QC, Philippines

Lili (Mangosing) & Gene
    Evangelista
Fairfax, VA

Lino & Maureen (Holazo)
    Faelnar
Las Piñas, Philippines

Susan (Rodriguez) & Dick Fagan
New York, NY

Dette Feliciano
Los Angeles, CA

Lisa Filler
Norwalk, CA

Temy (Dapilos) Gamboa
Patchogue, NY

Malu (Barrios) & Oids Garcia
Cerritos, CA

Pepito & May (Miñosa) Gatchalian
Quezon City, Philippines

Divsy (Astraquillo) & Ken Geoge
Shorewood, WI

Danny & Lisa (Señeris) Gil
Artesia, CA

Erwin & Alita Gomez
Valparaiso, IN

Narita Gonzalez
UP Diliman, QC Philippines

Ibarra Gonzalez
San Jose, CA

Ruben & Maria Habito
Dallas, TX

Effie (Sta Romana) Hall
Bettendorf, IA

Chit Inciong
Flushing, NY

Jessica Infante
Los Angeles, CA

Jess & Jessie (Quinto) Javelona
Muntinglupa, Philippines

Nanette (Ortega) & Benny Jongco
South Orange, NJ

Godofredo & Deng Juliano
Alabang, Philippines

Christie (Borromeo) & Don Kawal
Albuquerque, NM

Helen (Ybanez) Kluck
Gloucester, MA

Lallie (de Vera) Lacaba
Pateros, Philippines

Clara (Reyes) & Bart Lapus
San Juan, Philippines

Raquel (Celera) & Ric Lejano
Torrance, CA

Loida (Nicolas) Lewis
New York, NY 10019

Cheche (Lim) & Delfin Lazaro
Makati, Philippines

Gus & Toti (Yuson) de Leon
Quezon City, Philippines

Dante & Baby V. Liban
Quezon City, Philippines

Flora Libay
New York, NY

Lenore (Raque-Santos) Lim
New York, NY

Poch Macaranas
Makati, Philippines

Eddie & Josie Magtoto
Parañaque, Philippines

Mario & Myrna Manansala
La Palma, CA

Romy & Edna (Zapanta) Manlapaz
Quezon City, Philippines

Melvyn & Susan (Paulin) Martin
Ayala Alabang, Philippines

Mart Martell
Jersey City, NJ

Jess Martinez
Freeport, IL 61032

John & Cecille (Gordon) Mullen
Alexandria, VA 22310

Roly & Evelyn Miranda
UP Diliman, Philippines

Bernie (de Castro) & Jurg Muller
Geneva, Switzerland

Clemencia Natividad
Toronto, Ontario, Canada

Tony & Bernadette Nievera
Babylon, NY

Beth (Arcellana) & Bong Nuqui
Diliman, QC, Philippines

Jimmy & Ting Ong
Bo Kapitolyo, Pasig, Phils

Rachel (Zaraspe) Ordoñez
New York, NY

Oca & Tatish Palabyab
Makati, Philippines.

Ernie & Jessie (Raqueño) Pangilinan
Mission Hills, CA

Eileen (Morales) Pelaez
Cherry Hill, NJ
(

Ramon & Mimi Pasicolan
Ayala Hts, QC, Philippines

Renan Pineda
North Plainfield, NJ

Ed & Lina (Soliman) Plantilla
Brooklyn, NY

Priscilla (Bautista) Perez
Bronx, NY 10467

Susan Po
San Francisco, CA

Emily (Bacaltos) Popp
West Palm Beach, FL

Gene & Violy Pulmano
Roseland, NJ

Sonia (Valenzuela) & Dietrich Quast
Sao Pablo, Brazil

Amelia (Bascon) Rasalan
New York, NY

Hermie (Manoto) & Jess Rabe
Cerritos, CA

Zeny (Roxas) & Sixto Ramirez
Los Angeles, CA

Nel Reformina
Nanuet, NY

Johnny & Mila (Garcia) Reyes
Belle Mead, NJ

Guia (San Juan) Rijk
Pasig City, Philippines

Ruben & Naida (Uy) Rivera
Filinvest II, QC, Philippines

Portia Salvacion
Los Angeles, CA

Maya (Arroyo) Santiano
Quezon City, Philippines

Greg Santillan
Pasadena, CA

Angel & Stella Sta Maria
Pasadena, CA

Bing (Pascual) & Nem Santos
Whittier, CA 90601

Linda (Rojas) Santos
Denver, CO

Miren (Dumlao) & Alex Santos
UP Campus, QC, Philippines

Berryl Silva
Long Beach, CA 90808

Noel & Angge (Alday) Soriano
Quezon City, Philippiness

Susan Sulit
Manila, Phils

Ping & Merle (Custodio) Tan
Quezon City, Philippines

Pete & Merle Tandoc
Canton, MI

Thelma (Ibañez) Teves
Rowland Heights, CA

Dell & Julz Tocong
Bellflower, CA

Bernie (Abrera) Tjarks
Dallas, TX

Danny Uy
Westminster, CA

Girlie (Alzona) & Tito Valbuena
Astoria, NY

Lina Valcarcel
San Juan, Philippines

Sari Valenzuela
Brooklyn, NY

Jemz & Nora Valera
North York, Ontario, Canada

Fred Valera
Chatsworth, CA

Mila (Arevalo) Vales
Yorba Linda, CA

Arlene Vallesteros
Makati, Philippines

Jose de Vera
Granada Hills, CA

JC (Chit) de Vera
Vorhees, NJ

Mon & Eva (Singson) de Veyra
Marikina, Philippines

Vic & Vickie Vitug
Richmond Hill, NY

Priscilla (Javier) Weber
Manhattan Beach, CA

Elizabeth (Zaraspe) Yoo
Los Angeles, CA

-o-o-o-o-o-

EMAILS AND TEL NUM ERASED

UPSCA *Alumni Association Newsletter*

Staleletters   Nobrainers   Portrayals

A M D G   Vol 4, Num 14   Summer 2001

LAKBAYAN AGAIN IN 2003, IN PROVENCE?

Reactions to the Special Edition of the Newsletter on the Lakbayan were lively and animated. Firstly, it was unanimous that indeed there'd be another Lakbayan, but the question was where?

The suggestion of **Johnny** that England might be better than France quickly escalated the division between the Anglophiles and the Francophiles. This was exacerbated by the emergence of **Ramon Casas** from his hiding in France.

See page 5 (French Connection).

-o-o-o-o-

A number of errors were also pointed out by **Vic Vitug** regarding **Mon Pasicolan**'s theory of crankiness.

See page 3 (Bladder).

-o-o-o-o-

There was a gathering of old-timers last May for the 40th wedding anniversary of UPSCA stalwarts **Noel** and **Angge Soriano**. A few weeks before the event she emailed the loop:

Where L O V E has gone....

Being with UPSCANs of all generations will be our way of celebrating our 40th Wedding Anniversary !

Please join us on 31 May 2001 (4-6 p.m.), Thursday at the Delaney Hall, U.P. Parish of the Holy Sacrifice, Diliman, Q.C.

Noel & Angge Soriano

Angge sent in a batch of pictures and a handwritten "Minutes of the Meeting". Excerpts:

REGISTRATION:

There were more than a hundred UPSCANs who came. For purposes of this general meeting, anyone who belonged to any of the following categories was considered an UPSCAn:

-Anyone who came and claimed to have been an UPSCAn whether inducted or not.

- Spouse of an UPSCAn.

- Professor, UP Employee, UP Community member close to the former chaplains or to UPSCAns.

- Former chaplain, priest or nun who worked closely with UPSCAns.

- UPSCA faculty advisers and spouses.

GREETINGS:

Angge accompanied everyone to greet Noel who was pure joy as he recognized those who came. Noel was in tears as he pointed to each one saying "oh! oh! oh!". He really wanted to say "It's you!" To help Noel, Angge uttered each name clearly so Noel could repeat the names.

VIEWING OF THE MEMORABILIA OF NOEL & ANGGE'S WEDDING:

A few interesting memos were displayed: the veil and cord, the photo album, guestbook, and the cake decor consisting of the usual miniature couple

and a scale model of the UP Chapel especially made by Ernie Santos who was then chairman of the UPSCA construction committee. The guest book showed the signatures of some of the UPSCAns who were at the 1961 wedding. Johnny Ramos was the best man, Ben de Leon and Ernie Santos were mass servers. Fr Pacifico Ortiz was officiating priest. UPSCA guests were (in the order in which they appeared):

Charito Quintos, Johnny Ramos, Nene Laraya, Flora Libay, Julie Celestino, Letty Allado, Helen Ybañez, Tercy Mortola, Lisa Señeris, Lina Valcarcel, Evelyn Mendoza, Lindus Carreon, Pilar Enriquez, Nancy Cruz, Baby Arao, Ester Alday, Rosemarie Juan, Zeny Roxas, Marcia Jacinto, Imelda Pulumbarit, Metty Vargas, Susan & Yolo Sulit, Fe Tan Torres, Fely Briones, Ben de Leon, Venus Salazar, Ramon de Veyra, Ma. Eva Singson, Raquel Zaraspe, D. Disini Jr, Manuel Espejo, Juanito Balaoing, Mr & Mrs Cesar Jesena Jr, Mr & Mrs Senen Miranda, Norma Egay, Alejandro de Leon, Baby Mangosing, Alampay the Not Too Great, Ernie Santos, Boy dela Cruz, Tony Racela, Art Ferrer, Hilda Reyes, Linda Aquino, Maurice Borromeo, Enteng Batas, Nonong Quero, Tinoy Desamito, Miraflor Parpan.

And from the gift list:

Tatay & Nanay Zafra, Siony Kalalo, Arthur Ludan, Enteng Limcauco, Erlinda & Patrocinio Valenzuela, Manny Ramos, Lolit Serrano, Tigi Barcelona, Fernando Lagua, Emmeline Quinio, Ibarra & Selma Gonzalez, Evelyn Lesaca, Lynn Colegado, Modi Collantes, Ludy Borlangan, Sonia Mayor, Fely Briones, Pepito & May Gatchalian, Dante Morales.

THE REUNION:

Many of those who came had not seen each other for many years. Brick Pascual and his wife Olive came all the way from Tarlac. Tony Pastor came from Batangas.

The old familiar UPSCA laughter pervaded the whole celebration.

Kuwentohan! Biruan! Sigawan!

FINAL HYMN:

Just before six o'clock, the Catholic Action song officially ended the celebration. As usual, the group sang with enthusiasm.

At the May 31 affair at DH, *L to R:* George Sta Maria (designer of Upsca pin), Modi Collantes, Lito Collantes, Mundy Gonzales, Josie Sta Maria, Tigi Barcelona, Louie Lagdameo, Charito Quintos-Guerzon, Olive Caoili, Blue Luna Lizaro, Lito Domingo, Ester Buenaventura, Letty Tison, Bel Cunanan, Arnie Santos, Becky Kalaw, Tita Acevedo, Sylvia Lacson, Edda Pena, Linda Madrid and Pearl Palma. Seated in front are Noel and Angge Alday-Soriano.

PS:

Mundy Gonzales who was obviously prepared with several nostalgic songs did not need much prodding. His rendition of "All the Things You Are" caused Bel Olivares-Cunanan, Ester Buenaventura and Pearl Palma to swoon as they sang along. It was suggested than an "oldies" choir be formed.

The 1961 guest list must have touched a nostalgic chord among the UPSCAns in the Loop, judging from the spirited responses. At least one was a case of mistaken identity:

Denverite **Erlinda Santos:** You may be interested to know that Art Ferrer is now communicating with me in Denver as he is a Colorado resident although he commutes from his work in Wyoming.

Danny: Hi Erlinda, must be a different Art Ferrer. The one mentioned is now a Jesuit, head of the Ateneo Law School in Makati.

-o-o-o-o-

CENTENARIAN CELEBRATION

From Upscan and Philippine Inquirer Columnist Bel Olivares Cunanan:

I haven't known too many people who celebrated their 100th birth anniversary. The most celebrated centenarian is the United Kingdom's Queen Mother Elizabeth, and then there was the late wife of former AFP Chief of Staff Gen. Mariano Castañeda, who was fondly known to all of us as "Mommy Castañeda."

Last Thursday [July 12] another lovely lady, whom the entire UP community has called "Nanay" for several generations now, celebrated her 100th birthday, but the big bash will be held at the QC Sports Club tomorrow, starting with an 11 a.m mass.

Prof. Luz Alzona Zafra, widow of the late UP history professor, Dr. Nicolas Zafra, and a member of the distinguished Alzona family that gave birth to one of the earliest feminists, her sister Encarnacion Alzona, was one of the earliest UP graduates. Luz became the first principal of the Far Eastern University Girls' High School and dean of the Institute of Education.

The Zafras were among the first families to move out to UP Diliman in 1949. According to her daughter, Fely Zafra-Reyes, this was how Nanay started serving the UP community: first as a "real-life labandera" to legendary UP chaplain John P. Delaney, then as a surrogate mother to countless students put in her care by Delaney. After Father Delaney died, she "inherited" all the other chaplains who

came after him, such as Fr Pacifico Ortiz, S.J. Countless UPSCAns, including this columnist, became close to her, and many of her alaga became the leaven in their own communities around the country and went on to become very distinguished in their fields.

-o-o-o-o-

UPSCANS HONORED

There's a "Noiseletter" newslet of a close-knit group of '65 to '70 UPSCAns. On May 1, they feted those in the group who are on the Arroyo cabinet:

"Dinky" Juliano-Soliman, sec of the Dept of Social Work and Welfare **Oscar Palabyab,** undersec of the Dept of Tourism **Vicky Sisante-Bataclang,** asst sec of the Dept of Foreign Affairs

We offer our congrats and best wishes, too. Dinky is the younger sister of Godo Juliano, our contemporary. Also in the Arroyo cabinet is early '60s Upscan **Isagani Cruz,** undersec of Education; and **Heidi Yorac,** head of the PCGG (Pres Comm on Good Gov't), though she is a few years ahead of us. Ombudsman Desierto was even of an earlier era, a Delaney Upscan.

-o-o-o-o-

OBITUARIES

Frankie "Jun" Abao, Oct 2000, of colon cancer in Manila.

As reported by Mercy: His last few months were spent at home under the care of his family. He knew it was coming and it was his choice to spend his last months at home. He is lucky to have a young and faithful wife who loves him. According to Brenda, Jun loved reminiscing about UPSCA days so that our names became familiar in the retelling. Jun, unlike many in the broadcast arena here in the Philippines was a faithful husband. His last words to his wife was: I love you. Nakakaiyak.

(Jun started out in pre-med in the early '60s, but shifted, and ended up in the broadcast media.)

Mian Chanco-Sison, Oct 2000, of cancer in Manila.

As reported by Tigi: The family of Mian Chanco Sison has designated tomorrow night, November 2, as Friend's Night. They are requesting Mian's friends to come and hold vigil.

(Mian appeared in the 1964 Philippinensian, College of Law, cum laude, and was active in the UPSCA Law chapter).

Marc Abrera Somerstein, youngest son of Rory, Mar 2001, in a car accident in upstate NY.

As reported by Sari Valenzuela: I am not sure if Rory Abrera Campbell would mind my sharing this sad news, but I just heard from Priscilla Bautista-Perez that Rory's son, Marc Somerstein, 18 years old, died last Sunday (March 11, 2001). He was a passenger and the only casualty in a vehicular accident. There may be friends who live in the area and might be interested in going to the Funeral Home.

From Rory:

Dear Danny, Lisa and all our UPSCA friends,

Thank you for all your prayers and condolences for Marc. At a time like this, our family is coping because we have friends like you who pray for us and give us comfort in our sorrow. He was a wonderful young man, possessed a joy for living and loved people. We still do not understand why he was taken so early in life, but God gave, and he took away. We have faith that He had a good reason for taking Marc at the stage of his life when the world was there for him to explore and discover. Perhaps eventually we will realize why. In the meantime everybody's prayers and our own sustain us and keep us strong. Our deepest thanks to all.

Prayerfully, Rory.

Col Juan Arroyo, father of UPSCAn Yeng Arroyo, and Maya Arroyo-Santiano (widow of Fredie), on July 23rd at the age of 88.

(the report of JOng, referring to earlier departed Upscans, elicited a raft of responses). From JOng:

Hi Danny,

Heavens, how time flies.

Last night at the wake for Maya Santiano's father, we realized that this year, Fredie [Santiano]-- the first among our gang to kick the bucket -- will have been gone 10 years. And it's been 6 years since Gerry [Gil] left. We pick up the pieces and move on; how inexorably, was brought home to us when we met Ariel and Dax, Fredie's eldest and youngest, and learned that all three sons are working, Ariel for the past seven years.

We still miss these two most mischievous of gangmates, and not just at wakes and anniversaries. Each get-together is minus a few laughs, for lack of Fredie's inspired heckling. And Gerry's absence is most painful when the political carnival seems most bizarre. Each Gloria flipflop, each Angara obscurantism, each release of Pimentel bile and bitterness, simply begs to be punctured by Gerry's scalpel wit.

JOng

LAKBAYAN DIARY

Johnny's "Lakbayan Diary" drew a series of responses, in a similar manner to his accurate and factual reporting, and fiction writing. However, some readers couldn't decide which was which. On the section which went, thus:

It *is interesting to note that on the evening of May 10, only two weeks after the Lakbayan exercise, a Mafia hit team walked into Mon Pasicolan's Carnegie Deli, climbed the stairs, entered an apartment on the second floor, and executed five individuals gangland-style.*

Cynthia Calejesan wrote:

Sheesh, Johnny, your imagination soars even higher than the pastrami and corned beef sandwiches we dove into at the Carnegie Deli. Didn't realize what those pickles were doing to you. Can you imagine what might have happened if Jun had been allowed to pass the matzoh ball soup around?

Jun added:

There has to be a connection. I knew there was a reason why Mon was so particular about where he wanted to get his pastrami.

Johnny sets the record straight:

I am also mailing you a photocopy of the news item about the Carnegie Deli killings. Some Lakviajeros believe I made the story up and I'm flattered by the compliments about my "imagination," but I don't really deserve credit for the story.

Indeed, Johnny sent a photo copy of the news clipping about the murders. And it certainly wasn't bogus because Lisa did see a news item on the internet about that incident. Good thing we Lakviajeros were two weeks early!

-o-o-o-o-

Another rejoinder from Vic Vitug:

BLADDER:

I am curious about a line from Mon's e-mail in the Newslet which read: "3. The trade-off between gall bladder capacity and crankiness."

Initially, I thought that Mon might have misspoken and meant the urinary bladder *(pantog)* rather than the gall bladder *(apdo)*.

But then, I remembered a Pampango phrase *"alang apdo"* which literally meant "no gall bladder" implying the lack of a certain social grace. Also, there is the English expression "a lot of gall" which means a lot of cheek or gumption, if you will.

Unfortunately, I do not remember what social grace was being referred to by the Pampango phrase and I am not particularly clear about the English phrase, either.

Perhaps Mon can clear this up for me? Is his statement somewhat related to the Pampango phrase? i.e. lack of a Social grace? (like peeing in one's pants?). Or, does he mean: Those with small gall bladders (less gall) or large gall bladders (meaning a lot of gall) tend to be cranky, perhaps surly and demanding to pee ? What does gall have to do with peeing anyway?

If so, could the engineers derive a mathematical formula that would explain the relationship between gall bladder capacity and crankiness?

I suppose, in the final analysis, the question to be answered is: To Pee or Not To Pee?

Regards, Vic

That indeed is the question!

-o-o-o-o-

WHODUNNIT

The Lakbayan trip even spawned a short mystery story. Edited version:

Dear Danny,

You recall during my last night in LA before I flew back to Manila, you and Lisa came to my brother-in-law's house and requested me to bring back to Manila a "Neiman-Marcus" package containing a black, lacy bra, a black undie and a pair of black trouser socks. This package was left behind in Babette's house in New Jersey.

I figured it probably belonged to one of the girls who because of the frenetic outlet shopping and the equally frenetic packing into bursting-at-the-seams-luggage, waylaid the black, lacy and sexy items.

I also figured at our age and predispositions (us guys, I mean), buying such black, lacy and sexy items would be a waste, even at such ridiculously low 80% discount deals in Neiman Marcus.

But "hope still springs eternal". Since our flight from LA was delayed by three hours and I had read all the papers, the nagging question was, who bought and invested in this black, lacy and sexy items?

I immediately discounted Mimi. She has considered me like the Alamo, a lost cause.

While flying over the Polar route, at the edge of Alaska, I considered Mercy, but dismissed it as well. Those black, lacy sexy items for Gemino? As they say in Español, no puede. Victoria's Secret was still a secret when I landed in Osaka.

Since we were delayed, we were rushed by those actuality-freak Japanese, no time to flex those "many, tiny cells" as Poirot would put it. I almost forgot Cynthia C. She and Jun stayed with us in Babette's house, for they were in rush to drive back home to Pittsburgh the the day after we saw Loida. But they bought the tickets and did not go shopping. Besides Jun is a metallurgical engineer, and it does not compute. Those black, lacy sexy undies are unalloyed.

So there. Elimination, elimination, over Sequijor, just after we hit a turbulence, wallah . . for sure those black lacy sexy undies belong to Ting. First, they were in a rush to go and attend a wedding. And weddings are bad vibes, man!

Not that Jong is viciously unromantic, he knows all the Broadway love songs by heart from "Younger than Springtime"; the poetic refrain of "If Ever I Would Leave You" to one his favorites "I've Grown Accustomed To Her Face." Jong has a side hobby: he used to deliver a lively discourse on "How to Say I love YOU" alá Broadway. All the SMC girls adore him whenever he gives those lectures, complete with background music and his occasional grumpy and elusive smiles (I understand, Ting has a small but precious collection of them).

And my final proof, that Jong was the intended target of those black, lacy sexy undies, was in one of those evening conversations when we reminisced about our friends and their exploits like Tigi, etc. I recall we talked about Gerry Gil and his secret loves and his attitude about women. Jong, in a philosophical mood revealed that he and Gerry are so much alike except that Gerry is Colonel Pickering and he is Henry Higgins. Just you wait. . . those black, lacy sexy undies!

With the mystery solved, I went to pick my luggage and once again saw how unlit the streets of Tramo and EDSA at 11:00p.m. Back to reality.

So I called Ting the next day. She says, not mine, try Mercy. So Henry Higgins lives to wait another day. Back to my cogitation. And for first time this pseudo-Poirot is out of his elements. What if Mercy says not mine too? Time to look for other unlikely suspects. Or think of another theory for the "tiny brain cells" to worry about.

Is there a *lurking, pathological Cross-Dresser among us?*

Is it Jimmy Abad, who in a moment of self-revelation took poetic license and in-between delirious moments at Half-Price Bookstore took that lazy but committed step to Neiman-Marcus?

Or is it Tony Estrera, whose secret but quiet passion for anything cantilevered finally collapsed. Or is it really JOng, whose pygmalion-like wish in life is to simply to have "a room somewhere." Or is it me, for I want to be Marlene Dietrich.

But all our secrets are safe for now until Provence.

For Mercy, the all-knowing, all-understanding, and all-merciful Suprema, owned up to those black, lacy, sexy undies.

Mon

***

Hi, Mon.

Congratulations on that masterpiece of deductive logic, perfect all the way up to the finish line, in which you note that Gemino bought a lot of books. This negates everything. Mercy admits, in her last e-mail to Tony Estrera and me, that Gemino fondles books, not undies.

But maybe the sentiment "hope springs eternal" burns in Mercy's heart as it does in your brain; as Joan Crawford told Norma Shearer in *The Women*, "when anything I wear doesn't please Stephen, I take it off." (Or, should Gemino shift his gaze from poetry tome to black lace, she could try Grace Kelly's offer of picnic chicken to Cary Grant in *To Catch a Thief*, "Do you want a leg or a breast?")

JOng

***

Fron Johnny Reyes:

Congratulations to Ramon for a brilliant piece of analysis. The suspense was killing me! Too bad you had to reveal the culprit at the end, before we all had a chance to solve the mystery ourselves.

But I'm still not quite sure I understand -- were the black lacy thingies for Mercy or for Gemino?

***

From Erwin:

What a great piece of detective work, Mon, and supremely entertaining. Being acquainted with the cast of characters from both the U.S. and the Philippines, either from direct communication or by loop e-mail, I would propose that anyone of these persons, either singly or as a couple, could have fitted the profile of "black lace undie purchaser." This includes Jun and Cynthia, except that they would have ordered it from E-Bay, using Jun's computer and engineering know-how combined with Cynthia's literary talents.

If J.E. Alzona were with you, because of his Russian interests even he would have been suspect, since we all know from Cyd Charisse in "Silk Stockings" that such merchandise is hard to come by in Moscow or dreary Siberia, and thus a purchase from Nieman-Marcus is logical.

The "cross-dresser" theory is intriguing, but could probably be discarded off the bat, unless you have a suspect about whom we haven't heard much over the long years, especially if he has a strong French accent.

The clue however, as JOng picked up quite astutely, was not in Mon's story, but in Mercy's e-mail of 6/10, wherein she described Gemino being "in nirvana fondling his new hoard of books."

I always thought this was an odd description, coming from a writer's spouse who is an engineer. Now with Mon's ruminations this Freudian slip makes complete sense: these days Gemino is reading the wrong books!

P.S.: In the next Lakbayan which I hope not to miss, in order to avoid a serious mishap of this sort, for sure I will hand-carry the set of whips, handcuffs and feather duster which I plan to buy in France.

***

From Tony:

(paraphrasing Erwin's "these days Gemino is *reading* the wrong books!"). Erwin, I guess you meant *fondling* the wrong books!

***

From Mon:

Now Erwin is really into it! My earlier suspicion of a "cross-dresser" in the group, is now coupled with a "Dominatrix" persona complete with "whips, handcuffs and feather duster". If only Mon Casas knew what awaits him when he hosts this group in France. Add

to that are the *[above]* mysterious "figures" hidden in the closets at Johnny's house in Belle Mead. Tony Perkins in Psycho would have smirked with hideous delight.

-o-o-o-o-

EMAIL FROM ALL OVER

Rachel (Zaraspe) Ordonez: Thank you very much for initiating and maintaining the Upsca loop. This is an incredibly great service! Although many times I may not be able to respond or join you in the conversations, it warms my heart to listen to the talks and to keep up with the events occurring in the lives of so many friends. My UPSCA era is one great period in my life that has influenced in a very very significant way my values - what and where I am now.

***

Lenore Raquel-Santos Lim: Hello. Thank you for the UPSCA Alumni Association Newsletter. I enjoyed reading about UPSCA & the alumni.

In the Spring Summer issue, page 7 - the newsclipping from the scrapbook of Dette Feliciano - Alexi Antonio is in San Francisco, he's married to Willy Yotoko and they have 3 children.

Lynn Raquel-Santos is married to Rene Sunico, also from UP, College of Engineering. Lynn & Rene have 3 sons. Lynn & Rene own The Makati Skyline (catering & restaurant business) in the Philippines.

Cora de Jesus is married to Chet Tan and they live in the Philippines. They have 2 daughters who are both here in Manhattan.

I am fourth from left in the picture, Nore Raquel Santos (Lynn's sister) now married to Jose Lim. After I got married, we moved to Vancouver, Canada, and lived there for 12 years. We moved to New York and have been here for the past 12 years. I am a faculty member of the United Nations international School. We have 2 children, Marie Claire, 24 years old, a graduate of Yale, and Justin who's 20 years old, currently a senior at McGill University.

***

Alex Dacanay: Hi everybody. Glad to meet you guys after all these years -- thanks to Vic Vitug, Danny Gil, and DAU. Great stuff, this Loop. Okay. I'm a post-Delaney UPSCAN ('62-'65) who cut classes with Vic, played chess with Ani Cruz and Jimmy Ong, read poetry with Frank Abao and Jimmy Abad, admired the CAFA singers (Nonong Pedero, Malou, Beryll), stood in awe of Tigi Barcelona, Gerry Gil, discussed philosophy with Ruben (Habito, Villote), lost my head in The Divine Milieu of Teihard de Chardin, and my heart to Luz (who married someone else but that's another story...) Just to complete the sentimental jag: Steppenwolf strolls with Ed Orozco, Tony Pangilinan, and Bobby Manzano. Dreamy hours with Effie Sta. Romana, Digna Dacanay, Ging Mauleon. Ping pong conversations with Roger Hipolito, Lito Domingo. There, have I proved my credentials?...The past couple of decades? Got married (to Barbara Mae Naredo whose UP High class I used to teach catechism to), produced four children, found a job as journalist (the next best thing to literature and besides, what other profession except priesthood will accept prodigals). Will spare you the details (except if you ask)...Recently caught up with Vic in New York who told me about the Loop and gave me a copy of the Newsletter. How times have changed. How they've remained the same. God, how I miss those days!

***

Action & Reaction!!!

Letters, faxes, e-mail, anecdotes, conversations . .

THE FRENCH CONNECTION

Hi Johnny,

It's me resucitado despues de haber leido your Lacbayan Diary. I'm seriously considering joining the next gathering of crazy individuals who spent hours and hours of their lives in Diliman. Cynthia Reyes answered my message and hinted about a next Lacbayan in Europe. You, however, favor the ghostly horizons of the English countryside. While je suis d'accord avec toi that such trip would be worth the effort, if only because of the natural and historic valeur que cela implique, I beg to disagree when you deny whatever value there is in Central Europe's culture, specially French littérature mondialement appréciée. Ask Jimmy (A or O), Cynthia Reyes, etc....if they did not enjoy reading des romans français, even if translated into anglais.

You are indeed very culto; you would even be more if you don't downgrade les valeurs de la culture et civilisation françaises. This message is just pour provoquer a word from you.

Cheers. *Mon Casas de Strasbourg*

***

Hi Mon,

Je fais des excuses pour la réponse retardée. We just got back from a long week-end -- Monday was a holiday here.

Quelle surprise plaisante! Nice to hear from you again after a lapse of more than thirty years! Mila and I hope you and your family are all well. How long have you been living in Strasbourg? How many children? Any grandchildren yet? Too bad you missed the latest adventure on the East Coast involving UPSCA Alumni both from the home country and from the U.S.

By the way, I wasn't intending to put down the culture of your adoptive country. Queest-ce que vous a donné cette impression? All I said was that French culture is less vicariously familiar to us Filipinos than English.

Actually, I have enjoyed France and logged more miles -- I mean, quilometres -- within that beautiful country (Calais, Paris, Versailles, Chartres, Fontainebleau, Lourdes, Nevers, Lyons, Grasse, Nice) than in Great Britain. (And Bonaparte is one of my idols.) But somehow the places of interest and their names didn't elicit quite the same thrill as did the land of Shakespeare, Tennyson, Dickens, Bronte, Conan Doyle, Chesterton, and the rest of the guys we were made to read in high school. Sure we also enjoyed Dumas, Hugo, De Maupassant, and Mauriac during our time, but it was like reading Rizal in translation -- we could never really appreciate the diction, the rhythm, and the power of the originals.

I guess the choice of which language and culture -- English or French -- would become the universal one was decided in that little piece of undulating farmland on the outskirts of Bruxelles in 1815. After recently exploring the site (on foot), I became convinced that if only Napoleon had had the benefit of two-way radio contact with his field commander on that miserable day, the tide of battle and that of history would have been completely different. But the military genius (who was also suffering from an upset stomach at the time) could not get an accurate view of what was happening on the field, while his field commander could not see the overall picture. So things turned out as they turned out -- the indisposed emperor misread the terrain and the situation, his vastly superior army was outmaneuvered and broken -- and since then the French spirit seems to have been broken as well, all the way through World War II and Dien Bien Phu (although their talent for fermenting good spirits remains unequalled).

Lilliput or Blefuscu? It's really up to the Lakviajeros of 2003 -- the comparative costs will influence the final itinerary a lot -- but the point I'm making is that everything else being equal, a Filipino tourist who has unlimited choices of places to visit, but has limited time and resources to do so, is better off going where the action is (the land of Guinevere, Elizabeth I, and Victoria) than ending up in the wrong country (the nation of Inspector Clouseau).

Please don't get offended. I was only having a little fun with the French. J'espère que vous n'êtes pas picon.

Best regards. *Johnny and Mila*

-o-o-o-o-

LANGUAGES, ACCENTS, HUMOR *(Lino Faelnar recently joined the Loop and met up with Johnny's playfulness). Excerpts:*

Hi, Lino!

Nice to hear from you. Regards to you and Maureen. By the way, could you send me an English translation of your article on blaming religion? (What I got was the Sanskrit version -- see attached excerpt below)   *Johnny & Mila*

We <DIV></DIV>> > >should all remember that whether we like it or not, we will all be held <DIV> </DIV>> > >accountable.....

***

Hi, people,

Johnny Reyes tells me something was wrong with the first transmission. It was in Sanskrit. I'm resending through the loop. Regards,   *Lino*

***

Hi Lino,

That's better. At least it's now in Swahili -- which I can read. Regards,   *Johnny*

***

Hi Lino,

Good 'ol Johnny's rejoinder merely highlights the need to "cut and paste". Many emailers merely "forward" an email, and oftentimes, especially with certain ISPs (like hotmail), lots of excess baggage is added (<<DIV></DIV>> > &gt ,>>> etc. etc). As the relayed email gets forwarded again, the baggage gets exponentially longer, especially with varying wrap-arounds and page breaks inherent in different systems. So we try to "clean it up" by highlighting only the message (no addressees and other headers), and copying it to a blank new email screen. Cheers,   *Danny*

***

Lino sent Johnny something in French. Johnny's reply:

Lino,

Ci è male qualcosa con il vostro calcolatore. I vostri messaggi vengono sempre fuori in una lingua straniera. Veda prego il vostro proprio messaggio qui sotto come lo ho ricevuto. Chieda al vostro fornitore di Internet che cosa il problema è. Riguardi,   *Johnny*

***

Cher Johnny,

Ou avez vous apris italienne? Mais a revenir au probleme, peut etre qui'l y a qulque chose avec votre computeur. Les autres a qui j'ai envoye l'article l'ont bien recu. Peut etre c'est votre computeur. Veuillez accepter mes sentiments tres agreables.

Lino

Lino und Maureen,

Ich hörte, daß sie Neues Jersey im August besuchen werden. Was ist ihr reiseweg? Unsere adresse und telefonnummer sind wie folgen:

   1606 Taggert Drive
   Belle Mead, NJ 08502
   (908) 431-1929

Unser warmer respekt,   *Johann und Mila*

***

From Danny to Lino and Johnny:

What is this! First it's Sanskrit, then Swahili, French perhaps, and now German? Domo arigato gusai mashta! *Duh-knee*

***

Danny, the problem seems to be coming from Lino Faelnar's computer. I send messages in perfect English, then >pouf!< he gets them in some strange language. I have suggested that he check his Control Panel settings. Regards.   *Johnny*

***

Johnny, where'd you learn all these languages? Is somebody helping you? I lost my German and my French is rusty, both through non-use. The only other language I'm comfortable with these days is Spanish. Lo ho perdutto e olvidutto molto. Non posso mai scrivere, non posso parlare queste lingue. Domaggio.   *Lino*

***

Actually, Lino, the secret is that I'm using an old WW II U.S. Army French Phrase Book. As a matter of fact, I've nearly exhausted all the phrases supplied, and the only ones I still haven't used on you are the following (I'm waiting for the appropriate situation to provide the opportunity):

Y-a-t-il des troupes pres d'ici?
Combien d'hommes y-a-t-il votre compagnie?
Ou est le champ d'aviation?
Le pont supportera-t-il ce poids?

Are there any troops around here?
How many men are there in your company?
Where is the airfield?
Will the bridge support this load?

Regards. *Johnny*

                    ***   *Pic file Johnny sent*

To ramon.casas, ferngil, and thereyeses

Cher Mon, Johnny Reyes est Tres "kalog". He really got me there.   *Lino*

-o-o-o-o-

As it turned out, Johnny took all of us for a ride. It was Tony, who, acting on a tip from Johnny, found the website where anyone can translate phrases from English to French, German, Spanish, etc. and vice versa. But no Tagalog. Pardon my French:

Attaquons-nous et surfons au wesite **http://systranaol.com/systran**

-o-o-o-o-

But before all of this happened, Mercy already was having fun with the Erap Impeachment proceedings. Her email:

It is now chic to have a Visayan accent thanks to the impeachment trial where many of the prosecutors, Chief Justice Davide and Nene Pimentel carried on with genuine Visayan accents. One prosecutor Cong Apostol terrified the women because he kept on saying "Madam Wetness". Then on one occasion he said "have you seen this document Ki-ki 2 (KK2)" which of course was met with laughter from the gallery. Then much later on he said "and when was this mating?"   *Mercy*

THE AMAG EPISODE

Sometime last year, Tigi wrote to all:

Dear Guys,

I need help. I have a number of 3 inch floppy discs that contain some rather important documentation. Some are a year old, some about two years old, some a few weeks old. They cannot be read. Everytime I put them into the disc drive I get the message that: " No disc in the drive.......etc.etc."   Tigi

A number of people responded; one classic reply was from Vic Vitug, with all the technical geekiness he innocently mustered. But more classic was Susan Po's reply, about **amag** *in the disks, and the hilarious exchanges between her and Liliosa. Mon Pasicolan wrapped it up, referring respectively to Tigi, Vic, Susan and Liliosa:*

Dear Danny, if you plan to have a ten best list in the Upsca newsletter of Great Exchanges for Category 2, these should be among them: "The Most Reverend Amag"......"The Good Samaritan Geek" and the two "Most Irreverent Amag-Slayers" ——— ranks up there. Really made my day.   Mon Pasicolan

Vic missed the point:

Is there a joke somewhere here? If there is, could someone please share it with me?

Danny:

Yes, there's a joke. Tigi is the most senior in the barkada. So, baka may-amag. When we were talking before about somebody to handle the Delaney archives, someone suggested that Tigi be the archive, and a talking one at that!

A few weeks passed, then Tigi wrote again:

Dear Guys,

I need help. I have a number of 3 inch floppy discs that contain some rather important documentation. . . People I have consulted here say that may **amag** daw, my drive is okay . . .   Tigi

Susan:

Wh-a-a-a-t ah-gain?!?!?! (Hindi lang amag ang problema dito, folks)

Liliosa:

Tigi, mukhang malala ang problema ng discs mo. Your eMail is dated January 1970! Sorry I can't be of help.

Mon:

Can you hear the background music.....we just entered The Twilight Zone.....circa 1969......

Liliosa:

Tingting Calejesan, you are mucho calocojan! But seriously, did you notice the date on Tigi's eMail? Could it be that he is having problems because the date on his PC has been moved back 30 years, and anything he saved since then is in limbo? As Susan says, I may not be a techkie (sp?), but I know when a date is laos na.

-o-o-o-o-

The close comaraderie and loyalty to each other amongst these core of Upscan friends (referred to by Mon as Category 2) allow them to rib each other mercilessly without any fear of generating ill will or feelings. All for a good laugh!

MORE AGAIN ON TRAVEL (excerpts):

From Lenore (Raquel-Santos) Lim:

Hello. I'm back from the Philippines. I had an art exhibit at the UP College of Fine Arts Gallery and I also did a workshop on printmaking for the Fine Arts faculty other printmakers. **Tiggy Barcelona, Betty Nable de Vera** and **Bochie Tapales Santiago** (from my UPSCA days) attended the opening reception. I also met **Manya Alvendia Rodriguez** & **Rogel Rodriguez** (Manya's mother passed away a month ago) and **Nonong Pedero** whose father passed away last July 25, just a few days before I left.

From Erwin Gomez:

Reading about the Eastern Lakbayan tour really makes me really sorry I missed it for all the UPSCAns I haven't seen nor heard of since I left Diliman. But it was great seeing you guys and gals in LA and Las Vegas.

But after my son Victor and I left Las Vegas, we flew to Paris with my daughter Gaea, then went on to Sevilla via Madrid. My kids and I had a blast in Sevilla, wandering around tiny alleys just about every night to hit flamenco bars and gorge on abundant seafood and tapas washed down with sangria and cervesa CruzCampo, while listening and clapping in rhythm with the flamenco guitar, singer, and dancer. (This seems to be the Sevilla version of the Chicago Blues or jazz bars, or the little coffeehouses we used to see in Manila with a small informal band.)

But one lesson I discovered is that it's always the people that make the place interesting. I love Charlie Trotter and his exquisite and expensive cuisine, but I had almost just as much fun eating the dinner that my son's foster family in Sevilla prepared for us on our brief visit. Or mixing with the rowdy crowd at the corrida and flamenco bars with what little Andalusian Español I could blurt out with my son's help. This is why eating French cuisine in Paris rather than Chicago, or buying books in London rather than LA, becomes a different experience.

I was in Paris for a few hours at CDG airport, and contrary to what my kids told me, I found the French quite friendly and accommodating. (Actually almost half of the French staff in the United Airlines terminal in CDG are Filipinos, and they were really very helpful.) I think if Mon Casas would take us around Paris it may be a great experience. At saka culto pa! Sign me in for the European lakbayan: I suggest France, Spain, Tuscany region.

From Johnny Reyes:

Last Saturday, Mila and I were invited to a reunion of **Liliosa Evangelista**'s Clan at the Paramus mansion of Dr. Philip Mangosing. Also present at the party was a long-lost UPSCA alumna: Dr. **Frances Tolete-Velcheck** (and her gregarious Croatian husband, Dr. Velcheck). Frances would like to attend future reunions of East Coast UPSCA Alumni, and would like to be included in the official mailing list of the UPSCA Newsletter. The Velcheck couple have a villa in Croatia and are offering to take the Lakviajeros yachting in the Adriatic if we decide to go there in 2003.

From Susan Po:

I picked up JOng at the corner of Market St and Virgin Records (that's the way we give directions around here - mixing up streets and buildings) and drove to a waterfront restaurant run by Zen monks-on-the-verge-of-whatever (San Francisco being the place for anyone on the verge of something).

Over a glass of wine (for JOng), artichoke lasagna, vegetarian griddle cakes, apple pie with their "home-made" berry ice cream, and cups of peony white tea - JOng and I reminisced about the good old days at UPSCA: "deconstructing" and then again, reassessing old personalities we knew, etc, etc.

From Nancy (Cruz) & Gerry Dienel:

The Lakbayan was a great success! Thanks for all your work on the newslet. Thanks, also, for the pictures. Received them today.

Gerry and I went to a meeting in Norway two weeks ago, beautiful country; a bit chilly and rainy. We both came down with the flu and all the works after we came back. Still recovering. Best regards.

From Bernie (de Castro) Muller:

Mga kaibigan, I am resurfacing and am now in Paris, at the Embassy (Minister without a Church!) and have continued to receive the Newsletter (Merci, Danny - but my address has changed ten years ago, and now that our old mailman has retired, I would have to give you my new address in Switzerland- 3, chemin des Pléiades, 1206 Geneva, Switzerland).

I read with interest, and a twinge of "inggit", the account of Lakbayan 2001 and realized how much I still share with you guys after all these years, above all, "crankiness". Or has that evolved through the years, from less to more?

Other than getting soaked through and flooded in Paris (the rainiest year in more than a hundred years - climate change - US friends, do I thank George W. for this?), I am enjoying myself immensely (nearer Geneva for one), much less travel (I like it less with age - all that cramped intimacy for 16 hours!), and after all, this is Paris. Plus less work - I marry people, for one (to each other, of course), and give counsel (I will give you a discourse once on the downside of the OCWs, our so-called "heroes" and "heroines", at least those that did not make it here abroad - the total deterioration of moral and family values that cannot be quantified in terms of remittances back home). But not soon, no fear.

In the meanwhile, you might think of the next Lakbayan over here in Yurroop, less total space (including home space), but more to see per square meter. If we plan it well, we might even see some operas and concerts and get you guys turned "cultos" finally, and end Mon's greatest regret (that was Casas, not Pasicolan, of course).

-o-o-o-o-o-

JOKETIME (from a statistician):

THE TOP TEN REASONS TO BECOME A STATISTICIAN
　　Deviation is considered normal.
　　We feel complete and sufficient.
　　We are "mean" lovers.
　　Statisticians do it discretely and continuously.
　　We are right 95% of the time.
　　We can legally comment on someone's posterior distribution.
　　We may not be normal but we are transformable.
　　We never have to say we are certain.
　　We are honestly significantly different.
　　No one wants our jobs.

HOW STATISTICIANS DO IT
　　Statisticians probably do it.
　　Statisticians do it continuously but discretely.
　　Statisticians do it when it counts.
　　Statisticians do it with large numbers.
　　Statisticians do it with significance.
　　Statisticians do it on random walks.
　　Statisticians do it stochastically.
　　Statisticians do it. After all, it's only normal.
　　Statisticians do it with standard deviations.
　　Statisticians do it with 95% confidence.
　　Statisticians do it with only a 5% chance of being rejected.

From the archive files of Bing Caguioa-Snow, dating back to the mid '60s. Left photo, L-R: Bing, Val Tiu (non Upscan) Dinky Juliano, now with the Arroyo cabinet, and Punch Gavino. Right photo: Bing Caguioa, Girlie Alzona, Vangie de Castro and Berryl Silva. Bing is now in Illinois, Girlie in NY, Vangie in Manila, and Berryl in LA. The following Bings have appeared in the newslets: Pascual, Fragante, Ferrer and Caguioa.

April 2001 Lakbayan at the Quisumbing residence near DC. Front L-R: Johnny, Danny, Lisa, Mercy, Jimmy and JOng. Middle row: Mimi and Ting. Standing: Mila, Liliosa, hostess Cely, Cynthia and Jun. Does anybody appear to be sitting on somebody else's lap?

July 2000 LA party honoring Rory and her sis Bernie who was visiting from Texas: Front L-R: Tessie, Rory, Bernie, Josie, Angel, Manny. Standing: Danny, Johnny, Stella, Malu, Oids, Thelma, Mario, Dette, Lilly, Bing and Lisa.

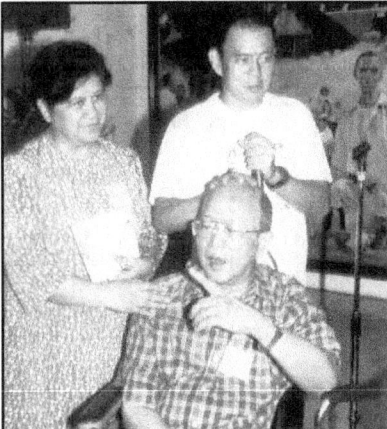

Fr Reyes (the running priest), and UP Chaplain, praying over Noel, with Angge, at the 40th wedding anniversary of the Sorianos. On 31 May 2001, at the DH. Notice mural in background with Fr Delaney.

EDSA DOS. Mabuhay ang Filipinas! This shows the tremendous enthusiasm of the people in ousting Erap, and ushering in whoever was the legal heir, who happened to be Gloria Arroyo. View shows the Edsa Shrine on the lower right, the Edsa overpass on Ortigas Ave, with La Salle Greenhills Coliseum on upper left.

EDITORIAL BOX

The UPSCA Alumni Newsletter is published ill-frequently in Los Angeles. Send in your pictures, comments, anecdotes and trivia to Danny Gil at 19002 Horst Ave, Artesia, CA 90701, tel/fax (562) 402-5098, e-mail ferngil@aol.com, so there'll be incentive to have another issue.

This issue, as are the earlier 13 issues, will also be posted on the Upsca website (http://upsca.org) maintained by webmaster Danny Uy.

Other acknowledgements: thanks to Tony Estrera, Malu Garcia, Johnny Reyes and Rory Campbell for helping out on the postage and other expenses, and to Mercy Abad for same on the Manila end.

UPSCA
Alumni Association Newsletter

Stale news   New news   No use

A M D G   Vol 4, Num 15   Late Summer 2003

PHOENIX? RESURRECTION? WE'RE BACK!

EDITORIAL

It's been almost a two-year hiatus since the last UPSCA Newsletter, and many thought, rightly so, that is was curtains.

But no! Just like the Phoenix or Lazarus, it's back in business. In the past, making a newsletter was relatively easy. It involved reading all the email from the Loop, saving the more interesting ones into a folder, then stringing them all together as text in a preformatted QuarkXpress desktop publishing file, then editing it, adding pictures, then printing 200 sets or so. Ideally, this was supposed to be every quarter. And the longer the delay, the bigger the inertia to start.

That's what exactly happened, due to a number of factors: the move to the East coast, the novelty of the new environs, new friends and activities, the enormous email exchanges for the Lakbayan 2003, the trip itself; in short, this was information overload of the highest degree!

So here now is UPSCA Alumni Newslet #15, in it's 8th year running, with the theme of OLD and NEW, or better yet, THEN and NOW.

Tony Nievera took this picture at the Arles Plaza, before an old Roman building. *Up front:* Danny Gil. *Next row:* Lisa Gil, Mercy Abad, Bernie Muller, Jimmy Abad, Ting Ong, Bernie Nievera. *Back row:* Lili Evangelista, Mimi Pasicolan, Mon Pasicolan, Jimmy Ong.

From the Travelogue of Liliosa, first part:

Lakbayan 2003 Takes Shape

At the close of the lobster dinner in the New York 5th Avenue residence of **Loida Nicolas-Lewis**, when Lakbayan 2001 ended, we bade each other goodbye with the rallying cry, "See you in Provençe!" Much discussion by e-mail followed to determine where we should hold Lakbayan 2003, with France and England the strongest contenders. But it was **Bernie de Castro-Muller** who clinched the final decision, when as newly appointed Consul-General of the Philippine Embassy in Paris, she wrote, "I am now a Minister without a church ... when are you coming over?" Little did Bernie know then that what lay ahead would tax to the fullest her extraordinary talents and expertise in international affairs.

Then there was our beloved friend, **Ramon Orense Casas**, who lived with his family in Strasbourg for many years. News of his recent illness spurred us to accelerate plans for our French odyssey. Sadly, we did not reach our goal. Ramon passed away just a few days before we arrived, as if to say "now that you are coming, you will finally become 'culto' and my work is done." Instead of a reunion with him, Lakbayan 2003 became a memorial to his legacy of caring and friendship.

Timing of Lakbayan considered several factors, among these the end of the school year in Manila (April) so Jimmy Ong could turn in his students' final grades. It also had to take place before June 1st, when airline rates would precipitously rise for the tourist high season. Bernie needed time to prepare for her daughter's wedding in August. I requested **Johnny Reyes**, appointed as trip organizer despite his vigorous campaign for England, if Lakbayan could be scheduled after May 17, when my son would graduate. Together, these constraints presented a very narrow window of opportunity between May 18 and June 1.

But the US war against Saddam Hussein (and the staunch refusal of the French to be an ally) nearly upset our plans. Despite **Danny Gil**'s brave "War or no war!" declarations, the threat of war and terrorism put our plans on hold, although not seriously enough for anyone to take out flight cancellation insurance. By the end of April, when the events of war finally took a denouement, preparations were enthusiastically resumed, with e-mail messages titled "Countdown" proliferating our Inboxes, and the itinerary and cast of characters finalized.

The Cast of Characters

Traveling must be an incurable bug, because the veterans of Lakbayan 2001 ventured to make this trip again. From Manila, **Mercy and Jimmy Abad, Ting and Jimmy "Jong" Ong, Mimi and Mon Pasicolan** signed up early on. From the US, commitments came in from **Danny and Lisa Gil** of New Jersey, **Erwin Gomez** of Indiana, and **Tony and Bernie** (henceforth to be referred here as BerNiev) **Nievera** of New York, and me in Virginia. In France, there was Bernie de Castro Muller (**BernieM**); **Ramon Casas** was willing to meet us in Paris despite his illness. Some others considered, including **Arthur** and **Cherrie Adiarte** of Minnesota, **Cynthia** and **Jun Calejesan** of Pittsburgh, **Tony Estrera** in Los Angeles, **Beth** and **Bong Nuqui** in in Manila, then in the end all regretfully declined. **Johnny** and **Mila Reyes**, also of New Jersey, first pledged 57% certainty, then reduced this to zero, but only after Johnny gallantly fulfilled his duties as trip organizer. The various locations of all these participants alone made planning a very complicated task, so e-mail proved to be the indispensable means to get everyone organized.

Tony Nievera expounding on the merits of sidewalk cafes, in Arles, Provençe, while Mon, Ting and Mercy attentively listen.

The Itinerary

Johnny's proposed itinerary was mulled over, incorporating ideas from BernieM and others. Later on, the skeleton of the plan was fleshed out with the help of **Carlos "Choy" Arnaldo**, a retired UNESCO officer and longtime resident of Paris, and friend of several UPSCAns, including being a former drinking buddy of Gerry Gil. Earlier in April, a "pre-reunion" reunion took place in the Long Island home of the Nieveras, where a visit by Choy to New York provided an opportunity for the trip planners to get together and bond, a task easily accomplished with the help of the gourmet Filipino lunch prepared by Tony and BerNiev, and the copious flow of red wine that presaged the forthcoming French culinary experience.

The ten-day limitation provided the structure for a trip that would start with a two-day tour of Paris, a drive out west to Normandy to see Claude Monet's estate in Giverny, the hometown of St. Therese of the Child Jesus in Lisieux, and to spend the night in the picturesque and medieval port town of Honfleur. The next day we would swing out to the coast of Brittany to see the tapestry of Bayeaux, the mystical site of Mont St. Michel, and then back to the center of France to see the "mother of cathedrals" in Chartres, which Johnny suggested in place of Amiens and Rouen. From Chartres, we hoped to have a picnic lunch by the Loire River, possibly see

Orleans, the city of Joan of Arc, and then decide if there would be time to visit Nevers, where the incorrupt body of St. Bernadette Soubirous is enshrined, especially since there are two Bernadettes in the group. To break up the long ride to Provence, we would stay overnight at Clermont-Ferrand, capital of the Auxerre region, and located in the Central Massif's mountainous and volcanic area. Once in Provence, we would stay for three nights in Arles, with planned day trips to Aix, Avignon, the Camargues, Marseilles, and other areas deemed appropriate by the tour leaders. The final leg of the journey would consist of a return along an easterly auto route, stopping for lunch in Lyon (the gastronomic capital of the world), an overnight stay in Beaune (near Dijon, capital of the Burgundy region and famous for mustard), and then a look at Fontainebleau, Napoleon's favorite chateau, before spending our last night in Paris.

What actually happened is a totally different story that Liliosa is writing about in a forthcoming book.

-ooo-

Michelin is known here as a tire, but apparently in Europe, it is also a Guide for hotels, restaurants, etc. The detailed French map I bought in Barnes & Noble was "Michelin Atlas of France". Mon Casas emailed us his version, all of 2 pages long, herein excerpted below:

GUIDE MICHELIN:

So you are coming to France, à Paris? Zat is very good: for you to become cultivé. Why affraid of ansrax? The Steel and Coal Community is fini with the naissance of the Union Européenne. Only outre-atlantique zere is bactérie du charbon.

Anyway, no problème, you must drink and drink, wine first, of course, and then beaucoup, beaucoup d'eau. No need of Evian or Perrier. In Paris the plumbing is centuries old and noisy, it goes tap,tap, tap when you open le robinet, so you have authentique tap water, zat is very good.

O, Paris, Paris, ton âme m'envahit et m'engloutit, évanescence de mon être! When you are in Paris, you are confondu avec l'air, la terre et la Seine. You want a promenade romantique ? No pay, so you save euros; you walk and walk, of course

Mon Pasicolan takes a breather from walking

bras dessous, bras dessus and in autumn you are sure to have la caresse of a falling feuille morte on your cheeks.

(This advice we followed: walk, walk, walk, mainly because for the first 2 days, we were without the rental vans, and our hotel was half a mile away from the nearest Metro Station. The first two times we negotiated that distance, we got lost and meandered almost a mile. We did take cabs when we could, but hailing a cab in Paris is even more difficult than finding one in Los Angeles)

You may skip the old pieces of greek marbles and egyptian mommies, coins, etc. which you see all over the world. But at least you must seek the great masterpieces in sculpture as well as in painting. Not too much temps? Eh bien, at least theses famous works of art:

Venus de Milo: masterpiece of opulent flesh, as was the critère de la beauté féminine grecque. Do not mind if the sculpture is incomplete: zis was bicauze Venus tried to pary with her arms the attempt of a greek soldier to touch her. Zaat is when this soldier unsheathed his sword and cut her arms

La Joconde: Merveilleuse Mona Lisa. French intellectuals sink she iz crezy bicauz she is always smiling since she was snatched from Leonardo.

-ooo-

The first ETAP Hotel misadventure occurred in the port town of Honfleur when at 3:00 in the morning, Tony & BierNev awoke to find the floor under 3 inches of water. Then the others awoke to the sound of firemen. There was a break in the water main, and not a fire, fortunately. The Nievera's clothes got wet, and since this was an overnight stay, there was no time to go to a laundrymat, hence the improvised *sampayan* in van #2, driven by Tony.

BernieM negotiated with the sourpussed hotel clerk, and it was agreed that Tony will get insurance compensation for all the damage, real or imagined. So the suggested list grew to include the Louis Viton bags, the digital camera, etc. As to whether all those claims were finally sent in, and if Tony indeed got them, we don't know. We'll perhaps know in Lakbayan 05

Honfleur is an old town catering to many of the rich Parisiennes who maintain stately houses on the hills overlooking the port, and the 13th century castle.

We had a fine time eating clams, among others, at the local restaurant.

Hi, Johnny.

Notwithstanding Liliosa's otherwise comprehensive reportage, I'm not sure if you've gotten a satisfactory answer to your query on Etap hotels. Here's my two centimes worth:

If you think of a hotel's core service as a bed that you rent for the night, and everything else as supplements that entice you to stay longer, I'd say that Etap hotels were an eminently suitable choice.

Etap is designed to be a low-cost operation, with a minimum of overhead, and electronic technology to make up for the absence of manpower.

Someone is at the reception area if you check in before noon or between 5-9 pm, otherwise you're on your own, and must punch your reservation number and credit card into a thingamajig on the wall, which spews out in turn a sheet of paper containing your room assignment and the code number that works as your key to your bedroom. The same room code number allows you to open the hotel gate and front door, so there's no need for a security guard, and no parking valet either.

Breakfast, if you checked in electronically the night before, is the very first sign that the hotel provides employment to human beings. At about 6 am, someone starts laying out the sumptuous repast of coffee, tea, milk, orange juice, 4-5 kinds of bread, butter, honey, and 4-5 kinds of jam. That same someone hisses murderously at you if you look like you intend to sit down at a table before the scheduled time (6:30 am M-F, an hour later on weekends, and the hell with you if jet lag woke you up at 4:30 am); and that same someone checks your documents that show that your breakfast has been prepaid. Once that's done, you can eat. One morning you try the sliced white bread with butter and apricot jam; then the next day if you want to live it up you have a baguette with butter and peach jam. Until I got to France I did not know it was possible to survive 12 mornings without corned beef, but voila! it can be done.

After breakfast, checking out requires no leavetaking, no signing of receipts or checking of what you've consumed from the mini-bar, because you've prepaid and there's no mini-bar. You lug your bags out of the door and into the van, and off you go. Not a bad deal, for what we paid. In retrospect, we could have chosen classier lodgings, easier to find and more generous with towels, but they would probably have sliced something like 300 euros from the shopping budget.

Does the whole thing work without a hitch? Not entirely. Due to Tony Nievera's non-existent French, he lost two Etap rooms he'd reserved earlier, and he ended up staying at the Ibis next door for two nights or so, paying maybe 40 percent more because Ibis is two-star, though for 6 euros instead of 4, they got ham and eggs for breakfast. Due to everybody else's nonexistent French, reservations at

Honfleur Etap and everywhere else gave us twice as many rooms as we needed. And then there was this Etap (Chartres? Clermont Ferrand?) where, after Mon and Mimi's bags were already inside their room, the room code number refused to work. But we had BernieM to straighten things out in impeccable French. Without her, we could have stayed in 5-star hotels all the way, and still come to grief.

JOng

But Jimmy Abad needed his ham and eggs for breakfast badly, so at Arles, where we stayed the longest, 3 days, we ate breakfast out.

After all, he changed the flat tire of van #2 when Tony hit a curb. We drove almost a thousand kilometers without a spare, then Yankee (or Pinoy) ingenuity made us hammer back the bent rim into shape, pump air in, and voila, back in business.

-ooo-

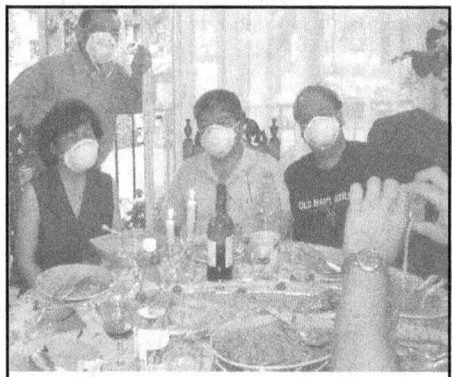

At Bernie's Paris apartment, we demonstrated how we came prepared for SARS.

5/13/03

Dear friends,

I do not know how to tell you except in this direct way: Mon Casas died yesterday afternoon. I just learned about it this afternoon. I understand he died at the hospital, in his sleep, very peacefully. I am trying to get more details to see if I can attend his funeral. I was so looking forward to having him with us for the dinner on 22 May. It becomes all the more important for us to see each other again for this Lakbayan.

See you soon, Bernie

-ooo-

Condolence Excerpts for Ramon:

He was one of our gangmates in UPSCA in the 60's. He finished Foreign Service cum laude, after his Philosophy summa

cum laude in UST. He played the piano beautifully, spoke perfect Spanish, and was truly culto. And he was such great company. He moved to France years ago, settled down and raised a family. *Danny & Lisa.*

Mon was old school in the best sense of the word, one of the finest gentlemen I ever met. Culture oozed from every pore and yet he was never stuffy. A good guy. I'm sorry our paths never crossed again after college. *Jun & Cynthia Calejesan.*

More on Lakbayan!

From the super digital camera of Erwin: Danny, Lisa, Mon, Lili, Bernie, Jimmy, Mercy, JOng and Ting. Erwin didn't show up in Paris, and we all figured he must have had some really good reason for the no-show. But on the fourth day, when en route to Arles, we got a call on the cell phone. He was making *pa-habol*, and could we pick him up at the train station. Turns out he had been deputized to sit in some medical court hearing that had to do with some sordid and interesting sexual case, which he couldn't turn down. But neither could he also have turned down the Lakbayan trip. In the background is the Arles local ETAP hotel, of remarkable fame (or infame). See the analysis of JOng on page 3.

Erwin posing beside the famed Pont du Gard Aqueduct, a 2nd century Roman engineering marvel built to convey water to the City of Nimes "The Rome of Gaul." There is a canal at the top where the water flows by gravity over an ever so gentle slope that astounds present day engineers. Nimes is known for fabrics, and reportedly was the origin of the word "demin".

A visiting Manileña and two Parisiennes. Mercy making a toast to everybody's health, with Choy Almado and Bernie de Castro-Muller, at Bernie's Paris place.

That's a budding van Gogh demonstrating his fast and remarkable painting prowess. Tony doing impromptu painting at the sidewalk cafe. He promised each couple a painting, and did come across. Jimmy and Ting watch intently. No, his subjects are not nudes, but just landscapes (*sabi daw*).

Pasicolan antics: emulating Samson (arms not long enough) at the Nimes Coliseum; playing Pope in the Avignon Cathedral.

An interesting email exchange ensued after the above picture was circulated, and it was all about how Bernie appeared to be flirting with the police officer (to which she later retorted "you ain't seen nothin' yet"), as Mon's body language gleefully points out. But as the other photo shows, Jimmy was more suave. He approached a maniquin.

EDITORIAL BOX

The UPSCA Alumni Newsletter used to be published ill-frequently in Los Angeles, but now the publisher has moved to Jersey City, NJ. Send in your pictures, comments, anecdotes and trivia to Danny Gil at 126 Ogden Ave., Jersey City, NY 07307, tel/fax (201) 659-4695, or e-mail ferngil@aol.com. Perhaps there'll be incentive to have another issue.

This issue, as are the earlier 14 issues, will also be posted on the Upsca website (http://www.upsca.org) maintained by webmaster Danny Uy.

On this same spot in the last issue, credits were given to those who helped out. Vic Vitug's name was inadvertently omitted. Thanks, Vic.

PAST AND FORTHCOMING EVENTS:

UPSCANS CONNECT UP TO FR VIC SALANGA

Mercy emailed about how she and Jimmy listen to Vic Salanga ". . . now a renowned Theologian. He gives night classes to working people. Jimmy and I attended one course on Christology and it really added depth to our understanding of Christ and his mission.".

I eventually connected up to him through my Ma, since he's a cousin. Excerpts:

From Vic to Danny:

Thank you for your e-mail message. I do remember your name when I was in U.P.; you may have been in third or fourth year and I was in freshman year. I suspected that we were distant cousins, but then I wasn't sure and we hardly met and I left it at that. Yes, I was a quiet person then. Friends of mine today do not believe that I was very shy then. I entered the novitiate after my freshman year together with Ruben Habito and Rene Ocampo.

That was thirty-eight years ago.

As I look back and reflect on the UPSCAns who joined the Society, suddenly I realize that I am the only one left from our generation: Esguerra left the Society after one year in the novitiate. Bobby Neri left the Society last year; however, he remains a priest. Ibarra Gonzalez got his "dismissal" papers just last year and is now married. Ruben Habito left probably about ten years ago. Rene Ocampo, ang pambato ng aming generation because he became provincial superior, is dead. So, that leaves me.

From Danny to Vic:

I'm taking the liberty of excerpting your email and cc'ing some of the Upscans in the Loop whom I'm sure will be glad to hear from/about you: Ruben Habito in Dallas; Johnny Reyes, your next door neighbor in San Juan; Bing Caguioa-Snow in Illinois, Bing Ferrer-Dubitsky in DC, and Malu Barrios-Garcia in LA — three of whom had asked for your email address. I also will cc the "inner Loop" of about a dozen who form the core of our lively, frequent and enduring cyber friendship.

And while you mention about being the last SJ in your generation, one might stretch the point about the definition of a generation: though they were a few years ahead of me, I did meet and know Art Ferrer and Matt Sanchez. I never met Archie Intengan, but from what I understand, he was well on his way to be a surgeon before he entered the novitiate. They, too, are Jesuits going strong.

Malu started a drive to collect funds for Fr Vic's project. Please contact Malu oids2000@yahoo.com.

-ooo-

MAINLY UP GROUP — 62ND STREET FORUM LAUNCHED

As a result of a chance meeting with our UP Physics Prof Dr Amador Muriel, a "Discussion group" was formed. Excerpts from Johnny's email:

We learned a lot during the 6th lecture evening of the series at Amador Muriel's 62nd Street residence in Manhattan. You will recall that on April 12, the group listened to an exposition on "The Meaning of Art" by renowned 80-year-old painter Manuel Rodriguez, and on May 17 to a dissertation on "The Paper Tiger Economies of Asia and How the Philippines Can Immolate Them" by successful economist Norman Madrid. Last night, we enjoyed a talk on the intricacies of "The Camera and Landscape Photography" by Carlos Esguerra, systems analyst by profession, connoisseur landscape photographer by avocation, and disciple of the great Edsel Adams by inclination.

The very entertaining lecture was attended by a sellout crowd of 15 — amazing, considering the foul weather outside — I only had an audience of 10 when I gave my lecture on "Oil Refining in Tabangao." Aside from hosts Amador and his wife Gloria and regulars Bert and Eva Florentino, Norman and Sandy Madrid, Danny and Lisa Gil, and Johnny and Mila Reyes, also present were four ladies accomplished in their own right — each eminently capable of delivering the next lecture: Carlos' architect wife Arlene Esguerra, mathematician-and-musician Cynthia De Leon, and physician Reggie Cruz-Cailao.

Reggie, an UPSCA alumna, was actually a house guest of the Muriels together with her aunt, the famous pediatrician Dr. Fe Del Mundo, founder of the Children's

At the 62nd St Forum in Amador Muriel's house. Reggie listening to the lecture.

Medical Center on Banawe Street in Quezon City, now in her early 90's but still on her feet and mentally alert. In fact, she is presently in the U.S. to actively raise funds for her non-governmental humanitarian projects promoting the health and well-being of children in the Philippines, and Reggie, a pediatrician herself and heir apparent of the doctor's practice, is assisting her. Later in the evening, off-Broadway playwright Linda Faigao-Hall, whose Ma-Yi play just completed several sellout performances and who is planning another one entitled

"Pusong Babayi," also showed up as promised. (She has been stirring up the DILA loop lately, as has Norman Madrid.)

It was at one of these meetings that we met and old UP friend, Mars Custodio, and his wife former Upscan Cora Yabut.

-ooo-

MORE UPSCA LOOPERS JOIN DILA LOOP

The freewheeling forum on Yahoo-Groups named DILA (Defending the Indigenous Languages of the Archipelago) got more members as Danny Gil, long time member, endorsed not only Upsca Loop members Johnny Reyes, Gene Pulmano but also 62nd Street Forum members Norman Madrid, Amador Muriel, Linda Faigao, among others.

For those interested in Linguistics surf at <http://groups.yahoo.com/group/dila-philippines>

-ooo-

OCTOBER 26 PERFORMANCE FOR THE FILIPINO CHILDREN'S FUND (FCF)

Michael Dadap will have a concert at the Merkin Concert Hall in New York City as a benefit performance for the FCF, a non-profit charitable organization, established in the U.S. 18 years ago solely to help indigent children and families in the Philippines.

As FCF President Ross (Chit) Inciong writes, [the concert] will introduce a New York rave (and a UP alumnus) in the person of Michael Dadap, who is quite singular in his many accomplishments not only as a classical guitar master, but also as a composer, a conductor and a lecturer on the subject of guitar, the rondalla, and the many aspects of orchestral performance.

The benefit concert will feature Victor Santiago Asuncion (a young but celebrated orchestral piano and harpsichord soloist and assistant professor of piano at the University of Memphis), Lani Misenas (a coloratura soprano), George Magno (baritone-tenor), and the Kayumanggi Chorale (sponsors of the first Filipino-American Choral Competition at Lincoln Center in NY). The show will also feature the works of Filipino composers Lucio San Pedro, Felipe de Leon and Michael Dadap.

A suggested donation of $50.00 will get not only a seat but a chance to join the post performance reception in house. Contact numbers are 646 227 8463, or FCF co-volunteers, Josephine at 212 984 5434 and Kristine at 201 413 2217.

-ooo-

UPSCA REUNION SET TENTATIVELY SET OCTOBER 11

Due to an as yet unconfirmed visit by Bernie de Castro-Muller to NY, the Upscans headed by Tony Nievera plan a party at Tony's Babylon residence. Call Tony at 631 321-4981.

Action & Reaction ! ! !

News clips, letters, faxes, e-mail, anecdotes, conversations . .

NOW, FOR THE REALLY OLD STUFF

In the party last year at the Manila Sunset restaurant in Jersey City to honor the transplants from Los Angeles, a number of out-of-towners attended, including Effie Sta Romana-Hall, Liliosa Mangosing-Evangelista, and Rory Abrera-Campbell. Rory brought her old picture albums and scrapbooks. They were so fascinating we asked her to make copies, which she obligingly did.

Here now are selections from that treasure trove of the 60's:

The Action
July 10, 1961

TRAINING OUR BOMBSIGHTS

By Eddie Manlapig

Incidentally our first joust with UPSCA this semester satisfied our gastronomical gusto when we "caught" Tony Estrera giving his birthday blow-out at the Sawali Corner. The posters committee members: Rory Abrera, Lindus Carreon, Bay Villavicencio, Tessie Chua Chiaco, Leonor Garcia, Joey Añel, Mila Abad, Baby Mangosing, Arthur Adiarte, Oca Calacal, Danny Dequito, Alexi Antonio, Alex Villaflor, and Danny de Guzman were present with two other squatters who smelled their way in, Eddie Manlapig and Gerry Gil, Jr.

The Midnight Fraternity, an affiliate of the NAACP (National Association for the Advancement of Colored People) experienced a great loss when its Grand Midnight, Noel Soriano, gave way to Cupid's stupidity by getting "hooked for life" with Angge Alday. Noel was sentenced to "hard labor for life" by UPSCA's adviser Fr. Pacifico Ortiz at the Sta. Rita Chapel, Philamlife Compound. We wonder how Angge will handle the problem of "looking after" her husband who has the asset of having a natural built-in camouflage.

Gallivanting at the college of Arts and Sciences we silhouetted "Black (K)night" Ernie Santos teaching Algebra. Asked whether he is joining the "territory"(society of instructors dubbed as TERRORS) his response was, "Just wait till next semester and you'll see who will be the most talked about instructor in the University College!"

It has been said that "Many are called but few are chosen". But in Ely's case he was neither "called nor chosen"; he volunteered! UPSCA's jester, old guard Ely Alampay Jr. finally decided to join the "come follow me' club composed of former UPSCAns Jimmy Cruz, Romy Manlapaz, and formerly Ernest Belamide. Ely wrote a letter entitled "The Epistle of the Prophet Elisian's to the Dilimaniacs" saying how great his loss to UPSCA is and how probably UPSCA's missing him with his incomparable wit, humor and trash!"

The following is an excerpt from prophet Elisian's Epistle"!

FACTS ABOUT THE SEMINARY AND THE SEMINARIANS YOU NEVER WOULD HAVE KNOWN IF I HAD NOT WRITTEN TO YOU
1. Seminarians could go on for weeks without thinking of money.
2. Coke is more precious here than Jacqueline is to Kennedy.
3. It's nice to tell stories during sacred silence.
4. We're not allowed to take baths here. Only showers.
5. Some seminarians do not take showers.
6. There arc no girls here-I think.
7. Seminarians study a lot. They learn very little.
8. I still have to shine my shoes without someone asking if I were going to the dance.
9. Manualia means when you clean the toilet, be manual about it. Use your hand!
10. We're not allowed to use pomade, oil, or any artificial beautifier. That's why we all look like male witches. (It's bad enough to be a female witch!)
11. If you want to give up smoking, give it up here, they'll give you up.
12. I do not miss the movies, the comics, but I miss the ROOK, those who play it, and those who don't.

Editor's Notes:
Eddie Manlapig was that tall, slim fellow who went around with co-engineering student and equally lanky Romy Manlapaz (before he also entered the seminary), and this prompted the wags to dub them Manlapaz and Manlapis.

Ely didn't stay long in the seminary . . . a matter of just a few months, much to the relief of quite a number.

Which prompts an anecdote about another Upscan who went in and left early on. His then GF had reportedly said I'm happy that he entered, but would be happier if he didn't.

But Romy stayed on and on, until he became a scholastic, then left just before taking the vows, and another external event.

There were others who also entered later on, and most also left, but others stayed the course, and became Jesuits.

-ooo-

THE ACTION
December, 1960

PERSONALITY

When UPSCA receives its applicants this corning January, it will be taking in a special personality: Johnny M. Reyes. At 18, Johnny is like any typical teenager. His favorite sports are basketball (he roots for La Salle) and swimming. He likes to read when time permits. "I studied a lot when I was in high school." This probably explains his black-rimmed eye-glasses. Besides being a typical teenager, Johnny's hopes and ideals make him a mature Catholic gentleman. He attends Mass regularly and hopes to make the UPSCA in order to continue the apostolic work he began in high school.

Johnny entered UP as a Science Foundation scholar, after having passed an examination which both private and public school applicants took. He decided to take the bachelor of science course in physics and became a college scholar at the end of the first semester. Johnny is now a sophomore and has three more years to go.

His education at St. John's Academy and La Salle are filled with funny incidents but Johnny considers them "unprintable." During his high school days. Johnny was a member of the SCA and the Sodality, as well as being a newspaper reporter and an artist for the La Salle annual. His activities in the UPSCA include his membership in the CIL, posters and choir committees. Besides English, he is fluent in Tagalog — his father is from Bulacan.

At present Johnny's subjects are botany and speech I.

He plans to work in a commercial firm after lie graduates.

When we asked him about the girl he had in mind he said, "She must he natural and an extrovert." Johnny tends to be quiet arid observant — and funny at the proper time — we know he'll win her by his charms.

The Action Staff then: Fredie Santiano, Bay Villavicencio, Rosario de Joya, Rory Abrera, Gerry Gil, Susan Paulin, Cynthia Reyes, Tessie Chua-Chiaco, Lino Faelnar, Primalee Haresco, Mila Abad, Liliosa Mangosing, Melvyn Martin.

Now, who among the Staffers wrote about Johnny?

MORE OLD STUFF, CONTINUED

The Action
May 6, 1960

UPSCA Dramatic Guild to present "Glass Menagerie" on May 8, 11, 12, 1961

The UPSCA Dramatic Guild has for its summer presentation, Tennessee William's "The Glass Menagerie". The play will make its opening performance on May 8, at the Ateneo de San Pablo and then at the UP Engineering Theatre on May 11 and 12. Included in the cast are Robert Arevalo as Toni; Jessica Infante and Aurora Abrera, alternating for the part of Amanda; Heidi de Ocampo and Barbara Gordon, taking turns as Laura and Benjamin Barrera, Jr. as Jim.

This memory play revolves around a mother's loss of the sense of beauty and the ever constant search for it in ugliness. It tells of a daughter's search for herself in the world where glass figures easily break and human hearts more tenderly burst. It tells of a man dreaming of magic impossibilities grasping at the rim of his dreams only to find them dripping to little drops of sea-foam. It tells, finally, of a man who might have changed the lives of these three but did not because he was being himself. Lastly, it tells of blueness.

Plans are underway for having "Glass Menagerie" perform at the De La Salle College and Cebu City.

Responsible for the production is UPSCA Dramatic Guild chairman, Danilo Dequito; along with Alexi Antonio, cast and stage manager; Manny Espejo and Yu-Kuo-Nan, Construction committee; Racquel Zaraspe, Ushering and Refreshments; Boy dela Cruz, lights; Bingo Borromeo and Aida Lava, make-up; Danny Gil and Arthur Adiarte, publicity; Mian Chanco, Pictorials; Susan Rodriguez and Aurora Achacoso, props and sets; Roger Hipol and Rex Baquiran, Scripts; Nanette Ortega and Mila Espejo, prompters; and Mila Abad, Finance. Tickets are available from any Upscan.

Talking more about the busy Dramatic Guild, it is also planning to hold a repeat performance of "MEDEA". Considering the crowd which enjoyed this performance last March, another full-house run is expected when it is presented again, this time at the Ateneo Auditorium at Padre Faura. The same will appear in this performance, with Linda Caedo as "Medea". Robert Arevato as Jason, ably supported by Jessie Infante, Rene Nepomuceno, Antonio Reyes, Danilo Dequito, Pamela Torre, Evelvn Machan and Liliosa Mangosing.

An early play of Tennesee Williams, lately of New York and the inner Sancti of the best psychiatrists, "Glass" was written about two decades ago. Williams revolutionized stage techniques by combining story-line and mechanics into an exciting and quite promising play on poetry. The late Laurette Taylor played Amanda on Broadway and was an instant success. Hollywood beckoned and a talented cast was assembled composed of (the-first-lady-of-the-marquees) Gertrude Lawrence known also for her Anna role in "The King and I", Jane Wyman who earlier had won an Oscar for "Johnny Belinda", Arthur Kennedy who brilliantly recreated his *Jim*, and a young unknown, Kirk Douglas. Well received by the critics, it rated a fair treatment at the box office.

(The article goes on to describe the original Broadway performances, alá Rex Reed)

Ghost Cast in Gauche Case

The cast is unknown but lucid.

Jessica Infante, a virtual unknown except for a bubbly throat and penetrating walk of a few months back, monologized a Nurse in "Media." For three nights, a standing room audience sniffed to Creusa's Tragedy. lnfante was in. As Amanda, Infant Terrifique radiates a charm rarely seen on stage.

Rory Abrera, discovered via a Spanish play where her forte was steaming off a succession of now dazzling, now-inviolate, now-decaying "Tses!", emits the frail, vague, tremendous paranoia of Amanda with tempered aplomb.

Robert Arevalo had no dramatic experience until last year. A BSBA graduate of Ateneo de Manila, his room is lettered with trophies and testimonies to an up-grade I.Q., and a talent for after-dinner chats. Then, the movies came. "Huwag Mo Akong Limutia" made him, and his producers seek him out for "intelligent" roles. Consenting to play Jason to "Medea" three months ago, he professes to enjoy UPSCA so much he might again consent to a part in the tentative play billed for July. "Long Day's Journey Into Night".

Heidi de Ocampo, small, piquant, cheery and partial to mushrooms and strawberries alternates with Barbara Gordon for Laura. Gordon, either in blue, red or cherry white, cavorts impishly with a shy charm that bespeaks of milk at midnight, roses at dawn. Both react to Benjamin Barrera's Jim with the fragility and sweetness Laura is ban with. Barrera, soda guzzler, party-habitue, and a man's man to boot, exudes the boyish frankness of JIM that will surely have the girls in the back row squealing with delight.

Now, who in the Action Staff wrote that review? Seems like there were parts lifted off from somewhere.

-ooo-

Manila Bulletin, Friday, November 10, 1961

Family Theater Features UP Dramatic Group Tonight

"Family Theatre," a weekly television program, will introduce the University of the Philippines Student Catholic Action Dramatic Guild on TV when it presents Ernest Kinoy's "Goodbye to the Clown" today, Nov. 10 at 7:30 over Channel 3. Produced by Maria Isabel Diaz with Fr. Federico Escaler, S.J. as moderator, the play takes its place among the "Family Theatre's" list of serious plays.

Stage directed by Kit Santos Jr., the Kinoy play is a psychological study of a small girl who has a fixation and imagines she has a clown for a constant friend. The most recent plays that Santos directed for the Guild were "Watch on the Rhine" and "Voice of the Turtle."

Heading the cast are Cecile Gordon as Peggy, the little heroine who is detached from reality, and Benjamin Barrera Jr. as the clown. Miss Gordon recently scored as Sally in the Druten play, while Benjie Barrera is an UPSCA mainstay.

Also playing important roles are Lani Villareal as the distraught and highly sensitive mother, and Butch Kalaw-Katigbak as Uncle George, an affectionate, understanding man. Fernando Gil appears as Dr. Benson, the man who tries to help Peggy out. Booth Anson makes a guest appearance as Miss Erwin, Peggy's teacher.

"Family Theatre" has lined up the following for its production staff: television director Arturo Ramos; sets, Jose Roxas; music, Ernesto Zarate; make-up and costumes, Luz Sangco; props, Roberto Bartolome and Ricardo Herrera. The producers of the program have also announced a play-writing contest in connection with its coming anniversary.

The officers of the UPSCA Dramatic Guild include Jimmy Abad, Danny Dequito and Aurora Abrera. This will be the Guild's fifth presentation for the academic year.

Strange how time really dims the memory. Until I reread this news item, I only vaguely remember having acted on TV, and that was under my mistaken notion that I had to stand in for Robert Arevalo (or maybe I really did). Now, I can rightly say I was an actor alongside Robert Arevalo and Boots Anson-Roa! But alas, another thing I distinctly remember was the way director Kit Santos kept pleading with me during rehearsals to "emote!, emote!" I must have been a really bad ham.

-ooo-

Now, for the pictures of the thespians. Next page, please.

MANILA BULLETIN, WED., MAY 3, 1961

'GLASS MENAGERIE.' This is a scene from Tennessee Williams' 'Glass Menagerie,' which will be presented by the U.P. Student Catholic action on May 11. From left: Benjie Barrera, Aurora Abrera, and Robert Arevalo.

Robert Arevalo, a guest, hostess Rory Abrera, and Kit Santos.

At the debut of Rory. Leftmost, Tony Bautista IV, very active in the UP Dramatics Club. Center is Rory. Rightmost is Rudy Magdangal. Tony Bautista and Donnie Montelibano were a bit hit in the Samuel Beckett play "Waiting for Godot", directed by Leon Maria Guerrero. Who are the others?

This is not at Rory's party. Place and year unknown, but that's Lallie de Vera, Jessie Quinto, Jess Javelona, and Jimmy Abad. This probably is after 1967 because Jess' T-shirt indicates he already was working at PRC.

Where are all these friends now? Rory Abrera-Campbell is in Dallas, running a string of Children's schools both locally and in NY, Robert Arevalo is still the big movie name, Kit Santos was last heard of in Canada, Lino Faelnar retired from the ADB in Manila. Mila Abad is working for the Gov't in Manila, Tessie Chua-Chiaco still plays the piano beautifully and resides in Los Angeles, Jess & Jessie Javelona are in Manila and Jessie is the treasurer of the Opus Dei, Lallie de Vera-Lacaba is in Manila, Jimmy Abad is a UP professor. Jessica Infante, long time LA resident, is now retired in Basilan. As to the others, who knows? Any volunteered info?

At Rory's 1961 debut, seated L-R are Lino Faelnar, Olga Cruz, ???, Mila Abad, Tessie Chua-Chiaco.

Sitting foreground, L-R: Danny Dequito, ???, ???, Alexi Antonio, Manya Alvendia, Anaco Castro?, Olga Cruz. *Standing, L-R:* Alex Villaflor, Rogel Rodriguez. Lurking behind Rogel is Fredie Santiano.

Rory Abrera, Rudy Magdangal, Bay Gordon, Betty Nable and Alma Roque. Snapshot at a Dramatic Club rehearsal.

All pictures taken from Rory Abrera-Campbell's scrapbook, mainly showing 1960's parties at her place. Gives credence to the AMDG acronym of *Ang Mga Demonyon Gutom.*

Seated left to right: Alexi Antonio, Baby Mangosing, Rory Abrera, Danny Gil, Susan Paulin, Cynthia Reyes. *Standing:* Gerry Gil, Jess Javelona, Divi Astraquillo, Tessie Chua-Chiaco, Bernadette Abrera, Willie Abrera, Melvyn Martin, Jimmy Abad, Danny Dequito.

L-R, regardless of depth: Jimmy Banaag, ???, Tom Aquino?, Ric Yabes, Manny Espejo, Fredie Santiano, Enteng Batas, Jimmy Abad, Godo Juliano, ???, Johnny Reyes partly hidden, Ernie Pangilinan, Arthur Adiarte, ???, Rory's cousin Caloy Abrera, Tony Estrera, Danny Gil.

The following is a mailing list of all the Upscans whose postal addresses are current

Jimmy & Mercy (Rivera) Abad
Antipolo, Philippines

Arthur & Cherrie Adiarte
St Paul, MN

Vyva Aguirre
U.P. Campus, QC, Philippines

Ofie (Peñaflorida) & Ken Aid
Lakewood, CA

Letty (Ramirez) Ajodah
Queens Village, NY

Ely & Sonia (Alday) Alampay
Diliman, QC, Philippines

Arsenio & Maricon Alfiler, Jr
Diliman, QC, Philippines

Rico Alfiler
McLane, VA 22101

José Alzona
Glendale, CA 91206

Evelym (Machan) Andamo
Huntington Beach, CA

Nanette (Gadi) & Boy Angeles
Monroeville, PA

Lolly Aquino
Los Angeles, CA

Myrna Aquitania
Camarillo, CA

Primo & Lindus (Carreon)
    Arambulo
Rockville, MD

Lito Arong, OMI
Oakland, CA

Noli & Rosita Arong
Arleta, CA

Sisoy & Cecile Arong
Houston, TX

Marylou Fermin Aurelio
San Nicolas, Ilocos Norte, Phils

Alda Balaoing
Los Angeles, CA

Lito & Tita (Teaño) Balucano
Cerritos, CA

Remy Baluyot
Los Angeles, CA

Nina Los Baños
Las Vegas, NV

Tigi & Nora Barcelona
San Juan, Philippines

Olga (Cruz) Barrios
Williamsville, NY

George Bartolome
Vallejo, CA

Enteng & Mely Batas
Los Angeles, CA

Lennie (Abellera) & John Blair
Libertyville, IL

Maurice Borromeo
Quezon City, Philippines

Reggie & Eddie Cailao
Marikina, Philippines

Jun & Cynthia (Reyes)
    Calejesan
Monaca, PA

Rory (Abrera) Campbell
Southlake, TX

Manny Castillo
Brea, CA

Delfin Castro
Bowie, MD

Rey Cendeño
Marikina, Philippines

Tessie Chua Chiaco
North Hollywood, CA

Remy & Anching Chica
Northridge, CA

Norma Cornelio
Marikina, Philippines

Celia (Morales) Cornelio
San Diego, CA

Ludy Corrales
Basking Ridge, NJ

Baby dela Cruz
Los Angeles, CA

Boy dela Cruz
Cottage Grove, MN.

Isagani & Medy Cruz
Malate, Philippines

Nilo & Muni Cruz
Las Vegas, NV

Rene Cruz
Diamond Bar, CA

Alex Dacanay
Quezon City, Philippines

Rene & Lydia Dawis
Minneapolis, MN

Bing (Ferrer) & Tony Dubitsky
Riverdale, MD

Carmen Dungca
Moorpark, CA

Enedina (Garcia) de Guzman
Chesnut Ridge, NJ

Nancy (Cruz) & Gerry Dienel
Little Rock, AR

Georgina (Reyes) & Melvyn
    Encanto
Quezon City, Philippines

Cir & Rose (Lacebal) & Engay
Los Angeles, CA

Manny & Lee Espejo
Saugus, CA

Tony & Josie (Angeles)
    Estrera
Cerritos, CA

Liliosa (Mangosing)
    Evengelista
Fairfax, VA

Lino & Maureen (Holazo)
    Faelnar
Las Pinas, Philippines

Susan (Rodriguez) & Dick
    Fagan
New York, NY

Dette Feliciano
Los Angeles, CA

Lisa Filler
Norwalk, CA

Temy (Dapilos) Gamboa
Patchogue, NY

Malu (Barrios) & Oids Garcia
Cerritos, CA

Pepito & May (Miñosa)
    Gatchalian
Quezon City, Philippines

Divsy (Astraquillo) & Ken
    Geoge
Shorewood, WI

Danny & Lisa (Señeris) Gil
Jersey City, NJ

Erwin & Alita Gomez
Valparaiso, IN

Ruben & Maria Habito
Dallas, TX

Effie (Sta Romana) Hall
Bettendorf, IA

Chit Inciong
Flushing, NY

Jess & Jessie (Quinto) Javelona
Muntinglupa, Philippines

Nanette (Ortega) & Benny
    Jongco
South Orange, NJ

Godofredo & Deng Juliano
Alabang, Philippines

Christie (Borromeo) & Don
    Kawal
Albuquerque, NM

Helen (Ybanez) Kluck
Gloucester, MA

Lallie (de Vera) Lacaba
Pateros, Philippines

Clara (Reyes) & Bart Lapus
San Juan, Philippines

Loida (Nicolas) Lewis
New York, NY 10019

Gus & Toti (Yuson) de Leon
Quezon City, Philippines

Dante & Baby V. Liban
Quezon City, Philippines

Flora Libay
New York, NY

Lenore (Raquel-Santos) Lim
New York, NY

Poch Macaranas
Makati, Philippines

Eddie & Josie Magtoto
Parañaque, Philippines

Mario & Myrna Manansala
La Palma, CA

Romy & Edna Manlapaz
Makati, Philippines

Melvyn & Susan (Paulin)
    Martin
Ayala Alabang, Philippines

Mart Martell
Jersey City, NJ

Jess Martinez
Freeport, IL 61032

John & Cecille (Gordon)
    Mullen
Alexandria, VA

Roly & Evelyn Miranda
UP Diliman, Philippines

Bernie (de Castro) & Jurg
    Muller
Paris, France

Vangie (de Castro)
Quezon City, Philippines

Clemencia Natividad
Toronto, Ontario, Canada

Ernie & Tess Natividad
Tustin Ranch, CA

Tony & Bernadette Nievera
Babylon, NY

Beth (Arcellana) & Bong
    Nuqui
Diliman, QC, Philippines

Jimmy & Ting Ong
Bo Kapitolyo, Pasig, Phils

Rachel (Zaraspe) Ordoñez
New York, NY

Oca & Tatish Palabyab
Makati, Philippines.

Ernie & Jessie (Raqueño)
    Pangilinan
Mission Hills, CA

Eileen (Morales) Pelaez
Cherry Hill, NJ

Ramon & Mimi Pasicolan
Ayala Hts, QC, Philippines

Renan Pineda
North Plainfield, NJ

Ed & Lina (Soliman) Plantilla
Brooklyn, NY

Priscilla (Bautista) Perez
Bronx, NY 10467

Susan Po
San Francisco, CA

Emily (Bacaltos) Popp
West Palm Beach, FL

Gene & Violy Pulmano
Roseland, NJ

Sonia (Valenzuela) &
    Dietrich Quast
Sao Pablo, Brazil

Amelia (Bascon) Rasalan
New York, NY

Zeny (Roxas) & Sixto Ramirez
Los Angeles, CA

Charito Ramirez
Amsterdam, Holland

Nel Reformina
Nanuet, NY

Johnny & Mila (Garcia) Reyes
Belle Mead, NJ

Ruben & Naida (Uy) Rivera
Filinvest II, QC, Philippines

Vic Salanga, SJ
Quezon City, Philippines

Portia Salvacion
Los Angeles, CA

Maya (Arroyo) Santiano
Quezon City, Philippines

Greg Santillan
Pasadena, CA

Angel & Stella Sta Maria
Pasadena, CA

Bing (Pascual) & Nem Santos
Whittier, CA 90601

Linda (Rojas) Santos
Denver, CO

Miren (Dumlao) & Alex Santos
UP Campus, QC, Philippines

Noel & Angge (Alday) Soriano
Quezon City, Philippines

Susan Sulit
Manila, Phils

Ping & Merle (Custodio) Tan
Quezon City, Philippines

Pete & Merle Tandoc
Canton, MI

Thelma (Ibañez) Teves
Rowland Heights, CA

Dell & Julz Tocong
Bellflower, CA

Bernie (Abrera) Tjarks
Dallas, TX

Danny Uy
Westminster, CA

Girlie (Alzona) & Tito
    Valbuena
Astoria, NY

Lina Valcarcel
San Juan, Philippines

Sari Valenzuela
Brooklyn, NY

Jemz & Nora Valera
North York, Ontario, Canada

Fred Valera
Chatsworth, CA

Mila (Arevalo) Vales
Yorba Linda, CA

Arlene Vallesteros
Makati, Philippines

Jose de Vera
Granada Hills, CA

JC (Chit) de Vera
Vorhees, NJ

Mon & Eva (Singson) de Veyra
Marikina, Philippines

Vic & Vickie Vitug
Richmond Hill, NY

Priscilla (Javier) Weber
Manhattan Beach, CA

Elizabeth (Zaraspe) Yoo
Los Angeles, CA

AMDG

UPSCA NEWSLETTER

RESURECTADO
Issue 16, March, 2007

Special Edition
On Batanes Lakbay

Published irregularly and whimsically . . . . send in your news, trivia, photos.

In emailable, printable color PDF format

Hello, everybody!

After almost a 4 year hiatus, the Upscan Alumni bunch of the mid '60s have come back with a vengeance on reporting to the others what's going on, especially on their recent peregrinations, in this new format of the Newsletter.

As usual, let us quote from email exchanges excerpted below:

From Danny to Johnny: Lakviajeros leave for Batanes early tomorrow morning, allow me to give some running commentary. After I hit the send button, I will close the laptop, and will be incommunicado for the next 6 days, unless Basco, Batanes has an internet cafe. Hopefully, Johnny's scenario of having to send messages in a floating bottle will not come to pass.

Early on, Johnny had admonished us: See you in ten months. Don't forget to take ample supplies of Gillette shavers, empty coke bottles, cork stoppers, writing paper, and ball pens. Wait for the current to shift southwards before launching any sea-mail.

And Mercy threw in a whodunit mystery: You do not know who else is coming. But that is my final surprise!!! He he he, as Gerry would say, control your passions.

Even the day before, I had to email all: Mercy still refuses to divulge who is the mystery lakviajero(s) who will be joining us, thus rounding out the group to 15. Abangan ang susonod!

The surprise couple was Romy & Edna Zapanta-Manlapaz. In a sense, Mercy's hints were true; we haven't seen them in quite some time, and we knew them from way back.

We all somehow managed to be at the airport at about 5 in the morning for the 6 o'clock flight on Air Spirit to Basco, Batanes. It was a 2-engined turboprop plane, certainly not new, but it didn't look too old either.

These discussions had prompted Bernie earlier to relate a true story about how her friend got on a really old plane on some hick airline in Africa and when she expressed concern about it, the flight attendant soothingly said not to worry because at least the pilot is new.

According to the flight attendant, there were 48 adults, and 2 children. Yet, we saw still a number of empty seats. So obviously Batanes isn't such an off-the-beaten-track destination.

The flight was surprisingly smooth, all 1 hr 50 minutes, despite the fact that we flew only at 17,000 ft, almost half the height of modern jets which fly over the weather fronts.

When we touched down, our tourist guide and her crew were very efficient; they took care of getting our bags through checkout, loading them on one jeepney that served as the baggage vehicle, and loading us on a second stretched-version jeepney that served as our limo. But our general impressions of the airport were all positive: the structure was new and modern, and the restrooms were clean, and even had running water and TP. And there was a cell phone network (we later found this true for the entire island and even in the adjacent island).

There were two people who were at our service, a lady manager/proprietor named Luz, and a young and energetic and versatile tour guide named Roger. Under them worked a team of assistants: drivers, cooks, attendants, etc. We quickly got to see that the fee for the entire tour package of P7000 for each of us (not including airfare) was very reasonable for the 5 day-stay.

Airfare, on the other hand, was not that much of a bargain. But considering the Airline had a monopoly, it was not too surprising.

Fifteen Upsca Lakviajeros all, but seventeen in picture. Discounting the two extra guests who joined the boat trip, they are L to R, kneeling, Danny Gil & Jimmy Abad; standing, guest1, Erwin's son Victor, Erwin Gomez, Mon Pasicolan, Mercy Abad, Edna Manlapaz, Romy Manlapaz, guest2, Jessie Javelona, Bernie Muller, Lisa Gil, Jess Javelona, Mimi Pasicolan, Jun Calejesan and Cynthia Calejesan. Yes, life vests were mandatory.

Edna and Erwin deplaning, with Victor already on the ground. Behind Erwin was one of the two foreigners on board. Roger tells us that most residents fly rather then take the ill-frequent boat trip to Manila, or to Laoag, then bus to Manila.

About 4 km away was the next town of Mahatao. We stopped for breakfast of coffee and hamburger and cheese, presumably from the local beef farms. After another stop at the church and the town plaza with a funny looking statue of Rizal, we motored to our quarters, a rustic set of cottages just outside town.

The roads were mostly winding narrow ribbons of concrete or dirt cut through the mountain cliffs that make the most of the island's shoreline. Shown above is a typical coastal road.

There would be two couples to a cottage, so we quickly chose who'd be cottage mates. The Gil's shared a relatively large cottage with Erwin and Victor. The other odd couple was Bernie with the Javelonas. The Pasicolans and Calejesans took the third, which eventually became the gathering place for meals and just chatting. The fourth cottage was occupied by the Abads and Manlapaz'.

The first step upon arrival at any place is to unpack suitcases, hang up clothes and put the toiletries in the bathroom or dresser. Once done, a person starts to feel at home. That's exactly what we did the first hour we were ensconced in the cottages by the sea at Disvayangan barrio in town of Mahatao.

Then lunch was delivered: clam chowder soup, heaps of "paco" fern salad, a big tray of escabeche fish, and enough pork chops to make round two for all. And the plates were those native trays topped with a large leaf.

Having gotten up at the unholy hour of 2 or 3 a.,m., most of the lakviajeros desperately needed a nap. That accomplished, it was decided not to waste any time. There was so much to see on the island. Roger and Luz had everything planned. We drove around for a general look-see, noting the hedge rows that locals use to demarcate their properties and gardens. This was like the rice terraces on top of mountains but differently shaped. They were best admired from afar or from atop a mountain.

The first thing that struck us was the Ivatan language has so many "v"s, and "f"s. And it is totally unlike Ilocano. According to Roger, the northern most island has its own language that is barely intelligible to them. Ivatan has nor vowel "e", since "i" is pronounced like a hard "e". As a matter of fact, the sound "i" as a prefix means "from", so Ivatan literally means "from Batan" All these data were copiously being noted down by Jimmy.

We drove to the lovely artist's home of Pacita Abad in the mountains, isolated from the neighbors except for her brother Butch (used to be Cabinet Secretary under Cory, Congressman from Batanes and Secretary of Education under Gloria Macapagal-Arroyo eventually resigning as part of the Hyatt 10 Group).

Entering the Museum that used to be Pacita Abad's house.

It was a lovely home that she and her foreigner husband built. Every window looked out a marvelous sight. We saw the gallery of paintings upstairs, including some self-portraits showing a beautiful vibrant lady. We wondered why she never received the National Artist award. Someone supposed that she was better known abroad than in her homeland. Regretfully, Pacita Abad and her husband only got to live for two months in the home. She passed away from cancer a few years ago but painted valiantly to the end.

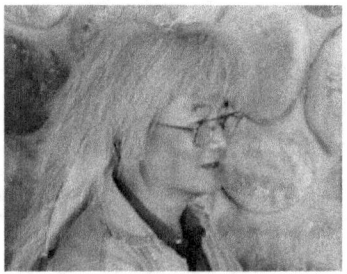

In the kitchen of the Abad home, Jess, Danny and Jun got their first glance of a "vakul". They took pictures wearing it and we think that's when they fell in love with the native raincoat made of the fiber "vuyavuy:" Later, Jess and Jun bought such raincoats and dubbed them as "Tina Turner". None of the wives got jealous.

From there, we proceeded to her brother's equally beautiful home.

Between the two homes are seated lovely life-size statues of Pacita's parents dressed in barong and terno. We were told that is where Pacita's ashes were scattered.

We first admired the gardens in the back, then soon found ourselves ushered into the terrace. Turns out Edna and Romy Manlapaz knew Butch and he graciously instructed the caretaker to serve us coffee. Rather luxurious and just the picker-upper.

We wound our way down to Basco to look at some handicrafts places and Lisa and Danny bought jackets because the weather had turned cold the very day we arrived. It was lovely for some people but freezing for some. Bernie who just came from her Kenya assignment wanted a jacket eventually, so pretty were the ones bought by the Gils.

It had been a long day so we headed home for an early dinner and an early bedtime. Tomorrow a boat ride awaits.

There are no gas stations on the island. The first one is under construction. Gasoline or diesel is brought in as barrels, and sold by retailers, often at sari-sari stores, in bottles such as two liter coke plastic containers. At left is the stretch SS jeepney, our limo, manned by Ramon.

A BOAT RIDE TO SABTANG, from Cynthia's write-up.

We were told by Luz and Roger that, if the weather was nice the next day, we would go to Sabtang, one of the three inhabited islands of Batanes Province. We were to be up and ready to go by 6 a.m. (which meant breakfast at 5:30 or so) because the earlier we went, the calmer the seas would be, the seas being South China Sea and the Pacific Ocean. Needless to say, we didn't get going till past 7:30 which was probably an achievement, considering we were a group of 8 couples plus 1, all dealing with various sleep deprivation from the day before. Not to worry – it was only a mere 30 minutes to Sabtang.

We were driven to the dock by our stretch jeep limo. There we saw

two boats side by side. The captain of one boat was positioning big bags of flour on one end to balance, he said, the passengers who always sat aft and center. The baker who was getting them delivered would be happy to know that he or she was getting certified all-purpose flour. While the crew of two was getting the boat ready, we were glad to see that each of us was getting a bright orange life vest for the trip. They were obviously aware of safety measures. Very reassuring.

Roger blithely announced that, if anyone had seasickness, now was the time to take medicine. I really didn't want Jun hearing this announcement because one, he does tend towards seasickness; two, it didn't seem like a good idea to use the power of suggestion at this time; and three, he hadn't brought any motion sickness medicine. After 39 years of marriage and without even looking at him, I knew Jun was starting to get apprehensive. Roger recommended going with the rhythm of the water – inhale with the rising wave and exhale with the falling one. Easier said than done. Jessie was not happy. Neither of the two boats tied to the dock had "katig" or outriggers. Not to worry, these are experienced boatmen and it's only a 30-minute boat ride. Finally, we were ready to board. Turns out, the first boat closest to the dock was only a stepping stone to the second one which we soon saw was old, decrepit and not one to inspire confidence at all. Nevertheless, trusting in the Lord, our husbands, tour guide and the euphoria of our planned excursion, we gamely trooped onto and into the boat, helped aboard by our solicitous guide and respective hubbies and what did we see? Right smack in the center of a gaping hole on the bottom of the boat was an old, evil looking engine, which would, in a few minutes be emitting smelly, dizzying, probably toxic fumes for all of us who had to sit on the narrow benches around it to inhale.

Pity the one whose legs had to swing freely because of his position right above the engine. I think the lucky man was Jess Javelona. As soon as the anchor was hauled aboard, the head boatman (no one called him captain) turned on the engine, his hand on an iron stick for maneuvering (no steering wheel here), and off we painfully chugged away. His lone crewman jumped down into the hole and began pumping away at the bilge. Okay, it's emptying water. That's good; we don't want to see too much water on the bottom of the boat.

Jessie quipped that this must be the slow boat to China because it was not going anywhere fast. We rose and fell with the waves. I glanced at Jun who had positioned himself in the very center of the boat on one end, away from the fumes and presumably inhaling freely of the fresh sea air. Like Jun, Mon and Mimi made sure they were as far away from the fumes as they could get.

The head boatman suddenly clapped his hands and pointed to the side of the boat. No need for words here. For one thing, the engine was making too much noise and for another, all of us, especially the engineers in the group (and we had an inordinate amount of engineers for such a small group!) had our ears perked for any signs of emergency. The crewman hung over the side of the boat, peering down as far as he could. All our eyes were trained on him. Never mind that the water was a beautiful shade of blue and sometimes green and off in the distance were the mountains that surround Batanes Islands.

Boatman 1 motioned to Boatman 2 to take the wheel while he took a turn at hanging over the side of the boat, checking and hoping, I'm sure, that whatever might be causing the problem had cleared up just like that. Again, he took the helm but kept looking down at the engine and around the boat, never saying a word or changing the expression on his face, but one would have had to be a dolt not to realize that something was amiss. Boatmen 1 and 2 changed places again. Boatman 1 frantically wiggled a plastic tube on the floor of the boat. Danny Gil, Jess Javelona, Erwin Gomez and Jimmy Abad, who are not even engineers, were craning their necks to see what was happening and what the heck the engine was doing. It didn't take too much imagination to see the boatman as Charon of the River Styx and the gaping hole became a hell that was to be abhorred.

We were getting closer to the middle of the channel where the South China Sea and the Pacific Ocean meet and thus, the waves got bigger and bigger. Romy, another engineer, albeit a chemical engineer, looked serene as always. (I wonder if he ever worried.) Edna's brow looked furrowed. I'm sure Lisa was concerned but since Danny was monitoring the situation, I suppose she thought there was no sense in her getting discombobulated as well. Bernie had her diplomat's face on, assessing the situation, I'm sure, and wondering about the options. Jessie hooked her arm through Jess' and turned to me saying: "I keep reciting the mysteries of the rosary but I don't know whether I'm starting or ending a decade." I, on the other hand, had been praying "Hail Mary" but for once it didn't comfort me, especially when I came to the part that said "Now and at the hour of my death". Oh, no, that wasn't what I wanted to hear just then. I shifted gears in a hurry and changed to another prayer, one that I say every time I receive Holy Communion.

> "Soul of Christ, sanctify me,
> Body of Christ, save me,

> Blood of Christ, inebriate me, (Being drunk might be
>   good just now)
> Water from the side of Christ, wash me,
> Passion of Christ, strengthen me,
> Oh, good Jesus, hear me,
> Within Thy wounds, hide me,
> Suffer me not to be separated from Thee,
> From the malignant enemy, defend me, (from these
>   waters and this old boat)
> In the hour of my death, call me (oh, no, again
>   this reference!)
> And bid me to come to Thee (Lord, I am not ready)...."

I had to change prayers again. Which one will comfort me just now? I dredge up a prayer from STC and Upsca days: "The Memorare"

"Remember, oh most gracious Virgin Mary, that never was it known, that anyone who fled to thy protection, implored thy help or sought thy intercession, was left unaided. Inspired with this confidence, I fly unto thee, oh virgin of virgins, my mother. To thee I come; before thee I stand, sinful and sorrowful,. Oh Mother of the Word Incarnate, despise not my petition, but in thy mercy, hear and answer me. Amen. Perfect!

Suddenly, Boatman 1 moves his stick. The boat makes a turn. At first, I thought we were heading for a nearby shore where I saw a church and some other buildings. OK, the timing is right, it's about 30 minutes, give or take. We soon realize the boat is going back where it came from. Bernie reacts quite simply and with the sweetest of smiles "We're going back? O.K." I told Jessie: "Let's make a pact. No more boat rides today." She readily agrees and 30 to 40 minutes later, the slow boat to China is back where it started.

Against our better judgment, we were guided into the other boat which we had just clambered over to get into the first. The boat was

We did make it to Sabtang on the other boat. Disembarking without a pier was quite a feat. At least there was a breakwater. Going back using the stairs in the breakwater was even more exciting when each of us had to time our leap to the heaving of the waves, and Mercy almost slipped.

certainly in better condition, even though the engine was still smack in the center (that must be where it's put in this part of the world) for all of us to see. This time, the boat had 4 crewmen in addition to the captain who looked rather young for the position. What fascinated those of us who were seated close by was the fact that while his head was sticking above the hole above his seat, his big toe and the next were maneuvering the iron stick quite adeptly. Several of us girls were thoroughly impressed. Bernie Mueller said she read that the foreigners who first came to this land found that the Asians (Filipinos included) were very adept in the use of their toes, using them to pick up objects or for games. Our fears were greatly allayed because the captain was calm, quiet in his movements and definitely in command of his vessel. There was still a guy pumping the bilge, but the engine sounded better tuned and chugged strongly and determinedly. Danny theorized that something had clogged in the intake valve of the other boat and that they had tried to fix it, but since they couldn't, they then made the decision to bring us back to the dock.

Off we started again. I told Bernie: "So much for a 30 minute ride. Here it was going on an hour and a half and we were still in the middle of the ocean. As we neared Sabtang, our fears returned. The boat was getting tossed about by increasingly strong waves. This was not just roller-coaster up and down waves; these were up and down and right and left and sometimes, one couldn't see the horizon at all. Instead, the waves we glimpsed were higher than the

Swells seemed 8 ft high

prow. The lady beside Jessie didn't make it over to the side of the boat. She threw up right then and there. We saw crewmen on either side of the boat rolling up what looked like thin ropes. They seemed to know what they were doing but I never did find out what they were doing. Not that it mattered. I was just happy to be nearing dry land. The captain never lost his imperturbability, maneuvering his boat where he thought it best and soon, we were safe at port. Everyone looked around at the others. Thumbs up and arms pumped together with sighs of "Yes" were greatly in evidence. I thought for sure Jessie would kiss the sand. I caught up with Jun who had disembarked ahead of everyone. He looked pale and haggard. I asked him how he was and, without a backward glance, he walked behind another boat and promptly threw up. Everyone wondered how the other boat would have fared had we continued on that journey.

Danny's notes after reading Cynthia's account: Actually, it wasn't that bad at all. Boats here are designed to be wide and flat bottomed, so to roll with the swells, hence they travel much slower, as compared to the outriggered banca-types that travel faster. Besides, the worst that could have happened in the first boat was the engine to conk out due to overheating since it's coolant system got partially clogged, but the boatman saw this and throttled the engine to near idle; that's why it took so long to go back. And if it did conk out, Luz or Roger or Charon the boatman could have whipped out their cell phones and called for rescue for the second boat, which incidentally had two engines. And all the engines were venerable Yanmar diesels, not any make-do Toyota. Lastly, what's wrong with some open-sea swimming with life vests?

SABTANG   (Notes from Mimi Pasicolan included)

As soon as we had doffed our life vests, a whole bunch of us headed to the rest rooms which were labeled "He" and "She". They were fairly clean for an isolated town, but no water and no T.P. Fortunately, we never travel unequipped or unprepared.

There were two jeeps waiting to drive us around Sabtang. Unlike Basco, where we came from, Sabtang was hot and sunny. As we drove around town, Roger made sure to point out the old,

traditional houses, some of them built in the last century. The walls were made of stones and corals for mortar. The roofs, called "atip" were made of date palm leaves (although cogon was also used) which were layered very heavily to keep the water from leaking. The cross brace on top of the house which kept everything in place was called "vuvong", a word quite similar to our Tagalog term for roof which is "bubong". Later, we noticed a predeliction for the letter "v" in their language as in "Ivatan", "Disvayangan" etc. Bernie found this curious since we don't have the letter "v" in the national language. Unlike the "bahay kubo" seen in other parts of the Philippines, the roof of their "bahay na bato" hangs very low and close to the house. There were windows, however, that allowed for cross breezes. The house had outdoor facilities for a kitchen, a bathroom and a garden. Nice use of space. Just outside the front of the house, we noticed a set of stairs that led nowhere. Turns out, that was a place where the family could store water for times when there were dry spells.

We entered one of the old houses just to see how people from those times lived. Basically, there was one big, multi-functioned room. There was a bed that could serve as a bench or a table.. Hanging from the ceiling was a long stick from which protruded dowels. We were told this was for food storage. I assumed this kept the food safe from small hands as well as flies and ants. I thought that hanger would have made a rather smart way to hang glasses behind a bar or in a modern kitchen. Roger pointed out that the cement walls were at least a meter thick so they were warm in cold weather and vice-versa. Roger recounted the evolution of the Batanes Bahay na Bato from all grass huts to a combination of grass and cement to those that were elevated to keep them safe from floods. Storage space was provided in a room at the back of the house as well as down in a dirt basement.

Roger encouraged us to walk around the town and get a sense of the townspeople's lifestyle. It must have been the season for garlic because it was everywhere. Mimi said garlic from here was supposed to taste sweeter and nicer so in no time, Mercy and Jessie and Mimi were making bids to buy a cache of garlic that was stacked in one of the houses. The lady of the house said they weren't selling them because they needed them for planting.

Sabtang houses, like those in the rest of the Batanes islands have an innate sense of order about them. The houses are built on either side of long, straight roads. Neatness is evident because there is no garbage strewn around and women constantly sweep the street, the garden and anywhere there is detritus. The houses are pretty uniform in size, shape and color. While there is a grayness about the town, this is relieved by the lovely flowers such as bougainvilla and San Francisco bushes that are planted in the gardens or hanging over fences.

Roger pointed out different flora and fauna – palo Maria used for making boats, umbrella trees whose nuts are edible, Talisay trees. We stopped on the sidewalk under a shady tree to drink fresh buko juice and eat its meat with homemade spoons. So refreshing.

One of the delights of walking in a small, strange town like Chavayan, whether here in the Philippines or in Europe perhaps is first, not getting too lost and second, the serendipitous discoveries waiting around the corner. Such was an intimate chapel sitting off to the side of a basketball court which a local man was more than willing to open up for us. He slid a big old log aside and gave us permission to admire the blue and beige altar with St. Thomas Aquinas prominently featured near the front. He was the patron saint, after all. Of course, we made the requisite three wishes, that being a new church. Jimmy and Mercy, who peeled off from the group for a little while, chanced on a small chapel called St. Rose of Lima. Roger had told us that Batanes is 90 to 95 % Catholic. It is obvious in the number of churches and chapels on the island.

Outside the church, we found Roger and Victor engaging in game of pick up basketball. Having played basketball in high school, Victor made several 3-pointers, much to his, Roger's and Erwin's delight (proud papa natch!) The local guy who had shown us the church said several times that he was related to this basketball star Hubalde in Manila. "Pinsang buo ko 'yon." He said they always won the basketball tourneys presumably because they were agile and tall.

Roger also wanted to make sure we met the Centennial man who, at 102 years of age, still fashions native hats from a certain plant.

There was one hat lying around and while Edna proposed to buy it for the group with the intent of raffling it off, Bernie ended up buying it for her husband's collection. She went home happy with her purchase.

We piled back into the jeeps to tour the countryside. It was indeed enchanting, standing on the ridges and taking in the blue, blue waters so reminiscent of the Mediterranean or Virgin Gorda in the Caribbean Sea. The jeeps followed apace while we gawked at the scenery. Jun and Victor decided to follow Roger down and up a mountain ridge. He raved about the pictures they got. Pretty soon, it was time for the lunch which had been prepared by some local women contacted by Luz. We headed for the beach called Murong in the adjoining town of Malakdang after picking up the cook and her staff, even loading the plastic chairs and tables which would be used for serving the meal atop the jeepneys. What a feast! Nilagang manok with cabbage, coconut crabs brimming with buttery aligue, (cholesterol never tasted so good and alluring!), fish with mayonnaise, "bulaklak ng sibuyas" (never knew onions had flowers), bananas and freshly picked buko. We ate to our heart's content after which some of us walked the beach looking for beautiful seashells and coral. Mon and Jessie had quite a collection. We wonder how they're bringing them home.

Time to report back to the pier. We knew that we had to be there soon after lunch if we expected the waves to be calm. We donned our orange vests once again and waited for the boat to be unloaded. Apparently, it had returned to Basco to pick up passengers and merchandise. It was amazing how much it contained – boxes and boxes of merchandise. Just when we thought we could start boarding, the crew realized that they had not unloaded the GI sheets and plywood which were on the top of the boat. Meantime, it was edging towards 3 p.m. and we saw the waves starting to crash ashore. The crew decided that it was not wise to pick us up from that part of the pier because it was sitting so close to the bottom of the sea causing them to get stuck in the sea bottom. Thus we were motioned to another part where there were stairs that the boat could position itself against. Even that was a decidedly risky proposition.

Naturally, it was the women who were supposed to go on first. We, who were loaded down with purses and shopping bags had to be supported on either side by Roger and some boatmen. The first two or three boarded without too much trouble. By the fourth one, they were having some problems. The boat wouldn't stay still long enough for the passengers to board. They started counting the waves which apparently have a rhythm to them. Big waves were followed by 5 or 6 little waves and so forth. Most of us were already on sitting on the narrow benches around the engine when we heard a cry. Apparently, Mercy had both her feet already in the boat when it suddenly lifted due to a high wave. The two men holding her had to hang on so as not to drop her. With a mighty effort, she was able to force her body over and she was in. Mercy swore that her guardian angel pushed her in. Jimmy, who didn't know angelic forces were at work and who was right beside her, stared in horror at the near accident and heaved a sigh of relief at the fortunate ending. By the time the guys got on the boat, they knew the routine and were able to board without incident.

The boat ride out of the channel was a bit choppy but nothing like the entry we had. Perhaps we are just too tuckered out because most of us fell asleep on the return home. We were happy to be back home by late afternoon.

Dinner of "pakbet", grilled flying fish and pork chop. Mimi said "burp, burp, burp. We were definitely ready for bed after that.

NORTHERN BATANES - Around the Island

Jessie has been a model of virtue. Because of her, we – Mercy and I – decided to accompany her to church at 5 every morning (Jessie went by herself the first day), armed with flashlights to see where we were going. It was a wonderful way to start the day when the stars and the moon were still out and few vehicles were out and about. We were pleasantly surprised to hear the Mass, homilies and hymns in English. American influence was certainly far reaching.

(to be cont'd - Marlborough country, fishing village, windmills)

Miscellaneous pictures below:

The picnic at Sabtang island, under a natural arch of volcanic rock.

To the left of the arch is the beach, which seems typical: an area of sand that slopes downward toward a tableland of coral (the darker portion), then the edge of the coral where the water is deep and the waves start to break.

Sunset and low tide at the beach in front of our cottages. The coral tableland teems with life, and we spent hours just wading across it. Swimming is best at high tide where the water reaches the sloped bank of sand, yet the waves still break at the far edge of the reef.

Having merienda at the cottage of the Pasicolans and Calejesans. The thatching on the left is the roof of their sleeping quarters. When not eating out or picnicking elsewhere, we always had meals at this spot. In the evenings, we'd invariably stay up there to chat.

Lisa testing her teeth on sugar cane. That's Roger behind the ancient cane press on Sabtang Island. Note stone-walled houses.

Out of the many churches in Batanes, this is the only one with a grass roof, in Chavayan town on Sabtang island. The grass is almost a foot thick and is buttressed in layers by reeds made from some local flora.

We were given a wake-up reprieve – 9 a.m. instead of 7. Of course, by the time we got going, it was closer to 9:30. We headed for Uyugan where, on the pretext of buying garlic, everyone who descended from the jeep, ended up buying pan de sal, round bread with 4 corners (you explain that!), water and soft drinks. Good merienda. Those who had been pining for the garlic finally found them at two different stalls so they bought P100 worth of the beautifully braided bulbs.

Continuing our drive around the island, we came upon the church called San Jose de Obrero. It stood on a slight knoll

with a roundabout in the front We don't quite know where Romy slipped and skinned his knees but he sported two bloody wounds all the way home. According to his narrative, Roger said this church was really too big for the people of Uyugan, a barrio of Ivana. The explanation was that the Spanish friars, instead of traveling to the different communities, forced the natives to move there from to facilitate their evangelization. After that was accomplished, the natives were then allowed to return to their island or town.

One of the sights along the way was hundreds of molded triangular devices, a Japanese design that Roger said were to be sunk in the seas to act as breakers. This would protect the coral reefs from breakage. They were obviously huge and heavy but Roger said they were concerned about robbery. Who would ever have the chutzpah to do that?

Roger made a big deal about the Honesty Canteen which was started by a kind-hearted lady named Elena. She apparently felt sorry for people waiting for the ill-frequent boat to Sabtang island but had nowhere to take a little coffee and bread. Since she had to go off and work in the fields, she left all the fixings for a simple breakfast in the hut along with a little container for the people to deposit their payment. Later, when the boat dock was moved to a more protected cove, the Canteen remained and actually expanded to include canned goods, drinks, household items, and a karaoke machine. We snapped up the braids of garlic and 2 bottles of special basi and paid them off by slipping the bills into a slotted money receptacle. Here, Victor is shown

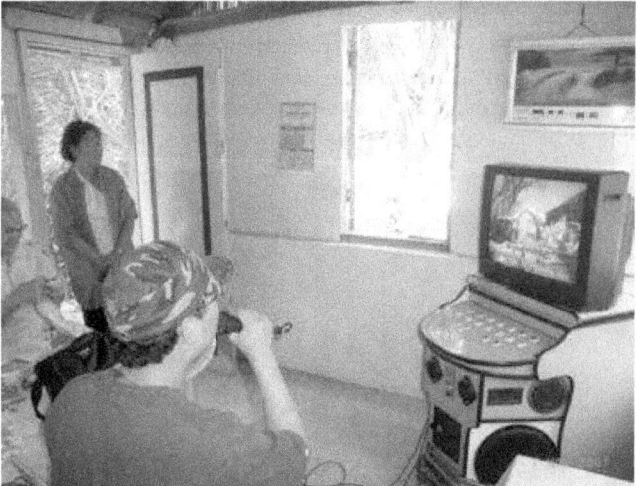

sampling the karaoke machine. It is a well known fact that people of Batanes are trustworthy and dependable. One can leave just about anything around and it will be exactly where it was left upon one's return. Would that they never lose that trait!

We drove through the smallest municipality named Ivana which turned out to be where Roger's father stayed every so often. We had heard of this fine gentleman who had fathered 8 children so to support them, Roger said, he would set his fishing nets at night, sometimes sleeping by the beach in a tent, then head for the fields to till the soil and harvest various fruits and vegetables which the children would have to sell to help meet expenses. Off he would go to his government job till 5, then it was back to fishing, farming and such. As if that weren't admirable enough, even with children and a wife to support, Mr. Doplito decided that Basco needed a veterinarian so he decided to go to U.P. in Diliman where he took Veterinary Medicine. He became the first Vet Med Dr. in Batanes. Hearing that we were mostly from UP, he emerged from the store where he was chatting with folks and came to our jeep to say hello. We asked him about several UPSCAns who might have been around when he was. He is 66 years old, not much older than people in our group, but oh, what an admirable life he has led!

We drove further on - remember, we were driving around the Batan island - and came upon a ghost village named "Songson". As the plaque on the roadside indicated, and as further explained by Roger, this was a thriving fishing village that got hard hit by a strong typhoon in the 1953, and finally finished off by a tsunami. This prompted Pres Magsaysay to offer the survivors land in Mindanao. Most took the offer, and only lately, many of the offspring have come back to rebuild the town.

Roger indicated that all this idea of Batanes being a gale swept wasteland is really exaggerated because the islands are always used as a reference for typhoons and the Batanes name always sticks, i.e., "typhoon so and so bearing westward now is located 300 kn south of Batanes.." That's 300 km away, says Roger. Another placename is Bicol.

We headed for a government-developed park in Itbud, fenced in to keep the goats from trespassing, but all to no avail. They still managed to get in and leave their droppings. Planted generously around the park were several yucca trees that had plentiful fruits similar to rosy red pineapples. The locals call

this plant "ujangu" on which coconut crabs feed. Bernie tried to break one open with her knife but nothing doing, The coconut crab beats her everytime. With the heat of the sun baking on our heads, we headed for the shade of the huts in the park. In one hut, there waited a young girl who when asked what was for lunch answered "It's a secret". Clever answer, we thought. We took note of the color coordinated dishes and napkins which we assigned to whatever people were wearing (when people have nothing better to do on their vacations, they do silly things like this!). Soon enough, a spanking white SUV disgorged some lovely ladies bearing nicely presented rice, yellow and white, the latter decorated

with peas and raisins. The last to alight was the town mayor herself, Mrs.Ibay ready to show us their unique brand of hospitality. They had soup, fish sarciado, lechon kawali with liver sauce, leafy vegetables and artfully carved tomatoes. Imagine, the town mayor being our food caterer. It was enough to touch our collective hearts. Then, it was nap time after this heavy meal, and we fell promptly asleep on benches, tables and, in a pinch, on the grass.

On our way to the barrio of Imnajbu, we passed the Chapel of San Lorenzo Ruiz. We also passed the abandoned American Loran station, now rendered obsolete with advent of GPS. Roger said there was always a contingent of Americans stationed there, and at least one has settled in town after marrying a local girl.

Then the jeep started climbing up the mountains to cut across back to Basco, as the northeastern portion of the island does not have a coastal road. Certain stretches were not yet paved. We were headed to Marborough Country.

It seemed like a Tour d'France road which wouldn't stop rising to the heavens. We were amazed at all the well cemented roads. Every corner brought a view of farm plots that had been planted with cassava, onions and other produce. When an outstanding skyline came into view, Roger asked Rufo to stop for some picture-taking. We concluded that

wherever we went, the cows and goats had beat us to it. We had to be extremely careful not to step on their trademark droppings. Someone remarked that was why the islands were extremely fertile. Along the way we stopped to taste some berries with big seeds called "alunot". In nearly the same spot, we espied a curious looking plant which looked just like a sugar cane except that it kept extending the more Jun pulled on it. It turned out to be rattan. The plant starts out looking like a palm tree but at some point, develops thorny edges that become this curvy piece of wood. Soon we could distinguish them from the other plants. We picked up something new from Roger again.

Marlboro Country was straight out of the movies. No horses, just cows with their calves. A gated area had a sign that said

this was a community grazing land. Animals have it good in these here parts. One wonders if the animals are tougher because they have to keep climbing hills and mountains. We took a lot of individual and group photos during those hills-are-alive moments.

At a tight fork on the road, Roger called out to Rufu the driver to take the turn and go toward a fishing village. After going downhill on a really narrow but concrete road, we finally entered town. The jeep was parked at the entrance to town, while we walked around the fishing village. Roads

were concrete and there were what appeared to be fishpens. It was sleepy and quiet although there were people busy at their pursuits. Roger had explained that there are certain traditions at the start of the fishing season, and that includes butchering a black pig. He said that as of today, no one may swim in the water anymore, as the boats go out the next day.

There was a man filling his boat with water to prevent shrinkage and thus leaky seams. Suddenly, we heard cries of alarm from those who were ahead of us. Apparently, a man on his bike, inebriated to begin with, lost his balance and fell headlong onto a gently sloping hillside along with his red and blue bike. He stayed there, head on elbows, peering up with glazed eyes every so often. The men near the boat said for us to pay him no mind because he was just drunk, perhaps a rather regular occurrence. Thankfully, he didn't seem gravely injured so, in a way, being drunk has its merits in a rather curious way. Jess theorized that when he saw the group coming, he couldn't decide with his drunken double vision where to pass so he chose to go to one side which, unfortunately, was the hillside.

So much for a little excitement. Roger called for us to hold up because a friendly looking woman was giving us "buko" to drink and white "ube" chips to nibble on. A friendly gesture but it also gave Jessie a chance to buy all the bags of ube chips she was selling. Good quid pro quo!

When we had our fill of ube chips and buko, I turned to 7 or 8 women who were looking at us curiously and said "Dios Mamahis" (thank goodness it came out right!) which, like a light switch, turned on their smiles. Thank goodness for Roger's patient instruction.

Then back to the main road for a really steep climb to one of the highest portions of the island, where the windmills are located.

We kept driving up, up, up. Jessie wondered whether our trusty jeep could handle it but not to worry. It had the heart of "The Little Engine That Could" and Rufo, our gentle driver, treated it with great care.

While the skyline was awesome, the beaches, coves and lagoons below were not to be disparaged. Perhaps in a few more years, like Boracay, they will be clean and free of rocks. Then again, that can only mean more tourists. It's a balancing act all right.

Finally, we got to the summit which felt indeed like the top of the world. There in front of us were three windmills, generating the power for the towns below. Roger showed us the winch which could be used to lower the windmill and position it on a cradle to wait out the bad weather. Breathtaking view but although scary to drive on, Roger nonetheless choose the shorter but steeper road back to Basco.

Night was falling by the time we reached Basco town proper. First, we drove up and down the streets looking for fish to buy. Fishermen and vendors just plunk themselves down on the street corners of Abad Street, the busiest commercial street in downtown Basco. Nothing but flying fish for sale.

Jun went down the street to look for flip-flops which he could use to the beach tomorrow. He came back waving his slippers – P100! – and with the announcement that there was an internet place down the street. Would I like to check my e-mail? Eager to hear from the kids, I said yes. We were there all of 10 minutes – P10 – but we had to hurry to Duques where dinner was a-waiting. We were the last to eat and dear Mon made sure we had samples of each dish – excellent eggdrop soup, paco salad, chicken, grilled fish steak, beefsteak, bola-bola made of banana root, and pinsec frito. We went home quite satisfied.

A LAZY DAY AT THE BEACH

Yesterday was declared a free day with swimming at the beach. The day before, we had driven by some beaches and indicated our choice of picnic place. We chose what looked like a secluded spot with a white sandy beach and huge rocks that looked like they had fallen from the nearby mountainside. The water was blue and inviting, teeming with the skinniest starfish we had ever seen.. Unfortunately, it was stony on the ocean floor and, in places, filled with kelp. Still, that didn't stop us from walking up and down the

beach, lying on the sand reading or taking naps, and wading in the water. Jimmy, Danny, Jun, Bernie, Mercy, Jessie and

Mimi went further into the water where there were rocks to sit on.

Later Bernie emerged with hives all over her; perhaps she was allergic to something in the water. Bernie wasn't the only one with bites. Roger, who had gone way out past the curling surf to catch some fish had jellyfish bites all over his body. Stalwart guy that he is, he didn't complain one bit. He came back with 3 medium-sized fish.

What is it about the beach that brings out the children in all of us? All of a sudden, frolicking in the waves or just sitting on a rock half-immersed in the water are perfectly acceptable. Looking for that colorful and different seashell, finding one that is occupied and hoping it abandons its house so we can take it home with us – what simple pleasures!

Every day, every meal has been a delight. We never know what awaits in the "palayok" – rice or soup or stew. Yesterday, it was soup, beefsteak, flying fish (certainly popular here), lumpiang frito, gabi trunk and bola-bola. Our plates were lined with giant leaves (we're particularly

enamored of the antipolo leaves which are sturdy and fit the rattan holders just right). Bananas always round out the meal.

Jun had his heart set, it seemed, on going over the rocks that led to the lagoon around the bend. It seemed like a lovely place to enjoy private moments and a leisurely swim. Unfortunately, the water crashing in big waves on the rocks did not invite further exploration, so, even with Danny in

tow, they were not able to get where they wanted. Never mind. Most everyone found some interesting seashells, corals or rocks, except for Romy and Edna who wisely relaxed on their brown mat and read to their hearts' content.

We might have stayed a little longer but Mimi and I and soon the others, felt some raindrops so we gathered up our mats and towels and swim gear and got ready to depart the beach. Unfortunately, it was earlier than planned so it took a while for the single SUV that Luz had arranged for (apparently, our stretch limo jeepney was now engaged elsewhere) to get back to us and bring us home in two trips.

It was a good time to contemplate the water that went back and forth unceasingly, approaching us like a million hands ready to massage the shore. Sleep beckoned and was never more welcome when we arrived back at our cottages.

Course, come evening it was time for dinner again. Luz lovingly prepared galunggong wrapped in foil for each of us. Rice, salad, tomatoes, and bananas provide a healthy and balanced meal.

A TASTE FOR LECHON

When we were Siargao several years ago, a healthy little piglet crossed our path unwittingly while we were on our way to church. Little did he know that his hours were numbered and he would soon end up as "lechon" on our table. The same idea occurred to our group so today, Roger and company arose early to get the pig ready for lunch.

Late in the morning, some of us realized that the pig would take longer than we expected to cook so I was told they volunteered to take a turn at the spit. Actually, Mimi reported that each was just looking out for their favorite part like the tail for Jessie, the hocks and feet for Lisa and the head for Erwin and Mimi. Since it takes a while to cook lechon on the spit (even though it was only 15 kilo "bi-ik", the pig did not get cooked until past lunchtime so we ate soup, rice, fish and greens with carrots and tomatoes, apples and peanut brittle first, and followed all that up with a crisp, crackling baby pig, Cholesterol never tasted so good! The meat was tender, the skin divine. It was demolished in no time but we left enough for "paksiw" this evening.

It's pack-up time. We have more dirty clothes than clean, flying fish dried for daing, garlic buds, ube chips that are white, fans and baskets and tons of shells to bring (that is, if the local authorities let us – actually, Jimmy's ploy was best – he stuck them in his shoes in his maleta). We have had a lovely, unique, once-in-a-lifetime experience and it'll be a while before it's repeated.

Each of us was asked to sum up what Batanes means for us. Here are the replies:

"God's own country!" ……..Jimmy Abad
"Unspoiled by civilization"….Mercy Abad

"Nature and progress in balance"…..Jun Calejesan
"People in harmony with their environment"… Cynthia Calejesan

"Cliffs and zigzag roads"……Lisa Gil
"Windmill electrical farm, wow!"….Danny Gil

"Unspoiled, beautiful land; very nice people"…Erwin Gomez
"God made a beautiful place to make people happy"…Victor Gomez

"Baguio + Palawan; Tina Turner"…Jess and Jessie Javelona

"High and mighty – the waves of Batanes"….Edna and Romy Manlapaz

"Breath-taking scenery"……………Bernie Mueller

"Hermosa! Batanes"…..Mon Pasicolan
"A simple life"………..Mimi Pasicolan

---ooooo---

The 2007 Batanes Lakviajeros, zigzagging ID from front: Jessie, Jess, Victor, Jimmy, Mercy, Mimi, Mon, Erwin, Jun, Edna, Cynthia, Danny, Lisa, Bernie and Romy.

Notes: The above write-up starting from halfway on page 2 was made primarily by Cynthia in collaboration with Mimi, and Jimmy for all the place names from his copious notes, and Danny who did the final editing and typesetting with pictures. The first portion had previously been posted by Danny on the loop from a Batanes internet café, taken from the memory stick copied from his laptop. Cynthia saw the email and remarked that she also had her laptop and was writing up the events. On the last day in Batanes, Danny copied Cynthia's write-up then noticed a few days later that it was the incomplete version. From Surigao, Cynthia emailed Danny the rest. By then, Danny had sent out to family a few pictorials, with emphasis on miscellaneous views. These are now appended in the next 3 pages.

The home address for the 5 day duration.

The stretch of sand in our cove, looking south. Cottages on left.

Our cottage, three king sized mattresses side by side on a common platform, sand/gravel floor, shelvings all around, and a dinning room beyond. Toilet bath is separate outside.

Wading in the shallower section, that extends on some sort of coral tableland until the sudden deep end where the waves break. We never swam to that portion.

Our beach is like a cove, with adequate sandy area, with north end terminating during low tide in rocky portion. It takes some maneuvering going through wave-dashed rocks to go to another cove further beyond which is inaccessible from the road because of high cliffs. We didn't venture that far.

One of the 4 sets of cottages we rented. I think there are about 7 or 8 in all, privately owned by different people, but managed by a cooperative. This version has a separate dinning area, which we always used together for our meals and gatherings. There are more modern hotels and structures nearer town, 4 km north.

Getting off the bucking bronco boat at the more primitive island of Sabtang was one thing. First boat had engine trouble and turned back. Above shows us getting back mid-afernoon.

This is the only church among all the many in the province where the walls are stone and the roof still is thatched grass.

But the serenity of old structures such as this abandoned stone house with thatched roof (typical), and the small church shown above right, and the picnic on beach shown below made the trip to Sabtang Island well worth it.

The outline of a lady's face is quite evident on the mountain.

A fort of the pre-Spanish Ivatan people, with mountain walls cut further to make a difficult and steep access. There are sixteen in all.

A more virgin beach on Sabtang island. The mountains beyond belong to the main Basco island where we boated over from.

Back on the main Basco island, to more serenity. Not fully shown is the looming outline of Mt Iraya, dormant volcano. This is at the estate of the Abads: good politicians and artists.

Spectacular view of the late Artist Pacita Abad museum.

A view from the other house, owned by Congressman Butch Abad.

The cultivated fields from as seen from the Abad estate.

The winding road to the wind farm: literally a narrow concrete ribbon straddling the mountain crest. We met no other vehicle.

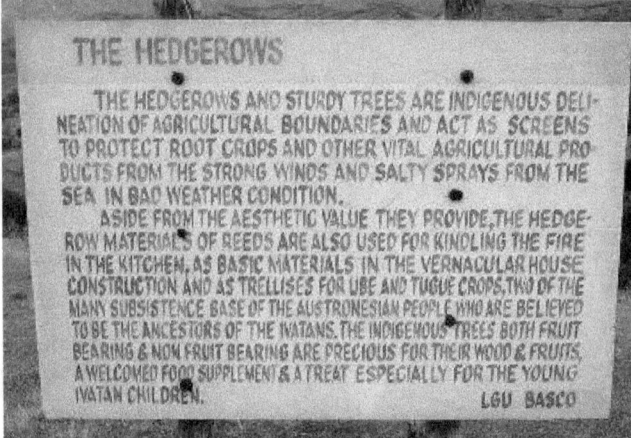

THE HEDGEROWS

THE HEDGEROWS AND STURDY TREES ARE INDIGENOUS DELINEATION OF AGRICULTURAL BOUNDARIES AND ACT AS SCREENS TO PROTECT ROOT CROPS AND OTHER VITAL AGRICULTURAL PRODUCTS FROM THE STRONG WINDS AND SALTY SPRAYS FROM THE SEA IN BAD WEATHER CONDITION.

ASIDE FROM THE AESTHETIC VALUE THEY PROVIDE, THE HEDGEROW MATERIALS OF REEDS ARE ALSO USED FOR KINDLING THE FIRE IN THE KITCHEN, AS BASIC MATERIALS IN THE VERNACULAR HOUSE CONSTRUCTION AND AS TRELLISES FOR UBE AND TUGUE CROPS, TWO OF THE MANY SUBSISTENCE BASE OF THE AUSTRONESIAN PEOPLE WHO ARE BELIEVED TO BE THE ANCESTORS OF THE IVATANS. THE INDIGENOUS TREES BOTH FRUIT BEARING & NON FRUIT BEARING ARE PRECIOUS FOR THEIR WOOD & FRUITS, A WELCOMED FOOD SUPPLEMENT & A TREAT ESPECIALLY FOR THE YOUNG IVATAN CHILDREN.
LGU BASCO

The view of the cultivated area has a plaque of what's it all about.

Two windmills, of the three in the area, generating about 20% of the Island's power. Only 3 years old, this was a venture by a French outfit and the Ayala group. There is talk about a wind farm on the northernmost island with undersea power cables to Taiwan.

Basco from the plane. Lighthouse on extreme left.

A fishing village with fish pens. Roads are concrete.

The stretch limo jeepney that had a powerful Isuzu engine, and a very careful driver. On two occasions, the destination was a turn off from the main road, terminating in a dead end too tight for maneuvering the vehicle around. So Rufu backed up all the way; at one place it must have been for about half a kilometer, on a narrow winding road. There were a bunch of cows that overtook us.

Part of the coast was sheer volcanic rock terminating into the sea, while others, like our resort area, was sandy shore and coral reefs.

The Batanes island group was a critical area during WW2, as it was a good watchpoint. The Japanese fortified the area with tunnels like the one above. The sign indicates a 250 meter long series of tunnels bifurcating to 5 exits with various rooms and a water tank.

At one of the more rocky shores. No swimming here for sure.

We didn't explore the tunnel; only three of us ventured into the anteroom. In contrast, the lighthouse near town, though built in the last century, now obsolete, was all spruced up, and climbable, all 53 steps to the top, which half of us managed to do. A restaurant was being constructed nearby.

Looking at what our guide Roger caught: fish and sea urchins.

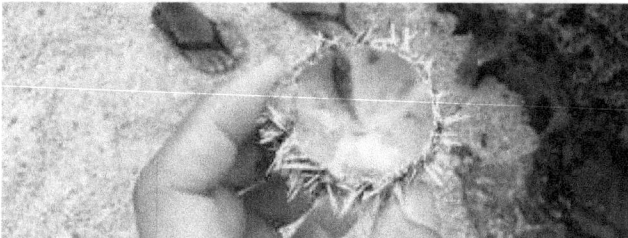

A new gustatory adventure: sea urchin cracked open, innards scooped up, and the remaining roe spooned out, to eat raw or with some lemon and vinegar. Ummm, delicious.

UPSCA *Alumni Association Newsletter*

Published whimsically when in the mood and there is occasion

AMDG   Issue Number 17   Fall 2014

The Great Philadelphia Gate Crash

Would you believe it but it has been seven (7) years since the last newsletter issue?

That issue was a special one exclusively reporting the "Lakbayan" adventures of a group of Upscan old friends on their weeks' trip to Batanes. And it was the first issue posted in the internet in color PDF.

Previous issues, all 15 of them, were hardcopy B&W prints mailed out to members and friends, oftentimes numbering up to 200 per print run.

They contained news, photos, jokes, trivia, and other entertaining items culled from the exchanges between UPSCA Loop members on the internet.

A popular series then were the stories spun by engineer-turned-writer Johnny Reyes.

He lately has been at it again, hence, the call for this latest issue, most likely the last

Here is what he emailed to the loop in 2 installments, with title shown on the headline. I added the pictures.

Danny Gil

--oOo--

Howdy, folks!

Last Saturday, I saw an opportunity to meet friends again whom I hadn't seen for many years, and also to connect again in some indirect little way with our good friend JOng who'd left us so quickly and unexpectedly recently. I was actually feeling guilty for having missed all the activities commemorating the prematurely-ended life of this brilliant and amazing guy. Now that his wife Ting is scheduling his inurnment (no, that wasn't a typo), the timing seemed appropriate for meeting his kid sister Avo again.

Danny Gil was in the process of doing his corporal works of mercy visiting the sick - me. His wife Lisa had already left for the Philippines the day before. Tony Estrera was supposed to come along with Danny to my home in Belle Mead NJ, but he cancelled at the last minute because of a bad cold. Danny came anyway, and I dressed appropriately for the occasion by putting on my robe and sitting in our living room with my wooden crutches and self-standing walking stick beside me, a hot-water bolsa on my head, and an old-fashioned mercury thermometer sticking out of my mouth (but no labatiba). When it was time for us to go, I was planning to get up, throw away my walking aids, and shout to the heavens, Mila! I can walk! But without Tony there I couldn't fool Danny, and after Mila said, John, will you stop that foolishness and get up out of that chair! off we went to the neighborhood Thai restaurant for lunch.

Then the opportunity came! Danny had learned that retired brain-transplant specialist Erwin Gomez was in Philadelphia and had been invited by Avo and her husband David Jones to dinner that evening. Danny was considering joining them, but was of two minds about going all the way to Philadelphia when he had to return to Brooklyn that night. He said, unless you two would also like to go with me. As I'd hinted earlier I was interested, but I simply glanced at Mila and said, don't look at me, Danny, in this household my wife makes the minor decisions on whether we go out for dinner or not. I only make the major decisions, for example on whether we send ground troops to West Africa to prevent ebola from breaking out here or not. Danny didn't pursue the subject further.

Mila   Johnny   Evelyn   Jaime   Cerina   Erwin   Avo   David

But as we were about to go back to our car after a nice spicy meal (Mila to drive), out of the blue I asked her, How would you like to go to Philadelphia tonight? To our surprise she replied Sure! Anytime! And the re-energized Danny proceeded to happily engineer the great New Jersey/Pennsylvania gatecrash exercise. We subsequently learned that Erwin was bringing his granddaughter to the dinner - last time we'd seen her she was a 9-year-old kid in that fairy-tale Martha's Vineyard cottage in the woods - now she was a pretty coed going to college in Drexel University in Philly! Also coming with Erwin was his younger sister Evelyn and her husband Jaime who was going to have a heart bypass operation in a couple of days. With three more of us joining the party and increasing the attendance by 50 %, Danny thought he would bring extra food and he ordered some takeout from the Thai restaurant where we still were. Having tested the quality beforehand, he was confident Erwin, Avo, and David would enjoy it too. Mila found some equally-proven wine-of-the-month Merlot from Bottle King in our basement, and after I'd wrapped it in my signature "Ace Hardware" brown paper bag, we were all set.

With Danny at the wheel, Mila and I had no qualms we'd find Avo's house in Philadelphia easily, but just to make sure (just like Superman always wears an extra pair of briefs outside his long johns), we activated the following additional layers of navigational aids: my personal knowledge of the city (the place turned out to be within 2 miles of my late brother's house); my Tom-Tom GPS device; a Yahoo map and step-by-step directions printed out by Danny; Google real-time tracking on Danny's i-phone; and on-the-spot telephone guidance from David himself. Unfortunately, we hit the height of peak hours, but traffic was moving continuously albeit slowly, and we were only an hour late for our 6-o'clock gatecrashing appointment.

We found the street at last, a tree-lined avenue where your parallel-parking skills will really be tested (not good for the Parkinson's brigade -- nowadays, my ideal parking arrangement is a double slot, one in front of the other, with both slots still unoccupied -- I call the front slot a Parkinson's parking slot, which you don't have to back out of). Anyway, I envied Danny as he slid gracefully and effortlessly into one of the available curbside slots between two cars, with minimal clearance front and back and on the side facing the sidewalk. According to David, there was a gigantic Gingko tree directly in front of their house. (Later, when we asked if there was a Kapre monster resident among the thick foliage on top of it, David said the only monsters frequenting that tree were the squirrels who continually make a mess and damage their eaves. I understand there have also been attempts in the past to market the sap of this tree as a short-term memory-improving drug.) Anyway, we watched out for the landmark, and sure enough David was under the tree looking out for us.

He is actually the third David Jones Mila and I have known. The first was a high-class department store in the city of Parramatta on the outskirts of Sydney (sort of equivalent to Bloomingdale's in America). The second was the son of my boss Bill Jones in Shell Tabangao, a tough but technically brilliant Englishman who gave his colleagues hell in Pulau Bukom Refinery (Singapore) where he was Operations Manager, and in Geerlong Refinery (Australia) where he was General Manager). He had already mellowed by the time he was assigned to Tabangao in 1995, where he successfully managed the safe start-up of the new state-of-the-art crude oil refinery with a thermal cracker during the heady days when the highly-competent Fidel Ramos was President of the Philippines (before Erap's turn). Bill Jones' only son David, who was still a teenager during our stay in Tabangao, was the apple of his dad's eye.

David Jones III turned out to be a very likable Philadelphian who grew up near the Main Line. This clean-shaven late sexagenarian/borderline septuagenarian didn't look a day over 50, and although he was a college professor he didn't have that characteristic stoop they usually acquire. Instead, he had a spring in his step and a spark in his eye, so that after a few minutes you forget the gray hair and the eyeglasses, but see only his smiling face. And he still had a full head of hair.

Erwin   Johnny

There was another guy approaching 70 in the room when we arrived, and with his hairdo and his brand-new and very becoming beard (which must be taking hours to trim and which he must be combing carefully every night), the guy was a dead ringer for that famous New York talk-show host and Constitutional expert - The Great One, Mark Levin! The resemblance was amazing, and so were the facial mannerisms they had in common. But as we all know, Erwin Gomez was not a lawyer but merely a retired cardiovascular surgeon.

As the great Walt Kelly (who is way up there with Al Capp, as far as I am concerned) used to say, there's nothing mere about a retired cardiovascular surgeon! Erwin has been our close friend all these years, and he's still the same dignified and shy gentleman with impressive professional accomplishments and surprising expertise in a number of unexpected and extraordinary fields. If you want to see what he looks like nowadays, just Google his doppelganger's name "mark levin" and then click on "Images."

Sitting beside Erwin was a pretty young lady, and for a while I was trying to make out whether it could be Nina, his daughter whom we had met in Martha's Vineyard some years ago, when Erwin had invited a group of UPSCA alumni for a couple of nights stay at her place. At that time not too long ago, as I said earlier, the island still seemed like fairyland, but I understand that recently the place has been taken over by some unwanted vacationists who keep coming back every year, and there went the neighborhood. Perhaps we can ask Erwin to confirm (or contradict) my understanding. But the girl seated beside him tonight must be only a teenager, too young to be Nina. Guess what - time certainly flies -- it was Nina's daughter Cerina, Erwin's granddaughter!

Speaking of look-alikes, I'm sure both Mila and Danny will agree with me that Erwin's younger sister and her husband bear an uncanny resemblance to each other, as many married couples do. Were such couples attracted to each other because they saw themselves in their partner, or did they start becoming like her or him after having looked at their partner every day and loving what they saw? With Evelyn and Jaime, maybe it's the individual features, or the shape of the eyes, or simply the facial expression. I wonder if anybody else has ever made this observation before? Anyway, Jaime seemed pretty calm, and otherwise rather fit, for someone who was going to undergo heart surgery soon. But if I had a brother-in-law like Erwin around, that would certainly be wonderful moral support, wouldn't it? By the way, Erwin, do you have any more siblings with names starting with "E" and ending with "n"?

Danny   David   Avo

Finally, our hostess Avo. I'd met her only briefly many years ago at a party in JOng's San Juan manor house, when I believe JOng was still a freshman UPSCA member (I was sophomore, but only just joining too, fulfilling a condition imposed by my high school principal and my parish priest for going to college in that Godless institution in the dark wilderness of Dilimán on the remote edges of Quezon City. After that, this attractive "bratty-looking" teenager just seemed to have disappeared.

Tonight, I was curious to see what Avo looked like now, and where she'd been all these years. When I first spotted her after David welcomed us to their home on Kenilworth Street, she definitely reminded me of JOng, but I couldn't pinpoint why, because there was absolutely no resemblance between the two siblings. C'mon, JOng, with all due respect to you, there can't be any resemblance, because Avo is a very attractive young lady!

Welcoming us latecomers into their home, David was showing Mila framed pictures of the family arrayed on a side table, including that of his son by his late first wife. Then I showed him in return a portrait of our family, comprising Mila, myself, and three of our eight grandchildren, printed on my T-shirt (see Danny's photo, attached somewhere to this thread).

All of a sudden, Avo and Danny intimidated us all by speaking to each other in loud, fluent, and fully-accented Sugbuanon -- the language of Dumaguete, Tanjáy, Cagayán De Oro, and their Mother City Cebú, and the second most widely-spoken language in the Philippines after Tagalog! As their conversation reverberated throughout the house, we started thinking

We all know that Danny is G.I. (Genuine Ilocano). Avo is a native of San Juan, Rizal (pure Tagalog, of Chinese ancestry with lineage traceable all the way back to the seafaring bandit Li-Ma-Ong). [Incidentally, I've heard that in Australia too, proof of relationship to any of the old-time convicts is now a valuable status symbol. Were you aware that Oz was a penal colony in the late 18th century, and that London jail cell prisoners convicted of crimes as serious as stealing a loaf of bread to feed family, were being transported there in leg irons, with little hope of ever returning home again alive, or ever seeing their folks again in this life, and that these convicts exiled there from England eventually became the first Australians?]

Wait, let's have a little geography check: The Province of Negros Occidental (that means "West," doesn't it?) Why couldn't the American colonial administrators simply have called it West Negros? Why did they have to translate "municipios" to "municipal buildings" instead of to the more straightforward term "town halls"? [Nowadays, when the Top Management of a company wish to speak with the entire staff and hold an open forum, do they call for a "municipal building" meeting?] Why did these bureaucratic and pompous people in the 30's label that faux-classical Greek structure situated near the mouth of the Pasig River as the "Post Office Building"? Wasn't it obvious it was a building? Would not "Post Office" (or, if they wished, "Central Post Office") have been sufficient?

Anyway, back to our geography check - so Negros with Bacolod as capital) west toward Iloilo, and its inhabitants speak Hiligaynón. Negros Oriental (East Negros to me, with Dumaguete as capital) faces east towards Cebú, and its inhabitants speak Sugbuanon. Very easy to remember, if you go through that little mnemonic exercise, but you've got to know how each of the Visayan Islands is positioned relative to all the other (after God finished playing Rubik's Cube with them when He got bored waiting for the flood waters to recede.)

Also very easy to get distracted and sidetracked (two words which happen to mean exactly the same thing). So, if neither Avo nor Danny grew up in a province where the lingua franca was Sugbuanon, a,k,a. Cebuano, a.k.a. Bisayà, how was that little exchange above possible, and how did the Dynamic Duo become fluent instantly in our other national language? I had a hunch other questions percolating inside our minds were going to be answered soon. Nice to be an ocioso, isn't it?

At this point, ladies and gentlemen, allow me to welcome you all to the Lola Basyang portion of my narrative. This is not how it actually happened., but how it could very well have happened. I take no responsibility for the veracity of the contents of the next X paragraphs, because it is based only on a combination of information overheard by a hard-of-hearing old geezer and conclusions he jumped to hastily and without any basis except the "halo effect," whereby the bad guys in a story can do nothing right, and the good guys can do nothing wrong. Serendipitously, the answers to other questions mulling in my mind are also coming to the surface at last.

THE DULL STRAIGHT FACTS

1. Avo moved to Cagayán De Oro with her Cebuano-speaking husband and lived there happily for 17 years, visiting her family in San Juan from time to time.

2. While visiting Melbourne in the early 70's, JOng had met an old friend from his Stanford days who was now a professor in that Australian city. As a young United Nations hotshot scouting on behalf of his boss (some obscure UN bureaucrat) for prospective presentors in a forthcoming UNESCO symposium to be held in Manila. As usual, the topic was swathed in heavy bureaucratic legalese but completely useless in the real world. And as JOng pondered the day's events in his hotel room that night, weak and weary from his frustrations, JOng suddenly smiled because he just had an interesting idea. [Do not confuse UNESCO with UNICEF, that dear old United Nations agency in charge of promoting the welfare of the world's poor children - they used to raise extra funds by marketing the magical and beautiful Christmas cards featuring children's painted art work - until the leftists of this world made Christmas unfashionable and taboo. And UNESCO was already a far-left United Nations agency even at that time, busy "improving" the world's educational textbooks and systems.]

Next day, David was in First Class on a plane bound for Manila, pleased and excited but still trying to make sense of the urgent telex in his hands from the Assistant First Vice-Secretary of UNESCO inviting him, all expenses paid, to present a 45-minute paper on a subject which had no connection with his field of expertise, but which any intelligent student could competently discuss if he could put together a sufficient amount of trivia. David had 80% of such trivia already in his head, and if he only had time to go to the public library before his plane was scheduled to leave, he could have cinched the last 20% and made a complete and perfect presentation. (There was no Internet in the 70's.) But he thought, was it worthwhile to fly in all those delegates from around the world to listen to such a trivial presentation? He wasn't planning to complain.

Soon he checked into the Manila Hotel, and was mildly annoyed when what he understood to be a local VIP, also with a pencil-thin moustache like him, cut into the line ahead of him with all the members of his entourage. David could hear the conversation with the desk clerk, but of course he did not understand. "Check in kayó, Sir?" "Dehin! Dehin! Noy-pi akó! 'Di mo ba kilala ang Mayor ng San Juan?" "Ay! Sorry, Sir!"

In his 4th floor hotel room finally, David realized that he was sharing it with an East German delegate, to save the U.N. some costs. The Communist delegate (think Robert Shaw in "From Russia With Love," or Dolph Lundgren in "Rocky IV") was all muscle and no fat, and was exercising continuously in the hotel room to keep his magnificent body in shape (he was standing on his head when David arrived). When the East German left the room to attend the buffet dinner at the hotel lobby, David thought he would skip the activity as he still felt full from all the meals they served on the Qantas airliner. He had found it funny that all the stewardesses were male - they had to be, in order to be capable of physically stopping fist fights among the Aussie passengers who had had too much to drink. But tonight, David also needed some quiet time to organize and polish up his presentation for tomorrow, and to create some decent visual aids to make it more interesting.

Two minutes after the East German delegate had stepped out the door, two Filipino men in gym suits came in and one of them said to David in a voice so full of authority that he had no choice but to obey, "We've got to get you out of here quickly. Please do exactly as we say!" Soon they were out of the window at the end of the hall and rappelling four stories to the ground, where a black limousine was waiting with its engine running. Thirty minutes later, David was in JOng's plush dining room in San Juan enjoying a nightcap of fine Bourbon whisky, reminiscing about their old times in Stanford, and discussing possible employment with the U.N., in offices located along Isaac Peral Street in Manila. Subsequently, David met JOng's sister Avo at their home, and since both of them were now available again, married each other and lived happily to date.

NOT HOW IT ACTUALLY HAPPENED

1. Avo rebelled against her strict and monolithic family, eloped with her Cebuano-speaking boyfriend to Cagayán De Oro, and hid among the pineapple plants to avoid her kinsmen bristling with spears sent by her tough old warlord father to search for her and bring her back. [Background music: "On the Isle of Filla-Lilla."] Meanwhile, her boyfriend called on his own kinsmen to come and help defend them against attacks by Avo's clansmen, led now by her hotheaded brother JOng. Marked by occasional vicious skirmishes, this stalemated siege held for 17 years, breaking the record set by Helen of Troy for resisting recapture and repatriation (10 years).

2. David was one of the mercenaries JOng had recruited in his campaign to get his sister back and bring her home again, whether she liked it or not. At that time, David's hair was pitch black, longish as was the fashion in the 70's, and he had a pencil-thin moustache, like Errol Flynn's and Cary Elwes'. As back-to-back champion for the past two years in the All-Melbourne Epee & Rapier Fencing Club Ladder Tournament, he was in perfect physical condition, and you'd never suspect he was the same person as he supplements his income by working as a professor of motion picture arts in an everyday sort of secret.

The final duel between David and Avo's boyfriend took place in the upper galleries of the Grand Ballroom of the Manila Hotel, among the drapes and the chandeliers, where the expert swordsman from Cagayán de Oro more than held his own against the foreign invader. But at last David had the upper hand, and sensing this, the Cebuano protagonist grabbed Avo and fled with her aboard his Moro vinta, pursued by David in a two-masted schooner. When the two watercraft pulled abreast, David shouted, "I'll send you down to the locker of Davey Jones!" [I guess that must be the Fourth] and after slaying his opponent, he wiped his pencil-thin moustache on his sleeve and collected Avo.

--oOo--

End of story, by Johnny Reyes

The responses were immediate:

Hello, Johnny,

I thoroughly agree with Mercy and Lenny that you are a story-teller par excellence! I daresay, with your engineering background and your writing prowess, you could easily qualify for a Renaissance man in the 21st Century!

I truly enjoyed all the details of your narrative, from your plan to dress appropriately for Danny's arrival to your preparation of all variety of GPS aids in order to find your way to Avo and Davy's house. I especially liked the

role of your beautiful, efficient and dutiful wife who knows exactly when to order you around and when to accede quite disarmingly. Please do give her our sincerest regards and a big bear hug!
Cynthia

It even spawned a debate on the language issue:

Juan, Lino Faelnar will not forgive you for saying that Cebuano is the second most spoken language in the Pinas. On the contrary Senyor Juan, it is the most widely spoken language around these islands that is why Cebuanos cannot accept that Tagalog was declared the lingua franca.

Other than that, your story casts a spell, is so entertaining and as usual your exaggerations tickle the funny bone. Keep on writing please. We miss you.
Mercy

With due respect, I beg to disagree with Lino. He may have been correct during President Quezon's time. But that was more seventy years ago.

However, nowadays, Pilipino, in its Tagalog form, is spoken by more people in the country than any other language. When you travel around the country you can generally communicate in Tagalog (aka Pilipino). I am sure, in your most extensive travel around the country, you have noted this change, Mercy.

In my travels to Visayas and Mindanao in the sixties, I had to have some basic knowledge of the local language. In the next fifty years, as time went along, I noticed a steady increase in local familiarity with Pilipino. Now, I find some Tausugs/Maguindanaos being interviewed in TV who are even more fluent in "Pilipino" than myself (who grew up in Southern Tagalog)!

Back in the fifties, whenever I traveled to Pampanga with my dad, he would always ask somebody to accompany me to be able to communicate with sellers of goodies that I craved for.
Ed Magtoto

You are right Ed, more Filipinos can speak Tagalog now. But if you did a survey and asked what dialects can you speak, you will be surprised - Cebuanos outnumber Tagalog speaking. At least this was how it looked 7 years ago before I retired.
Mercy

But wait. Johnny told me candidly that he indeed will be publishing more of his writings, and this time, it will be on Amazon, perhaps even under a pseudonym.

Folks would recall cyber friend Jobo Elizes, an Amazon sub-contractor, writer-publisher. I know they have been in touch. Jobo treated me to dinner two days ago.

NOW FOR THE MORE NEWSY PORTIONS:

I have been in Brooklyn, NY, since September 26, following Lisa's and my sudden and unplanned trip here to help out our son Ramon, who had a triple bypass operation.

We had asked for prayers, and the response was very moving. We thank you all who responded. He now is

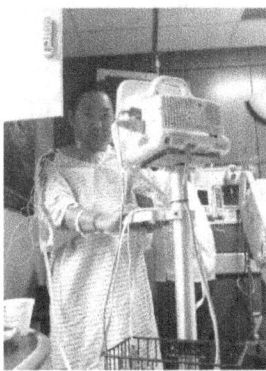

doing very well. The day after his operation, he was made to walk, as shown in the picture, then was discharged from the hospital after 5 days. Later on in the following week, he started doing his free-lance work, including attending a comic convention.

This is where my main role lay, as being driver, especially for the two grandkids who attend school in Manhattan.

The doctor said he can drive by mid November, and I shall head back home to Manila, then Tanjay shortly after. Lisa stayed here only 3 weeks.

Four months earlier, I also made an appeal to help Ramon's Kickstarter Project in a fundraiser for publishing a comic book series using mainly Filipino talent. The goal was reached, and again many thanks to all who helped.

So what have I been doing the past 1-1/2 months in between the weekday morning and afternoon driving schedules for the grandkids, and free time afterwards?

I make the most out of NYC. Drive or walk around, see new places. Visit old friends, etc.

The NYC Marathon ran right past my son's place in Brooklyn and I took pictures and video right from the window overlooking the street. Here below left is a photo of a wheel-chair bound handicapped person being pushed by his robust caregiver.

Above, a selfie with Vic Vitug who treated me to a great Chinese buffet in Queens.

Above is a shot taken at the off-Broadway Imelda musical "Here Lies Love" It was a blast. In the first place, it was an "interactive" play, where the audience moved around with the cast. And the approach was all disco type; with the flashing strobe lights, monstrous loudspeakers and music, and of course dancing. We old fogeys opted for the balcony seats where we sat though.

Early on, Lisa and I visited Amador & Gloria Muriel at their 62nd Street brownstone. They have taken over the top floors again, and their daughter Marie is running the place as a classy bed & breakfast. Amador still is doing his Physics.

Amador was enthusiastic about reviving the 62nd Forum. Below is a screen capture of the masthead of the

 **62nd Street FORUM**
"Where ideas flourish"
NEWSLETTER   NEWSLETTER   NEWSLETTER

Volume Num 2 | Published by the NY 62nd Street Forum | April, 2007

New Issues for Past Lectures - Bandurria

2007 newsletter which featured many of the writings of Johnny Reyes on the 36 or so lectures of the Forum.

Since many of the 62nd Forum members also are Upscans, this issue might just as well be considered also a 62nd Forum newsletter, and most likely also the last.

I told Amador it is too late to revive the Forum. Many of the active members have left town.

Lisa and I have been retired in Tanjay for the past 8 years.

Vic & Vicky Vitug retired and moved to Indiana, but recently found the pull of NYC in their Flushing house as irresistible, and have moved back.

Tony & Bernie Nievera have been in Las Vegas since early on, and Tony is most active on the internet with both Upsca and 62nd cyber loops, relating his various hobbies on photography, astronomy, food, travel. and guns

The ever-interesting writer Chay Lumba also moved to Las Vegas, and maintains his postings to a number of cyber groups.

Gene & Violy Pulmano now are in Hawaii, and he is most prolific in his emails on economics and health.

Award winning photographer Carlos & Arlene Esguerra still are based in NY, but at the moment, Carlos is in the Philippines where he has another exhibit. But a good portion of his time is also spent in Belgium with one of his children and their family.

Economist Hery Brillantes and Mila now are in Arizona. Their waterfront house on the NJ side of the Hudson was the venue for many a small get-together of some Forum members such as, among others Mars & Cora Custodio, Frank Jimenez, Gene Pulmano, Ninotchka Rosca.

From what we gleam from Facebook postings, Mars and Cora travel a lot and spend the cold months in the Philippines. Seems as if they recently were in Machu Picchu with Ham & Mayu Gonzales.

Frank Jimenez still is in NJ and occasionally joins the email threads on photography posted by Tony and Carlos. He of course comes out once in a while with postings that show his unique sense of humor.

Bert Peronilla & Maryann still also are in NJ, nearby to Frank, and Bert is the computer expert on any Yahoo problem regarding both cyber loops.

Bert & Eva Florentino are in Oregon, according to Amador. And Bert is quite "not together" up there, which is understandable at his age.

Nel Reformina, in NY, is also very visible in both loops, with his advocacies on education in the Bicol.

There are many other names that should be accounted for among those old friends we've had in the tri-state area during those 5 years we lived there, but we've lost touch.

For old times' sake, here is a 7 year old group photo at a barbeque in Bert & Maryann Peronilla's house. IDs seem discernible. In a subsequent redo, I cloned in a number of other active members, but unfortunately, I don't have that pic file on my present laptop.

Linda Faigao-Hall, playwright, retired to Ireland with her husband, who soon passed away. Last we heard was that she would teach in Silliman in Dumagete for a semester or two, in between her visits to hometown Cebu.

One transferee to Damaguete is Thelma Ibañez-Teves, who moved from LA. Though from Luzon, she prefers the easy and slower provincial life there. Besides, her husband, Dennis Teves, has kin.

Mike Dadap is one we often see in Dumaguete. He visits at least once a year. But once there, he is busy in a whirlwind of activities from concerts to workshops, etc. We missed him last July when we were in Manila.

Jane Orendain comes in often on the loop with her posts on little known but significant Philippine historical events. Though based in NY, she moves back and forth to the Philippines.

Ninotchka Rosca, also NY based, often posts about her advocacies. She co-authored a book with Amador.

Lenore Rachel Santos Lim occasionally posts schedules on her various print exhibits in the NY art scene.

Johnny Reyes in Belle Mead NJ (near Princeton) and Erwin Gomez in Indiana of course are up and about and doing well, (as the first 2 pages of this newsletter attests); Johnny from his brain implants (I kid you not), and Erwin from his "second-hand" kidney. But all these were discussed in previous loop postings.

I wish there were occasions to meet up with more of the UPSCA crowd, but time is short. Last year, the girls, spearheaded by Sari Valenzuela, Priscilla Bautista-Perez, and Cebu visitor Aissa Arambulo-Cruz (together with their UP college-mates) invited us to a posh restaurant in mid Manhattan. Below is the group photo.

Like the newsletters of old, forthcoming events are posted. On Dec 7, Ting Ong is having an "inurnment" rite in Manila, where a whole lot of the Upsca friends of JOng will be attending.

In February, some of the group plan on a local Lakbayan cruise or trek to some interesting place. We understand that Bernie from Switzerland, Erwin from Indiana, TonyN from Las Vegas, and TonyE from LA will be in town, and are all gung ho for it.

Last week end, I was in Boston. This week end, I hope to see a close high school friend in NJ, then homeward I go mid week.

Danny Gil, temporarily in NYC, 14 Nov 2014

Printed in March 2016 by
Self-Publisher - Tatay Jobo Elizes
In the United States of America under ISBN codes below.
ISBN-13: 978 - 1530201198   +   ISBN-10: 1530201195

Book List - Buy online as paperback or kindle,
Contact: job_elizes@yahoo.com, tatay@usa.com
Websites: http://tinyurl.com/mj76ccq + www.jobelizes.webs.com + www.tatayjoboelizes.webs.com

Writings 1 Book, 2012 , Articles by Bambi Harper + Butch Jiimenez + Dr. Phil Stack + Noel Alegre + Toto Causing +_ Melanie Ferrer + Susie Barbieri _ Rodel Ramos + Sylvia Salvador + Tatay Jobo Elizes + + Writings 2 Book, 2012, Artices by Gov. Grace Padaca + Melanie Aquino + Toto Causing + Rodel Rodis + Cesar Torres + Joey Concepcion + Charity Guides + Cesar Lumba +_Casiano Mayor Jr. + Sonny Coloma + Anonymous.+ +

Writings 3A Book, 2012, Articles by Norman Madrid + Dr. Rene Azurin + Ernie Delfin + Toto Causing + Dr. Jose Abueva + MarVic Cagurangan + Casiano Mayor Jr + Rod Garcia + Roy Gaane + Tatay Jobo Elizes + + Writings 3B Book, 2012, Articles by Ceres Busa + John Reyes + Bert Guiang. + + Writings 4A Book, 2012, Articles by Dr Jose Abueva + Col. Dennis Acop + Fred Natividad + Irineo P. Goce, KaPule2 + Miguel Reynadlo + Marjorie Ann Elizes Reyes+ +

Writings 4B Book, 2012, 1. Mi Ultimo Adios (My Last Farewell), *Dr. Jose P. Rizal* + 2. Aling Pagibig Sa Tinubuang Bayan, *Gat. Andres Bonifacio* + Articles by Irineo P. Goce or KaPule2 + + Writings 5 Book - "Best Hopes" 2010 (About President P-Noy), Articles by Tony Meloto + F.SionilJose + Juan L. Mercado + OFWs Letter + Marcelo Tecson + Cesar Torres+ Perry Diaz + Dr. Philip S. Chua + Ernie Delfin + Atty. Ted Laguatan + Frank Wenceslao Jaileen F. Jimeno + Tatay Jobo Elizes + +

Writings 6 Book, 2010 + I. SONA - State Of Nation Address - English - *Pres. Benigno Aquino III* + II. SONA - State of Nation Address - Pilipino - *Pres. Benigno Aquino III* + III. First 100 Days peech - Pilipino - *Pres. Benigno Aquino III* + *Artiucles by Bert Guiang + Tony Meloto + Felicito or Tong C. Payumo + Cesar Lumba + Flor Lacanilao + Juan DelaCruz or Txtmanika + Dr. Ramon Marquez + Joey Jamito + Percival Cruz + Rod Garcia + Orion Perez Dumdum + Sarah Raymundo.* + + Writings 7 Book, 2010 - My Vintage Pics - Pictorials & Family, Tatay Jobo Elizes + + Writings 8 Book, 2010, Articles by Gel Santos Relos + Ms.Mike Portes + Jose Ma. Montelibano + Tony Meloto + Dr. Philip S. Chua + Dr. Cesar D. Candari + Dr. Eliseo Serina + Greg B. Macabenta + Irineo P. Goce or KaPule2 + Percival Cruz + Juan DelaCruz or Textmani + Demosthenes B. Donato. + +

Writings 9 Book, April 2011, Articles by Judge Simeon dumdum Jr + Gemma Cruz Araneta + Larry Henares Jr + Tony Joaquin + Allen Gaborro + Atty. Toto Causing + Mar-Vic Cagurangn + Emily Espanol Derry, Poet + Elyn Jean Felarca, Poet + Naysan A. Albaytar + Laura Wade, Blogger + Perter Allan Mariano + Marge Trajeco-Aberasturi + Julia Carreon Lagoc + Irineo P. Goce or KaPulle2 + Anonymous. + + Writings 10 Book, July, 2010, Articles by Atty.Ted Lagutan + Percival C. Cruz + Allen Gaborro + Peter Allan Mariano + M.L. Munoz + Alvib T. Tabaniag + Resty Odon + Dr. Phili S. Chua + Dr. Cesar D. Candari + Anonymous. + +

Writings 11 Book, August, 2011 + 1, SONA In English and Filipino, by President Benigno Aquino III (P-Noy) + 2, Telltale Signs: SONA and the Dogfight Over Spratlys, by Rodel Rodis + Atty. Ted Laguatan + Tatay Jobo Elizes + Jeremiah M. Opiniano + OFW Journalists + Bob & Carol Hammerslag + Roger P. Olivares + Rob Ceralvo + Anonymous + Irineo P. Goce or KaPule2 + Random. + + Writings 12 Book, April 2012 + Articles By Orion Perez Dumdum + Julia C. Lagoc + Honorio M. Cruz, MD + Ben Gonzales, MD + Mar-Vic Cagurangan + Marisa Lerias + Gerry Partido + Dr. Cesar D. Candari + Erwin De Leon + Jovelyn B. Revilla + Tatay Jobo Elizes + +

Writings 13 Book, July 2012 + Articles by Raymundo E. Narag + M.L. Munoz + Sonia Barbara gl Munoz + Pamela Joy Agtoto + Percival C. Cruz + Tatay Jobo Elizes + Jhakie Eslit Bayobay + Reygel Saplad Perales. + + Timely Writings 14, 2013 + Articles by Cesar F. Lumba + Eugenio Pulmano + Late Jesse Robredo + Antonio Nievera + Alvin T. Tabaniag + Kevin L. Nadal + Anonymous + Fred Natividad + Anonymous + Ellen Tordesillas + Lat Capt. Rene N. Jarque + +

Timeless Writings-15 (TW15), 2014 + Articles by SC Justice Antonio T. Carpio + Atty Dodel Rodis + Atty. Ted Laguatan + Sona by Pres. Benigno Aquino III + F. Sionil Jose + Dr. Philipi Stack + Racz Kelly, Padilla + Bert Armada.+ + Timeless Writings-16 (TW16), 2014 + Articles about The Martyrs of Camarines Norte + by Rodel Rodis + R.A.Gubalane + Robert Bernardo + Pres. Aquino's SONA 2014 + + Timeless Writings-17 (TW17), 2014 + Articles by Rodel Rodis+ Jose P. Rizal+ Irineo Goce+ Julia Lagos + Alvin Tabaniag+ Ragubalane + Red Butterfly+ Cesar Torres + + Timeless Writings-18 (TW18) + Articles by Rodel Rodis + Raul Manglapus + Ragubalane + Allen Gaborro + Manuel Vergara + + Timeless Writings-19 (TW19) + Articles by Atty. Ted Laguatan + Romely Bacsain + Charlie Chaplin + Orlando Carvajal + Allen Gaborro + Rodel Rodis + Primitivo Mijares + Krip Yuson + +

Solo Authored Books: + + +

Book A, Turning Points, *Job Elizes Sr,1968 (Reissue 2009)* + + + Book B, Be Considerate For Once, *Tatay Jobo Elizes (Jr), 2013* Book C, Piglets Unlimited - Wealth, *Tatay Jobo Elizes, 2009* + + + Book D, Out of the Misty Sea We Must, *Cesar Lumba, 2010* + + + Book E, Fulfilled – *Gonzales Reynaldo, Editor, 2010* + + + Book F - Reflections - *Bert Guiang, 2010* + + + Book G, Writings 7 - My Vintage Pics, *Tatay Jobo Elizes, 2010* +

Book H, May Bagwis Ang Pag-ibig, *Percival C. Cruz* + + + Book I, Letters To Matrimony, *Irineo P. Goce, Ka Pule2, 2011* + Book J, Songs I Wish You Knew, *Soledad R. Juan, 2011* + + + Book K, Make My Day, *Larry Henares Jr., 1993, Re-issue 2011* + Book L, Our Guerrero Family, *Tatay Jobo Elizes, 2010* + + + Book M, Handy Jokes, *Tatay J. Elizes, 2011* + Book N, FaveArt 1, *Tatay Jobo Elizes, 2011* + +

Book O, Beyond idle thoughts, *MLMunoz, Sept,2011* + + + Book P, Cracks In The Armor, *Mariano Ngan, Oct 2011* + + + Book Q, FaveArt 2, *Tatay Jobo Elizes, 2011* + + Book R, Balitang Kutsero, *Perry Diaz, Jan 2012* + + + Book S, FaveArt3, *Tatay Jobo, 2011* + + + Book T, FaveArt4 ,2012, *Tatay Jobo* + + + Book U, Stack Family Journals, *Phil & Fe Stack, 2012* + + + Book V, Emily, An Adoption Journey, *Romerl Elizes, 2012* + + +

Book W, Hermes Alegre Art Gallery, *TJ & Hermes, 2012* + + + Book X, Masaya Din, Malungkot Din, *Jovelyn B. Revilla, 2012* Book Y, Tiis, Sipag At Tiyaga, *Raquel Delfin Padilla, 2012* + + + Book Z, Until I Meet You, *Jhackie Eslit Bayobay, 2012* + + + Book AA, Buhay At Pag-ibig, *Argel Lucero Tamayo, 2012* + + + Book AB, Hail to the Second Best, *Dr. Philip Stack, 2012* + + + Book AC, Life Bus, *Mommy Joyce Pineda-Faulmino, 2012* + + + Book AD, My Candid Musings, *Monette Dioquino Calugay, 2012* + Book AE, Tickets to Life, *Maria Lourdes Jesalva, 2012* + + + Book AF, The Dove Files, *Mike Portes, 2012* + + + Book AG, Nursing Vignettes, *Jocelyn Cerrudo Sese, 2012* + Book AH, Poor Ba Us, *R.A. Gubalane, 2012* + + +

Book AI, Summer Idyll, *Avelina Gil, 2012* + + Book AJ, Legacy (Pamana), *Rachel Astrero, 2012* + + Book AK, Narratives Old & New, *Avelina J. Gil, 2013* + + Book AL, Buhay Saudi, *Adele J. Esic, 2013* + + Book AM, Buhay Ofw Atbp, *Jessica Napat, 2013* + + Book AN, Mga Tula Ng Buhay, *Angelita C. Esguerra, 2013* + + Book AO, Not by Bread Alone, *Judge Lily V. Magtolis, 2013* + + Book AP, Jokes Collection-2, *Tatay Jobo Elizes, 2013* + + +

Book AR, *My Writings Sometimes, Tatay Jobo Elizes, 2013* + + Book AS, Sa 'Yo Na Ako, *Shayne A. Martinez, 2013* + + Book AT, My Kin's Family Trees, *Tatay Jobo Elizes, 2013* + + Book AU, Rizal Family Tree & Others, *Tatay Jobo Elizes, 2013* + + Book AV, Make My Day-2, Nice & Nasty, *L. Henares, 2013 (1993)* + + Book AW, Make My Day-3, Cecilia, Love, *L.Henares, 2013 (1993)*Book AX, Handy Lyrics-1, *Tatay Jobo Elizes, 2013* + +

Book AY, Ang Biblos, *Rev. Dr. Eugenio Guerrero, 2014 (1929)* + + Book AZ, Make My Day-4, *Sweet & Sour, L. Henares, 2014 (1993)* + + Book BA, Life's Journey, True Stories, *Dr. Phil Stack, 2014* + + Book BB, Gerry Gil Writings, 2014, *Danny Gil* + + Book BC, Mr. President, *Hermie Rotea, 2014* + + Book BD, Nostalgic Pics 1, *Tatay Jobo Elizes, 2014* + + Book BE, MakeMyDay-5, Saints & Sinners, *Henares, 2014 (1993)* + +

Book BF, MakeMyDay-6, Villains & Heroes, *Henares, 2014 (1993)* + + Book BG, Nostalgic Pics 2 (ElizesClan), *TatayJE, 2014* + + Book BH, MakeMyDay-7, Tough & Tender, *Henares, 2014(1993)* + + Book BI, MakeMyDay-8, Light & Shadow, *Henares, 2014(1993)* + + Book BJ, MakeMyDay-9, Give & Take, *Henares, 2014(1993)* + + Book BK, MakeMyDay-10, ToBeOrNotToBe, *Henares, 2014(1993)* +

Book BL,Emily Forever In Love, Poems,*Emily Espanol Derry, 2013* + + Book BM, The Sinatra Songbook, *Henares, 2014* + + Book BN, The Gaborro Reader, *Allen Gaborro, 2010* + + Book BO, Ramon H. Lopez - Art Gallery, *2014* + + Book BP, Philippines Via Old Pics-1, *Tatay Jobo, 2014* + + Book BQ, Ronna Manansala - Art Gallery, *2014* + + Book BR, Philippines Via Old Pics-2, *Tatay Jobo, 2014* + + *Book BS*, Being Good-A Medley Of Love, *Dr. Phil Stack, 2014* + + Book BT, Lifestream Fisherman, A Filipino Odyssey, *Paul Dalde, Jul2014* + + Book BU, Kristina Reed Manansala, Art Gallery-1, *August 2014.* + +

Book BV, Hermes Art Gallery-2, *Sep2014,* + + Book BW, Fave Art-5, *Tatay Jobo, Sep2014* + + Book BX, Cash & Credits, Make My Day-11, *Larry Henares, Sept 2014* + + Book BY, Rise & Fall, Make My Day-12, *Larry Henares, Oct 2014* + + Book BZ, Swans & Swine, Make My Day-13, *Larry Henares, Oct 2014* + + Book CA, Touch & Go, Make My Day-14, *Larry Henares, Oct 2014* + + Book CB, Life & Death, Make My Day-15, *Larry Henares, Oct2014* +

Book CC, Kiss & Bite, Make My day -16, *Larry Henares, Oct 2014* + + Book CD, Good & Evil, Make My Day-17, *Larry Henares, Oct2014* + + Book CE, Beast & Beauty, Make My Day-18, *Larry Henares, 2014* + + Book CF, Beggar & King, Make My Day-19, *Larry Henares,*

Oct 2014 + + Book CG, Trash & Treasures, Make My Day-20, Larry Henares, Oct 2014 + + Book CH, Wear & Tear, Make My Day-21, Larry Henares, Oct 2014 + + Book CI, Why Blame the President, Irineo P. Goce, Oct 2014 + +

Book CJ, Angel & Devil, Make My Day-22, *Larry Henares, Oct 2014 + +* Book CK, Pretty Ugly, Make My Day-23, *Larry Henares, Oct 2014 + +* Book CL, Salvation & Damnation, Make My Day-24, *Larry Henares, Oct 2014 + +* Book CM, Don Daniel Maramba, *Larry Henarez & Edith Perez de Tagle, Oct 2014 + +* Book CN, Hilarion G. Henares, *Larry Henares & Edith Perez de Tagle, Oct 2014 + +* Book CO, FaveArt-5 ++ Book CP, FaveArt-6, Book CQ, FaveArt-7, Book CR, FaveArt-8 *(All FaveArt books by Tatay Jobo), 2014 + +*

Book CS, Minsan May Isang Puta, *Ms.Mike Portes, 2014 + +* Book CT, Ramblings A, Danny Gil, 2014 + + *Book CU, Ramblings-B, Danny Gil, 2014 + +* Book CV, Grace Esmeralda Album, by her, 2014 + + *Book CW, Secrets of a Romantic Man, Dr. Phil Stack, 2014 + +* Book CX, Ramblings-C, Danny Gil, 2014 + + *Book CY, Ramblings-D, Danny Gil, 2014 + +* Book CZ, Ramblings-E, Danny Gil, 2014 ++ *Book DA, Tenacious Nurse-1, Gretheline Bolandrina, 2014 + +* Book DB, Tenacious Nurse-2, Gretheline Ramos-Bolandrina, 2015 + + *Book DC, Of Words I Have Found, Dan Jimenez (danmeljim), 2015 + +*

Book DD, Tanjay East Coast Magazine, Issue 1, Feb 2015 + + Book DE, Tanjay East Coast Magazine, Issue 2, April 2015 + + Book DF, Catechism Manual, Dr. Latorre, April 2015 + + Book DG, Tanjay East Coast Magazine, Extra Issue 2A, April 2015 + + Book DH, Wedding Album, Anita & Barry, May 2015 + + Book DI, Tanjay E. Coast Magazine, Poconos, May 2015 + + Book DJ, Baptism Guidebook, Dr. Latorre, May 2015 + + Book DK, Chita, a Memoir, Tony Joaquin + + Book DL, A Journey Unto Peace, Dr. Phil Stack, June2015+ + Book DM, Jokes Collection-3, Tatay Jobo Elizes, July2015 + + Book DN, Jokes Collection-4, Tatay Jobo Elizes, Aug2015 + + Book DO, Jokes Collection-5, Tatay Jobo Elizes, Sep2015 + + Book DP, Beautiful Lie, Joecel Jayme, Jan 2016 + + Book DQ, The Conjugal Dictatorship of the Marcoses, Primitivo Mijares (1976), Reprint 2016 + +

Permission had been granted by the author/authors/heirs to print their books under my free self-publishing and reprint services. They own copyrights to their works. Interested reader may request free reading/viewing of any of my booklist via online reading or ebook. Just email me.

Why I Publish and Reprint Books
by Tatay Jobo Elizes

Writings are timeless documents and they act as mirrors of history. I publish and reprint books as they remain relevant anytime. Good and memorable articles need to be published. I collect them to come up with a collection in order to complete a fairly good-size book. I produce also solo-author books, columns, novels, opinions, essays, art books, pictorial albums, family trees, joke books, songhits, biographies, travelogues, reunions, in color or black/white, etc.

Why put writings in a hardcopy or book? And not just in the internet. Well, the hardcopy is there for posterity and availability. Not all use the internet. Sometimes, internet has problems.

I publish or reprint free of charge under POD system (Print-On-Demand). Print is always available and for all eternity, unless the owner or author chooses to halt its publication.